Resort City in the Sunbelt

Nevada Studies in History and Political Science

Eleanore Bushnell and
Don W. Driggs
*The Nevada Constitution: Origin and
Growth* (6th ed., 1984)

Ralph J. Roske
*His Own Counsel: The Life and Times
of Lyman Trumbull* (1979)

Mary Ellen Glass
*Nevada's Turbulent '50s: Decade of
Political and Economic Change*
(1981)

Joseph A. Fry
*Henry S. Sanford: Diplomacy and
Business in Nineteenth-Century
America* (1982)

Jerome E. Edwards
*Pat McCarran: Political Boss of
Nevada* (1982)

Russell R. Elliott
*Servant of Power: A Political
Biography of Senator William M.
Stewart* (1983)

Donald R. Abbe
*Austin and the Reese River Mining
District: Nevada's Forgotten Frontier*
(1985)

Anne B. Howard
*The Long Campaign: A Biography of
Anne Martin* (1985)

Sally Zanjani and Guy Louis Rocha
*The Ignoble Conspiracy: Radicalism
on Trial in Nevada* (1986)

James W. Hulse
*Forty Years in the Wilderness:
Impressions of Nevada, 1940–1980*
(1986)

Jacqueline Baker Barnhart
*The Fair but Frail: Prostitution in San
Francisco, 1849–1900* (1986)

Marion Merriman and Warren Lerude
*American Commander in Spain:
Robert Hale Merriman and the
Abraham Lincoln Brigade* (1986)

A. Costandina Titus
*Bombs in the Backyard: Atomic
Testing and American Politics* (1986)

Wilbur S. Shepperson, ed.
*East of Eden, West of Zion: Essays on
Nevada* (1989)

John Dombrink and
William N. Thompson
*The Last Resort: Success and Failure
in Campaigns for Casinos* (1989)

Kevin J. Mullen
*Let Justice Be Done: Crime and
Politics in Early San Francisco* (1989)

Eugene P. Moehring
*Resort City in the Sunbelt: Las Vegas,
1930–1970* (1989)

A Nevada
Humanities Committee
Selection

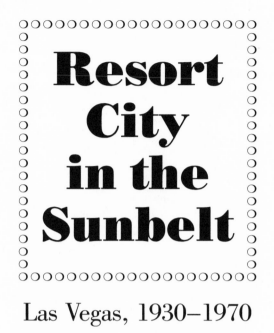

Resort City in the Sunbelt

Las Vegas, 1930–1970

EUGENE P. MOEHRING

University of Nevada Press

Reno and Las Vegas

F
849
L35
M64
1989

NEVADA STUDIES IN HISTORY
AND POLITICAL SCIENCE NO. 29

Studies Editor
Wilbur S. Shepperson

Library of Congress Cataloging-in-Publication Data

Moehring, Eugene P.
Resort city in the Sunbelt : Las Vegas, 1930–1970 / Eugene P.
Moehring.
p. cm. — (Nevada studies in history and political science :
no. 29)
Bibliography: p.
Includes index.
ISBN 0-87417-147-4 (alk. paper)
1. Las Vegas (Nev.)—History. 2. Resorts—Nevada—Las Vegas—
History. 3. Tourist trade—Nevada—Las Vegas—History. I. Title.
II. Series.
F849.L35M64   1989
979.3′135033—dc20   89-9130

The paper used in this book meets the requirements of American National
Standard for Information Sciences—Permanence of Paper for Printed Library
Materials, ANSI Z39.48-1984. The binding is sewn for strength and durability.

University of Nevada Press, Reno, Nevada 89557 USA

Designed by Richard Hendel

Printed in the United States of America

9 8 7 6 5 4 3 2 1

This book is a Nevada Humanities Committee Selection and has been
funded in part by a generous contribution from Wilbur S. Shepperson, the
Grace A. Griffen Chair in History. Additional funds were provided by a
grant from the Nevada Humanities Committee, an affiliate of the National
Endowment for the Humanities.

For Richard C. Wade

Mentor and Friend

Contents

Preface

For half a century, Las Vegas has been the subject of many books and articles directed largely at a popular audience. Works proclaiming Las Vegas as a glamorous, "fun in the sun" tourist mecca have shared the spotlight with searing exposés, portraying the town as a bastion of vice and organized crime. While entertaining and informative, neither approach has presented a balanced view of local development. More recently, scholars have begun investigating the city's past, especially the relationship between casino gambling and the community's economic and social systems. John Findlay, in particular, has spearheaded an effort to place Las Vegas in the larger context of modern American society. However, while his and other works have been helpful, none has systematically traced the historical development of Las Vegas and its suburbs.

Part of the reason for this neglect lies in the tendency of many writers to dismiss Las Vegas as an anomaly. Indeed, Las Vegas has been strangely absent from much of the urban sunbelt literature of the past decade. Yet past assumptions about the town's exceptionalism are largely unfounded. As a sunbelt city, Las Vegas has exhibited many political and economic tendencies found in Phoenix, San Antonio, and other metropolises along the "southern rim." As a resort city, Las Vegas has built a tourist infrastructure remarkably similar to those in Miami Beach and Honolulu. And, as a casino city, it has struggled with an abnormally high crime rate, just like its seaside counterpart in New Jersey.

Nevertheless, much of Las Vegas's historical development is typical not only of sunbelt, resort, and casino cities, but of all cities in general. So one must avoid the temptation of attributing virtually every development to the town's gambling economy or sunbelt status. To help minimize this determinism, I have refrained from imposing an overall conceptual design upon the story in favor of identifying those specific instances when gambling or sunbelt forces influenced events. Still, the book's overarching purpose remains clear: despite its traditionally scandalous reputation, Las Vegas deserves to be studied as a dynamic resort city and one of the fastest growing sunbelt centers in postwar America.

This work is not intended as a comprehensive history of Las Vegas. Instead, the book employs a largely thematic approach and focuses on the rise of Las Vegas from roughly the first days of Hoover Dam until the completion of the MGM Grand Hotel—with particular emphasis on the city of Las Vegas and the Strip. Special attention is paid to political issues and agendas, resort development, suburbanization, economic diversification, municipal services, civil rights, and other events which shaped the valley's development. Besides encouraging an appreciation for the city-building side of the Las Vegas story, it is my hope that this introductory volume will inspire more research on individual topics. For this reason, the book is aimed at a broad audience. In addition to the reading public and students, scholars will also find many sections of interest.

I am indebted to many people for their help, especially John Findlay, who read the manuscript in its entirety and suggested many useful revisions. Thanks also go to Carl Abbott, Brad Luckingham, Ralph Roske, Michael Green, Frank Wright, Leonard Goodall, Roosevelt Fitzgerald, and Roger Foley, who read all or part of the manuscript. Ken Jackson was supportive of my ideas about the Strip as a suburb, but I also benefited from the useful suggestions of Howard Rabinowitz, Mark Rose, and my mentor, Richard C. Wade. A number of other people also provided helpful information regarding specific details. These include: Robert LaPoint and Sid Burns of the Nevada Power Company, Barbara Lord of the Clark County Clerk's Office, former Las Vegas City Clerk Edweena Cole, Jack De Bolske of the League of Arizona Cities and Towns, Gary Elliott, and the late John Cahlan and George Franklin.

Librarians, of course, are crucial to the success of any research project. I was fortunate to have known and been helped greatly by the late Anna Dean Kepper, whose devotion to document collection was an inspiration to us all. Also contributing their time and effort were Sue Jarvis and the Special Collections staff at the James R. Dickinson Library, University of Nevada, Las Vegas, as well as David Millman and his associates at the Nevada Historical Society. Nevada State Archivist Guy Louis Rocha and his staff in Carson City have been encouraging and helpful.

Special thanks also go to those who aided in the preparation of this manuscript, including Joan Dussault, Diane Andersson, Michael Green, Monique Kimball, and particularly Joyce Nelson-Leaf, as well as Dr. Wilbur Shepperson and the staff of the University of Nevada Press. Lastly, a special word of appreciation to my colleagues for their encouragement, and especially to Joseph Fry and Thomas Wright for allowing me a much-needed course reduction to finish my research.

Prologue:
Before the Dam

From its earliest days, Las Vegas catered to travelers. In the nineteenth century it served as an oasis on the road to California. Prior to the 1820s, travelers plying the Old Spanish Trail between New Mexico and California swung south of present-day Nevada, following the eastern banks of the Colorado River up to the Needles area and then westward along the Mohave River toward Los Angeles. In the 1820s, explorers like the American fur trapper, Jedediah Smith, blazed new trails through what is today northern Arizona and southwestern Utah, which established Nevada as the new gateway to southern California.

While the first white travelers through the Las Vegas Valley were part of Antonio Armijo's 1829–1830 expedition, the Muddy-Las Vegas-Amargosa River route was not heavily traveled until the late 1840s. Following the Mexican War, the number of American wagoners multiplied.[1] Beginning in April 1854, travel became even more regularized when Congress established a monthly mail run from Salt Lake City to San Diego through as yet uninhabited Las Vegas and San Bernardino, a town settled by the Mormons just three years earlier. At the same time, Washington acted to safeguard the route by appropriating $25,000 to construct a military road from Salt Lake to the California border. Though unpaved, the thoroughfare was widened and graded to permit the rapid deployment of troops, horses, and military freight wagons. A year later, the Mormons reinforced the trail's permanence by founding a settlement at Las Vegas to provision travelers plying the so-called Mormon Corridor between Utah and the church's outpost in San Bernardino.

In April 1855, Brigham Young announced plans to colonize Las Vegas (then part of the New Mexico Territory) as part of his policy to extend Mormon influence southwest to California and provide travelers with safe havens along the way. William Bringhurst was chosen to lead a group of settlers "called" to establish the new mission. The party left Salt Lake in May 1855 with the two-fold goal of proselytizing the local Indians while also raising crops to provision needy travelers. After roughly a month's journey, thirty men, forty wagons, and animals arrived at Las Vegas. After a brief survey, Bringhurst chose a settlement site about four miles east of Big Springs on a promontory overlooking the northeast end of the valley.

For the next year, the men struggled to build a fort large enough to protect their animals, store their crops, and house their mission. The colonists worked throughout the summer preparing adobe bricks. In September construction began on an adobe corral for mules, cows, and other animals. Work then commenced on the large fort, complete with walls ranging from nine to fourteen feet in height with eight two-story houses and a storage building inside.[2]

By February 1856, the building had progressed to the point where the colonists could leave the rest of its construction until spring. The settlers nourished themselves all winter with corn, melons, and other crops planted during that first summer in 1855. The next two years saw the Mormons struggle with their missionary work, instructing their neighbors in religion and agriculture. Although the Indians were largely cooperative, many undoubtedly agreed to be baptized in return for promised gifts of food and clothing. To be sure, the Paiutes were a hungry lot; their frequent forays into the mission's grain fields eventually forced the Mormons to post guards. After a while, the settlers kept all of their farm implements, seed, animals, and other valuables behind the fort walls for protection.

Despite much tribulation, the Mormons persevered, extending their fields farther out from the fort walls in 1856. As the colony assumed more of a permanent stature, the Utah government established a post office, "Bringhurst," in honor of the settlement's leader ("Las Vegas" was not used because Las Vegas, New Mexico already existed). The colony's sudden prominence was short-lived. Within a year, Brigham Young would release the settlers from their "call," to end political factionalism which threatened to split the community apart. By August 1858, most of the Mormons had returned to Utah, abandoning Las Vegas to the Indians who now feasted on that year's harvest.[3]

The white man's absence would be brief. Nevada's famous Comstock boom began little more than a year later. Within months, as San Francisco-bound freight wagons hauled tons of silver and gold bullion across the Sierra, a mining fever gripped the territory including southern Nevada. In 1861, an old Mormon lead mine at Mt. Potosi began yielding traces of silver, and a new smelter was built. Prospectors then reported a large gold strike in El Dorado Canyon near the Colorado below the present site of Hoover Dam. Once again, Las Vegas became the focus of interest, because both mining camps were relatively isolated and therefore in need of food and supplies. There was no permanent settlement there until 1865

when a group of men, including Octavius Decatur Gass (a former El
Dorado prospector), acquired the rights to the Old Mormon Fort. Gass
eventually repaired the old adobe building, renamed it the "Los" Vegas
Rancho (to avoid confusion with Las Vegas, New Mexico), and bought out
his partners. Gass recognized that the fertile fields and abundant springs
could supply the needs of the mushrooming passenger traffic along the Los
Angeles-Salt Lake wagon road, while also provisioning the region's mining camps. Throughout the 1860s Gass provided lodging as well as fresh
fruit, vegetables, and hay from his orchards and fields which supplemented a steady trade in supplies and livestock for the distant mining
camps. While business was brisk, Gass, a restless prospector at heart,
longed for California's mining frontier. His failure to repay a debt eventually put the rancho in the hands of Archibald Stewart, a freight operator
from Pioche, Nevada.[4]

In spring 1882, Stewart and his wife Helen moved south to Las Vegas
for what was intended to be a temporary stay. However, Stewart was
mortally wounded a short time later in a shoot-out at the nearby Kiel
Ranch. Mrs. Stewart, now a widow with children, could not afford to
abandon the ranch, so she remained on the property with her family,
managing the farm, store, and hostelry. All the while, she looked for a
buyer. Several prospective deals fell through before she finally sold the
ranch in 1902 to Montana Senator William Clark.[5]

The growth of Los Angeles was the key to this transaction as well as
later development in the Las Vegas Valley. By 1900, western economic
growth demanded greater access to southern California markets from the
Salt Lake-Chicago-New York trade route. Clark had already begun to
acquire rights-of-way for his proposed San Pedro, Los Angeles, & Salt
Lake Railroad linking the Union Pacific mainline in Utah with southern
California. Purchase of the 2,000-acre Stewart Ranch, along with its
water rights, was crucial for several reasons. First, engineers already
knew that the valley networks between Los Angeles and Salt Lake lined
up in such a way as to make the Las Vegas Valley the most cost-efficient
route. Second, Las Vegas lay roughly midway between the two cities,
which made it an ideal site for a railroad "division point" where crews and
locomotives could be changed. Third, Las Vegas, the route's traditional
oasis, alone possessed enough water to service not only the steam locomotives, but the new town itself.[6]

After a brief struggle with the Union Pacific (which also wanted to build
along the line), Clark negotiated a compromise which awarded his com-

pany the right to construct the railroad. The next two years saw feverish construction through Utah, Arizona, and California into Nevada, approaching the Las Vegas Valley from both directions. As early as 1904, grading work had begun in the region, and Clark's men were utilizing the Stewart ranch as a source of food and water. The railroad itself was completed on January 30, 1905. While plans were announced for the sale of lots in May at "Clark's Las Vegas Townsite," a small community already existed nearby. A year earlier, J. T. McWilliams, a surveyor and valley resident since the 1890s, had purchased land west of Clark's tracks, platted a townsite, and sold lots (see Map 1). The so-called Original Townsite served as a camp for railroad workers as well as barbers, grocers, saloon-keepers, and dozens of other businessmen who comprised the service sector of the fledgling economy. Moreover, the enterprising McWilliams intended to outflank Clark's town by securing even more settlers from southern California. Throughout 1904, Los Angeles newspapers carried McWilliams's advertisements promoting the town's "splendid climate" and "plentiful supply of the purest water." Lot prices were a major inducement: "first-class, inside business lots" went for $200 and less.[7]

McWilliams' Townsite (which later became West Las Vegas or simply the Westside) continued to attract settlers through the spring of 1905. While Clark's men drove in pegs to mark the lots of their newly platted community, business continued booming across the tracks. Even though railroad crews had departed, the Westside continued as a prosperous staging area for oxen and muleteams carrying lumber, food, and other supplies to Bullfrog, Rhyolite, and other boomtowns in the mining districts northwest of Las Vegas. Once the railroad was completed, more settlers thronged McWilliams's town, pitching their tents in anticipation of lot sales east of the tracks. As the day of the Clark's Townsite opening approached, the railroad announced that a heavy advance demand for lots would force an auction sale on May 15, 1905. This decision only heightened the land fever, encouraging still more squatters to camp along the banks of Las Vegas Creek. Adding to the excitement was a trainload of investors who arrived from Los Angeles on May 14, encouraged no doubt by the railroad's promise to refund the round-trip fare of any passenger buying land. On May 15, the large crowd and prevailing optimism combined to produce a flurry of sales. Speculators, prospective storeowners, out-of-state banks, and businessmen all contributed to the railroad's coffers. Of course, the carrier itself did not conduct the auction. A few weeks earlier, the railroad had formed a subsidiary, the Las Vegas Land & Water Company, which handled all land transactions.[8]

Map 1: Clark's Las Vegas Townsite, 1905

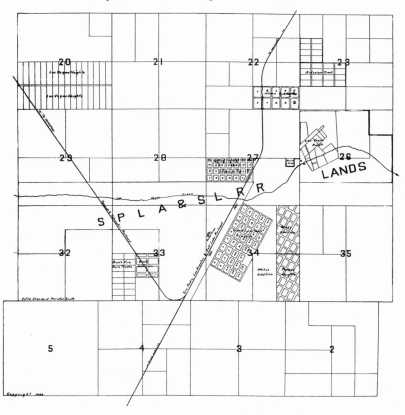

On May 16, the day after the auction, hundreds of plots were sold, bringing the final total to a little more than half of the townsite's twelve hundred lots. Almost immediately, "Clark's Las Vegas Townsite" bustled with activity as tents and tent-framed buildings were erected along the community's main thoroughfare, Fremont Street (named for "The Pathfinder," John C. Frémont). A parlor car was rolled to the head of Fremont to serve as the temporary railroad station. Almost immediately, passengers and freight began arriving to reinforce the community's infant economy. In addition, dozens of Westside residents, suddenly recognizing the barrier to wagon traffic posed by the railroad crossing, now moved across the tracks and pitched their tent houses and stores on newly purchased lots in Clark's Townsite.[9]

Aside from the predictable growth occasioned by the settlement of a new town, Las Vegas enjoyed added prosperity thanks to Senator Clark's decision to build a branching railroad out of Las Vegas to tap the silver boom districts of Bullfrog and Rhyolite. Track construction for that line began almost immediately in 1905, with Clark's Townsite as the staging area for the lumber, steel, food, and other provisions needed to supply the construction crews. Overnight, Las Vegas became a major transshipment point, as supplies from California and Utah arriving by train were briefly stored before being loaded onto wagons for the trip northwest to the advancing construction camps. As usual, progress was feverish. In 1906, the so-called Las Vegas & Tonopah Railroad reached Beatty and Rhyolite, Nevada; by 1907, it had arrived at its Goldfield terminus.

Las Vegas benefited further from Senator Clark's decision to build a repair center in town to service equipment on both his southern Nevada lines. As early as 1905, the railroad had provided Las Vegas with substantial facilities, including a station (replaced in 1940 by a more elegant successor) and two ice houses (the first was destroyed by fire and replaced by a new Armour Ice Plant in 1907) which for years supplied the needs of the freight trains and distant mining camps as well as Las Vegas's own resorts. As part of its construction program in 1909–1911, the railroad built Hanson Hall, a sprawling two-story concrete building. Surrounded by tracks and elevated loading docks, the structure served as both a warehouse and meeting hall. The company agent's house, located in the center of the yards near the main machine shops, came in 1911. Later, in 1915, the company added more to its complex, erecting a two-story concrete powerhouse just east of Hanson Hall in the yards. The decision in 1909 to build the repair shops in Las Vegas forced the railroad to expand the stock of workmen's housing. Since Las Vegas was, to some extent, a company town, the railroad felt a paternal obligation to provide its employees with affordable and comfortable housing. With this in mind, the railroad had reserved several blocks along South Second, Third, and Fourth streets. Between 1909 and 1912, the company planned to erect up to 120 cottages. In the end, though, management built only sixty-four, opting then to sell the remaining vacant lots to their employees and offer them liberal building loans.[10]

Thanks to the railroad, Las Vegas survived the Panic of 1907 and saw its payrolls swollen by additional train employees. Despite a brief recession occasioned by a track washout in 1910 (which briefly dropped the local population from 1200 to 800 people), the town prospered. By 1909, Las Vegas's appearance reflected its growing physical maturity. Fremont Street was paved, guttered, and flagged with sidewalks, while over ten miles of secondary streets had at least been oiled to reduce the dust. A public school was organized as early as fall 1905; classes were held in a donated building. Then in July 1908, the railroad deeded a two-block parcel bordered by Bridger, Lewis, Fourth, and Fifth streets as a center for future school construction. Similar to education, water was another major concern—particularly in a new desert town. According to deed agreements, the railroad promised to provide the town with an abundant supply. Thus, in August 1905, the Las Vegas Land & Water Company announced plans to build a network of redwood pipes to transport water from the railroad's main line at Main and Clark streets. The first pipes supplied the town's nascent resort industry; indeed, John F. Miller's Hotel at Fremont and Main was the first to receive service. Subsequent months saw pipes laid down Fremont and through the alleys to the secondary streets north and south of the commercial district. Of course, wooden mains were the railroad's cheap solution to a complex problem. Between 1905 and 1912, pressure dropped repeatedly because of leaks and breaks. In fact, a major line burst in 1912, leaving the entire town without water for a day. Even the power plant had to be closed when the lack of water made it impossible to make steam in the generator.[11]

Reliance upon the railroad for service made some local promoters uneasy. In 1907, determined to expand the town's water supply and liberate themselves partially from the restraints of railroad dependency, a group of local businessmen, including developer and future mayor Peter Buol, banker John S. Park, and others, formed the Vegas Artesian Water Syndicate for the avowed purpose of "boring for artesian water in the Las

Vegas Valley." The group drilled its first well in the Westside in July 1907, hitting water at the 300-foot level. This proved to be the first of hundreds more artesian wells drilled in the valley over the next six decades. The discovery encouraged the creation of an agricultural plan to develop the valley's crop potential. Unfortunately, the soil and lack of effective irrigation would eventually discourage large-scale farming.

However, residential growth more than offset it. The completion of the new railroad repair shops in 1911 provided a new impetus for urbanization, because the railroad announced its intention of boosting the local work force from 175 to 400 men. The anticipated surge in the housing market immediately led to the platting of new additions in the city's residential zone north and south of Fremont Street. Within months, Mayor Peter Buol opened his own Buck's Addition (between Fifth, Tenth, Linden, and Stewart streets) while Doherty-Sumner prepared the Fairview Tract (Ninth to Fourteenth, Mesquite to Fremont streets) and James Ladd readied his own addition (stretching from Twelfth to Fifteenth streets and Clark to Fremont). With lot prices ranging below $100 and the railroad unwilling to provide water for tracts beyond its townsite, artesian drilling was critical to Las Vegas's future development. [12]

The same booster spirit which inspired the search for water and land promotion also fueled the desire for better government. Local businessmen and land investors particularly resented the 300-mile round-trip to the Lincoln County seat at Pioche. In an age before superhighways, traversing the Nevada desert by car or wagon was an ordeal. As early as 1905, Charles "Pop" Squires, Ed Clark, and other civic leaders had lobbied for either the removal of the Lincoln County seat from Pioche to Las Vegas or the creation of an entirely new county. In August 1908 John S. Park, John F. Miller, and other prominent businessmen formed the County Division Committee and enlisted the help of Senator Clark and the railroad to carve a new southern county out of sprawling Lincoln County. A month later, with the railroad's support, the committee succeeded in convincing the county Democratic and Republican party conventions to endorse a division bill. The 1909 state legislature complied with Las Vegas's request and created a new county (named for Senator Clark) with Las Vegas as county seat. [13]

Flushed with this victory, local business leaders welcomed the new court and administrative sectors of Las Vegas's economy and formed a chamber of commerce to promote the town further. As one of their first steps in this direction, Ed Clark, Pop Squires, John S. Park, and others in the chamber proposed the incorporation of Las Vegas as a city complete with a charter providing for commission government. At the time, only about one hundred cities in America had adopted the commission form. Clearly, the town's elite, anxious to appeal to businessmen around the west, saw commission government as the kind of positive, forward-looking image that Las Vegas needed to project if it was to attract the interest of American industry.

Crucial to the success of these endeavors were Las Vegas's newspapers. Chief among them was the *Las Vegas Age*. Created as an independent weekly a month before the town's birth in May 1905, the *Age* struggled along until 1908 when it was purchased by Charles Pemberton Squires, a Wisconsin native, whose Las Vegas holdings already included shares in a hotel, bank, and lumberyard as well as interests in the town's power and phone company. A devout Republican, Squires trumpeted the conservative party line for over forty years. The *Age* was eventually challenged by the *Clark County Review*, although the intense rivalry between the two organs would not begin until the arrival of Al Cahlan in 1926. Born in Reno in 1899, Albert Edmunds Cahlan attended the University of Nevada, earning a degree in electrical engineering. A mathematics teacher and coach at Las Vegas High, he gradually developed an interest in journalism. In 1922, he became editor and business manager of the triweekly *Elko Free Press* before returning to southern Nevada in June 1926 to accept a similar position at the *Clark County Review*. Established in 1909 by former *Age* editor Charles C. "Corky" Corkhill, the weekly underwent several changes of ownership before being purchased by Frank Garside in April 1926. Garside, a longtime newspaperman and Democrat, wanted an editor whose views coincided with his own. Cahlan was the man. Within three years, the aggressive Cahlan had expanded the *Review* to a daily (forcing Squires in 1931 to do the same with the *Age*). Two years earlier, the *Review* had absorbed former Governor James Scrugham's short-lived *Journal*—hence the newspaper's new title, the *Evening Review-Journal*. For the next two decades the paper would be a loyal mouthpiece for the New Deal, Pat McCarran, and the state's Democratic leadership. [14]

Buoyed by a strong booster press and a progressive business leadership, adolescent Las Vegas eyed the future with optimism. Between 1911 and 1918, the new city enjoyed a welcome burst of prosperity as the Rhyolite-Goldfield-Tonopah-Bullfrog mining districts (along with Goodsprings and other nearby camps) continued producing substantial although steadily decreasing loads of ore. World War I briefly invigorated the mines, as worldwide and nationwide shortages of copper, tungsten, silver, and gold raised prices to the point where even low-grade ores were profitable. The boom, however, soon ran its course. As the ore gave out, mining districts near Goldfield eventually closed down, forcing the Las Vegas and Tonopah to cease operations in 1919. Subsequent months saw the railroad tear up its tracks and sell the iron and steel for scrap.

The gloom continued a while longer, as the immediate postwar recession cut rail traffic somewhat. An additional blow came in May 1921 when railroad officials announced Senator Clark's impending sale of the San Pedro, Los Angeles & Salt Lake Railroad to the Union Pacific in return for stock. The transfer of control portended dramatic changes for Las Vegas. While Clark's control of the town had been firm but benevolent, the Union Pacific's hierarchy in New York and Omaha was concerned more with revenues than paternalism. This became obvious in the fall of 1921 after the Union Pacific took control and immediately fired sixty repair shop employees. A local strike order set for November was rescinded, but Las Vegas workers enthusiastically supported the great railroad strike of 1922 which idled trains across the country. Violence flared in Las Vegas a week after the strike began when scab crews arrived in town. Eighteen strikers were arrested in the yards for interfering with scab operations and the Federated Shop Craft Union had to bail them out. For several weeks thereafter no trains moved through Las Vegas and the town's economy plummeted as stores closed, freight piled up on sidings, and supplies went unsold. Following the strike, the local economy absorbed another blow when the vindictive railroad moved its repair yards from Las Vegas to Caliente—an action which cost the city three hundred jobs.[15]

Despite the loss of the railroad yards, the town survived. Expansion of the Union Pacific's local stockyards combined with increased rail traffic to keep the town's economy relatively healthy. In the meantime, residents valiantly tried to attract more industry. As part of its promotional effort, Las Vegas sought to improve its physical appearance and attractions. In 1925, the city commission voted to pave Fremont Street from Main to Fifth, and then approved an additional $6,000 to match federal funding for the paving of Fifth Street (the Los Angeles Highway) from Fremont two miles south to the city limits at San Francisco Street (today Sahara Avenue). A drive was also launched to secure federal legislation which would permit more generous national funding for road construction to make Las Vegas more accessible to Californians. In fact, efforts were under way as early as 1914 to improve auto transportation between southern California and Las Vegas. Between 1914 and 1916, officials of Clark and San Bernardino counties discussed plans for improving the roads between their two jurisdictions. Supported by these authorities and local automobile clubs, the states of Nevada and California pressured the federal government for funds to oil portions of Highway 91 linking Los Angeles with Las Vegas (the Los Angeles Highway). Improved accessibility also sparked a movement to open an airfield near Las Vegas. In 1926, the town supported efforts by Western Air Express (later, Western Airlines) to begin regular service between Los Angeles and Salt Lake. City leaders encouraged the diversion of flight operations from the original field south of town (today between the Sahara and Hilton hotels) to a new strip and terminal ten miles northeast of the city (today Nellis Air Force base).[16]

The transportation initiative was part of an overall attempt to diversify the town's economy. Part of this strategy involved the marketing of Las Vegas as a "resort city." Since 1905, the town's boisterous clubs had played host to thousands of railroad passengers on train layovers. By railroad order, the sale of intoxicating liquors was limited to Blocks 16 and 17, a zone conveniently located on Fremont Street near the railroad station. Within a few years of the town's founding, the area had evolved into a red-light district as well. During Prohibition, the speakeasies masqueraded as clubs.

Aside from the wide-open atmosphere downtown, Las Vegans also hoped to imitate Tucson and Palm Springs by parlaying their year-round sunshine into something lucrative. There were a number of efforts to promote spas and tourism. In 1924, Edward Taylor, an eastern capitalist, purchased the old Kyle (Kiel) Ranch (a few miles north of the Mormon fort) with the avowed goal of building a dude ranch for vacationers and prospective divorcees. In the meantime, David Lorenzi had already begun construction on his "high class resort" northwest of town. Workers had already dug twin lakes for boating and swimming and were beginning work on a dance hall and tavern. Then, in 1927, Las Vegas began development of its first golf course on a tract just south of town (today the Las Vegas Hilton Hotel). Although it would be several more years before the town could boast of an 18-hole golf course, the dirt facility served its purpose.[17]

While these early efforts to lure tourists were mostly unsuccessful, Las

Vegans had already begun to glimpse the potential of adding a resort dimension to their transportation economy. Slowly, in the late 1920s, a series of events combined to enhance the tourist industry. A decade of lobbying for better roads paid off in 1927 with passage of the Oddie-Colton Highway Act. With its budget now substantially enlarged, the federal government's Bureau of Public Roads announced that it would fund the widening (from twenty-one to twenty-four feet) and oiling of the Arrowhead Trail (the Los Angeles Highway). The announcement of Hoover Dam's approval only speeded up the effort. By 1931, work on the great highway was largely completed (although some sections were not finished until the New Deal), and Angelenos could easily drive up for a weekend visit to the little casino town. With the legalization of casino gambling in that same year, the stage was now set for the building of the world's premier entertainment city.

The Federal
Trigger

Las Vegas's triumph as a world resort was never assured. Virtually no one in the 1920s would have expected the town to blossom into the metropolis that it is today. Lack of water, fertile land, productive mines, and heavy industry made it an unlikely candidate. But the same forces which forged the new west and lured millions of people to the sunbelt, also boosted Las Vegas. Reclamation projects, New Deal programs, defense spending, air conditioning, interstate highways, jet travel, right-to-work laws, low taxes—all of the factors that promoted Atlanta, Houston, Phoenix, Los Angeles, and other sunbelt cities, helped Las Vegas, too. Of course, the latter developed more slowly at first and along different lines. Although railroading, manufacturing, and especially defense programs all contributed to local growth, Las Vegans did not create the usual trading entrepot or industrial town. Instead, like their counterparts in Miami Beach and later Honolulu, they built a resort city—and, more significantly, a resort city based upon casino gambling.

The resort emphasis evolved slowly, not becoming the town's dominant business until the 1940s. It was only a decade earlier that Las Vegas had even begun moving in that direction. The national government was the key, just as it was throughout the sunbelt. Federal spending, and lots of it, triggered the rise of modern Las Vegas. Like towns across the sunbelt and west, Las Vegas benefited from a sudden outpouring of federal reclamation, relief, and after 1939, defense programs. More importantly, the dam builders, soldiers, and defense workers brought to town by Uncle Sam patronized the city's fledgling casinos, laying the foundation for Las Vegas's resort industry. Dam spending powered the early economy. Between 1930 and 1939, Washington pumped over $23 million into the area.

Of this amount, $19 million went to build Boulder (later Hoover) Dam and Boulder City. In addition, Franklin Roosevelt's New Deal pledged millions more to outfit Las Vegas with new streets, sewers, and other improvements. By 1940, Hitler's invasion of Europe brought new rounds of spending just as it had in Los Angeles, Phoenix, Tucson, and other sunbelt centers. Within two years, Las Vegas had an air base, a magnesium plant, and a new suburb to house defense workers. In just over ten years Las Vegas was transformed from a sleepy whistle-stop to a city with prospects. [1]

Boulder Dam's construction sustained the initial prosperity. Paradoxically, as New York, Chicago, and thousands of smaller towns reeled from the effects of the Great Depression, Las Vegas boomed as a dam construction center. The great project symbolized the national government's dream of harnessing the west's major rivers to control flooding and provide cheap water and power. Under the New Deal, Las Vegas became part of a larger story: the federal effort to combat massive unemployment and broaden the nation's industrial base by developing southern and western natural resources.

Dam building provided a bracing stimulus for the growth-hungry town. Following passage of the Boulder Canyon Act in 1928, Las Vegas witnessed nothing short of a revolution: land values soared, population jumped, and construction skyrocketed. Why all this change? In one stroke, Hoover Dam magnified Las Vegas's strategic importance. For a quarter century the town had prospered as a transshipment point, receiving ore and forwarding supplies to southern Nevada's remote mining camps, while also serving as a through route for cargoes traversing the Los Angeles-Salt Lake rail corridor. The dam immediately multiplied Las Vegas's economic assets, awarding the town a substantial water, power, and construction hinterland to the southeast. Blessed suddenly with these new advantages, Las Vegans took the initiative, improving their government, developing new industry, and pursuing New Deal funds to expand their town's infrastructure.

Overnight, Las Vegas tried to shed its wild frontier image. The town put on its best face in June 1929 to greet Interior Secretary Raymond Wilbur and Commissioner of Reclamation Elwood Mead who came by railroad to examine the dam site and decide where to base the construction force. Buildings were repainted, streets were washed, and Block 16 actually shut down temporarily. The city even erected an arch across Fremont Street with a large sign welcoming Wilbur who played along, smiling at the crowd and delighting officials with endless compliments and grand predictions for the town's future. But it was all in vain; privately, Wilbur had no intention of basing the huge construction force in Las Vegas. Instead, he preferred building a "government town" on land closer to the dam site. The Interior Department's official announcement came a month later and struck many as a ringing condemnation of Las Vegas and all that it stood for. The stern announcement proclaimed that "it is the intention of the government that the bootlegger or other law violator shall not interfere with the well-being of its workmen assigned to the task. . . . Instead of a boisterous frontier town, it is hoped that here simple homes, gardens with fruit and flowers, schools and playgrounds will make this a wholesome American community." The government wanted to avoid the rowdy, wide-open atmosphere so characteristic of traditional mining and railroad construction camps. Aside from morality, logistics also governed the decision. Las Vegas was simply too far from the construction site. Although the town was the perfect hub for routing supplies by rail or truck to the dam site, a sixty-mile daily round-trip for 5,000 construction workers was impractical. Though deprived of the payroll pie, Las Vegans still knew that their economy would profit handsomely from the millions of dollars' worth of supplies expected to be shipped through and stored locally.[2]

Townsmen braced for the impending boom. In 1930 alone, even after the government decided to build Boulder City, Las Vegas developers planned forty new buildings. As population mushroomed from 5,200 to 7,500 in just one year, authorities scrambled to handle the growth. In a daring move, stockholders of Consolidated Power & Telephone split their company into two utilities. While the new Southern Nevada Power made plans to modernize its grid, Southern Nevada Telephone implemented an immediate program to expand its network and add the city's first long-distance service. The city commission approved a series of municipal improvements, including the installation of ornamental streetlights, the purchase of modern sanitation trucks, adoption of the community's first zoning ordinance, expansion of the police department, construction of a new high school (approved by voters in a 1929 bond election) and extension of the original 1911 sewer system into the town's newer neighborhoods. These programs, together with Washington's promise of a large federal building and post office downtown, signified the dawn of a new age for southern Nevada.[3]

Aside from these improvements, Hoover Dam laid the foundation for a metropolitan growth by creating a new suburb southeast of town. To be sure, the optimism sweeping Las Vegas in 1930 was shared by a string of camps along the Colorado. As early as 1930, unemployed men, hopeful of securing a job on the dam, came with their families and erected tents, cardboard shanties, and other primitive housing along the riverbanks. In those first days, conditions were primitive and the heat almost unbearable. Families soaked bed sheets in the river to cool themselves while sleeping at night. Escape from the isolation was also difficult, since there were as yet no paved roads to Las Vegas. Contributing further to the gloom were snakes, lizards, little food, and no medical care. Conditions were hardly better in 1931 at Cape Horn, a barracks-like structure built high atop the canyon walls for those drilling the dam's diversion tunnels. Few modern conveniences eased the strain for these early crews who began work months before the construction of Boulder City.[4]

For many people on this rugged frontier thirty miles from Las Vegas, Boulder City was built none too soon. On March 16, 1931, five days after the government awarded the dam contract to Six Companies, Inc., work began on the temporary camp to house the men who would build the town. Two weeks earlier on March 1, Las Vegas paving contractor Pat Cline had begun paving the Boulder Highway, linking his town with the proposed Boulder City. Construction of the latter formally began in April based on a design prepared by noted Denver city planner S. R. DeBoer. Although topography and budget restraints forced some modifications, the Interior Department generally followed DeBoer's suggestions about the size of homes and lots, the street system, utility networks, and location of government and administration buildings. Blueprints called for a community capable of handling up to 5,000 people. Plans provided for a hospital, general store, recreation hall, commissary, and plenty of housing. Six Companies, the dam's major contractor, built 250 one-room cottages for married couples ($15 monthly rent), 260 two-room houses ($19), 123 three-room houses ($30), and 14 other buildings ranging from three to five rooms each. Single men lived in 8 two-story dormitory buildings which dominated the residential center of town. Food was served at the Anderson Brothers Mess Hall where employees used their "meal tickets" three times a day. A soda fountain and lunch counter served the town's massive recreation hall where the men gathered to use the pool tables and gym. As the community grew, additional facilities became available. By February 1933, residents could play at the new Boulder City golf course southeast of town, or take the ever-popular ride to Las Vegas.[5]

Municipal government also came quickly. From the beginning, federal control of the town was complete. The first show of strength followed an August 31 strike by Wobblies and other "union agitators," when U.S. marshalls secured the reservation with a fence and gate on the Boulder Highway. Guards searched all cars and only people with official permits were allowed in. Strike leaders were immediately discharged and, except for a brief walkout in 1935, the city was never again torn by labor turbulence. With 42,000 applications for less than 6,000 jobs, management had the upper hand. The government tightened its control further in October 1931 with the arrival of Sims Ely, a skilled administrator and martinet, who assumed the duties of city manager. Ely served for ten years, settling domestic disputes and firing drunkards while imposing a strict bible-belt morality upon the town. Though Ely's dictatorial policies were often controversial, they nevertheless maintained an atmosphere which promoted peace and productivity. [6]

Between 1931 and the completion of the dam in 1935, Boulder City efficiently provided for the needs of workers and their dependents. Unfortunately for Las Vegas, retailing was no exception to this rule. In addition to several private shops, the massive Boulder City Company Store (a subsidiary of Six Companies, Inc.) catered to residents. At the time, it was the largest department store in Nevada and conveniently accepted shopper's payments in U.S. currency or Six Company scrip. The latter, however, was not transferable. This, together with the store's practice of advancing credit to workers in company scrip, eventually sparked a fiery protest from Las Vegas merchants who objected to this "unfair competition." Eventually, these businessmen, anxious for a share of the dam's $500,000 monthly payroll, successfully pressured federal officials into allowing workers to be paid in U.S. currency. Of course, the Interior Department responded to many of Las Vegas's concerns about Six Companies' policies by insisting that Boulder City was only a temporary town. Following the dam's completion, it was expected that the administration and municipal buildings would become the permanent headquarters of a small Bureau of Reclamation crew with perhaps an office or two for California Edison and other utilities connected with power generation. But it soon became apparent that many workers wanted to stay, continuing to rent their homes until the government agreed to sell. And, why not? By 1932, the town had its own school, cemetery, police station, post office, and train station. In fact, as the Anderson Mess Hall prepared to close for good on New Year's Eve 1935, dozens of prospective merchants were already waiting for business licenses to cash in on the expected tourist trade. [7]

Everyone knew the tiny community would become a popular tourist mecca. From its inception, the dam had attracted thousands of visitors. Almost 100,000 came during the first full year of construction in 1932 while double that amount visited Las Vegas. In 1933, the dam drew 132,000 people and Las Vegas 230,000. Recognizing the magnetic value of the new "world wonder," the latter's chamber of commerce began to bill Las Vegas as "the gateway to Hoover Dam." And it was; by 1934 the numbers ballooned to 265,000 and 300,000, respectively. Throughout the 1930s, 75 percent of those visiting Hoover Dam also stopped in Las Vegas, and these totals grew every year. The reason was obvious: Hoover Dam was a tribute to modern engineering. Towering 726 feet high, it was 300 feet taller than any other dam in the world. Its mere construction was a spectacle. As early as May 1931, visitors watched in awe as hundreds of workers struggled to build the coffer dam, lay Boulder's foundation, and drill the tunnels to divert the Colorado around the construction site. The work force grew to 4,200 by April 1932 before peaking at 5,251 in July 1934. Of course, the story of the dam's construction and the trials faced by the men who built it lies beyond the focus of this book, but their work literally reclaimed the southwest and rescued Las Vegas from a whistle-stop fate. [8]

In every way the dam transformed the little desert town. The physical dimension was obvious, as warehouses and yards multiplied along the railroad tracks north and south of Fremont Street to meet the demand for building supplies. Las Vegas also became an administrative hub. Even though the town had failed to secure the base camp for the construction force, it nevertheless functioned as the hiring center. In the fall of 1930 Leonard Blood, the superintendent of the U.S. Employment Office in Las Vegas, began processing job applications for work on the project. Within days the hiring hall on North Main Street began filling up with hopeful applicants lured from around the country by prospects of good-paying jobs. The influx of workers immediately overwhelmed the town's limited housing stock. Within weeks a "Hoover City" of shacks, tents, and shanties sprang up on North Fifth Street near the Woodlawn Cemetery. Although many men eventually gained employment, thousands more were disappointed. The dam brought unprecedented prosperity and notoriety to Las Vegas while also inundating the town with thousands of desperate people from around the nation. Ill equipped to handle the massive relief effort, local government buckled under the strain. In 1932 and 1933 the Clark County indigent fund was depleted. City funds were also consumed to the point where the mayor and other city officials took voluntary pay cuts until newly elected President Franklin D. Roosevelt finally established a camp to feed the homeless in September 1933. By January 1934, New Deal agencies would spend an average of $75,000 per month for relief and public works programs to relieve the situation.[9]

Despite the recession for a portion of the city's population, most residents enjoyed unparalleled prosperity. From the beginning, investors recognized that Boulder Dam would enlarge Las Vegas. In 1930, developers built over $1.2 million worth of new structures. Many were small houses whose rooms could be easily partitioned off to form several apartments. Dozens of landlords were local businessmen who merely speculated in lots located in the newer additions south and east of town. Some tracts were also built by investors and recent migrants from California, Arizona, and Utah. Aside from dwellings, the construction boom also included new office and warehouse structures. Between 1930 and 1932, many of the old wooden frame buildings downtown yielded to taller, more substantial successors. The Union Pacific, for example, upgraded its facilities by spending $400,000 for yard improvements and a more spacious terminal while local Masons erected a modern temple valued at $110,000. Clark County commissioners approved an $80,000 loan for a courthouse addition designed to service the increased caseload resulting from the local population increase.

Everyone knew that even if Boulder City housed the work force, the dam would still accelerate the urbanization of Las Vegas. The rippling effects of increased wholesaling, retailing, warehousing, administration, and tourism would inevitably boost the railhead's population, thereby forcing the expansion of the business and residential districts. To prepare for these changes, the city commission in 1931 authorized bond issues of $165,000 to pave, widen, and extend existing streets and $150,000 to expand the current sewer system into the town's new additions. At the same time, the city was completing a large new high school to handle the growing number of students expected from Boulder City and the nascent subdivisions on the edges of Las Vegas. Expanded medical care was another priority. In December 1931, local physicians met that challenge by opening the modern, new Las Vegas Hospital at Eighth and Ogden. In addition to these local efforts, Washington also contributed to the town's physical plant by spending $300,000 for an impressive post office. This project was related to the construction of the new federal building in City Hall Park, which confirmed Las Vegas as the administrative center for all federal offices in southern Nevada. This move, combined with the town's county seat status, added a valuable administrative dimension to the local economy for years to come, as legal offices, accounting firms, and related businesses clustered around the downtown area.[10]

Aside from these improvements, the dam inspired the enlargement of the business district surrounding Fremont Street. Much of the new downtown construction involved hotels, as Nevada's recent legalization of gambling teamed with the population growth occasioned by the dam to fuel a recreation boom. Anxious to control and derive revenues from the state's substantial underground gaming industry, Nevada's legislature legalized gambling in February 1931. The move energized the economies of both Reno and Las Vegas. Of course, legalized gambling had flourished in Nevada long before 1931: even before statehood and despite the best efforts of mining districts to outlaw it, gambling had been a popular tradition on Nevada's frontier. Beginning in 1869 and for the next forty years, legalized gaming flourished in the silver state until a wave of reform sentiment during the so-called Progressive Era resulted in a 1911 law closing all casinos. Public outcries led to a 1915 amended version exempting card games (where the deal changed after each hand) and slot machines (provided the prize was not monetary). For the next fifteen years the law was lightly enforced. By the early 1930s, the depressed state was ready to legalize the industry again. While license revenues were an incentive, state leaders at the time were more concerned with controlling the substantial underground business which existed. Fear of national reaction was no longer a major concern, because Nevada already enjoyed a maverick image, thanks to its liberal marriage and divorce laws.[11]

When the legislature legalized gambling again in 1931, it awarded cities and counties full power to collect taxes and issue gaming licenses. In Las Vegas, like Reno, major club owners, anxious to retain their customers, wanted to be licensed. Clark County commissioners first issued gaming licenses for slot machines only; permits for other games came later. The first license went to J. H. Morgan and Mayme Stocker, longtime operators of the famed Northern Club on Fremont Street. Tony Cornero's Meadows Club on the Boulder Highway followed soon after. For its part, the city of Las Vegas acted cautiously, issuing only six licenses in April 1931. While the number of licensees was eventually expanded, early permits were mostly restricted to slot machines and even their number was strictly regulated. Obviously, city fathers did not foresee gaming as the town's economic savior—even the location of gaming clubs was limited. The municipality passed a red-lining ordinance confining the industry to Fremont Street between First and Third streets. Subsequent years saw the district expanded to Fifth Street and beyond, but (except for the Moulin Rouge in 1955) town authorities were careful to prevent casino activity from spilling over into residential neighborhoods. Despite the restrictions, gambling quickly became a dynamic new industry in Las Vegas, thanks to thousands of dam workers who provided a ready market for casinos. [12]

Although most of the early clubs opened in temporary quarters on Fremont Street, a few were farther out. Perhaps the nicest was located on the Boulder Highway beyond the city limits. On May 2, 1931, California gambler Tony Cornero and his brothers opened The Meadows Club, an elaborate casino and cabaret. Set in a plush atmosphere, their $31,000 establishment offered a variety of games, including faro, twenty-one, roulette, craps, and poker. The Corneros hired Jack Laughlin, of New York and Hollywood fame, to produce the "Meadows Revue" in the showroom; music was provided by the "Meadow Larks," a Los Angeles band. Plans called for hotel construction to begin immediately with the goal of making The Meadows "the finest resort . . . in Nevada." As the dam project boosted the town's population, more clubs and casinos appeared downtown, on Highway 91 (the Los Angeles Highway), and along Boulder Highway. Eventually, the nightly merriment in the early thirties inspired someone to coin the phrase: "every night is New Year's Eve in Las Vegas." By the mid-thirties, major clubs like The Meadows and Pair-O-Dice (later the 91-Club), on the as yet unnamed "Strip," vied with the lively Apache Bar and Golden Camel downtown. But Las Vegas did not yet possess the ultramodern resort image of later years. As newswoman Florence Lee Jones later remembered, "the storefronts were more typical of the western frontier than of the modern resort familiar to residents today." Still, as early as the 1930s, Las Vegas's nascent recreational economy began to shape the town's urbanization. Aside from growth downtown, The Meadows, along with a group of new clubs scattered along the Boulder Highway catering to dam workers, stretched Las Vegas's urbanized zone to the southeast. To accommodate The Meadows and other club employees who needed housing near their jobs, homebuilders in 1931 began the new Sunrise Addition which, in the words of one contemporary, was "located at the end of Fremont Street on the road to the new casino." [13]

Aside from residential development, the dam-inspired influx of tourists, workers, and contractors exposed the town's appalling shortage of hotel rooms. To ease the strain, existing hotels expanded. The two-story Nevada Hotel near the railroad station added a third floor in 1931, while farther down Fremont, the MacDonald added sixteen more rooms and The Meadows fifty. Besides more rooms, Las Vegas desperately needed a first-class hotel. Fortunately, investors rushed in to fill both pressing needs. In July 1931, pioneer businessman Cyril Wengert sold his home on Fifth and Carson for $30,000 to the Virginia Hotel Corporation, which soon erected a building. In fact, the rapid change of land use from residential to commercial-recreational, forced many pioneer families into the nearby suburbs. The town's first "luxury" hotel, the Apache, opened on March 19, 1932. It contained the city's first elevator, which carried guests to an elaborate third-floor banquet room which seated 300 people. The Apache Bar and Casino, outfitted with $50,000 worth of furnishings, was easily the most elegant in southern Nevada. Thanks to the impetus of Hoover Dam, Las Vegas began to recognize the importance of building better hotels to attract a more affluent clientele.[14]

As the 1930s wore on, the dam and the hotels combined to attract other industries to town. A direct by-product of population and club growth was Coca Cola's decision in 1934 to build a bottling plant to service residents and guests. Food distributors and small hotel supply firms also began to cluster in town. Eventually, the growing resort industry supported a small convention business. Las Vegas's first major convention, consisting of 5,000 southern California Shriners, came in November 1935, with the Union Pacific ferrying the delegation up from Los Angeles. Such meetings were not only profitable for the hotels but residents as well, since almost half the town's inhabitants regularly rented out spare rooms to visitors.

Technological advances enhanced the town's popularity. New "cooling systems" were a case in point. First developed for theatres, department stores, and other large concerns, "swamp coolers" began appearing in homes by 1930. Nowhere was the new device embraced more universally than in Las Vegas. Thanks to Hoover Dam's cheap electricity, swamp coolers revolutionized living in the desert town. In earlier decades women and children had retreated in the summer months to California or Mt. Charleston, leaving the heat to the men, but swamp coolers and later air conditioning ended this practice. In addition, the new technology actually promoted Las Vegas tourism because, as Florence Lee Jones has observed, while such systems in 1938 were "almost unknown in many parts of the nation, every hotel, auto court, restaurant, business establishment and home in Las Vegas was now cooled."[15]

The increased tourism and physical expansion induced by Hoover Dam made city government more important. With leadership and policy suddenly major issues, the 1931 municipal election took on added significance. This was especially true after the then current Mayor Fred Hesse was arrested and nearly recalled from office in 1930 for violating the Volstead Act. Two major candidates vied for his office in 1931: City Commissioner Lou Hansell and Ernie Cragin, a prominent insurance broker and part-owner of the El Portal Theatre. Since municipal elections in Nevada traditionally were conducted on a nonpartisan basis, neither candidate wore a party label, but instead emphasized local issues and programs. In his campaign, Hansell touted the importance of road improvements as a tool for coping with urban growth while, at the same time, enhancing the town's appearance. To this end, he advocated the elimination of the "dust and mud nuisance" by allocating street department funds to gravel outlying streets for light traffic until the suburban population grew large enough to support a bond issue or assessments to oil the thoroughfares on a permanent basis. Hansell's running mate for city commission, Phil Bettelheim, promised to organize a "uniformed" police force and a small, paid fire department to supplement the volunteers. To promote the modernization of Las Vegas, he urged the creation of a downtown "business zone" complete with sidewalks, gutters, curbs, and streetlights. [16]

Opposing these two were three prominent businessmen, Cragin (for mayor), and W. C. German and William Mundy (for commission). A respected community leader, Cragin supported Franklin D. Roosevelt's bid for the presidency in 1932, a move which endeared him to Al Cahlan of the influential *Evening Review-Journal*. While the pro-Republican *Age* and its editor Charles "Pop" Squires maintained a cautious neutrality in the election, Cahlan vigorously boosted the candidacy of the Cragin team. Appealing to the booster spirit of all Las Vegans, Cahlan characterized the election of an "honest business administration" as the essential first step, "if . . . we hope to become the city which will take its place along with Phoenix, Salt Lake and Denver as great inland population and industrial centers." For its part, the Cragin team pledged citizens "an honest [and] efficient business administration." Noting that previous administrations had been charged with political favoritism, the three reformers claimed to be independent of all "cliques" and swore to uphold the "public interest." [17]

Another election issue saw Cahlan and Squires close ranks in a rare moment of unanimity. Both newspapers urged approval of a $160,000 bond issue to expand the capacity of the town's original 1911 sewer system. Contending that the bonds were "not an attempt to further burden taxpayers with a luxury," the *Review-Journal* explained that as dam construction boosted the town's population and extended the building canvas, public health demanded that the sewer facilities keep pace. Squires also supported the bonds, warning that "any of several of the large building operations being planned may be delayed by the inadequacy of our sewer system." Then, in an effort to convert prospective suburban residents and investors, he wondered aloud: "What will the many who desire to build homes in the outlying portions of the city do?" Clearly the impending dam exerted an influence. Not only did it succeed in bringing organizational order to the power and water distribution networks of the southwest but, closer to home, it also inspired the gateway town of Las Vegas to develop a much-needed public works program for modernizing its street, sewer, and utility systems. To virtually no one's surprise, the election produced a landslide victory for Cragin who buried his opponent by nearly an 8 to 1 margin (1,736 to 232). Mundy and German also won easily, as did the sewer bonds (1,152 to 546).[18]

The new officials took office in the midst of the great building fever which accompanied the start of dam construction. Clearly, the city's expansion demanded the enlargement of its infrastructure and physical plant. The Cragin team spent most of 1931 shoring up understaffed departments such as streets and police, while preparing an agenda of public works initiatives designed to meet the dictates of current and future growth. Finally on January 4, 1932, the mayor announced that work on the $160,000 expanded sewer system would begin in a few weeks. Thanks to the dam boom, Las Vegas was aggressively extending its physical boundaries at a time when most depression-struck cities were not. But even with the population growth and prosperity, city officials had to cut spending. The rising number of indigents in town, together with the need for police and other municipal services strained the budget and forced spending cutbacks. While engineering surveys and planning for the new waste network continued, the national depression worsened, drying up capital for bond issues. By 1933, Cragin had already ordered salary cuts for himself and other top officials. In some cases, two offices were combined into one, and some employees were furloughed. While the town was still committed to the sewer improvements, Cragin recognized that it might have to be a scaled-down version of the original program with work progressing slowly until the national depression subsided.[19]

The election of Franklin D. Roosevelt, however, dramatically changed this outlook. By the spring of 1933, the president's braintrust had already mapped out an ambitious strategy to promote relief and recovery. Within months, the New Deal boldly came to the aid of cities across the nation in building bridges, subways, freeways, and airports. Sunbelt cities were major beneficiaries, especially the urban southwest. As Bradford Luckingham and other historians have noted, El Paso, Tucson, Albuquerque, and especially Phoenix secured new schools, parks, and miles of badly needed streets and sewers. Smaller towns like Las Vegas and even North Las Vegas (which gained a water system in 1934) also benefited from the federal largesse. With funds in short supply, Mayor Cragin, the city commission, and the chamber of commerce wasted no time lobbying Nevada's congressional delegation, especially influential Democratic Senators Key Pittman and Pat McCarran, for federal help for the sewer project. Negotiations with the Civil Works Administration's (CWA) regional office in Salt Lake City continued throughout the summer of 1933. Estimates put the project's cost at $110,000, including labor and materials. Under the proposed formula, Washington would bear 30 percent of the expense and would loan the rest at low interest. Such liberal terms offered townsmen the rare opportunity to finance a badly needed improvement at little cost to local taxpayers. Within a year, CWA crews were hard at work extending waste networks in "all the built-up area including the Westside." Thanks to New Deal funding, the city was able to extend its sewer system to service all the new suburban neighborhoods created by the dam boom.[20]

During the next six years, federal spending funded more public works projects, which improved the city's quality of life and provided a foundation to support new rounds of expansion in the 1940s. With Senators Pittman and McCarran casting vital swing votes for many New Deal programs, the Roosevelt Administration was particularly responsive to the needs of Las Vegas, Reno, and other Nevada communities. Between 1934 and 1935, CWA and Federal Emergency Relief Administration (FERA) workers had repaved over fifty-eight blocks. Much of the work was in the suburbs, where the "dust menace" had long been a problem. But this was not all. Cragin's strong alliance with McCarran and the Democratic party brought other improvements. The New Deal "finished" the half-built City Park (located on the old fairgrounds between Stewart, Washington, Fifth, and Main), equipping it with trees, driveways, baseball fields, and other recreational facilities. Then, following a major fire in May 1934 which gutted the city's old high school (which now functions as a grade school), Public Works Administration (PWA) officials agreed to build a new grade school at Fourth and Bridger (today the Clark County Courthouse Annex).[21]

The city's efforts to secure federal help for the construction of needed buildings did not end with the school project. Having already acquired a new post office and federal building, Mayor Cragin and other leaders of the emerging recreation city now pushed for a convention center. With Boulder Dam scheduled for completion in 1936, everyone knew that tourists would eventually have to replace the construction workers if the town's fledgling casinos were to prosper. For several years a convention center had been supported by Las Vegas's forty or more fraternal lodges who had repeatedly suggested that the town build a multistoried structure with a hall and offices sufficient to host large convention meetings. Financing would come from the lodges renting space. But it would not be enough. A solution was finally reached in the fall of 1934 when the town's American Legion Post #8 agreed to build a War Memorial Building in honor of local veterans. The city donated a parcel of land (today the site of city hall) and the Legion pledged $5,000. Construction, however, could not begin until another $80,000 could be secured. Enter the federal government. Satisfied that the building would qualify as a "civic auditorium" and thus fulfill its project guidelines, the Works Progress Administration (WPA) contributed $80,000 worth of free labor and materials. When it opened in 1936, the War Memorial Building provided Las Vegas with its first major venue for conventions—a major step toward developing a full-scale resort economy.[22]

The New Deal continued to build facilities that would eventually contribute to Las Vegas's emergence as a resort city. Thanks to the WPA, a public golf course and fish hatchery (in the City Park) for newly created Boulder Lake (today Lake Mead) both opened in 1937. Access to Las Vegas was also improved when New Deal funding finished the paving and widening of the Los Angeles Highway—an event which forever abolished southern Nevada's remoteness. Of course, townsmen recognized that airplanes were the key to smashing the desert barrier between California and Las Vegas. Spirited efforts by Mayor Cragin and his successors to secure WPA or PWA funding for a modern new airport met with enthusiasm in Washington. But Western Air Express, owner of the existing municipal facility north of town, proved a formidable opponent. Unwilling to surrender its monopoly of Las Vegas air travel, Western successfully thwarted every city initiative in Washington—until World War II began in 1939.[23]

The New Deal not only shaped the city's physical plant but its political system as well. In his 1935 bid for re-election, Mayor Ernie Cragin credited his close contacts with the Roosevelt administration (and Senator McCarran) with helping him "save . . . individual property owners over $100,000 in street, park, sidewalk and curb and gutter improvements." Moreover, Cragin boasted that his re-election would only ensure more public improvements. Indeed, he promised to "complete the pavement of our streets at low cost . . . finish our municipal park [and] proceed with sidewalk and curb and gutter improvements . . . [which] will provide employment for many of our citizens who are now out of work."[24]

Ironically, it was a controversial New Deal project which resulted in Cragin's defeat. In 1934, City Commissioner Leonard Arnett (a club owner) and other businessmen, convinced that Southern Nevada Power's electric rates were too high, began a campaign to secure New Deal funding for a public power plant and transmission line from the dam to Las Vegas. Cragin, long an associate of C. C. Ronnow, Samuel Lawson, and other local businessmen who owned the utility, was slow to join the public power bandwagon. Charges of political favoritism for New Deal contracts teamed with the power issue and his friendship with partisan *Review-Journal* editor Al Cahlan to ensure his defeat. Despite a considerable record of accomplishments in just four years, Cragin could not shake the pro-utility image which Arnett had fashioned in the public mind. On May 6, 1935, city voters elected Leonard Arnett mayor by a majority of almost 400 votes against Cragin (1,472 to 1,093). In addition Cragin's cohorts, W. C. German and C. V. T. Gilbert, lost their commission seats to public power advocates Gene Ward and Henry Marble.[25]

Upon taking office, Mayor Arnett and the new commissioners immediately authorized a survey of Southern Nevada Power's current system to estimate its value and the cost of building a competing city network. By August 1935 consulting engineer, Barry Dibble, had completed his report which put the cost of buying Nevada Power's works at $150,000 plus another $100,000 for building a transmission line from the dam. Later, using Dibble's figures, the city prepared a FERA project application calling for $250,000 "to aid in financing the construction or purchase and remodeling of a municipal power system and incidental facilities." The commission also empowered Arnett to petition the Colorado River Commission "for a sufficient allotment of the power to supply the inhabitants of the city of Las Vegas, as, if and when, it is ascertained the amount of power which will be required to supply the inhabitants of the city of Las Vegas." But executives at Southern Nevada Power were determined to oppose any purchase of their facilities. In their view, the utility had served the town faithfully for thirty years and the new line to Hoover Dam would, by 1937, give Las Vegas nearly the lowest rates in the country.[26]

The utility's opposition combined with a worsening local recession to stop the public power initiative. In April 1937, the mayor warned that cuts in city tax revenues by both the county and state seriously threatened the town's meager surplus and raised the dreaded prospect of seeking emergency loans just to meet the payroll. The time hardly seemed right for pursuing an expensive power project, but Arnett insisted on proceeding with a bond election for the enterprise. Once again, as in 1935, controversy swirled about the issue. In the forefront of opposition was Nevada Power and the Las Vegas Taxpayer's League, led by future Mayor John Russell and others, who argued that the town had already reached its taxable limit and further outlays would overburden property owners. Arnett countered that the project was the key to lowering electric rates—a crucial prerequisite for future growth. The campaign was bitterly fought on both sides, but, in the end, the bond issue carried by 1,041 to 884.[27]

Arnett's apparent victory was only a prelude to his defeat. Revenues fell steadily throughout the latter 1930s as a mild recession signaled the end of the Boulder Dam bonanza. Between 1935 and 1940 Las Vegas revenues from property taxes collected within Clark County dropped from $1.50 per $5.00 of assessed valuation to $1.05. Gaming, gasoline, and other tourist-related taxes kept the town afloat, reinforcing the view of many local business leaders that continued prosperity could best be ensured by developing a recreational economy. But Mayor Arnett's dreams of building that economy and luring other industries with low-cost public power died in the spring of 1938. Clearly, with a new recession on the rise statewide, revenues would continue to decline. And with the city's bonded indebtedness reaching its legal limits, a new bond issue seemed unwise. These doubts led commissioners to appoint a Las Vegas Power Board composed of prominent civic and business leaders to investigate the problem. After some study, the group recommended postponing the power project. City commissioners and other officials reluctantly agreed. But an irate Mayor Arnett first rejected the board's view and then, as a gesture of disgust, resigned his office on May 4, 1938. He was immediately replaced by City Commissioner Henry Marble who, the next day, voted with the commission to postpone the PWA application in order "to permit the matter to rest until conditions appear more favorable for the successful consummation of the plan."[28]

The departure of thousands of dam workers and their families coupled with a reduction of New Deal spending in 1937 to slow the Las Vegas economy. With the effort to lure industry with low-cost public power temporarily stalled, local promoters focused their sights on tourism. As the "gateway to Hoover Dam," Las Vegas was already attracting 300,000 tourists annually. In an attempt to attract more, local Elks in 1935 announced plans to exploit the town's wide-open frontier image with a "Helldorado" rodeo. The local response was positive, as most of the town's population pitched in to help by building signs, manning booths, and cheering the parade. The next year saw construction of a Helldorado Village complete with wooden sidewalks, hitching posts, watering troughs, town pumps, and other western artifacts. The first Helldorado, along with succeeding ones, symbolized the community's determination to promote Las Vegas and make it a permanent tourist attraction. A similar commitment made the first Boulder Dam Regatta a success. In November 1936, as Boulder Lake (later named Lake Mead in honor of Reclamation Commissioner Elwood Mead) filled completely behind the newly finished dam, Las Vegans staged their second regatta featuring seventy-five boats and thousands of spectators. Future years would see the town exploit the sporting and recreational advantages of the lake and its shoreline to diversify its market strategy beyond the dam and frontier images to attract more summer vacationers.[29]

The divorce business also became a growing source of revenue for Las Vegas in the late 1930s. While the sheer number of cases became more significant after World War II, one cannot underestimate the publicity value gained in the late thirties from such celebrated media events as the Clark Gable-Ria Langham divorce. Bursting upon Las Vegas in early 1939 to fulfill Nevada's six-week residency requirement, Mrs. Gable became the focus of national attention. According to historian Phillip Earl, while Gable cavorted in Hollywood with Carole Lombard, Ria played the gay divorcée role in Las Vegas, "dealing craps, roulette and blackjack at Frank Houskey's Apache Club on Fremont Street and cruising Lake Mead on his yacht. She also took horseback rides into the surrounding deserts, hosted big names from Hollywood at her home and boosted Las Vegas in interviews with the national press." Local casino owners were quick to cash in on the media attention. Former Los Angeles gambler Guy McAfee timed the opening of his 91-Club to coincide with the Gable divorce publicity, while owners of Fremont Street's big four casinos—the Las Vegas Club, Apache, Northern, and Boulder clubs—all announced significant expansion and programs. In the months following the Gable divorce decree (on March 7, 1939), "all the world began to show up to get their own divorces where Ria and Clark got theirs." Celebrities, industrialists, and middle-class Californians descended upon Las Vegas by the thousands during the war years and beyond. To handle the influx, investors remodeled the old Kyle Ranch north of town in 1939 and created Las Vegas's first haven for prospective divorcées, the Boulderado Dude Ranch.[30]

Tourism teamed with the old standby, railroading, to keep the town alive in the late 1930s. Nevertheless, the local economy sputtered in the absence of federal spending. The political crisis of 1938 only reinforced the sense of gloom. Declining revenues strengthened the position of conservative taxpayers who opposed expensive public works and an activist city government. Not surprisingly, John Russell of the Las Vegas Taxpayer's League, won the mayoral election of 1939. A prominent landowner and longtime resident, Russell reassured voters by proposing a "sound financial policy, keeping municipal expenditures at the lowest point consistent with progressive policies." Following a campaign largely devoid of the usual name calling, voters elected Russell. In the commission races, newcomer Al Corradetti and pioneer Westside merchant C. V. T. Gilbert also won. It seemed that the political bickering was over. In a post-election editorial a relieved Al Cahlan observed that with the new team of Russell, Corradetti, and Gilbert joining talented incumbents Joe Ronnow and Herb Krause, "the city is assured a business administration for the next two years."[31]

To almost everyone's surprise, the next year was marked by unprecedented chaos. Within months Mayor Russell and the Board were at odds on virtually every major question. According to *Age* editor Pop Squires, the clashes stemmed more from personalities than issues, as the intractable mayor brooked no opposition to his policies. Moreover, his penchant for charging dissenting commissioners with graft and stupidity only exacerbated tensions. By the fall of 1940, a major crisis arose over the size of the city tax rate. Russell wanted it set at $1.05 per $1,000 of assessed valuation while the board preferred $1.25. Russell's figure, of course, created the illusion of lower taxes, but since the total city, county, school district, and state property tax was limited by law to $5.00, the issue was largely moot. The state's slice of the pie was set initially by the legislature, the city then chose its share, and the county got the rest. Since Las Vegas, with the highest assessed property in the county, contributed mightily to the latter anyway, the commissioners wanted the $1.25 rate to boost the municipal treasury. As Pop Squires observed, "since the full rate will prevail anyhow, the question resolved itself into whether the city or county commissioners shall have the expenditure of the major portion of the funds. . . . So, if the county board can jockey the city into accepting a low tax rate, the county gets most of the money to spend for county purposes outside the city." While the commissioners' stand may have reflected the conventional wisdom regarding the issue, the tax-conscious Russell would not bend. These and other petty disputes sparked further intransigence on both sides. For the next year the mayor and commissioners battled in the worst political crisis in Las Vegas history. Shouting matches, lawsuits, recall efforts, and mass resignations embarrassed the city and brought government to a virtual standstill. In the end, Russell was removed as mayor in a trial conducted by the commissioners, and businessman Howell Garrison was appointed to finish his term. In addition, the four commissioners themselves either resigned or were defeated as a house-cleaning fever swept the community.[32]

The political controversy had to be settled and a measure of stability restored, because Las Vegas once again had become the object of federal interest. Following Hitler's invasion of Europe and the British retreat from Dunkirk, the Roosevelt Administration was preparing for possible war. With the advent of modern bombers and their threat to coastal cities, Las Vegas, Pocatello, Salt Lake, Phoenix, Albuquerque, and other western cities became ideal locations for defense plants and military installations. Moreover, the sunbelt, with its year-round flying weather, was well suited for the training of pilots, gunners, and bombardiers. In the end, World War II would change the American west forever. As Gerald Nash has demonstrated, the national emergency would diversify the region's economy from the earlier reliance on mining and agriculture to an expanded role in manufacturing and science. Las Vegas would participate in these events, acquiring a magnesium factory, an air base and, ultimately, a proving ground for nuclear weapons. More especially, the war would stimulate casino gambling and urbanization while also helping the city polish a glittering new image.[33]

To some extent, the city's effusive support for Hoover Dam, President Roosevelt (who carried the town handily in every election), and the New Deal encouraged the War Department to build in the region. The militarization of the Las Vegas area dates from June 1940 when the War Department began constructing a small marine auxiliary base at Boulder City's airport consisting of a hangar, storage tanks, and a dormitory for crews servicing navy planes. Of greater importance, however, was the new airport Las Vegas hoped to receive as a by-product of President Roosevelt's program to strengthen western air defenses. For the previous five years, Western Air Express had successfully blocked efforts to use New Deal funding to build a municipal airport on its property. Now, with American security threatened by Hitler, federal officials brushed aside the company's interests. In the summer of 1940 the Civil Aeronautics Authority pledged $340,000 to help purchase and upgrade Western's facility eight miles northeast of town (today Nellis Air Force Base) for joint commercial and military use. Supported by the Junior Chamber of Commerce and other civic organizations, city and county officials pursued the offer. On October 5, 1940, the city of Las Vegas offered the airport to the Army Air Corps for a dollar a year rental. By early January 1941, the city had acquired the site from Western and so, on January 23 of that year the air corps signed a lease with the town. Army officials approved building plans in March. Ultimately, the army spent over $25 million, providing the base with hangars, storage facilities, barracks, fuel tanks, a 4,000-foot east-west runway and a 5,900-foot north-south counterpart. A third runway plus grading, drainage, and hangars finally gave Las Vegas a decent airport for joint military and commercial airline use. Gradually, the War Department revealed its plans for the field. It was not to be an air base but an air training school—a million-acre shooting range to prepare army pilots and gunners for airborne combat.[34]

Townsmen rejoiced as they contemplated the vast payroll harvest that Clark County casinos and businesses would reap. By October 1941, with land condemnations finalized by the courts and federal marshalls clearing the last stragglers out of southeastern Nye County, the new center began operations.[35] During the next few months hundreds of recruits arrived at the base, swelling the population of North Las Vegas and, for the duration of the war, partially offsetting the tourist loss on Fremont Street. Actual air-to-air training began soon after Pearl Harbor on January 13, 1942. As the Pacific war intensified and America prepared for its great counterattack following the Battle of the Coral Sea, the Las Vegas Air Gunnery School trained gunners at a frantic pace. By May 1942, the program graduated classes of 4,000 students every six weeks! Then in 1944, as the United States prepared for the eventual invasion of Iwo Jima, Okinawa, and Japan itself, the base's vast gunnery ranges were expanded to almost 3.3 million acres. In the spring of 1945 fighter planes joined the bombers at Las Vegas and the nearby Indian Springs base, bringing the gunnery school's manpower to almost 13,000 men and women. But there was more. Thanks to the efforts of Nevada Senator Pat McCarran and utility officials, the army also began erecting barracks at Boulder City to house troops assigned to protect Boulder Dam from saboteurs. It was expected that, when completed, "Camp Sibert" would support over 700 men—another payroll boost for the local economy.[36] By 1941, Camp Sibert, the gunnery school, and a growing number of bases in the government's Desert Warfare Center in Arizona, southeastern California, and southern Nevada would dramatically swell revenues for Las Vegas's emerging casino industry.

But soldiers were not the only new players at the tables. In 1941, the federal government announced plans to build a giant magnesium plant near town. Once again, Las Vegas was part of a larger story. Because of feverish dam construction programs in the 1930s, southern and western cities—with their new sources of cheap power and water—had become prime sites for war industries. Thanks to the influence of Arizona Senator Carl Hayden, for instance, Phoenix had already been ringed with air bases and was in the process of securing a huge aluminum extrusion plant. Similar projects were also under way in New Mexico, Texas, California, and southeastern sunbelt states. Aside from Pat McCarran, the driving force behind the Las Vegas factory was Howard Eells, an obscure Cleveland businessman whose firm held the patent for a particular type of refractory which could be manufactured from either magnesite or brucite. In the 1930s Eells's company, Basic Refractories, manufactured heat-resistant bricks for the inner walls of high-temperature furnaces. Anxious to locate a large, dependable supply of the needed raw materials, Eells's geologists examined deposits from around the west. Impressed by the high grade and size of the brucite and magnesite deposits on public lands near Gabbs, Nevada, Eells acquired the mineral rights and began shipping the ore to Ohio in 1936.[37]

Once World War II began, Eells recognized the potential value of his deposits for the manufacture of war materiel. He dreamed of making record profits, but two major companies blocked his way. Prior to the war, Dow Chemical and Alcoa Aluminum had largely monopolized magnesium production and fabrication in the United States. These firms, along with their British and German counterparts, controlled the valuable patents for chemical processes used to transform magnesium into tracer bullets, flares, bomb casings, fuselage components, and other key defense products. Smaller concerns like Basic Refractories were normally excluded from these activities. But World War II suddenly changed everything.[38]

In 1941, while Germany's Luftwaffe was pounding London, Eells met Major C. J. P. Ball, president of Magnesium Elecktron, Ltd., a British firm. Prior to meeting Eells, Ball had traveled to Canada in hopes of building a plant far removed from Nazi bombers. Ball, however, was impressed by Basic's holdings in Nevada. An alliance was inevitable; Eells controlled an unlimited supply of raw materials and Ball the refining know-how. Both men needed a factory, and Nevada's congressional delegation had the clout to build it. Efficiency would have dictated that the ore be hauled to existing plants in California, but then Nevada would have lost the factory. Efficiency might also have demanded that the magnesium deposits in nearby Overton (only fifty miles from Las Vegas) be used, but then Eells owned the deposits at Gabbs, 350 miles away. So, at first, the federal government paid an exorbitant price to transport Gabbs magnesite 1,100 miles by rail via Salt Lake City to Las Vegas. Eventually, Washington built road connections (including a new Las Vegas thoroughfare, Rancho Road, to prevent the heavy trucks from tearing up existing city roads), linking Gabbs with Las Vegas.[39]

For their part, Nevada officials allied with Eells to get the Basic plant near Las Vegas. For years chamber of commerce leaders, determined to minimize the boom and bust cycles associated with reliance upon the mining industry, had struggled to provide Las Vegas with an industrial base. Despite the proximity of low-cost dam power and Lake Mead water, no corporation had been willing to invest the $7 million required to build a pipeline, pumping station, and power transmission lines. Enter Nevada Senators Key Pittman, Pat McCarran, and veteran Congressman James Scrugham. This influential trio allied with former Nevada Senator Charles Henderson, now chairman of the powerful Reconstruction Finance Corporation, to push federal funding of the factory. Actually, the factory should never have been built. California had the plant capacity, and American firms owned the patents (which they would not share with Eells) to chemical processes more efficient than Ball's. Nevertheless, the Roosevelt administration approved RFC funding for the factory in southern Nevada.[40]

On July 5, 1941, the U.S. Defense Plant Corporation, a subsidiary of the Reconstruction Finance Corporation, signed a contract with Eells's new firm, Basic Magnesium, Inc., to build a plant to produce 33.6 million pounds of magnesium (the amount was later increased to 112 million tons) per year. The projected output would be ten times Germany's total production for 1940. The contract specified that the federal government would own all buildings, land, equipment, and magnesium. The Defense Plant Corporation even reserved the right to approve all sales and stockpiling of the metal. BMI only managed the operations. As compensation, Eells's firm received $1 per ton. Basic administered all personnel matters, including hiring and firing; although the U.S. treasury paid workers' salaries.[41]

Ultimately, the magnesium project would spawn a new industrial suburb—Henderson. The original plans in 1940 did not provide for a town, just a large factory fifteen miles southeast of Las Vegas on a barren hillside west of Boulder Highway. While Las Vegas expected to house the work force, Eells preferred Boulder City whose atmosphere was more conducive to discipline. The Bureau of Reclamation, however, balked at the scheme, claiming that little Boulder City lacked the housing and services to accommodate an extra 10,000 workers and their families. Throughout the summer of 1941 Las Vegas city leaders fought to prevent the construction of a new town near the magnesium factory. Naturally, federal officials were also anxious to avoid the expense, but by fall government surveys clearly demonstrated that Las Vegas lacked the water, sewer, and other utilities necessary to service an immediate population increase of 10,000 people. To a large extent, the gunnery school's drain on local services convinced the government (more specifically the Office of Price Management) in November of 1941 to build the Basic Townsite. To forestall this move, the city commission pledged support for a bond election to finance a new sewage treatment plant, but it was too late. Las Vegas should have expanded its capacity years earlier: the sudden war boom had caught the town by surprise. Nevertheless, Las Vegas businessmen, having been deprived a decade earlier of Hoover Dam housing, demanded that Washington lift wartime building restrictions locally and provide funding to extend the city's infrastructure. Under prodding from Senator McCarran, the Defense Plant Corporation (an RFC subsidiary) struck a compromise, approving a separate but "temporary" townsite of "demountable homes" while also granting one thousand additional building permits for Las Vegas.[42]

Given little choice, Eells agreed to erect some housing near the plant, but he opposed building an entire town. He soon changed his mind when the Defense Plant Corporation and other federal agencies refused to approve funding for employee housing unless U.S. Public Health Service standards were met. These required streets, sewers, stores, and recreational facilities for the men as well as water, power, and gas supplies. Faced with these obligations, Eells had to build a company town. In September 1941, McNeil Construction Company of Los Angeles began work on the plant and Basic Townsite (later named Henderson in honor of RFC Chairman and former Nevada Senator Charles B. Henderson). Even before construction began, Las Vegas boosters recognized that the factory, together with the gunnery school and the city's strategic location along key truck, rail, and air routes between the Rockies and southern California, guaranteed a housing and population boom of enormous proportions. Already by December 1941, retail sales, rentals, and construction soared, while on a regional scale, mining, farming, and ranching were again paying the kind of dividends reminiscent of 1917.[43]

Actual construction of BMI was a massive undertaking. At one point, 13,000 workers (10 percent of Nevada's population!) toiled on the project. Though originally designed as a modest operation, the plant's capacity was enlarged by tenfold in response to federal concerns over dwindling supplies of ammunition. Revised blueprints called for the construction of a gargantuan structure, stretching nearly two miles in length and a mile in width, to house the largest metallic magnesium plant in America. Groundbreaking occurred in September 1941 at a 2,800-acre site midway between Las Vegas and Boulder City. As noted, the Defense Plant Corporation had signed a contract with Eells's newly formed Basic Magnesium Industries to build the great complex. Basic, in turn, had subcontracted with McNeil Construction of Los Angeles to build the plant, townsite, power lines from Hoover Dam, and the 14-mile-long water pipeline from Lake Mead. Thanks to a feverish construction pace, production began by the fall of 1942, as the first magnesium ingots rolled out of the plant along a special railroad spur connecting with the Union Pacific's main line just south of Las Vegas. Between September 1942 and November 1944 (when production ceased), the factory shipped over 166 million pounds of magnesium ingots to Los Angeles factories. As early as 1942, the symbiotic relationship between the two "martial cities" was evident. Las Vegas provided the electricity and magnesium to feed southern California's aerospace and munitions factories, while Los Angeles provided the defense workers and troops who thronged Las Vegas's casinos throughout the war.[44]

As was the case in the dam era, federal spending for World War II triggered suburban growth in and around the city of Las Vegas. The construction of the Basic Magnesium plant resulted in the creation of Henderson, while the army gunnery school expanded North Las Vegas. Following the attack on Pearl Harbor, special emphasis was given to the emerging magnesium town southeast of Las Vegas. During the spring of 1942, 13,000 construction workers toiled at the factory site, living in an adjacent tent city with no power, flush toilets, or running water. By October 1942, only three of the projected ten separate cells of the Basic Magnesium plant were finished. By now, 1,000 men (from both BMI and McNeil Construction) lived in homes near Las Vegas, but 4,800 still slept in army tents. In September 1942, the *Review-Journal* reported that of 9,000 McNeil employees surveyed, 61 percent lived in Las Vegas, North Las Vegas, and the Westside; 3.5 percent in Boulder City; and 12 percent in the Boulder Highway hamlets of Pittman and East Las Vegas. The next year, however, brought a substantial out-migration. By May 1944, with Basic Townsite completed (the town was named "Henderson" when the post office opened on January 10, 1944), a new survey showed that over 53 percent of the chemical workers now lived in Henderson and only 35 percent in the Las Vegas area.[45]

As more cells came on line, the federal government struggled to complete the 300-unit Victory Village complex. Begun in 1942, the project contained a school, recreation center, apartments, and dormitories; a year later it also had a cafeteria, day nursery, community center, several food markets, and a department store. Yet, it was not enough. Plagued by a chronic shortage of defense workers, BMI eventually had to import black employees from Arkansas, Mississippi, and elsewhere. This move forced the construction in 1943 of Carver Park, a 324-unit housing facility (to the east across the Boulder Highway) for blacks with one-, two-, and three-bedroom apartments for families, dormitories for the unmarried, plus an athletic field, recreation hall, and grammar school. These separate facilities made Basic a racially divided community. The town's two grade schools were racially segregated (as were plant restrooms, the commissary, and even water fountains), although the high school admitted black and white students. While helpful, these housing projects could not handle the eventual flood of defense workers entering Clark County. As a result, many families found themselves living in motor courts, trailer parks, shanties, tents, and mine shafts, prompting three years of complaints from A.F. of L. and C.I.O. union leaders. In fact, the housing issue became such a concern that controversy even surrounded the planning stages of Carver Park and Victory Village, as union officials pressured a reluctant, cost-conscious Defense Housing Corporation to revise preliminary blueprints and install air conditioning, electrical refrigeration, and "fireproof construction" for the residents. [46]

With help from both the federal government and Las Vegas residents, a new town rose in just over a year. At the time, few realized it would become a permanent Nevada city, but the indications were there. Within a few months of settlement, Basic residents began forming organizations to heighten their sense of community. In October 1942, for instance, a local American Legion post sponsored creation of the town's first Boy Scout troop in the new BMI school. In that same year, Railroad Pass School District officials and faculty joined Las Vegas members of the Nevada Congress of Parents and Teachers in calling a meeting of mothers to launch a P.T.A. chapter for the school. In education, housing, and business, leaders of nearby cities helped the fledgling town organize its institutional life. By early 1943 its social calendar bulged with club meetings, sewing classes, arts and crafts, orchestra rehearsals, and other weekly events typical of small towns across the nation. [47]

Thanks to the army gunnery school, North Las Vegas underwent a similar though less spectacular transformation. The community actually began in 1917 when Thomas L. Williams, a Eureka, Utah rancher, moved his family to southern Nevada. Preferring the wide open spaces to urban congestion, Williams bought 140 acres several miles north of Fremont Street. Imbued perhaps with the idea of establishing a small ranch to supply Las Vegas with meat, Williams dug an artesian well. Then, in an effort to diversify his investment, Williams reserved 40 acres for himself and subdivided the remaining 100 into approximately 80 lots. He then began advertising his homesites, luring residents with promises of no taxes, no building restrictions, no licenses—in short, a laissez-faire community reminiscent of the old west. The only restriction was, to some, an appealing one: by law every deed contained a clause banning property sales to blacks. Throughout the 1920s the area grew slowly, a reflection of stagnant conditions before the dam. Yet the small community prospered, thanks to an underground economy. During Prohibition, North Las Vegas thrived as a "bootleg suburb," surreptitiously supplying Las Vegas speakeasies on Block 17 with illegal spirits. The community's artesian well supply made it a perfect site for distilling and bottling alcohol. [48]

During the flush years of dam construction, the growth and development of Las Vegas encouraged residents of Williams's townsite to organize and exploit the boom. At a public meeting inhabitants agreed to name their community Vegas Verdes, but public sentiment soon changed in favor of exploiting the now famous moniker of their neighbor to the south. Thus, in

1932, the community's first post office opened with the postmark "North Las Vegas." Content with its growth in the 1930s, Las Vegas made no concerted effort to annex its northern suburb, perhaps because most residents generally dismissed the place as a den of thieves, bootleggers, and riff-raff. Moreover, the area's property values were too low to boost the city's tax base significantly. In the long run, however, failure to annex North Las Vegas was a fateful mistake. By the 1960s, that suburb would be strong enough to block Las Vegas's imperialistic designs to the north for the rest of the century. Beginning in the 1930s, North Las Vegas began to grow stronger, playing a larger role in the metropolitan area as a low-cost housing zone for lower-income workers and their families. Throughout the 1930s, its population grew slowly, reaching 2,000 by 1941. World War II only accelerated its growth. Thanks to the stimulus of the nearby air gunnery school and later Nellis Air Force Base, construction soared and the town mushroomed. By 1940, North Las Vegas's population had nearly doubled and a decade of Cold War spending drove it over 18,000 by 1960. This growth brought an expansion of government functions, forcing an end to the laissez-faire tradition. In an effort to provide efficient fire and police protection as well as streets, sewers, and other municipal services, residents incorporated their city in 1946, approved their city charter in 1952, and modernized their municipal administration by adopting the council-manager form of government.[49]

Like Los Angeles, Phoenix, Houston, and other young sunbelt centers, Las Vegas was so overwhelmed by the flood of soldiers and defense workers that it escaped the wartime building restrictions which shackled growth in many frostbelt cities. As a result, residential construction boomed in Las Vegas as well as in Henderson and North Las Vegas. As early as fall 1941, the Federal Housing Administration approved the construction of eight hundred new homes in town. Thanks to the gunnery school and BMI, federal officials authorized the development of the Mayfair, Biltmore, and Huntridge additions. Most of the activity centered in the latter zone south of Charleston Boulevard along the newly created Maryland Parkway. Here McNeil Construction, builder of BMI, erected dwellings mainly for defense workers. To some extent, the sudden boom strained municipal services. In particular, the water and power companies were not prepared for such major developments. Southern Nevada Power actually refused to string its lines, citing the inevitable diaspora of families after the war. A threatened lawsuit by the city against the utility finally defused this intransigence. Similar understandings had to be worked out with the water company. Despite the confusion, the effects of federal wartime spending were magical. Within four years, the town's physical plant and housing supply had expanded enormously, laying a powerful base for the postwar years when a vibrant resort economy would team with Cold War spending to produce a substantial metropolis.[50]

Defense spending was an obvious by-product of the worldwide conflict. But, like the dam earlier, World War II also strengthened the town's recreational economy. Between 1940 and war's end, thousands of soldiers and their dependents thronged local casinos as did thousands more defense workers from Basic Magnesium and southern California factories. For their part, the casinos not only provided entertainment for a war-weary public, but also contributed to the overall war effort by supporting relief efforts, contributing to scrap drives, and hosting numerous shows boosting war bond sales. Of course, the industry also lost some business. Beginning in November 1942 the military curfews (which closed casinos and bars from 2 to 10 a.m.) cut profits, as did the Office of Price Administration's (OPA) meat rationing system which forced many local restaurants to close. But, overall, the war strengthened the emerging resort economy. By partially depriving the city of tourists for almost four years, the war magnified their importance in the minds of promoters. At the same time, the substantial casino play by defense workers and visiting troops confirmed gambling as Las Vegas's main postwar industry.[51]

Clearly, the national emergency created many problems for Las Vegas. Yet, like the railroad and Hoover Dam before it, World War II represented a bonanza for the small town's economy. The upgrading of airport facilities, construction of BMI, creation of Basic Townsite, the new housing, roads, sewers, and other improvements, along with military and defense payrolls all exerted a multiplier effect. Moreover, with the fall of the Iron Curtain just a year later, two wartime legacies would play key roles in the city's subsequent development. In 1949 the old gunnery school and range would become Nellis Air Force Base, the nation's primary tactical weapons training center, and in 1951 the atom bomb would find a home at the nearby Nevada Test Site. The war tried, tested, and transformed Las Vegas. The seemingly endless rounds of rationing, shortages, scrap drives, and fund-raising measured the community's resolve. But, as it did for cities in California, New Mexico, Texas, and other sunbelt states, World War II both created and confirmed the strategic importance of Las Vegas, thereby enhancing its chances of attracting future defense programs. Fifteen years of frantic federal spending changed Las Vegas forever.

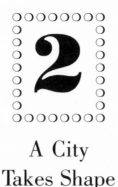

A City
Takes Shape

As wartime federal spending energized the city's resort and defense economies, Las Vegas finally ended its lifelong dependence on the railroad. Throughout the 1940s, gamblers from California, Texas, and other states transformed the little clubs downtown into spacious casinos just as other investors invaded the suburban lands south of town to erect the first Strip resorts. In response to the wartime and postwar growth of business, the state of Nevada would strengthen its regulation of gaming while the city would struggle to modernize government and expand to meet the demands of casino-driven growth. Spirited campaigns would also be undertaken to safeguard public health, end prostitution, and control spending. At the same time, municipal and county officials would attempt to widen the area's tax base by promoting tourism, saving Basic Magnesium's factory, and re-opening the army air base. In a similar vein, Las Vegas would fight to annex the Strip and its emerging suburbs to the south.

Despite the town's prospects, Las Vegas was not prepared for the population boom occasioned by the war. With limited water and sewer networks, a primeval telephone system, an overworked volunteer fire department, and understaffed police force, the city struggled to cope with the onslaught of new visitors and residents. A strange ambivalence gripped municipal leaders who welcomed the growth but bemoaned the problems it created. Still, the future looked bright. Economic diversification finally seemed in the offing as BMI president Howard Eells predicted that Las Vegas would become the "hub" of America's light metals industry and that "the whole area will be built up into one great city." But the jump from city to metropolis would involve much effort. Even well-wishers like

Charles A. Bennett, Los Angeles director of planning, warned local leaders in 1942 that "Las Vegas must shed its rompers and get into the swing of things." He and others urged City Hall to abandon its laissez-faire tradition of hodgepodge development and adopt a master plan for schools, rights-of-way, street networks, and commercial and residential zones.[1]

While politicians readily acknowledged the need, they were slow to adopt these reforms. Two major factors delayed action. First, the Russell crisis and its aftermath hampered city government from 1940 until 1943 when Ernie Cragin was elected. Second, the dramatic development of the casino-resort industry during the war accelerated the urbanization of Las Vegas, briefly overwhelming local government's ability to cope with the physical expansion. By the time of Pearl Harbor, not only was the Las Vegas area in the midst of a defense boom, but the casino sector of the local economy was also undergoing a dramatic expansion. To some extent, these events antedated the war. Even before the world conflict flooded Las Vegas with soldiers and defense workers who permanently revived the fledgling gaming industry, events in Los Angeles presaged a new era. For two decades (and especially during the administration of Mayor Frank Shaw), prostitution and gambling had flourished in the City of the Angels. Gamblers like Tony Cornero, Guy McAfee, and others ran their operations with little police interference until the election of reform Mayor Fletcher Bowron in 1938. Once in power, Bowron declared war on the city's illegal brothels, closing many of them down. Illegal casinos were the next target. As the moral crusade intensified, police Captain Guy McAfee, a vice squad commander and longtime operator, was forced to resign or face prosecution on gambling charges. Pressured out of southern California, McAfee and other gamblers migrated to Las Vegas in 1938 where their expertise in casino management was welcomed. McAfee invested immediately, purchasing the Pair-O-Dice Club (renamed the 91-Club) on the Los Angeles Highway. He moved to Las Vegas permanently in 1939 to run his roadhouse south of town. In fact, it was McAfee who first referred to the four-mile strip of Highway 91 south of town as "the Strip"—a reference to the Sunset Strip he had so often traveled between Beverly Hills and Hollywood.[2]

Although casino gambling was legal in the silver state, the Las Vegas gambling market paled in comparison to southern California's. But World War II encouraged the industry's growth in Las Vegas. By 1942, the war had inundated the town with soldiers and defense workers, encouraging

McAfee to expand his interests to downtown and purchase the Pioneer Club. The success of McAfee and others ultimately lured more California gamblers to town. Tony Cornero, who earlier had operated The Meadows and then the SS *Rex* gambling ship off Santa Monica, returned to open the Rex Club in Las Vegas, while San Diego gambler Wilbur Clark (builder of the Desert Inn) opened his Monte Carlo Club downtown just as the war ended. By 1945, Fremont Street was ablaze in neon with the Boulder, Pioneer, Frontier, Monte Carlo, El Cortez, and Las Vegas clubs, supplemented by a variety of smaller enterprises.

While Fremont Street glittered as the gambling hub of wartime Las Vegas, another casino area developed slowly. South of town on lonely Highway 91, a few clubs like the Pair-O-Dice (the area was named Paradise) sprang up in the 1930s, catering to tourists who preferred less congested spots to play and park their cars. For several years city fathers, dazzled by their own surging revenues on Fremont Street, ignored the few small roadhouses on Highway 91. City commissioners, like most residents, customers, and even club owners, did not foresee the events to come. But in 1940, California hotelman Thomas Hull launched a movement which would transform the town. Prior to his arrival in Las Vegas, Hull had made and lost several fortunes in various hotel ventures. In the early 1930s he had operated several California hotels, including the Belleview in San Francisco and the Mayfair in Los Angeles. Substantial profits from the latter enabled him to bid for the coveted Hollywood Roosevelt—an acquisition which proved elusive. The Roosevelt's owner, financier Lou Lurie, would not sell the property to Hull, but agreed to let him operate it on a lease agreement. By the late 1930s, Hull's success in Hollywood funded his dream of building his own hotel chain. Adopting a motif reminiscent of old Mexico, Hull first opened the El Rancho Fresno and later the El Rancho Sacramento.[3]

Hull's interest in Las Vegas was sparked by land developer Robert Griffith and car dealer James Cashman. Convinced that Las Vegas needed both the presence and capital of a California hotel chain, the two contacted Hull (who was on a business trip in nearby Bakersfield) and invited him to Las Vegas in early 1940. Within weeks of his stay, Hull decided to build a resort in southern Nevada. World War II played a major role in his decision. As early as January 1939, southern California's economy had begun to roar thanks to Allied orders for planes and munitions. Thousands of defense workers not only contributed to California's tourism but to southern Nevada's as well. Hull recognized that Hitler's blitz of western

Europe was a potential bonanza for the golden state's defense industry and therefore to Las Vegas's gambling economy. Moreover, the entrepreneurial Hull longed to supplement his hotel balance sheets with the added profits from casino gambling.

To everyone's amazement, Hull agreed to build a resort, but not in Las Vegas proper! Anxious to avoid Las Vegas's higher taxes while also securing spacious ground at low cost, Hull bought a tract on the southwest corner of Highway 91 and San Francisco Street (today Sahara Avenue) a few feet south of the city line. He then commissioned the Los Angeles architecture firm of McAllister and McAllister to design a sprawling, ranchlike complex built in Spanish mission style. Boasting a rustic interior, the main building housed a casino, restaurant (later the Stage Door Steakhouse), Opera House Showroom, and several shops. Low-rise bungalow and cottage buildings radiated outward from the main structure. A large pool and lush gardens contributed further to the El Rancho's reputation as Las Vegas's first "resort hotel." The gala opening was April 3, 1941. Visionaries like Al Cahlan immediately grasped the event's significance. Noting that "for many years Las Vegas has bemoaned the absence of high type resort hotels and the wealthy class of people such would draw to us," Squires rejoiced that "now the ice is broken." Observing further that the El Rancho was not only the town's first swank hotel but also the first in a chain, Squires predicted that "through the close cooperation of the Hull system with the great hotel systems of the east, an even more widely spreading field of favorable publicity is opened to us."[4]

Entertainment in those first years consisted of a lively production show starring Frank Fay and the "El Rancho Starlets"—a chorus line of scantily clad dancers from California. Backed by the Garwood Van Orchestra, this show and others played to large audiences for many years. In fact, wartime business was so good that Hull added sixty more rooms, years ahead of schedule. Unfortunately, managerial problems plagued the resort, resulting in a constant turnover of staff. Personality conflicts and administrative squabbles vanquished thirteen managers in the first three years alone. In 1942, Hull sold the trouble-plagued resort which then changed owners several more times before falling into the hands of Beldon Katleman in 1947. Faced with stiff opposition from the Last Frontier and Flamingo, Katleman immediately began upgrading the property. Extensive redecoration diminished the old frontier image. While much of the Spanish exterior remained, Katleman refurnished the resort's interior in a French Provincial style. In addition, he not only expanded the restaurant and showroom, but added 220 rooms. The renovation was a master stroke which restored the El Rancho's original charm. For the next decade celebrities once again patronized the resort (Paul Newman and Joanne Woodward were even married there in 1958), hobnobbing with local dignitaries and guests. Yet, these halcyon days were short-lived. As the 1950s wore on, the El Rancho declined, outshined by its glittering new rivals on the Strip. A disastrous fire in 1960 mercifully closed the resort and it never reopened. But the El Rancho's significance to the city lived on. Indeed, Hull's bold decision to build south of town inspired development of the Las Vegas Strip, America's first "casino suburb." The El Rancho's early success demonstrated the feasibility of combining casino operations with a large resort hotel. Moreover, Hull convinced hotelmen everywhere that the spacious tracts bordering the Los Angeles Highway were ideal locations to build the mammoth resorts which eventually made the town famous.[5]

The El Rancho began inspiring resort development as early as 1941. Within weeks of Hull's opening on April 3 two southern California investors, Marion Hicks and John Grayson, announced plans to build a $245,000 hotel downtown. When it opened later in the year, the El Cortez became Fremont Street's first major resort. The El Rancho also encouraged another man, R. E. Griffith, to build on the Strip. At the time, Griffith's family owned a chain of 475 movie theatres in the south, midwest, and southwest. Griffith himself managed the company's southwest holdings. In 1941, he was returning to Dallas from California with his nephew William J. Moore after securing construction materials for a new theatre project in Deming, New Mexico (ironically, Hull also owned a theatre in Deming), when he stopped for the night at the El Rancho Vegas. By morning Griffith and Moore, convinced of the town's growth potential, had canceled their plans for Deming. While the California defense boom had played a major role in Hull's decision to build the El Rancho a year earlier, Griffith and Moore enjoyed additional incentives. Thanks to the intensification of the war, it was obvious in early 1941 that southern Nevada would also become a major defense zone. Griffith and Moore, like other investors, surely recognized that, once completed, the army gunnery school and Basic Magnesium would pour thousands more customers into Las Vegas's gambling saloons. With the El Rancho already booming, and Fremont Street lots in high demand, sound business dictated a highway location a bit farther out from Hull's resort. Within weeks, Griffith bought a large parcel of land about a mile south of the El Rancho.

Imitating Hull's western motif, Moore, an architect in his own right, designed a hotel showcasing the ultimate in western style. Like the El Rancho, Moore's blueprints featured a large main building housing a casino, showroom, restaurant, and bars. A series of low-rise buildings (with a total of 107 rooms) led away from the main structure. There the similarity ended. Unlike Hull, Moore spared no expense for interior design.[6]

At the Last Frontier's opening in October 1942, visitors gasped at the splendor. The decor was deliberately extravagant, awarding the resort instant notoriety. The main building contained a trophy room lined with large stuffed animals; inside was the Carillo Bar immortalizing the Cisco Kid's famed sidekick, actor Leo Carillo (a frequent patron). The Horn Room and Gay Nineties Bar were illuminated by lighting fixtures shaped in the form of wagon wheels suspended by chains hanging from the ceiling. The main banquet facility, the Ramona Room, seated 600 guests and was supported by expensive flagstones and large wooden beams. In the guest rooms, cowhorns adorned every bed. Complementing the western atmosphere was a touch of Palm Springs: a sundeck and large pool (everything was larger than the El Rancho) fronted the resort's entrance to attract passing motorists. In addition, the hotel provided guests with horseback and stagecoach rides, pack trips, a showroom seating 600 and parking for 400 cars. To reinforce the frontier ambience, Moore later added the Last Frontier Village, a small townsite filled with 900 tons of Robert "Doby Doc" Caudill's western artifacts imported from his warehouse in Elko, Nevada. This collection was extensive, consisting not only of wagons, antique firearms, bar stools, barber's chairs, and the like, but also big items, including a Chinese "Joss House" (i.e., a place of worship) constructed in the 1860s for workers building the Central Pacific Railroad, full-sized mining trains, and actual jails from Nevada's smaller mining camps. From the beginning, Moore's Frontier Village was a major attraction, drawing thousands of tourists and locals alike who reveled in the trappings of the old west.[7]

By 1951, however, Moore had tired of running the Frontier and wanted to sell the family property. Preoccupied with his new interest in the downtown El Cortez, Moore sold the Last Frontier in 1951 to Jacob "Jake" Kozloff, a Pennsylvania brewery owner, and the El Rancho's Beldon Katleman. Kozloff, who had learned the casino business from his mentor, Guy McAfee, immediately boosted profits by presenting big-name entertainers such as Liberace and the Will Mastin Trio (featuring Sammy

Davis, Jr.). Several years later, in an effort to match new Strip competition, Katleman and Kozloff decided to modernize the resort with a major face-lift and change of name. The so-called Hotel New Frontier opened on April 4, 1955. Soon afterwards Katleman and Kozloff, eager to recoup their investment and profit from the property's newly increased value, sold their interests.

Trouble plagued the resort for the next few years, as a series of leasees suffered cash flow problems relating to the hotel and their other business ventures as well. For a while, the casino was closed and the property functioned as a motel. Finally, in the late 1950s, Hacienda owner Warren Bayley re-opened the resort and made small but steady profits until his death in 1964. Within months, executives at Banker's Life Insurance Company, which had acquired the Frontier through Bayley's estate, recognized that modernization and expanded room capacity were the keys to profits. So, in 1965 they ordered the New Frontier razed, to be replaced by a 500-room hotel building and a larger casino. However by opening night, July 20, 1967, there was a new owner. Anxious to expand his emerging casino empire in southern Nevada, eccentric billionaire Howard Hughes bought the resort on July 12, 1967, thereby guaranteeing the Frontier a return to the prominence of earlier days.[8]

Both the El Rancho and Last Frontier appealed to Los Angeles syndicate boss Benjamin "Bugsy" Siegel, who first came to Las Vegas in 1941 with associate Moe Sedway as part of the effort by Meyer Lansky and others to install their own race wire in downtown clubs. From the beginning Siegel was impressed with the casino city and, once back in southern California, dreamed of building a resort even greater than the Beverly Hills Hotel—a resort destined to impress the likes of Cecil B. DeMille and Hollywood society. Obsessed with this goal, Siegel raised over $1 million by 1945 and even received Meyer Lansky's approval for the project. In an unusual move, Siegel engaged the Del Webb Construction Company of Phoenix to build his dream resort. The hotel was to be called the Flamingo (named either for his mistress, Virginia Hill, or for the birds at Florida's Hialeah Racetrack). Yet, despite Siegel's power and determination, there were problems. Due to the postwar shortage of building materials, construction was expensive. Cost overruns were hardly eased by Siegel's lavish whims (including his insistence that each room have its own private sewer line). Ultimately, the syndicate had to contribute millions more to finish the enterprise. Opening night in December 1946 featured Jimmy Durante and a star-studded audience at a half-finished

resort. While the casino, restaurant, and showroom were in full operation, the hotel itself was not completed. Siegel's impatience soon turned to
gloom when, just two weeks later, the casino closed after suffering heavy
losses.[9]

The formal re-opening came in March 1947 (only a few months before
Siegel's assassination). Now fully completed, the Flamingo was undeni-
ably the most glamorous hotel in Las Vegas, with 105 lavishly appointed
rooms, a health club, gym, steam rooms, tennis courts, and facilities for
squash, handball, and badminton. In addition, there were stables for
forty horses, a trapshooting range, swimming pool, 9-hole golf course,
and assorted shops. Complementing the magnificent three-story waterfall
in front were acres of beautifully landscaped grounds containing Oriental
date palms, rare Spanish cork trees, and other exotic species. To add
further to the pretension, Siegel clad his entire staff in tuxedos.

Perhaps more than anything else, it was Siegel's penchant for extrava-
gance, overspending, and arrogance which put him at odds with some
organized crime figures. His death that June disrupted management of the
hotel. Shortly after Siegel's murder, Meyer Lansky, Morris Rosen, Gus
Greenbaum, and Moe Sedway met with El Rancho owners Sanford Adler
and Charles Resnick to induce the latter (who were widely respected by
Nevada gaming authorities) to run the Flamingo. After this agreement fell
through in 1947, the syndicate imported the talented Gus Greenbaum
from its Phoenix operations to run the resort. Greenbaum, an expert
casino manager, turned a $4 million profit in the first year and the profits
continued. During the early 1950s, the farsighted Greenbaum met the
challenge from the Thunderbird, Desert Inn, and other new competition
by expanding and modernizing the resort. Like Kozloff and other Strip
moguls, he willingly spent thousands to attract the era's top headliners,
including Nat King Cole, Pearl Bailey, Lena Horne, and Ted Lewis, along
with Dean Martin and Jerry Lewis. In 1955, Greenbaum retired and the
hotel was sold to a group of thirty investors headed by Miami hotelman Al
Parvin and the El Rancho's Thomas Hull. By 1967, subsequent transfers
of ownership finally put the property in the hands of noted financier Kirk
Kerkorian, who used it as a training ground for staff slated to operate his
future hotel ventures. During his brief tenure as owner, Kerkorian added a
350-seat theatre and installed the famous electric mushroom sign at the
north end of the property before selling the resort to the Hilton chain in
1970.[10]

Despite his notorious life, Bugsy Siegel's contribution to Las Vegas was considerable. A decade earlier, only the visionaries had foreseen gambling as the town's major industry. Municipal leaders and even boosters like Al Cahlan had supported the idea of restricting clubs to Fremont Street. Until 1940, area clubs largely resembled the nineteenth-century saloons and betting parlors which had thrived along San Francisco's Barbary Coast. As late as 1945, these types of clubs dominated downtown Las Vegas; there were no truly elegant casinos on Fremont Street. Furthermore, while some hotels hosted gambling in a room off their lobby, there was no effort to house a casino within a resort hotel until Thomas Hull built the El Rancho.

While elegant in a western sense, the El Rancho and Last Frontier were little more than opulent dude ranches. The crucial event which transformed Las Vegas from a recreational to a full-fledged resort city was Bugsy Siegel's Flamingo Hotel. In a sense, the Flamingo was the turning point because it combined the sophisticated ambience of a Monte Carlo casino with the exotic luxury of a Miami Beach-Caribbean resort. The Flamingo liberated Las Vegas from the confines of its western heritage and established the pattern for a "diversity of images" embodied in future resorts like the Desert Inn, Thunderbird, Dunes, Tropicana, and Stardust. As the historian John Findlay has argued, "on the Strip gaming took place in a distinctly resort setting," where hotel owners, like their Hollywood clients, were skilled at mass producing a mixture of leisure and fantasy.[11]

Certainly, the Flamingo enjoyed a more prosperous history than its immediate successor. Begun by attorney Cliff Jones and builder Marion Hicks, the Thunderbird became the fourth hotel on the Strip. Earlier in 1946, the duo had tried and failed to purchase a casino in Reno. Rebuffed in northern Nevada, they bought a share of the Golden Nugget and made plans for acquiring a place on the Strip. Eager to duplicate the success of Griffith and Siegel, they purchased 1,100 feet of frontage on the Strip in 1948 as part of a huge tract stretching east to Paradise Road. Hicks, a mason who had earlier built the El Cortez, now constructed this newest resort. The "Thunderbird" itself was derived from ancient Navajo legend, and that motif dominated throughout. Native American portraits and earthen colors adorned the walls of the Wigwam Room and Navajo Room restaurants, and three fireplaces warmed public areas.

In the early 1950s, rising profits inspired Jones and Hicks to expand. To raise the needed capital, they brought in new partners, including Joe Wells (owner of Wells Cargo), Jack Lane (president of American Pipe and

Steel), Jake Kozloff, Guy McAfee, and other local investors. Kozloff's entrance subsequently led to revocation of the casino's license and a celebrated battle with the Nevada Tax Commission. Following a series of articles in the *Las Vegas Sun* alleging that Meyer Lansky and other underworld figures held hidden shares in the hotel, the tax commission revoked the Thunderbird's license in 1955. After a long court battle, the move was reversed, but the resort's image never fully recovered. Still, the Thunderbird prospered into the 1960s and even pioneered several innovations. It was, for instance, the first major hotel to hire a convention sales manager and actually host a convention (a delegation of air-conditioning experts). During the early 1950s, the famed Pow Wow Showroom featured such major stars as Hildegard and Louis Jourdan, and the dining room reserved booths for such regular patrons as Senator Pat McCarran, Howard Hughes, and the Desert Inn's Wilbur and Toni Clark. Profits eventually sagged in the face of increased competition. In a 1964 deal, the Del Webb Corporation, already expanding its Nevada interests with the Sahara, Mint, and Sahara Tahoe, bought the Thunderbird for $9.5 million. Unfortunately, the new management also failed to keep pace with newer and larger competitors surrounding the resort, and a 1972 sale to Caesars Palace owners did little to revive the aging resort. Finally in January 1977, Dunes owner Major Riddle bought the property, enlarged the casino, changed the name (to the Silverbird), added some restaurants and a maze of neon, and turned a profit until his death several years later. In 1981, veteran gamer Ed Torres purchased the resort, added bowling alleys and a Spanish mission front, and renamed it the El Rancho in honor of the Strip's first resort.[12]

Clearly, the flurry of hotel-casino development along the Strip and downtown reflected an unprecedented confidence in the town's future. Wartime and postwar growth inspired all kinds of plans. Famed cowboy star Roy Rogers talked of opening a dude ranch nearby, while Mae West and Frank Sinatra each considered resort hotels. In 1945, Guy McAfee expanded his operations from the Strip to downtown, opening the small Frontier Club on Fremont Street. He then used profits from the new club to acquire parcels of adjacent land "piece by piece." In August 1945, following months of construction, McAfee, Roscoe Thomas, and attorney Art Ham, Sr. (who had earlier owned the Frontier Club) opened the Golden Nugget, Las Vegas's largest casino—a gambling palace furnished in classic San Francisco-Barbary Coast motif. In 1948, McAfee made headlines again with a startling new innovation: a hundred-foot-high electrical sign which justified the Nugget's new billing as "the brightest night spot in the world." Responding to the higher standards of elegance being set by the Strip, McAfee's Golden Nugget became the archetype for the new image downtown. To achieve the new opulent look, older clubs were either remodeled or demolished and replaced by more pretentious successors. Thanks partly to McAfee, downtown Las Vegas had begun its forty-year struggle to keep pace with the trendsetting Strip.[13]

Aside from McAfee and Siegel, other Californians also contributed to the growth of Las Vegas during and after the war. Another Las Vegas legend, Sam Boyd, came to town in 1941. Born and raised in Oklahoma, Boyd moved with his family to Long Beach, California in 1924 at the age of thirteen. He began working amusement park concessions and quickly graduated to bingo. At age eighteen his talent netted him bingo jobs on the *Monte Carlo* and two other gambling ships off the California coast. The 1930s found him in Hawaii, running bingo operations for various gaming establishments in Hilo and Honolulu. He returned to the gambling ships in 1940. Then, during a brief Labor Day visit to Las Vegas in 1941, he met several of his old California cronies and decided to stay. At first, Boyd operated his own penny roulette concession where the Horseshoe Tower stands today. He learned more about the casino business through various stints at the El Rancho and El Cortez Hotels. Finally, in 1948, Boyd joined the town's ownership ranks, purchasing a share of the Club Bingo and later the Sahara Hotel.

In 1954, when the Sahara Nevada Corporation decided to build the Mint Hotel downtown, Boyd agreed to serve as a vice president. Following the sale of the Sahara and Mint to the Del Webb Corporation in 1963, Boyd remained briefly as vice president of operations. A few months later, after resigning over policy differences, he began developing his own gaming empire. In 1963, he and investor Frank Scott purchased the old railroad station at the foot of Fremont Street and opened the Union Plaza Hotel in 1971. Boyd also built the small Nevada Hotel across the street and the Eldorado Club, Henderson's largest casino. With profits from these ventures he built the California Hotel and Casino (one block north of the Mint) in 1974 and began construction in 1978 on Sam's Town, a western-style resort catering to locals. In a characteristically bold move, Boyd built the hotel on Boulder Highway about three miles south of the Showboat. Convinced that the road to Henderson and Boulder City would, in time, become the "next Strip," he has seen his original investment repaid several times over. Succeeding years have witnessed the Boyd investment group expand its interests, acquiring control of the Fremont Hotel downtown and the Stardust on the Strip.[14]

Of course, not all of the wartime capitalists were California gamblers. In 1946 famed Texas gambler Benny Binion came to town. Binion, a talented casino operator, had been harried out of Texas by authorities cracking down on illegal games. Eventually, Binion invested in J. Kell Houssels's Las Vegas Club, and worked there for a while before selling his interest to finance his own establishment, the Western Club. Business was good, but Binion recognized the property's limited capacities and opted for a more spacious Fremont Street location. So, after just a year, Binion sold the Western to George Eddy and bought the old Apache Hotel and Eldorado Club, enlarged them with a feverish construction program, and opened the world-famous Horseshoe Club in August 1951 (with the 1988 purchase of Del Webb's Mint, the Horseshoe was expanded to cover an entire city block). By 1951, Binion had lured many of his experienced dealers west to the new operation in Las Vegas. The Horseshoe quickly became a favorite hangout for high-stakes players, thanks to its daring $15,000 limit on individual bets. Aside from Binion, many other gamblers (some then or formerly associated with illegal operations) migrated to Las Vegas after 1950 when the highly publicized Kefauver hearings on organized crime activities inspired a wave of gambling crackdowns in Florida, New Orleans, Cincinnati, and elsewhere.[15]

The growth of casino gambling in the 1930s and especially during the war drew the mob to Las Vegas, eventually forcing the state of Nevada to play a larger role in both regulation and revenue collection. The growing presence of organized crime was the most immediate problem. Beginning in the mid-1940s, the state actively began regulating the gaming industry to discourage hidden ownership, tax skimming, and other activities linking Nevada gaming with organized crime. The move naturally upset some casino owners who viewed regulation as an alarming departure from the traditional policy of laissez-faire. Since 1931 state law had left the responsibility for collecting fees and granting licenses to the counties, and more specifically to the sheriffs. The state did not even involve itself in the licensing process until the 1940s.[16]

Among a host of events sparking this change of policy were complaints about syndicate infiltration of race wire services in Clark County. The story of organized crime's entry into Las Vegas dates from the late 1930s when the Capone-Luciano syndicate sent the flamboyant Benjamin "Bugsy" Siegel to Los Angeles to supervise the group's west coast operations. In

1941 Siegel was ordered to send trusted lieutenant Moe Sedway to Las Vegas to convert local horse racebooks to the syndicate's Trans-America Wire Service. At the time, Las Vegas operators were using James Ragen's Continental Wire Service. The syndicate, however, was not just emphasizing Las Vegas. Sedway's mission was part of a larger regional effort to establish Trans-America in all major western books. Gus Greenbaum was already pursuing the same course in Phoenix as was the notorious Mickey Cohen in San Francisco and Los Angeles. In fact, Sedway's victory in Las Vegas was hastened by Cohen's success, which forced Ragen to concentrate his attention on California where his most profitable operations were located. [17]

The presence of racebooks in Las Vegas casinos was relatively recent. In the late thirties and early forties Fremont Street casinos had added them to draw more daytime customers for the slots and card games. It was a long wait between races, and gamblers invariably killed the time at the tables. By 1941 the Las Vegas market, though small by California standards, merited the syndicate's attention. Sedway's tactics, at first, seemed innocent enough. In 1941, he gave every book his wire for a lower fee than Ragen's. Then in 1942—once organized crime had eliminated Ragen— Sedway, on orders from Siegel, suddenly raised his fees and even demanded a share of book profits. Lacking another source of race results, a few books (like the Fremont Club's) agreed to Sedway's terms. Major casinos like the Fremont capitulated because the racebooks (which only cleared $25,000 per month) boosted slot, craps, and card profits to the point where the loss was easily offset. Smaller clubs, however, complained about the monopoly to state authorities. But lawmakers, preoccupied with wartime problems, were slow to respond. As a result, Siegel quickly invested his new-found profits, buying interests in the casinos themselves! By 1945 he owned shares in the Golden Nugget and Frontier clubs. Siegel's growing monopoly prompted a flood of complaints to Carson City in 1945 and 1946. In Las Vegas, the Santa Anita Club and others protested that they could not obtain the race wire without acceding to Sedway's demands. [18]

Siegel's murder in 1947 (the syndicate controlled Ragen's Continental Service and Siegel began to compete with the mob using their old Trans-America wire) and other expected gangland violence finally drove the state legislature to take action. Anxious to avoid any link between the silver state and organized crime, state legislators that year enacted sweeping reforms which forced all gaming and racebook operators to obtain a state license. In addition, the Nevada Tax Commission was empowered to investigate, license, and monitor all applicants. In November 1948, the tax commission, determined to tighten its regulation of racebooks following Siegel's death, summoned all eleven Las Vegas racebook operators to appear at a series of hearings investigating race wire operations. Shortly thereafter, the Nevada Tax Commission suspended the gaming licenses of suspected underworld figures Moe Sedway and Willie Alderman. That December, the two pleaded in vain for reinstatement, claiming they had severed all ties with reputed mobster Connie Hurley and his Continental Press and Boulder News Wire.[19]

By the early 1950s, race wires had been outlawed in Las Vegas and local books instead obtained race results from a newswire off a local radio broadcast. Nevertheless, despite its occasionally tough stand, the state tax commission licensed a series of questionable people whose very presence in Las Vegas raised suspicions in police departments across the country. Lacking the cooperation of state gaming officials, city and county commissioners were powerless to halt the infiltration of hotel executives with reputed underworld ties. As County Commissioner Harley Harmon complained during the 1952 hearings surrounding the licensing of Sands entertainer director Jack Entratter, the state tax commission "has let every syndicate in the country into Las Vegas"—a statement seconded by District Attorney Roger Foley, Jr.[20]

Despite the skepticism of Las Vegas officials, the state legislature continued its effort to tighten control of the gaming industry. In 1955, in response to revelations uncovered by the Kefauver Committee on Organized Crime, alleged syndicate interests in the Thunderbird Hotel, threats of federal taxation, and other factors, Governor Charles Russell and the legislature tightened the state's gaming regulations further by creating the Gaming Control Board. This agency was designed to relieve the burden on the tax commission by acting as its investigative and enforcement unit. In 1959, the trend toward creating a state agency concerned solely with gaming regulation was strengthened when new Governor Grant Sawyer signed legislation to create a state gaming control commission—independent of the tax commission. Reasoning that the latter had enough work regarding equalization of property taxes, revenue disputes, and related tax matters, Sawyer had urged creation of a new state agency responsible only for gaming issues. Under the new state law, a five-member commission, appointed by the governor, made all policy relating to the enforcement of gaming laws and rules. In addition, it served as the final tribunal for license revocations. The Gaming Control Board continued to function as the investigative and enforcement arm which submitted recommendations for each license application or revocation to the commission. Then, in an effort to reduce further the influence of "undesirable persons" in Nevada casino operations, the two agencies in 1960 created the so-called Black Book, which listed the names of those people whose mere physical presence was banned on all casino properties in the state. The blacklist was sent to all gaming operators in Nevada; violators were subject to immediate license revocation. While regulatory procedures were generally tightened in the postwar era, Governor Paul Laxalt led the fight in the late 1960s for one significant liberalization. Prior to 1969, Nevada law required that all corporate stockholders be licensed. The policy effectively excluded most large companies whose stock was traded on Wall Street. Laxalt's new plan changed the law, requiring only the licensing of major stockholders. Thanks to the liberalization of regulations, companies like Hyatt, Hilton, Ramada, Holiday Inns, MGM, and Bally's have been able to pour millions of dollars into the Las Vegas and Reno hotel markets.[21]

In addition to a marked increase in state regulation after the war, Clark County's gaming industry also witnessed a substantial amount of self-regulation. In the wake of a disquieting price war in 1947–48 which saw slot odds liberalized to the point where profits were actually jeopardized, Las Vegas area casinos informally agreed to standardize odds on most games to prevent ruinous competition resulting from excessive payoffs. Moreover, the gaming moguls both downtown and on the Strip strengthened their collective security by standardizing most wages and prices as well (although the Strip continued to have higher operating costs). This informal collusion helped stabilize the industry by controlling expenses while guaranteeing a fair rate of return to all.

Beginning with the war years, the state not only intensified its regulation of the industry, but also its efforts to secure a larger slice of the revenue pie. For the first fifteen years after gaming was legalized, the state awarded Nevada's depressed cities and counties most of the income. Beginning in 1931, the state levied a "table tax" based on the number of games. Counties and cities did the same, but also received revenue from every slot machine (as did the federal government). County taxes were collected by the sheriffs, and the monies remained in the county of origin. City police chiefs or other law enforcement officials did the same within municipalities. Thus, hotels outside of city limits (like the Strip hotels in

Clark County) paid less gaming taxes than establishments in Reno and Las Vegas.[22]

The picture changed dramatically in 1945 when the state of Nevada, faced with soaring budgets and a severe postwar education crisis, reached for a piece of the revenue pie. In that year, state legislators levied a flat gross receipts tax of 1 percent on all casino winnings exceeding $3,000 annually. No expenses were deductible, including losses. Since these revenues were not enough to ease the fiscal crunch, Carson City doubled the tax in 1947 and added a table tax. While casino operators from Reno to Las Vegas howled in protest, lawmakers knew that Nevada's taxes were still far too low. Finally in 1955, the state implemented a graduated gross receipts tax ranging from 3 to 5.5 percent (casinos with annual profits over $400,000 paid the top rate). Although the big casinos in Reno and Las Vegas paid the highest amounts, the rural-dominated legislature added a provision that the total tax fund be equally divided among the seventeen counties. As a result, the state's two urban counties generated over 80 percent of Nevada's gaming revenue, but received only two-seventeenths of it—an inequity not rectified until after the court-ordered reapportionment of the state legislature in 1965.[23]

Lack of revenue coupled with wartime expansion required a more responsible leadership at city hall. Gone were the halcyon days when a small town of 4,000 could be easily governed. Even in the midst of World War II, Las Vegas faced an immediate crisis. There could be no more John Russells or Leonard Arnetts to disrupt the orderly functioning of government. With this in mind, voters took a giant step in 1943 toward guaranteeing a stable future for the town. Following the decision by appointed Mayor Howell Garrison not to seek a full term in office, former Mayor Ernie Cragin announced his candidacy. More than anyone else, the respected Cragin symbolized a return to normalcy. On a larger front, he represented the efficient, pro-business type of government which was becoming popular with voters in Dallas, Phoenix, and other cities across the sunbelt during the 1940s. Determined to avoid the chaos of the past while modernizing administration and policymaking at City Hall, Cragin enthusiastically endorsed a city charter amendment providing for a city manager. In this effort he was joined by commission candidate Walter Bates, a respected plumbing contractor, and the still-popular Al Corradetti. All three were experienced businessmen who recognized the value of delegating the day-to-day management of the growing town to a trained manager. The reform, boosted for years on the national level by the influential National Municipal League, had been widely adopted by many medium-sized cities by 1943.[24]

Nevertheless, some Las Vegans were not impressed, including incumbent City Commissioners M. C. Tinch and A. L. Rubidoux. The two men, understandably concerned about the prospects of seeing their power usurped by an aggressive executive, were clearly unenthusiastic. More outspoken was City Attorney Harry Austin, who urged voters to oppose the question "if you are afraid of 'selfish interests,' 'political cliques,' or a 'political machine.'" Citing sections of the proposed amendment which gave the manager policy-making powers, Austin warned that a coalition of just two commissioners and the manager could outvote the other two commissioners on any given issue. Theoretically then, a manager skilled in political intrigue could subvert majority rule. Cragin and other supporters countered that the city manager would have no vote, thereby voiding Austin's concerns.

The argument worked. On election day 1943, voters—anxious once again to restore the vigorous, progressive image of an earlier era—endorsed Cragin and the manager plan by convincing majorities. As in 1931, Cragin carried his two running mates, this time Corradetti and Bates, into office with him. Despite the support of the Las Vegas Typographical Union and other labor organizations, Tinch and Rubidoux's ambiguous stands on many issues apparently dismayed voters.[25]

Once in power, the new administration moved quickly to modernize the government. Following the election, Mayor Cragin and the commission hired Charles McCall as the first Las Vegas city manager. Taking office on January 1, 1944, McCall established the basic functions of the office and lines of authority before resigning a year later to accept a better paying job out of state. The commission replaced him with Tom H. Hennessy, who provided the dynamic administrative leadership which Cragin and other business-minded reformers had championed during the campaign. In a September 1945 report calling for sweeping reorganization of the municipal bureaucracy, Hennessy argued for implementing a strict system of cost accounting in the street department, thorough review of all department expenditures by the comptroller's office, and a comprehensive inventory of all city property. In addition, he proposed an ambitious program of public improvements, including a new police station, more streetlighting, and completion of both the new fire station and sewage treatment plant. Local reaction was swift; *Review-Journal* editor Al Cahlan spoke for many when he applauded Hennessy's effort, noting that the "majority of citizens concur" with city commission plans "to place the administration on a sound business-like basis." In the past, Cahlan explained, "laxity" had been tolerated in municipal government "because it didn't make any particular difference in the life of residents." But Hoover Dam, the gunnery school, BMI, and a dozen other events had transformed Las Vegas from the whistle-stop town of bygone years to a budding metropolis where municipal efficiency was paramount.[26]

Unlike the Arnett and Russell eras, an atmosphere of consensus and cooperation pervaded city politics following the Cragin landslide in 1943. Voters seemed content to give the new mayor and city manager time to develop their programs. As a result, Cragin enjoyed widespread support throughout the 1940s. The 1945 election, for instance, was largely devoid of the usual name calling and petty bickering. Once again, prominent businessmen triumphed. Pat Clark won re-election to his seat while political newcomer Bob Baskin edged incumbent Art Smith. Two years later, Cragin was again victorious in his bid for re-election. Facing a serious challenge by former City Commissioner Harve Perry, Cragin proposed an ambitious agenda of programs designed to assure the town's continued growth. In typically progressive fashion, he supported a $350,000 bond issue to retire the debt on new sewers built in 1941 for the new defense neighborhoods, another $350,000 bond issue to build a modern sewage disposal plant, a third bond for $250,000 worth of storm drains to handle storm water channeled to town by the proposed Charleston Boulevard underpass (under the railroad tracks), and another $250,000 issue to build a new police station. Then, in an appealing move, the mayor promised to pave and flag impoverished sections of town, including the black Westside (whose assessed valuations were too low to fund streets and sidewalks) by using gasoline tax revenues, "95 percent of which will be collected from our tourists." To assuage the concerns of spending critics, Cragin proposed "strengthening the city's tax base by cooperat[ing] with federal agencies to secure a permanent air base for this area."[27]

Despite its cost, Cragin's platform appealed to voters who once again returned him to office by a margin of 2,600 to 1,893 over Perry. The bond issues also passed, although two-term Commissioner Al Corradetti lost his seat. In eight years of dedicated public service, the strong-minded Corradetti had made his share of political enemies. But his contributions could not be denied—especially his efforts (along with County Commissioner Frank Gusewelle) to secure a new municipal airport south of town for Las Vegas. Voters, however, chose two talented men for the city board.

Popular Westside merchant Robert T. Moore and prominent Mormon banker Reed Whipple joined Cragin, Baskin, and Clark to assure the town a fiscally stable, business-oriented leadership for the next few years.[28]

Cragin's popularity between 1943 and 1951 reflected voter approval of his aggressive approach to Las Vegas's many problems. Waste removal was a case in point. The town's explosive growth eventually spawned a sanitary crisis, as wartime and postwar building centered along the retreating urban periphery beyond both the service zone of the 1911 sewer system and the New Deal networks of the 1930s. In addition, high-density apartment and hotel-motel construction around Fremont Street extending outward to Five Points (at Charleston and Eastern) had overwhelmed the earlier lines. More than anything else, the threat of a polio epidemic in September 1945 galvanized public opinion in support of sanitary reform. The immediate emergency (the feared outbreak never occurred) prompted municipal authorities to order a citywide cleanup and enforcement of sanitary ordinances. In a prophetic column, editor Al Cahlan deplored how "garbage cans, stacked full of stinking swill, are left for hours, with the big green flies and all their mates buzzing hither and yon." In particular, he denounced residents and business owners who, when cited by police, attacked the action in court as an infringement upon their liberty. With the dreaded polio virus menacing local children, a communitywide cleanup effort was essential. To Cahlan and other civic leaders, the sanitary crisis was real: perhaps "as bad as that of the hillbillies back in the Missouri hills." As the editors shamefully conceded, "we have back-yards which are a disgrace to a modern town." Obviously, the laissez-faire attitude toward waste removal, a relic of the city's frontier days, needed recasting. Over the next ten years, Las Vegas, like other modern cities, would expand municipal services and build an engineered infrastructure to remove wastes efficiently and safeguard public health.[29]

While a general cleanup eased the immediate emergency in 1945, it was obvious that wartime growth had overwhelmed the town's limited waste facilities. By 1948, the worsening crisis impelled Clark County Health Department officials to threaten a quarantine of the entire city if sanitary reforms were not soon enacted. This action plus the growing realization that an "unhealthy image" would divert prospective industry to other towns, prompted Hennessy, Cragin, and the commission to propose a bond issue in 1947 to enlarge main lines, extend sewer pipes into newer neighborhoods, and build a modern disposal plant east of town. Voters subsequently approved the bonds, but because of the town's precarious financial position, investors withheld financing until the city guaranteed payment through a new sewer rental ordinance in 1948. Within a year, the construction of the disposal plant was completed as were new waste tunnels reaching out to Las Vegas's southern border at San Francisco Street.[30]

Roads were another priority in the expanding town. Immediate street improvements were blocked, however, by city charter restrictions which prohibited property owners from being charged more than 20 percent of their property's assessed valuation. As a result, black Westside residents as well as many low-income white citizens could not equip their neighborhoods with the paving, widening, gutter, sidewalk, and lighting work needed to modernize their street systems. To circumvent this problem, Hennessy and his 1947 successor J. M. Murphy urged amending the city charter to ease the funding load by allowing the government to create "special assessment districts" to spread the costs over a broader area benefited by the improvements. Voters approved the change in 1949. Nevertheless, many expensive public works projects required some city support. Consequently, the municipality's bonded indebtedness crept upward in the 1940s, reflecting Las Vegas's new commitment to growth.[31]

As part of their drive to forge a progressive new image for Las Vegas, officials supplemented their government modernization and public works initiatives with a concerted effort to clean up the town's traditionally sordid reputation. To this end, community leaders fought a stubborn campaign in early 1946 against several local brothels. As previously noted, the city commission had closed the bordellos on the notorious Block 16 in 1942. Following the war's end, operators were determined to re-open: not downtown, but instead along the Boulder Highway just south and east of the city line. In January 1946, following reports that prostitution had resumed at the newly opened Formyle Club, concerned citizens organized a drive to pressure county leaders to crack down on the establishment. Chamber of Commerce President Maxwell Kelch and the Last Frontier's William J. Moore, led a chorus of voices "vigorously opposing legalized prostitution." In reassuring terms, County Commission Chairman Ira Earl vowed "there will be no legalized prostitution in Clark County if I can prevent it."[32]

For his part, Sheriff Glen Jones promised to revoke the Formyle Club's liquor license if county law was broken (it was temporarily closed in 1949). Other influential members of the community also joined the cause. Dr.

S. L. Hardy of the Las Vegas Hospital Association announced that since the closing of Block 16 in 1942 the local venereal disease rate had plunged. Supporting this view was School Superintendent Maude Frazier, who reported that until 1942 venereal disease had been a problem at Las Vegas High School, but since that time no student had been diagnosed or treated. Finally, Bryan Bunker, head of the local Boy Scouts, insisted that prostitution only gave Las Vegas a "black eye" at just the time when promoters were spending thousands of dollars to project a positive image to America.[33] The powerful influence of the Mormon and Catholic churches along with the Baptist, Presbyterian, Episcopal, and other denominations also played a major role in convincing county leaders to reject all efforts to re-legalize prostitution. In its march toward urban maturity, Las Vegas had finally discarded perhaps the most infamous legacy of its frontier past. Of course, prostitution would survive, but no longer in the more wide open, socially acceptable atmosphere of earlier days. Bolstered by community support, the police cracked down on suspected operators. In 1946, city vice squad officers raided the infamous Kassabian Ranch on the southern edge of town, and arrested two men and two women for operating a "commercial house." Initially, the county effort was also successful, although later years saw Sheriff Jones countenance a revival of the trade, especially in the early 1950s at Roxie's Club on the Boulder Highway near today's Sahara Avenue. Finally, in April 1954, newly sworn-in Sheriff R. E. "Butch" Leypoldt closed down the Formyle Club forever. A year later, in January 1955, Clark County commissioners finally passed an effective "rooming house ordinance."[34]

Part of the original motive for banning prostitution had been to support the military, and following the war Las Vegans were understandably concerned about the army's impending departure. While Las Vegans—like all Americans—rejoiced at war's end, there were nonetheless ambivalent feelings. The loss of troops and defense workers sparked fears of a new recession even worse than the 1937 downturn following the dam's completion. Residents, especially in North Las Vegas, glumly prepared for the gunnery school's deactivation. Fortunately, the process was gradual. Following the armistice, army officials announced that, while operations would be scaled down at the gunnery school, it would remain open on an interim basis as a separation center. This delay, combined with the growing intransigence of Joseph Stalin, fueled hopes of someday returning the base to active status. Throughout the fall of 1945, Senator McCarran exerted his full influence as chairman of the powerful Senate Appropriations Committee to persuade the Pentagon to consider the Las Vegas base. Pressed by McCarran and by an emerging Cold War in Greece, Turkey, and Iran, air corps officials deliberated. In the fall of 1946 Pentagon officials finally indicated their willingness to reactivate the base provided the city moved commercial flight operations to another facility.[35]

For years Las Vegas business and political leaders wanted a new airport closer to town. The obvious short-term solution to the Pentagon's sudden ultimatum was tiny Alamo Airport south of Las Vegas along the Los Angeles Highway. For a year, county commissioners dragged their feet on commiting the government to building a new terminal. The postwar drain on county finances for roads and schools was already substantial. A breakthrough finally came when an aggressive new county commission chairman took over. Within weeks, Frank Gusewelle had convinced the board to schedule a $750,000 bond election to finance the new facility. At once the booster press applauded the move, with the *Review-Journal* crediting Gusewelle for realizing "that talk will no longer appease the air forces," and for clearing "the decks for action." Despite local grumbling about rising taxes and indebtedness, the town needed the air force as much as it needed a modern new airport. Las Vegas promoters realized that with air travel becoming increasingly popular, all tourist centers would need to build modern terminals. Support for the issue rallied many local groups, including the Lions Club and other fraternal organizations. Meanwhile, the *Review-Journal* continued to hammer away at spending critics who raved about the cost, patiently explaining that the new base would not only provide a military payroll of at least $10 million per year, but would also employ hundreds of civilians. The creation of more jobs would only attract more population, which, according to the editor, "will mean additional visitors to the area and more publicity throughout the entire nation."[36]

As the May 1 election approached, the army demonstrated its good faith by announcing that it would spend $400,000 immediately to reconvert the old airfield barracks into modern base apartments. Pentagon officials even opened contractor bidding on the project, while at the same time making it clear that "any activity at the field [was] predicated upon the probable passage of the bond issue." Local boosters like Cahlan wasted no time portraying the action as a positive sign, reasoning that the Pentagon "is not likely, under the present economy drive in Congress to put $400,000 into a project which will not be permanent." The Pentagon's commitment to southern Nevada gained even more credibility in late April 1947, when naval officials expressed interest in establishing an armory in Las Vegas and a PT base at Lake Mead. Recognizing that such a move would be predicated upon the navy's ability to organize a reserve flying unit in Las Vegas, Cahlan again led the campaign, urging all patriotic young men to be prepared to volunteer. Clearly, Cahlan and a majority of Las Vegans increasingly saw defense as the key to economic diversification. By the end of April, support for the bond issue was overwhelming. Besides the community's fraternal organizations and chamber of commerce, major businesses like Cragin & Pike Insurance, the Golden Nugget, Las Vegas Club, Pioneer Club, and dozens of other concerns in both the recreational and commercial sectors of the economy supported construction of a new airport. On May 1, 1947, in one of the most lopsided elections in the city's history, voters delighted Senator Pat McCarran, the Defense Department, and local officials by passing the airport bond issue by a 10 to 1 margin.[37]

Following this election, the county bought out Western Airlines's lease for $35,000 and agreed to move the carrier's fuel storage tanks to the modern airport. The county built the new airfield on a site formerly occupied by Alamo Airport (a secondary facility for general aviation opened in the 1930s), just east of the Los Angeles Highway about four miles south of the Flamingo Hotel. Construction of the new McCarran Airport (today the site of the Hughes Air Terminal) continued throughout the year. Meanwhile the air force kept its end of the bargain. As early as April 1947, the old gunnery school had been partly reactivated as a standby facility for Williams Air Force Base in Arizona. Then, in late 1948, the air force formally announced plans to base a mixed fleet of one hundred prop and jet planes at Las Vegas for its new single engine training school. In May 1949, as expected, the air force expanded the base's functions by adding a gunnery school. A year later in May 1950, the Pentagon officially dedicated the base in honor of Army Air Corps First Lieutenant William H. Nellis, a former resident of nearby Searchlight, Nevada, who had been killed during World War II.[38]

Efforts to diversify Las Vegas's postwar economy were not just limited to securing a defense sector. A monumental battle was also fought to save the Basic Magnesium plant as the first step in attracting chemical industries to the metropolitan area. Earlier in November 1944, when the War Labor Board ordered an end to magnesium production, nearly all the workers were immediately laid off. The effect upon Henderson was devastating. School enrollment dropped by two-thirds, and half the town's houses were vacated as thousands of employees left the state. Although

Western Electro Chemical and Stauffer Chemical signed leases the following May to occupy part of the plant, Basic employment would never again reach wartime levels. Desperate to retain southern Nevada's meager industrial base, Mayor Cragin and other city, county, and chamber officials lobbied Senator Pat McCarran for help. For its part, the War Assets Administration (which assumed control of BMI from the Defense Plant Corporation after the war) preferred to cannibalize the complex, auctioning off equipment and building materials to the highest bidder. But Mayor Cragin and county leaders appealed once again to Senator McCarran. After months of lobbying, McCarran advised the Clark County legislative delegation in Carson City to introduce bills authorizing the state to purchase the plant from Uncle Sam. Following a fact-finding mission by northern Nevada lawmakers (who were wined and dined by Las Vegas's hotels), both the assembly and senate approved the measure in 1947, thereby demonstrating Nevada's good faith and strengthening McCarran's bargaining position. The latter's tenacity paid off in February 1948 when the new General Services Administration agreed to sell the complex (including the townsite) to Nevada for $24 million to be paid out of rental income over the next twenty years. On April 1, 1948, the property was transferred to Nevada, and the state's Colorado River Commission accepted the responsibility of securing tenants for the rest of the complex. The commission met its goal three years later and, in 1952, sold the plant to Basic Management, Inc.—a consortium comprising all the plant's tenants.[39]

Permanent operations at Basic finally realized the dreams of many longtime boosters. As early as 1930, Interior Secretary Ray Wilbur had echoed the views of many when he predicted that southern Nevada's share of low-cost Hoover Dam power would fuel a massive industrial migration to Las Vegas. So, after a decade of frustration, many residents viewed the construction of Basic in 1941 as a partial fulfillment of the town's manifest destiny—a triumph which no one wanted to forfeit after the war. Typical was the view of U.S. Senate candidate Berkeley Bunker who, in a 1946 campaign speech, spoke in glowing terms of Las Vegas's new image on the east coast, noting somewhat prophetically that if the Basic plant were developed and larger power contracts signed, "we may have the biggest chemical empire in the nation here." The confident Bunker then linked predictions about industrial development to others boosting tourism. Speaking in comparative terms about the town's resort potential, the candidate no doubt pleased his audience with the assertion that "we can make of southern Nevada what was made of Tucson, for we have more to sell than does that Arizona community."[40]

Even in the midst of war, city business leaders, sensing the inevitable victory, had begun dreaming of a postwar tourist bonanza. Las Vegas profited handsomely from the movement of troops to California. Thousands of midwestern and eastern men visited the town and spread the free publicity. Local newspapers contributed to the excitement, spicing their war coverage with columns praising the new El Rancho, the El Cortez, the Last Frontier—any new club or innovation contributing another dimension to the town's recreational economy. No event was too small to escape notice. In a 1941 column, for instance, *Age* editor Charles Squires praised the new municipal golf course built free of charge by the WPA, and credited the facility with "causing many tourists to remain in Las Vegas an additional day or two just for the novelty of playing our course." As Squires explained to his readers: "There are thousands of travelers who find pleasure in playing every course visited"—a fact not lost on the solons of Palm Springs and Scottsdale. It therefore came as no surprise to Squires when, in 1945 with the war scarcely over, the Las Vegas Chamber of Commerce announced plans to stage a $5,000 "pro-am" golf tournament to lure more tourists to Las Vegas (the Phoenix Open had already been established earlier, in 1932). This championship was a significant part of a marketing scheme which eventually culminated in the prestigious Tournament of Champions at the Desert Inn. As later years demonstrated, golf would play a significant role in the Strip hotels' marketing strategy, because of the game's magnetic appeal to upwardly mobile men—preferred customers for casino gambling.[41]

Aside from the nation's growing interest in golf, divorce also boosted tourism. The local boom dated from the Gable-Langham divorce of 1939 and continued during and after the war. To be sure, both Las Vegas and Reno profited from the postwar epidemic of broken marriages. Between July 1, 1945, and July 1946, Nevada granted more than 20,000 (New York had only 19,895) divorces. In the meantime, religious leaders across America decried the trend and searched for a solution. The worsening crisis led District Court Judge Clayton Parks of Minneapolis to predict that "four of every five war marriages" would end in divorce. Analysts attributed the rate to a number of factors, including too many wartime marriages following only a few days of courtship, housing shortages, postwar unemployment, religious decline, changing mores, growing affluence, and especially the increased availability of inexpensive, convenient, out-of-state divorces in places like Nevada. In response, states like Massachusetts and Rhode Island seriously considered outlawing divorce by decree. Nevada, of course, greeted such proposals with enthusiasm, hoping to monopolize the "industry" as much as possible. To some extent, residents of the silver state viewed national concerns about divorce with some amusement. In typical fashion, the *Review-Journal* bemusedly reported that "harried divorce judges" across the nation "worked overtime settling the postwar problems of those who failed to reconvert to peacetime matrimony."[42]

Throughout the 1940s, the chamber of commerce supplemented word-of-mouth promotion of the marriage, divorce, and gambling mecca with an increasingly powerful publicity campaign. Recognizing the crucial role played by propaganda in cementing support for the war, the Las Vegas Chamber of Commerce in late 1944 laid the foundations for their advertising campaign. Led by Chamber President and KENO radio station owner Maxwell Kelch, the chamber established the so-called Live Wire Fund in early 1945. Each chamber member agreed to contribute between 1 and 5 percent of his annual gross receipts, while the resorts pledged to match that figure up to $50,000. The money would then be used by the chamber to publicize Las Vegas. From its inception, the Live Wire campaign was a roaring success: $84,000 was raised that first year alone with greater amounts thereafter. In fact, Las Vegas raised more money per capita for publicity than any city in the United States! Armed with this war chest, the chamber wasted no time hiring J. Walter Thompson—one of the nation's top advertising agencies. To some extent, Thompson de-emphasized the traditional western theme and instead marketed Las Vegas in numerous national magazines as a desert paradise—the ideal getaway for those embracing the new, permissive morality popularized during World War II.[43]

In spite of the campaign's effectiveness, chamber officials switched agencies in 1947, contracting with the equally noted West-Marquis firm. West-Marquis once again emphasized the town's frontier heritage, inventing the friendly cowboy, "Vegas Vic," whose "Howdy Podner" greeting became a Las Vegas trademark for a generation of tourists. Despite this accomplishment, the impatient chamber again changed firms in 1948, this time choosing Steve Hannegan and Associates who handled publicity for the Union Pacific. The railroad, anxious to promote the economy of any town along its line, convinced chamber officials to choose the agency because of its recent success in packaging Sun Valley, Idaho as the premiere winter resort of the United States. In the next few months Hannegan and Associates pioneered several innovations, including the Desert Sea News Bureau, an office which provided local newspapers around the country with "hometown stories" featuring pictures of tourist couples basking in the sunshine, dancing under the stars, and winning at the tables, accompanied by the usual cheesecake shots of local beauties lounging around the pool. For the next few years, the Hannegan firm's publicity campaign etched this glamorous new image of Las Vegas in the minds of millions. At the same time, publicity resulting from the opening of still more Strip hotels only reinforced Las Vegas's growing reputation as the hottest new resort city in America.[44]

Clearly, Las Vegas succeeded in capturing the nation's attention. Virtually every postwar prediction by travel experts foresaw unprecedented growth for the city. Typical was a January 1947 meeting of executives from Western Airlines, LTR Stage Lines, Greyhound, American Express, the Southern California Auto Club, Kirkland Tours (of Kansas City), and the chamber of commerce at the plush new Flamingo Hotel to discuss the future of southwest tourism. In particular, Colonel Harry P. Dooley of Greyhound, asserting that the "Fabulous Flamingo" symbolized the southwest's potential as a tourist attraction, urged the tourist industry to unite "in selling this great area to the people." In a prophetic statement, Dooley argued that "the contacts millions of people made during the war will result in more travel." Moreover, he predicted that growing national affluence, once filtered down to the working classes, would expand the vacation industry. Even though Bugsy Siegel had designed the Flamingo for the opulent, Dooley insisted that "labor now realizes that it will be a potent guest of this hotel and people who, in the past have been deprived of relaxation, now will have the chance." He then concluded by recognizing the recent success of Las Vegas's Live Wire Fund, and congratulated the town for its unmatched efforts "to sell relaxation."[45]

The postwar challenge, however, was not merely limited to securing industry. Las Vegas's success at retaining the air base, developing BMI, and promoting tourism masked a growing urban crisis within Las Vegas. Mayor Cragin's ambitious public works agenda, fueled by a postwar population and building boom, put the government in financial straits. Municipal deficits reflected the story. The 1938 debt of $183,000 fell steadily throughout World War II (thanks to government restrictions on building materials) until it bottomed out at $88,000 in 1945. But the postwar years saw the city embark upon ambitious capital improvements which emptied the treasury. In 1946, the town's bonded indebtedness rose to $356,000 and skyrocketed the next year to an unprecedented $1.1 million. The seeds of the postwar crisis lay in the frantic growth of the early 1940s. While Las Vegas enjoyed a vibrant wartime economy, the city paid a price—physical deterioration. Overcrowding only aggravated a worsening space crisis. With construction handcuffed by wartime restrictions, downtown merchants, hotels, and clubs could not expand or modernize their buildings.[46]

Moreover, the power and telephone companies lacked the new wire, transformers, and other equipment needed to cope with the population explosion. And despite its swollen tax rolls, the city could not find the workers or materials to extend its sewer system, pave its streets, build its parks, or repair its overcrowded jail. In short, Las Vegas, like other cities, had to postpone its modernization, expansion, and other capital improvements until the late 1940s and early 1950s. Campaign promises reflected the sense of urgency. In a typical 1949 press release, city commission candidate Tom Jaggers, noting that postwar building restrictions had ended, advocated modernization and extension of the town's infrastructure. To this end, he urged adoption of "a program for curbs, sidewalks and pavement to be installed on all city streets." Furthermore, he demanded that "water and sewers should be made available to all city property to speed development of Las Vegas."[47]

Extension of municipal services was the goal of every politician, but Las Vegas lacked the money to fund every worthy project. Streets and sewers won priority attention. More police officers were hired and in 1943 a paid fire department was established, but schools, welfare, and other programs languished. The worsening debt, combined with the city's inability to expand its tax base through annexation, forced cutbacks in vital services. Under Mayor Cragin's leadership, the town made a valiant effort in the area of recreation, establishing a recreation department with a full-time director, and building two municipal pools (one each for blacks and whites) in 1947. But the city was still short of facilities when compared to other places of similar size. In 1948, Las Vegas had only two fully equipped playgrounds for its burgeoning number of children, while Reno had six. As Perry Kaufman has noted, the former had only 27 acres of parkland while its counterpart to the north had 50, including the picturesque riverside park along the Truckee River. Even more embarrassing was the Las Vegas library, whose holdings numbered less than one book per capita (1,000 books for a population of 24,000)! The poverty of public services was also reflected in meager city and county funding of welfare and medical care for indigents, as it was in other southwest cities where a lingering frontier spirit supported fiscal restraint.[48]

Expansion of the city's tax base offered the most immediate relief from the worsening fiscal crisis. Prospects for a time seemed bright because the casino boom of the 1940s was establishing a significant suburban area just south of Las Vegas. Ever since the El Rancho's opening in 1941, an increasing number of subdivisions had begun dotting the lots east of the Strip to service the housing needs of a growing work force. By war's end, builders had begun a series of expensive new developments to complement new hotel projects already on the drawing board. In April 1946, a full five years after the El Rancho's spectacular debut, the city of Las Vegas finally acted to extend its tax base by announcing its intention of annexing the four-mile Strip and lands bordering both sides of the highway back to a depth of 1,500 feet. Under the city charter, if a majority of residents did not object at an official "protest meeting" (scheduled for May 8), then Las Vegas could annex by ordinance. In an interview, Mayor Ernie Cragin characterized the move as "an effort to secure badly needed additional revenue to save our city streets, sewer system and other vital services." Already, casino gambling's success had fueled unprecedented urbanization which, in turn, required substantial public works. These huge capital investments put the city in a fiscal crisis. Eager to modernize its physical appearance, the town needed to raise $1.5 million to upgrade sections of its original 1911 sewer system, repave downtown streets, and build several new parks. In addition, a worsening school crisis threatened to absorb most of the area's property tax revenues, so Las Vegas desperately needed to capture the valuable Strip. Cragin, however, denied that the move was imperialistic, claiming instead that the El Rancho Vegas and Last Frontier were "actually part of Las Vegas." Reasoning that the real magnet which lured tourists to Las Vegas was the glittering club district along Fremont Street, Cragin concluded that since the Strip resorts "derived their revenues as part of Las Vegas," there was "no reason why they should not help pay the costs of maintaining our municipal government."[49]

The response was swift. At the May 8 meeting, over 90 percent of affected residents signed protest petitions. Attorney Frank McNamee, representing the resort owners, read the petition, which listed the group's objections. First, the hotelmen claimed that they would be subject to a special ad valorem city tax. Next, they emphasized "restrictive ordinances" which "redlined," or limited, those streets in the city where casinos could be located. Obviously, the Strip hotels feared that downtown casino interests, led by someone like J. Kell Houssels, might use their influence with the city commission to secure zoning measures aimed at restricting Strip growth and competition. Undoubtedly, Last Frontier, El Rancho, and Flamingo management felt more comfortable with the laissez-faire policies of county commissioners. On a larger scale, inhabitants of Paradise Valley (the unofficial name of the Strip area), like many later county residents, felt no need for sewers, paid fire protection, or other municipal services—much less the higher taxes required to support them. The rejection crushed Cragin, who argued in vain that Las Vegas was receiving only $.70 per $100 of assessed valuation off property tax. That year the city had raised only $180,000 in fees and fines, while the annual budget for the fire and police departments alone exceeded $160,000. Complaining justifiably that the state's tax structure was skewed against the cities, the mayor lamented that Nevada's towns were "the stepchildren of the tax family," getting whatever crumbs remained after the school district, the state, and county took their slices of the pie. Aside from taxes, bond issues were also devouring municipal revenues. In 1946 alone, Cragin predicted that bonds for new schools, a county courthouse addition, and hospital expansion would dry up funding further. Clearly, Las Vegas needed the Strip in 1946, but suburban forces held their ground and repulsed city hall.[50]

Anxious to remain part of the county, while still receiving some urban services, suburban residents quickly organized a number of pressure groups including the Paradise Valley Improvement Association. The latter lobbied county, state, and school board officials on a variety of matters. A major triumph came in May 1949 when President Norman White announced that the local school board would construct an elementary school for the area pending voter approval of a $100,000 bond issue. Following this victory, the Association's Road Committee prepared a prioritized list of needed street construction and began considering a master plan for the community. But suburban independence was not yet assured. Again in 1950, residents had to fend off a spirited annexation effort by the city. Nevada law stated that no muncipality could annex an unincorporated township without the approval of county commissioners. So, in the fall of 1950, as Las Vegas prepared to capture the Strip once and for all, Paradise Valley residents, led by Flamingo Hotel executive and reputed mobster Gus Greenbaum, hastily organized a petition campaign to create the unincorporated township of Paradise City. Victory came on December 8, 1950, when county commissioners, anxious to block the expansion of Las Vegas while enlarging their own tax and power bases, acceded to the petitioners' request. A year later county officials established a second unincorporated township—Winchester—further dashing Las Vegas's hopes of acquiring the Strip and its potentially opulent and populated (over 250,000 people by 1980) suburbs. Unlike Phoenix, Albuquerque, San Antonio, and scores of cities across the sunbelt, Las Vegas failed to expand its borders substantially through annexation.[51]

City hall's failure to annex the Strip combined with the town's soaring debt to spark a bitter reaction from spending critics during the 1949 municipal election. Charges of secret meetings, street projects to benefit casino interests, and licensing favoritism arose as they had in 1935 following Cragin's dynamic New Deal building programs. Since Cragin was not running in 1949, the brunt of the criticism fell on Commissioners Bob Baskin and Pat Clark. In a sharply worded attack, candidate Nate Randall charged the incumbents with deliberately excluding the press from their "Star Chamber" meetings of the city commission. Moreover, he insisted that during these covert sessions Baskin and Clark used their power to deny liquor licenses to political opponents. He also inferred that the two commissioners only approved street improvements bordering property "owned by various influential citizens." Indeed, Randall wondered aloud why the only paved street in the black Westside community was the road used by the bus line owned by their political cohort and prominent club owner, J. Kell Houssels.[52]

In a similar vein, Charles Pipkin, President of the Las Vegas Taxpayers' Association, blamed Baskin for the city's growing $300,000 deficit. Charging that Las Vegas was not being operated "on a sound financial basis," Pipkin questioned the recent request for a $103,000 "emergency loan" from the state. For Pipkin, the situation was clear: Baskin and his "playmate" Pat Clark were both key men in the "Houssels Machine"—a well-financed cabal of casino executives anxious to boost business by saddling area taxpayers with staggering bond issues to finance modernization projects. Furthermore Pipkin, like Randall, charged Baskin with using his office to control "the issuance of liquor licenses, gambling licenses and racebook licenses" to favor the Houssels interests. Noting that Clark and Houssels jointly owned the Nevada Beverage Co. (which wholesaled liquor and beer locally) and that Baskin and Houssels co-owned the Roundup Bar, Pipkin, in an election-eve column, implied that the two commissioners had used their power to reject any liquor or gaming license opposed by the Houssels interests. For its part, the *Review-Journal* steered clear of the allegations, praising the incumbents while characterizing their chief antagonists Wendell Bunker and Bill Peccole as "clear thinking businessmen." In the end, press support was not enough to save the incumbents. Charges of overspending apparently impressed an electorate which was already threatened by state and county tax increases. In May 1949, voters partially cleaned house, electing businessmen Bunker and Peccole over Baskin and Clark. Two years later, Cragin would also be turned out. It is unclear whether spending was the key issue in Cragin's fall, because voters in the 1950s would agree to spend unprecedented amounts for schools, streets, and other programs. Part of the mayor's problem was his loyalty to the statewide "McCarran machine." In addition, voters most likely perceived Cragin, Baskin, and Clark as part of the tired, old leadership, tied too closely to the casino interests which had run the town for too long. In many ways, the campaigns and rhetoric of Charles Pipkin and the Las Vegas Taxpayers' Association against Arnett, Russell, Cragin, and their commissioners duplicated the trend noted by Carl Abbott in his study of sunbelt cities. From North Carolina to California, "in one city after another, the new politicians lambasted entrenched cliques of officeholders as corrupt machines, promised to crack down on vice and end police corruption and argued for efficient planning and budgeting."[53] With the wartime emergency over and sunbelt urbanization on the rise, the postwar decade served as a period of transition, reorganization, and modernization as municipal governments struggled to cope with the demands of economic growth and physical expansion.

In Las Vegas the precise composition of competing elites for virtually all municipal elections prior to 1980 is still not clear. While the Taxpayers' Association and less formalized cliques mimicked the actions of good government leagues and other reform groups in larger cities across the sunbelt, the exact extent of the former's influence in Las Vegas elections will require substantial oral history research and vote profile analyses—a task beyond the scope of this book. Nevertheless, the trend in Las Vegas politics after 1945 was clear: like their counterparts across the urban sunbelt, local voters wanted a well-managed, business-oriented government with low taxes and a commitment to growth. The casinos along with local developers, bankers, and substantial businessmen formed the core of this support for Ernie Cragin and later Mayors C. D. Baker (although support was still strong for Cragin in 1951) and Oran Gragson.

"Boomtown
in the Desert"

Tourism and, to a lesser extent, defense fueled the urbanization of Las Vegas in the 1950s. Like cities in Florida, Texas, Arizona, and California, Las Vegas benefited from the shift of federal defense spending to the sunbelt. The town's main industry, however, was tourism. Of course, casino gambling was a two-edged sword. As gaming revenues skyrocketed, so did the threats to Las Vegas's new-found success. The Kefauver hearings, federal tax legislation, local scandals, casino bankruptcies, and gambling referenda in nearby states all menaced the city's fragile prosperity. Determined to ensure a prosperous future, Las Vegans countered by supporting a spacious, new convention center, expanded operations at Nellis, the opening of the nuclear test site, and construction of a modern interstate highway to southern California.

The spectacular development of the Las Vegas Strip was the paramount story of the 1950s. As early as 1948, it was obvious that the highway south of Las Vegas would need more than four resorts to handle the growing waves of Californians driving to and from the city. Only the undeveloped tracts south of town possessed the space for parking lots, tennis courts, swimming pools, riding stables, and the other amenities which resort guests had increasingly come to expect. The crowded downtown lots bordering Fremont Street simply lacked the room to compete with their suburban counterparts south of town. The 1950s witnessed a hotel-building fever which eventually made Las Vegas famous. In his recent work analyzing the relationship between gambling and society, John Findlay has provided a masterful overview of Las Vegas's place in America's postindustrial society. Upward mobility teamed with rising affluence, southern California's car culture, and new patterns of leisure to boost Nevada tourism in the decades following World War II. [1]

The seeds of the Strip's development lay in the 1940s with the spectacular success of the El Rancho, Last Frontier, Flamingo, and Thunderbird. Their triumphs inspired a generation of investors like Wilbur Clark. Having tasted a sample of the profits while a part-owner of the El Rancho in 1944, Clark dreamed of building the Strip's fifth resort, the Desert Inn. A native of Keyesport, Illinois, Clark first saw Las Vegas at the age of nineteen while en route to visit his father in San Diego. During the depression, he worked at a variety of jobs in California, including bartender, dealer (on the offshore gambling boats and in the town's underground gambling industry), and bellman at San Diego's Knickerbocker Hotel. An amiable man, Clark formed a series of friendships and partnerships which eventually netted him an owner's share of thirteen bars in the golden state. Following the election of reform Mayor Fletcher Bowron, he joined the migration of gamblers to Las Vegas. In 1944, he used profits from his earlier ventures to purchase a large share in the El Rancho plus two smaller casinos: the Monte Carlo (downtown) and the Player's Club (on Highway 91). All the while, he dreamed of owning something grander, a plush resort modeled after the Desert Inn Hotel in Palm Springs. With this in mind, he bought a large parcel of land across from the Hotel Last Frontier in 1945. Financing came from club profits and from his $1.5 million sale of the El Rancho in 1946. Within months, postwar building costs devoured his bankroll, and all work ceased on the project for almost two years. In 1948, he finally obtained the money needed to finish the job by selling 75 percent of his share in the resort to Detroit laundry kingpin Moe Dalitz and several of his Cleveland associates.[2]

With financing secured, Clark finished the enterprise in 1950. Opening night, April 24, was another grand event for the emerging Strip. Performers Edgar Bergen with Charlie McCarthy, actress Vivian Blaine, and the Donn Arden dancers played to a full house in the Painted Desert Showroom. The Desert Inn was truly the latest jewel in the Strip's glittering crown of plush resorts. The property's pastel appearance resembled the spas of Miami Beach and Havana. Bermuda pink buildings trimmed in green (with roofs of white tile chips) graced seventeen richly landscaped areas. Guests enjoyed all the modern conveniences, including air conditioning controlled by individual thermostats in every room. The gourmet restaurant served the cuisine of Chef Maurice Thominet, formerly of the Ritz Hotel in Paris. On the resort's third floor, the Sky Room featured nightly dancing. Large windows offered a panoramic view of the surrounding mountains while tiny star lights in the ceiling mimicked the night sky.

A white, oval fountain fronting the resort's driveway sprayed water sixty feet in the air, symbolizing Clark's commitment to excellence—as did the staff, which included N. E. Hoffert, former manager of San Francisco's renowned Clift Hotel and assistant manager Don Hoyle of Florida's Hollywood Beach Hotel. Allard Roen, a Dalitz associate (and later part-owner of California's La Costa resort) was casino credit manager, while publicity was eventually placed in the capable hands of Gene Murphy who, in 1953, helped organize the first Tournament of Champions golf event. This clever promotion, ostensibly designed to raise money for the Damon Runyon Cancer Fund in New York, enlisted the support of influential columnist Walter Winchell, a longtime Runyon associate, who used his column to promote the event. Sam Snead, Cary Middlecoff, Jimmy Demaret, and other golf champions mingled with Hollywood's leading stars to help make the event an immediate hit.

Clark, an amiable host and community leader, only added to the resort's popularity. For over a decade the Desert Inn was the Strip's premier resort, as Clark hosted visits by President-elect John F. Kennedy, the Duke and Duchess of Windsor, and a parade of other luminaries. Failing health eventually forced him to sell his share of the hotel in 1964 to the Dalitz interests. Then in November 1966, eccentric billionaire Howard Hughes arrived to begin his famous sojourn at the resort's top-floor penthouse. Pressed by casino executives to vacate his suite for incoming high rollers, the reclusive Hughes eventually bought the property for $14 million in April 1967. From that day onward, the Desert Inn prospered. Its 1987 sale to multimillionaire Kirk Kerkorian only solidified its position as a major Strip property.[3]

The Sahara, the Strip's sixth hotel, was originally the site of the old Club Bingo located directly across from the El Rancho. Technically, a group of investors (including alleged Oregon gamblers Al Winter and Milton Hyatt, plus Bobby Morris, Sam Rubin, Johnny Hughes, and Robert Gordon) bought the Club Bingo and prepared to build the Sahara, but the real force behind this endeavor was Los Angeles jeweler Milton Prell. Prell, who had operated the successful 30-Club in Butte, Montana, during the war, was also a founding partner of the Lady Luck Casino and the Mint Hotel (1957) downtown. By 1950, the Club Bingo had gone nearly bankrupt when Houston financier A. Pollard Simon (a Desert Inn partner) responded to Prell's pleas for help and contributed enough money to demolish the building and begin the Sahara. In a master stroke, Prell enticed Del Webb, the Phoenix contractor who earlier had built the

Flamingo, to erect the Sahara. Since Prell and the others were still short of cash, Webb built the hotel nearly at cost in return for a 20 percent share of the property. With this incentive, Webb finished the project ahead of schedule. The two-story, 276-room resort opened on December 2, 1952, in a lavish premiere starring dancer Ray Bolger. The Congo Showroom, Casbar Lounge and Caravan Restaurant combined with the Sahara camels in front to reflect the African motif Prell so admired. The hotel was an immediate success; in fact, business was brisk enough that first year to justify construction of 200 more rooms in 1953. Throughout the 1950s the resort was a hangout for stars and gamblers alike. John Wayne and Fred MacMurray frequently came and, even until his death, Elvis Presley (while he never headlined the Congo Room) often played the slots late into the night.

Prell guided the hotel until 1964 when he left town for a brief residence in Los Angeles. Earlier in 1961, he had sold his interests in the Sahara, Mint, and Sahara Nevada Corporation (which he had earlier formed) to Del Webb who, in 1966, added 200 more rooms by building a 14-story tower—then the tallest building in Nevada. Four years later, Webb built higher—a 24-story tower with 400 more rooms which became the new state record holder. Several years later, the company opened the "Sahara Space Center," a 44,000-square-foot, $3.5 million convention facility for hotel-based groups. Both projects helped the resort lure more customers while raising capital for Webb's expanding operations at Lake Tahoe.[4]

Just a few weeks after the Sahara's debut, another legendary resort, the Sands, opened on December 15, 1952. A virtual army of investors underwrote this project, including Texas gambler and oilman Jake Freedman, alleged Florida and Kentucky bookmaker Ed Levinson, reputed St. Louis bookmaker Sid Wyman, Boston restauranteur Hyman Abrams, former Stork Club bouncer Jack Entratter, and a motley array of Palm Springs residents who raised the suspicions of federal and state investigators alike. As a result, the licensing process was prolonged. Ultimately, Mack Kufferman and Jake Freedman were denied licenses by the state tax commission, although entertainers Frank Sinatra and Dean Martin subsequently embellished the hotel's image by purchasing minor interests.

Born in controversy, the Sands nevertheless prospered from the start. Opening night was a resounding success with Danny Thomas starring in the Copa Room. Appointment of the ever-popular Jack Entratter as entertainment director guaranteed the signing of top name performers and a steady flow of high rollers from New York, Philadelphia, and Boston.

Like the Desert Inn and Flamingo, the Sands's immaculately manicured lawns were graced by exotic palms and shrubs. The Garden Room Restaurant, a glass-sided coffee shop, gave diners a spectacular view of the pool and grounds. Like its predecessors, the original Sands was a series of low-rise structures. However, as business surged in the early sixties, management laid plans for expansion. Work began on a fifteen-story tower in 1963, and was fully completed in 1968 after Howard Hughes took over. Almost immediately, Hughes announced plans for the "new Sands"— a gargantuan 4,000-room resort—but the billionaire never followed through. The hotel remained a Hughes property, although leasing operators expanded the casino and remodeled many of the rooms.[5] Finally in 1988, convention manager Sheldon Adelson and associates purchased the hotel and laid plans for future expansion.

Despite the new Desert Inn, Sahara, and Sands, resort development continued unabated. In 1954 the Desert Showboat Motor Inn, a Mississippi riverboat gambler's delight complete with paddlewheel and smokestacks, opened its doors. The first resort hotel within the Las Vegas city limits, it was located on the Boulder Highway near the county line. The two-story, 100-room inn was financed by Last Frontier owner William J. Moore and longtime casino mogul J. Kell Houssels, owner of the Las Vegas Club, El Cortez, and later, the Tropicana. In an unusual arrangement, Wilbur Clark's Desert Inn managers ran the casino while Moore and Houssels operated the hotel. The early years saw the resort struggle, thanks mainly to its remote location, far from the Strip and Fremont's "Glitter Gulch." The investors originally chose the site based on contemporary economic surveys which erroneously predicted that the new center of town would be in the Showboat area. Fortunately, the town's frantic urbanization in the 1960s soon surrounded the property with populated neighborhoods and commercial zones.

Still, the process took time. The hotel's poor location condemned the resort to marginal profits for the early years. In response, enterprising management offered a variety of gimmicks to lure customers, including a $.49 breakfast special which drew locals who helped fill the "Boat's" 500-seat bingo parlor. Red ink finally turned to black once Joe Kelley, an Arkansas native and former California gambling boat dealer, became general manager. For the next thirty years, Kelley, who had worked for Houssels and Moore at their El Cortez downtown, guided the struggling resort. While profits gradually rose, the real breakthrough came in 1959 when Kelley and his associates built a 24-lane bowling alley at the hotel.

During that time, the bowling boom was just beginning to sweep the nation and Kelley exploited the trend. Marketing experts organized special Showboat leagues in the Phoenix and Los Angeles metropolitan areas, funding tournaments and offering teams and winners free trips to the hotel for championship playoffs. What golf did for the Desert Inn, bowling did for the Showboat. In 1960, the Boat hosted its first Las Vegas Open, one of only seven P.B.A. events at the time. Although bowling's national appeal eventually waned, the Showboat somehow escaped the decline, adding 12 more lanes in 1961 and 70 more in the next fifteen years. By 1979, the Showboat, with 106 lanes, was the third largest bowling center in America and the largest west of Pennsylvania. Catering to both a local and out-of-state, low- and middle-income clientele, the Showboat eventually became one of the most profitable casino operations in Las Vegas.[6]

The main focus of development, however, remained the Las Vegas Strip. On April 29, 1955, Nevada's first high-rise hotel, the Riviera, opened its doors. All previous resorts had consisted of low-rise motel or bungalow units in the architectural tradition of the old West. Builders had feared that the hardpan caliche soil, when combined with the valley's high water tables, would not support weighty, high-rise buildings. But the Riviera disproved the theory. Towering eleven stories above Highway 91, with its pretentious fleur de lis wallpaper, Cafe Noire Coffee Shop, and opening night star, Liberace, the Riviera added a decided European flavor to the Strip. Billed as a "self-contained vacation community," the $10 million resort combined the best of modern-day American luxury with "Mediterranean charm."

Despite the Riveria's elegance, profits were marginal from the beginning. Within months of the opening, the group of Miami investors who built the place had imported ex-Flamingo boss Gus Greenbaum to save the operation. Clearly, the mob had an interest in the property. A reluctant Greenbaum ended his semiretirement in Phoenix only after being threatened by Tony Accardo and Jake "Greasy Thumb" Guzik. The Chicago mob purchased the casino in 1955 (the hotel itself remained with the original investment company), and Greenbaum surrounded himself with a staff of mob associates and henchmen. Greenbaum, Elias Atol, "Little Icepick" Willie Alderman, Charlie "Kewpie" Rich, the notorious Davie Berman, Ben Goffstein, and others owned and managed the operation. In fact, the mob continued to control the resort even after Greenbaum's murder in 1958, although state and federal crackdowns eventually forced a sale. The Riviera changed hands several times in the 1960s before an investment group headed by New York multimillionaire Meshulam Riklis bought the property. Thanks to generous loans in the 1970s from the Nevada Public Employees Retirement System, Riklis expanded room and convention facilities, and generally rehabilitated the resort's sagging reputation.[7]

Like the Riviera, the Dunes also suffered cash-flow problems. Billed as the "miracle in the desert," the 194-room Dunes was the progeny of three men: Joe Sullivan, a Rhode Island restauranteur; Al Gottesman, an eastern theatre chain owner; and Bob Rice, a Beverly Hills costume jewelry maker. Opened on May 23, 1955, the hotel boasted a 90-foot-long swimming pool and 15-foot-long lagoon, along with a motif reminiscent of "Ali Baba and the Forty Thieves." A towering 30-foot-high Sultan, arms akimbo, stood in front like a sentinel. "Magic Carpet Revues," the brainchild of European producer Robert Nesbitt, graced the showroom nightly. Yet, despite all the elegance and entertainment, profits fell after the first few weeks. The "boomtown in the desert" myth which portrayed the Strip nationally as a glamorous bonanza of steadily flowing riches concealed the perilous risks of the casino business. Many hotels lost millions, especially in the mid-1950s when the Strip was overbuilt. The Dunes was a major victim. The gaming recession combined with the resort's unfortunate timing and location to spell disaster. The latter was especially troublesome: located diagonally across from the fabulous Flamingo, the Dunes could not compete with the established resort. Worse still, the newly opened Riviera and Royal Nevada only saturated the gambling market, undermining the Dunes. In a desperate move, Dunes owners agreed to let the Sands's management run the resort, but this too failed. As profits fell, management resorted to pirating customers from the Sands by offering them "comps" (free drinks, dinners, shows, etc.) at the Dunes. Yet, despite these efforts and $1.2 million in new loans, the hotel closed its casino after just one year in 1956, and began operating as a motel.[8]

Convinced that the Dunes could become a money-maker, Chicago shipping magnate and alleged mob associate Jake Gottlieb bought the property and, in an ingenious move, hired Major (his real first name) Arteburn Riddle, an Indiana trucking company owner, to turn the Dunes around. According to columnist George Stamos, Riddle made four key moves which saved the resort. First, he booked "Minsky's Follies," starring Lou Costello, for a six-week run. This was the first-ever Las Vegas production involving bare-breasted girls and, needless to say, it was an overnight sensation. In fact, with three performances nightly, the show drew 16,000 people in one week—a Las Vegas record for that time. "Vive Les Girls" seemed a natural successor, and Riddle later imported Frederick Apcar, a noted producer of European entertainment, to bring in the French spectacular "Casino de Paris," which played at the Dunes for over twenty years. Aside from providing spicy entertainment, Riddle built the Sultan's Table, a lavish gourmet restaurant inspired by the famed Villa Fontana of Mexico City.[9]

Then in 1961, he bought a huge rectangular piece of land (stretching between Dunes Road and Tropicana Avenue) from banker Jerry Mack and Mel Close for the 18-hole Dunes Golf Course, patterned after the Desert Inn facility he so admired. During the previous four years, Riddle had acquired a growing interest in the resort. Thanks to this foresight, he was able to raise millions in new capital quickly when he sold most of his interest in 1961 to outside investors. With these funds, Riddle financed his fourth great move: boosting room capacity. Recognizing that casino profits varied as a function of room capacity, Riddle opened the new 250-room Olympic Wing and pool which raised the Dunes to 450 rooms. Then in 1965, he and Irving Kahn (the other principal owner) finished their new 24-story high rise, which pushed the resort beyond 1,000 rooms. Strengthened by these improvements, the Dunes, joined later by Caesars Palace and the MGM Grand on the fabulous corner of Flamingo Road and the Strip, remained a money-maker until the early 1980s when debts and mismanagement again threatened its future. Finally in 1988, Japanese millionaire Masao Nangaku purchased the resort, promising a multimillion-dollar expansion program.[10]

While the Dunes's proximity to the Flamingo posed some initial problems, the Hacienda's location nearly two miles farther south was a greater barrier. The distant Hacienda was the brainchild of Warren Bayley, a syndicated travel columnist who later became chairman of the board of Standard Motels, Inc., a California-based chain. While the motel business was lucrative, especially in the postwar years when rising western affluence permitted more families to own a car and travel, Bayley aspired to providing motorists with something grander than standard motel units. Prior to his arrival in Las Vegas, Bayley and company opened their first Hacienda Hotel in California. The new concept, really a motor hotel, featured a substantial main building of Spanish design with motel wings radiating outward. The Hacienda provided bellmen, room service, and other frills traditionally associated with hotels. By 1954, the experiment's success led to the construction of a chain of Haciendas in Fresno, Bakersfield, and Indio, California. Buoyed by rising profits, "Doc" Bayley and his wife, Judy (a talented business manager who regularly attended the firm's high-level meetings), decided to add a casino dimension and therefore planned another Hacienda for the burgeoning Las Vegas Strip. Construction began in 1955. Blueprints did not provide for a large showroom or gourmet restaurants, because the owners realized that few Flamingo or Riviera high rollers would be traveling out to the distant resort. Instead, the Bayleys catered to the family market with a $17,000 quarter-midget racetrack for kids' go-carts, several pools, and similar attractions.[11]

The hotel itself opened in June 1956, managed by an able staff of executives drawn from the various Haciendas in California. The casino, however, remained closed. Bayley had insisted on naming Jake Kozloff as casino manager even though Nevada Gaming Control Board Chairman Robbins Cahill refused to approve Kozloff, citing the latter's known association with organized crime figures. Then, in a notorious blunder, Cahill defended the delay by arguing that Las Vegas would not miss the Hacienda since the Strip was already overbuilt. His implication that the control board might use its powers to control southern Nevada's casino development invited charges that the "Reno-dominated" board was trying to stunt southern Nevada's growth. Coming on the heels of the tax commission's effort to close the Thunderbird casino, Cahill's comments sparked a brief recall effort against Governor Charles Russell (a northerner), who had appointed Cahill. For their part, both Cahill and Russell denied the allegations. Eventually, the storm passed and, in a judicious move, Bayley dropped his bid to have Kozloff licensed.[12]

The casino opened in early 1957 and enjoyed moderate success. Lacking a significant pedestrian traffic, the Hacienda necessarily catered to locals and vacationing travelers. The Palomino Showroom, designed to handle small parties and shows, kept the hotel bustling, as did a number of successful marketing ploys. Perhaps the most famous was the "Hacienda Holiday" advertised on billboards along the Los Angeles Highway in Barstow, Victorville, and other California roadside towns. Customers paid only $16 to cover food and room expenses at the hotel and received a $10 refund in casino chips. The holiday was later extended to all of southern California. By the 1960s, the Hacienda maintained a fleet of thirty airplanes and even a helicopter for the convenience of customers.

Following its bumpy start, the resort continued to earn consistent profits in the decades thereafter. Prosperity continued into the 1980s under the guidance of financier Paul Lowden, who also purchased the Sahara from the Del Webb Corporation. [13]

By the mid-1950s, Las Vegas casinos were basically divided into two categories: "carpet joints" and "sawdust joints." Recognizing how the former had enthroned the Strip and drawn many of the best high rollers from downtown, Ed Levinson, a Chicago gambler, teamed with San Francisco financier and Miami hotelman Lou Lurie to build downtown's first refined hotel, the Fremont. Towering fifteen stories above Fremont and Second Streets, it was downtown's first high-rise property. The $6 million, 155-room hotel opened on May 18, 1956—an event timed for the middle of the annual Helldorado celebration. Crowds thronged the resort from the beginning. Many no doubt came to sample the fare in the Fremont's excellent gourmet rooms. In a clever move, Levinson snared Chef Shillig, formerly of Paris's Ritz Hotel and London's Savoy. Noted Chinese chef Billy Gwon was imported from New York, and the talented Ed Torres was made food and beverage manager (he had earlier been appointed publicity director). The Fremont was also the first hotel downtown to attract big-name entertainment, featuring Wayne Newton, Kay Starr, Pat Boone, Helen Reddy, and others in its rotating Carnival Lounge stage during their early nightclub years. Besides entertainment, Torres and Levinson masterminded a variety of other attractions to boost business. One stroke of genius was convincing KSHO-TV Channel 13 owner Morry Zenoff to locate his broadcasting studio inside the resort. The move drew hundreds of locals each week and provided customers with an added sense of excitement. Hotel expansion came in 1963, as management provided 200 more rooms by building the fourteen-story Ogden Tower, a parking garage (one of the first for downtown), the 650-seat Fiesta Theatre, and Nevada's first above-ground swimming pool. The Fremont remained a money-maker throughout the next two decades but, like the Stardust, acquired an unsavory reputation when purchased by Allen Glick and his Argent Corporation in 1974. Like the Stardust, the Fremont endured several changes of ownership (and licensing problems) before veteran gamer Sam Boyd bought the resort and ensured its continuing success with a series of improvements in the 1980s. [14]

When Tony Cornero died of a heart attack while gambling at the Desert Inn casino, his Stardust Hotel project was only three-fourths complete. As previously noted, Cornero and his brothers had first come to Las Vegas in 1931 and opened the sumptuous Meadows during the Hoover Dam boom. Following the dam's completion, The Meadows closed in 1936 and Cornero concentrated his attention on the SS *Lux*, the gambling boat he operated off Santa Monica prior to World War II. In 1946, Cornero tried and failed to deploy a new ship, the SS *Rex*. State and federal resistance (the Coast Guard impounded the boat as a menace to navigation) forced him back to Las Vegas. For several years, he operated a number of clubs downtown but, like Bayley, Jaffe, and others, Cornero recognized the growing importance of the Strip and longed for a piece of the action. Finally in 1954, Cornero paid Frank Fishman $650,000 for thirty-two acres directly north of the bankrupt Royal Nevada (just north of today's Frontier Hotel). He then formed a company, Stardust Inc., and actually sold $4 million worth of stock without registering it with the Securities and Exchange Commission. Compounding matters, Cornero proceeded to lose large amounts of his investors' money in casinos all over town.

Following Cornero's untimely death, John Factor, brother of cosmetics magnate Max Factor, sensing the Stardust's potential value, pumped $10 million into the hotel which finally opened on July 2, 1958. The resort's size reflected Cornero's personal extravagance. The Stardust's sprawling bungalow-style buildings and 1,000 rooms justified its billing as "the largest hotel in the world." The 105-foot-long pool and 16,500-square-foot casino were easily the largest in Nevada. Located in the rear was Horseman's Park, a rodeo facility equipped with over 300 stalls and corrals. In the 1960s, management built the massive Stardust Raceway for auto grand prix racing in western Las Vegas (today Spring Valley) several miles away. At about the same time, a golf course and country club were also constructed two miles east of the resort on Desert Inn Road. If these attractions were not enough, standing before the casino entrance was the largest electric sign in the world: 216 feet long and 27 feet high, the sign contained over 6 miles of wiring, 7,100 feet of neon tubing and 11,000 lamps. On a clear night it served as a great beacon for approaching cars sixty or more miles out on the dark desert roads.[15]

Aside from these novelties, the Stardust provided top quality entertainment. Its Cafe Continental Stage was technically the best equipped in town with six hydraulic lifts able to move props, musicians, and performers thirty feet below to ten feet above stage, making the theatre an excellent venue for large production shows. Complementing this were state-of-the-art lighting and sound systems which made the Stardust a natural home for the great Parisian extravaganza, "Lido de Paris." In

1958, famed producer Donn Arden brought the Lido (complete with the on-stage sinking of the Titanic) to the hotel, where it has remained for thirty years.

Throughout its history, the Stardust has survived a continuing swirl of controversy about its owners. Suspicions have been raised by the media as well as state and federal authorities first over Cornero and then, in the later fifties, over alleged proprietor Sam Giancana. Eventually, the Desert Inn's Moe Dalitz purchased the resort and, while state and local authorities were satisfied with Dalitz's integrity, insinuations made by investigative reporter Ovid Demaris and others were hardly comforting. Teamster loans in the 1960s and the subsequent purchase by Allen Glick, a suspected collaborator in underworld skimming operations, kept the Stardust in headlines as did Howard Hughes's celebrated effort to buy the resort—a monopolistic action successfully blocked by U.S. Attorney General Ramsey Clark and the state Gaming Control Board. Finally in the 1980s, the Stardust's acquisition by respected Las Vegas gamer Sam Boyd and his investment group cleared the hotel's image and laid the foundation for future success.[16]

The Strip's next resort, the Tropicana, owed its existence to the vision and drive of Ben Jaffe, the board chairman and part-owner of Miami Beach's Fountainbleu Hotel. In 1955, Jaffe came to Las Vegas and bought a 40-acre tract on the southeast corner of the Strip and Bond Road (today Tropicana Avenue). He organized the Bond Estates Company to build the resort and leased the casino operations to an associate, New Orleans gambler "Dandy" Phil Kastel. Like Bugsy Siegel before him, Jaffe wanted to erect the finest hotel in Las Vegas. Designed by architect M. Tony Sherman and built by Taylor Construction, both of Miami, the Tropicana exuded a Caribbean ambience reminiscent of old Havana. Guests could choose from four room decors: French Provincial, Far East, Italian Renaissance, and Drexel. In an unusual departure from Las Vegas tradition, room corridors bypassed the casino to maintain the quiet atmosphere of an elegant hotel, while exotic plants shielded the entrance and lobby from the bustle of slots and tables.[17]

Unfortunately for Jaffe, cost overruns delayed the resort's completion. Complicating matters was Tony Cornero's decision to pay construction workers double time wages to speed completion of his own Stardust. Cornero tied up every mason in town, forcing Jaffe to import more from California. Soaring costs eventually forced the latter to sell his interests in the Fountainbleu to raise another $5 million to finish the project. The

Tropicana finally opened on April 4, 1957, and immediately became the subject of controversy. On May 2, when gangworld leader Frank Costello was killed in New York, police found a note in his pocket bearing the figure $651,284—the gross profit for the Tropicana's first twenty-four days of business. The Nevada Gaming Control Board quickly traced the Costello link to Phil Kastel. Jaffe, himself a reputed punchboard operator and gambler in Mexico, had raised state suspicions earlier in 1956 when he had first proposed Kastel for licensing. Needless to say, Kastel was never approved.[18]

Anxious to mollify state authorities, Jaffe now turned to veteran Las Vegas gamer J. Kell Houssels, who agreed to manage the hotel. This was a sound move because Houssels was a respected member of the gaming fraternity who originally came to town as part of a surveying crew for the Hoover Dam project. Following the legalization of gambling in 1931, Houssels dealt blackjack before purchasing the Old Smokeshop (on the northeast corner of Main and Fremont), converting it into the famed Las Vegas Club. Later years saw him expand his interests, acquiring Las Vegas's first bus line and cab company (Lucky Cabs). He also purchased interests in other casinos, including the El Cortez in 1941, the Showboat, and the Union Plaza. Because Houssels had played a major role both on Fremont Street and behind the scenes at city hall to build Las Vegas into the nation's foremost casino city, his integrity was never in doubt.

Once licensed, Houssels, assisted by former El Rancho and Last Frontier general manager Robert O. Cannon, guided the "Trop" through a decade of prosperity. To be sure, the first years were shaky. On one night in 1957 when players' winnings emptied the casino cage, Houssels saved the day by rushing several hundred thousand dollars from the El Cortez's coffers over to the Tropicana in a shopping bag. By 1959, the struggle was over, and Houssels boosted his original 6 percent interest into a majority share by buying out Jaffe. Under the management of Houssels and Cannon, the hotel prospered from the late 1950s through the sixties. Entertainment Director Lou Walters (father of newswoman Barbara Walters) lured top stars like Eddie Fisher before importing the spectacular "Folies Bergere" from Paris in 1959 for a multidecade run in the hotel's main showroom. Aside from entertainment, the Tropicana's gourmet restaurants matched the Strip's best. Martin Appelt, the famed chef of the Waldorf Astoria, prepared sumptuous dishes while popular Los Angeles restaurateur Alexander Perino opened a Las Vegas branch of "Perino's" in the hotel.

Unfortunately, the Tropicana did not keep pace with the newer competition. While Houssels added another 315 rooms in various expansions during the 1960s, the resort's total capacity of 615 rooms in 1970 could not match Caesars Palace, the Las Vegas Hilton, and the impending MGM Grand. In 1968, the seventy-two-year-old Houssels, tired of the strain and anxious to concentrate his interests downtown, sold out to Trans-Texas Airways. The next few years saw the resort limp along through a series of owners including chemical heiress, Mizi Stauffer Briggs. Briggs, recognizing the need for a high-rise addition to compete with the other Strip hotels, began the 22-story Tiffany Tower in 1977. Within two years, however, declining profits and licensing problems forced a sale to the Ramada Corporation, which subsequently bankrolled a second tower and other improvements to guarantee the hotel a prosperous future.[19]

By 1955 it was obvious that Las Vegas would become a major resort and defense area. There were doubters, though, especially in the mid-fifties when the Strip boom seemed over. The 1955 bankruptcy of the small Royal Nevada casino combined with the well-publicized cash-flow problems at the Stardust, Dunes, Frontier, and Riviera to convince some that Las Vegas would never duplicate the smashing success of Miami Beach. But after a brief lull, the economy continued to grow. Crucial to Las Vegas's overall success was the cooperation of local unions. Unlike Reno, which suffered a calamitous strike by hotel workers on the Fourth of July weekend in 1949, Las Vegas did not experience a major hotel strike until 1976. From its founding in 1938, Culinary Union Local 226, representing hotel and restaurant employees, successfully negotiated wage, health, and pension fund agreements with hotels on the Strip and downtown. Thanks largely to the strong but prudent leadership of Al Bramlet, who became secretary-treasurer in 1953, the union permitted the hotels to operate continuously. While there were occasional work stoppages by bartenders, stagehands, and showgirls at individual resorts, no large conflicts threatened the industry. The same was true of construction. Fully organized by 1930 (the Clark County Central Labor Council was formed in 1929), Las Vegas's building trade unions staged occasional walkouts (e.g., the carpenters' strike of 1959), but none were lengthy enough to paralyze resort, commercial, or residential growth. While some violence flared during the 1949–50 campaign to unionize workers in local (intrastate) businesses not covered by the 1947 Taft-Hartley Act, these conflicts eased with passage of Nevada's right-to-work law in 1954. The

Teamsters too, were relatively quiescent. While there were strikes at the Nevada Test Site and in the city's bus system, truckers in the Jimmy Hoffa–led union rarely interrupted supply operations to Las Vegas's hotels. The resorts contributed further to labor peace by successfully fending off all efforts to unionize casino employees.[20]

As early as 1950, it was evident that the Strip would become a great tourist mecca. So, once again, the city of Las Vegas tried capturing the tax base. With the 1951 election looming, incumbent mayor Ernie Cragin needed more money to fund his ambitious building agenda and cover the town's spiraling debts. As previously noted, he was thwarted again when a group led by Flamingo executive Gus Greenbaum successfully lobbied the county commission for township status. On December 8, 1950, commissioners voted to create the unincorporated township of Paradise City. This move guaranteed protection for the suburb since, under Nevada law, no incorporated city could annex an unincorporated township without the approval of county commissioners. As will be shown later, beginning in 1950 and for decades thereafter, county officials pursued an aggressive policy of protecting their own tax base by creating a series of unincorporated towns, sanitation districts, and other entities to limit the growth not only of Las Vegas, but of Henderson and North Las Vegas as well.[21]

Of course, Las Vegas was not unique in this regard. The various conflicts between suburban and city residents over annexation were duplicated elsewhere in the urban south and west. As historian Carl Abbott found in his study of sunbelt cities, "the suburbanization of retailing, recreation and construction opened a gap between businessmen dependent upon inner city markets and real estate values and those whose property was tied to peripheral growth." To some extent, Las Vegas was an exception since some downtown clubowners also had Strip interests and most developers built in the city as well as the suburbs. Still, the divisions which Abbott found in Charlotte and other cities were, to some extent, operative in Las Vegas. As early as 1946, "suburban businessmen," especially strip hotel executives, saw annexation "as a tool for maintaining downtown dominance of local growth patterns."[22]

In 1951, the immediate reaction of Las Vegas was vindictive. Within ten days of the county vote to create "Paradise City," Mayor Ernie Cragin advised the Thunderbird Hotel, El Rancho Vegas, and Club Bingo that they would lose city sewer service once homes in the new Meadows Addition were built and "came on line." Cragin explained that, once occupied, the new tract would contribute an additional 200,000 gallons

per day of sewage which would overwhelm the town's disposal plant—
unless Paradise was disconnected. Then, with tongue in cheek, Cragin
advised the resorts either to seek county relief or form their own special
sewer district to absorb the full cost of enlarging the city's plant to treat
their wastes.[23]

As Las Vegas's fiscal crisis worsened in 1951, a worried Cragin bitterly
criticized the state's revenue structure which forced city taxpayers to
contribute more to the county than all other communities combined. He
noted, for example, that Las Vegans paid over 51 percent of all taxes
collected in Clark County for the state ($201,000 compared to $196,000
for the rest of the county). City residents paid $32,000 to the County Road
Fund compared to $30,000 by all other communities; $74,000 for the
county hospital (compared to $69,000 for others), and $68,000 for elementary schools (as opposed to $12,000 by the rest). Although 75 percent
of gas tax revenues came from the tourists and citizens of Las Vegas, the
city kept only 50 percent; the county and state split the other half. Thanks
to these inequities, the town could not expand its police and fire protection, install a modern infrastructure, or undertake other improvements to
accommodate its burgeoning growth. A gerrymandered tax structure had
combined with anti-annexation sentiment to cripple municipal administration.[24]

In fact, even county residents suffered. In spite of the Strip's spectacular growth in the 1950s, most of the gaming tax revenues went to rural
Nevada. As early as 1952, Clark County accounted for over two-thirds of
the state's gaming revenues. By April 1957, Clark and Washoe counties
contributed over 87 percent of license fee revenues, yet Nevada's fifteen
rural counties reaped most of the harvest since, under state law, gambling
revenues were shared equally by all seventeen counties. The Las Vegas
and Reno areas, therefore, received only two-seventeenths of the millions
of dollars they generated each year. This remained the case until the
reapportionment of the state legislature in the mid-1960s.[25]

Aside from the revenue losses to the state and county, Las Vegas faced
outside threats as well. As early as 1950, federal crackdowns against
Nevada gaming grew in response to Tennessee Senator Estes Kefauver's
probe into organized crime. Tensions reached fever pitch in Washington
when Kefauver threatened to charge underworld kingpin Meyer Lansky
with contempt of Congress for failing to testify about his relationship with
Lucky Luciano and Las Vegas casino interests. Later, in November 1950,
Kefauver's committee came to Las Vegas as part of its national fact-finding

tour. The senator and his associates stayed in Las Vegas less than two days, questioning several casino operators, including the Desert Inn's popular host, Wilbur Clark. Under oath, Clark conceded that he sold a 74 percent share of the resort to reputed Detroit gangland figure Moe Dalitz in return for money to complete the resort. The committee also grilled the Flamingo's Moe Sedway about his earlier relationship with the late Bugsy Siegel and Las Vegas racebook interests. Under questioning, Sedway openly admitted his role as the local representative for the Continental Press Service which ran the race wire allegedly controlled by the underworld. The committee, convinced that it had uncovered a major connection between organized crime and the local casinos, then left town for California to pursue its crusade. But the damage had been done; Kefauver had linked southern Nevada inextricably with the syndicate. Locals now braced themselves for the inevitable Kefauver bill regulating casino gambling. In 1951, the Tennessee senator proposed a measure which, among other things, would have levied a 10 percent federal tax on all wagering—enough to discourage most customers and effectively destroy the industry in Nevada. It took all of Senator Pat McCarran's considerable influence, but in the end Kefauver's bill was killed in committee, although the threat to Nevada (and Las Vegas) continued. In January 1955, Congressman Kenneth Keating (R-N.Y.) introduced a sweeping antigambling bill which exempted Nevada from only some provisions. Once again, the Nevada congressional delegation, consisting now of Senators George Malone, Alan Bible, and Congressman Cliff Young, struggled to kill the measure. After a lengthy and somewhat complicated process of negotiations, Keating was persuaded to withdraw his support.[26]

Even within the community there were crusading reformers who not only questioned the underworld ties of various hotels, but even challenged the power of Senator McCarran himself. Beginning in June 1950, a new city newspaper, the *Las Vegas Sun*, began raising issues which the *Review-Journal* mostly preferred to ignore. The power behind the *Sun* was flamboyant Hank Greenspun—an eastern liberal Republican whose opinions disrupted the staid political establishment of southern Nevada. Born in 1909 and raised primarily in the New York City area, Greenspun graduated with a law degree from St. John's University in 1934. Following his military discharge in 1945, he practiced law for a year before coming to Las Vegas. Greenspun originally planned to build a racetrack in Las Vegas with Joe Smoot, a former client of his law partner. While in town, Greenspun ran across an old law school chum, Ralph Pearl, who convinced him to publish "Las Vegas Life," a small magazine publicizing Las Vegas nightlife and entertainment. During his effort to secure advertising, Greenspun met Bugsy Siegel, who purchased a full-page ad for his newly opened Flamingo. Within weeks, Siegel hired Greenspun as the hotel's publicity man—a position which enabled the latter to make contacts all over town. Following Siegel's death, Greenspun left the Flamingo and invested with Wilbur Clark, purchasing a 15 percent share in the proposed Desert Inn Hotel and Casino. Between 1947 and his purchase of the *Sun* in 1950, Greenspun engaged in a variety of activities: buying KRAM radio in 1947, speculating in real estate, and even running guns to Israel during its civil war with Palestine (an act to which he later pleaded guilty).

In April 1950, Greenspun handled publicity for the Desert Inn's opening. At the time, the *Review-Journal*'s Don Reynolds (Reynolds had bought the paper from Cahlan and Frank Garside in 1949 although Cahlan remained managing director until December 1960) was engaged in a bitter contract dispute with the International Typographical Union and had just locked out his printers. The latter, in turn, had begun their own paper, the *Las Vegas Free Press*, to provide the city with a union voice and discourage (albeit unsuccessfully) statewide efforts to pass right-to-work legislation. A sympathetic Greenspun, who considered the monopolistic *Review-Journal* to be anti-union, anti-black, and even anti-Semitic, placed Desert Inn advertisements in the union organ—a move which incurred the wrath of hotel part-owner, Moe Dalitz. After all, Reynolds and especially Cahlan were close associates of Nevada's powerful Senator Pat McCarran, and Dalitz wanted no trouble.[27]

Unimpressed, Greenspun ultimately bought the union paper for $104,000 and renamed it the *Las Vegas Morning Sun*. A maverick at heart, Greenspun used the *Sun* as a vehicle for launching numerous crusades. As early as 1951, the feisty editor challenged the influence of Senator McCarran. Convinced that McCarran was behind a state policy to sell the BMI complex to Norman Biltz (a McCarran associate), Greenspun denounced the deal "that will make our grandchildren wonder where we were when the lights went out." Fearful that millionaire Biltz would control the water line that would eventually deliver Lake Mead water to Las Vegas, Greenspun demanded that the Senator secure federal funds for the project immediately. In the end, Basic's tenants bought the complex but Greenspun continued his attacks. Convinced that McCarran was anti-Semitic, Greenspun upbraided the Senator for his support of Joe McCarthy and the McCarran Internal Security Act. Greenspun then compounded matters by opposing McCarran's protégé, Alan Bible, in his 1952 senate campaign. Greenspun's championing of young Thomas Mechling provoked McCarran into organizing an advertising boycott of the *Sun* by Las Vegas's major hotels and clubs. Beginning in March 1952, all of the town's chief establishments, with the exception of Benny Binion's Horseshoe Club, pulled their ads from the *Sun*. Greenspun fought back with a lawsuit of his own. Charging McCarran and casino executives with attempted censorship, Greenspun pressed forward with his litigation, eventually breaking the boycott and winning an $80,000 settlement in 1953.

McCarran's intransigence only strengthened Greenspun's resolve. In October 1952, Wisconsin Senator Joe McCarthy visited Las Vegas to boost the campaign of Republican George Malone, who was opposing Mechling. Accompanied by Malone and McCarran, McCarthy spoke at the War Memorial Building downtown. During his speech, McCarthy strayed from his remarks to question Greenspun's patriotism, referring to him as an "ex-communist" and "ex-convict." In response, Greenspun sprang from the audience and approached the speaker's platform to challenge the senator's integrity, but Malone, McCarran, and McCarthy quickly exited the building. For the next few weeks, the *Sun* published a barrage of accusations, questioning (among other things) McCarthy's loyalty, sanity, honesty, and sexuality. At a time when both McCarthy and McCarran were at the height of their power, any challenge by a small-time Nevada editor was nothing short of heroic. While the *Sun* would never seriously threaten the *Review-Journal*'s circulation lead (except for a brief period in the late fifties and early sixties), Greenspun's newspaper nevertheless provided a needed counterpoint to Cahlan's political views.[28]

Moreover, the *Sun* played a vigilant role, ferreting out political corruption as well as underworld infiltration of Las Vegas gaming. In a celebrated 1954 exposé, Greenspun and reporter Ed Reid set up a sting operation to catch Clark County Sheriff Glen Jones, who had countenanced prostitution at Roxie's Club for years (even after an F.B.I. raid). Greenspun and Reid imported Pierre LaFitte, an undercover investigator from New York, to pose as Louis Tabet, an investor anxious to purchase Roxie's (the previous owners had been arrested in the F.B.I. raid). Closeted with a tape recorder in Tabet's hotel suite, Reid taped a series of incriminating conversations. In one, Roxie's owner reassured Tabet that Sheriff Jones would "protect" the brothel as long as the sheriff was paid off. Clark County Commissioner Rodney Colton also pledged his cooperation and accepted a "gift" from Tabet. Tabet also engaged Louis Weiner as an attorney and supposedly heard (the tapes were never produced) Weiner's law partner, then Nevada Lieutenant Governor Cliff Jones (brother-in-law of the *Review-Journal*'s John Cahlan, Al's brother), promise that Tabet would have no licensing problems once Democrat Vail Pittman was elected governor. On October 11, 1954, Greenspun's *Sun* began printing a series of articles based on the tapes. The bombshell wrecked the political career of Cliff Jones (who resigned as Nevada's Democratic committeeman), led to Governor Charles Russell's defeat of Vail Pittman, and sparked indictments against Sheriff Jones and Commissioner Colton. Subsequent testimony from Louis Weiner suggesting that reputed mobsters Jake and Meyer Lansky owned part of the Thunderbird Hotel with Cliff Jones triggered another series of articles from the ever-vigilant Greenspun. In the end, the Nevada Tax Commission revoked the Thunderbird's license, although the state supreme court later reinstated it. Despite the reversal, city and state politicians along with the gaming industry treaded carefully thereafter, anxious to avoid raising Greenspun's suspicions.[29]

Aside from Kefauver, Greenspun, the F.B.I., and others, Las Vegas officials and casino executives were also concerned in the 1950s about threats to the gaming industry from nearby California and Arizona. In November 1950, casino gambling referenda appeared on the ballot in both states. While some Las Vegas casino owners quietly supported the measures in hopes of expanding out of state, most southern Nevada business and political leaders were apprehensive. Undoubtedly, Las Vegas's well-publicized connection with organized crime was a major factor in the 1950 defeat of casino gambling questions in both states. Typical was an election-eve editorial in the *San Francisco Chronicle* which denounced Proposition 6, disputing the claims of supporters that revenues derived from casino gambling would help California's "blind and aged." The paper instead predicted that passage would empower casino executives "to turn this state lock, stock and barrel over to gamblers of their kind." Then, in an obvious reference to industry-barren Nevada, the editor insisted that "they will be in a position to smash the economy of this state. They will be the little Caesars of California and their composite record offers scant hope that their sense of responsibility will match their tremendous power." Obviously, the *Chronicle* reflected a statewide view; Proposition 6 lost in every county including Los Angeles (by a whopping 9 to 2 margin) where Las Vegas drew many of its customers. Election day 1950 saw Arizona voters defeat a similar proposal while Montana residents rejected slot machines. After a lull of several years, a new threat surfaced in May 1959 when businessman Charles Crittenden announced plans to place a new gaming question on the Arizona ballot. Supported by hotel-motel owners and various California investors, Crittenden expressed confidence he could reverse the 1950 vote, but the effort eventually failed as would all others until New Jersey finally approved the industry.[30]

These and other efforts to legalize gambling forced Las Vegas promoters to recognize that gambling alone could never fully support the city's resort industry. This realization led many casino executives and local boosters to advocate widening the town's market base beyond mere tourism by building a major convention center to rival the facilities in New York, Chicago, and Atlantic City. Since the late 1930s, Las Vegas had hosted small gatherings in the hall of the War Memorial Building. These meetings generally involved western groups such as the regional divisions of Pacific Telephone and Telegraph, the Small Brewers Association, the Union Oil Company, and the Brotherhood of Local Firemen and Enginemen. The conferences rarely drew more delegates than the city's hotels could handle, although they boosted casino play. Las Vegas really needed to attract national groups, but that effort required a larger convention facility. The origins of the Las Vegas Convention Center lay in the failed effort of the Las Vegas Thoroughbred Racing Association to promote horse racing in southern Nevada. In the spring of 1950 the association, led by President Joe Smoot, had begun construction of a track on 480 acres of land behind the Thunderbird Hotel. By September, the grandstand and clubhouse were half completed, and six months later the track was ready for racing. Opening day brought large, enthusiastic crowds, but the operation was doomed from the start. After only three days, the track closed for lack of a tote board, which made it almost impossible for fans to keep track of their bets. A series of other snafus kept the track closed along with the marked unenthusiasm of nearby Strip hotels which regarded horse racing as a threat to casino profits.[31]

Within weeks the track had closed, and the next few years witnessed several abortive efforts to re-open the facility. The property lay dormant for several years until 1955 when, in what proved to be a major contribution to the community, Horseshoe Club owner Joe W. Brown agreed to purchase the bankrupt track and transfer the 480 acres of land (today the site of the Convention Center, Hilton Hotel, and Las Vegas Country Club) to the city of Las Vegas for a convention center. In January 1955, a bankruptcy court judge ruled in favor of Brown's offer and against the bid of several Los Angeles investors who wanted the land for subdivisions. Brown made a $200,000 down payment to give municipal officials time to conduct a bond election. Initially, Las Vegas intended to annex the land between Sahara Avenue and Desert Inn Road for its convention center and fairgrounds. While the original deal gave county authorities little control over how the land would be developed, this soon changed because the area lay within the boundaries of Paradise and Winchester. Under state law the city could not annex any part of an unincorporated township without the county's approval, and that was not forthcoming. As a result, the Brown deal went through, but the eventual construction of a convention center was a joint city-county effort.[32]

In mid-January 1955, city-county leaders appointed the Convention Hall Subcommittee, comprised of Joe W. Brown, William J. Moore, and Ed Converse to begin the process of selecting a permanent site. While they considered a number of locations including a few closer to the airport, the three eventually chose a tract on Brown's land bordering Paradise Road. Ultimately, this location behind the Thunderbird awarded the Strip hotels a valuable advantage over their downtown counterparts. As larger conventions came to Las Vegas in the sixties and seventies, conventioneers invariably booked rooms in the nearby hotels, and confined their casino play to the Strip. As a result, the area's surging convention business helped boost the expansion of Strip hotel facilities compared to those along the less strategically located streets downtown. Not until the early 1980s would the city of Las Vegas, led by the Downtown Progress Association, push a large bond issue to construct the Cashman Convention Center.[33]

Plans for the valley's first major convention center moved along quickly once the site had been selected. A committee comprised of representatives from both the county and nearby cities worked on the details. Finally in January 1957, County Commission Chairman George "Bud" Albright announced that construction on the new $4.5 million domed Convention Meeting Hall would begin in the spring. A public hearing to determine how to finance the project was scheduled for mid-January. Blueprints called for the hall to contain 2,340 permanent seats, with a "temporary" capacity of 8,000. An exhibit hall with 90,000 square feet of space was scheduled to be built later. Parking for up to 1,800 cars was also included.[34]

From the beginning, local resorts and businesses recognized the multiplier effect that the new convention center would exert upon the local economy. It was therefore not surprising when, at the January 15, 1957, public meeting, no one objected to a funding formula which levied a 5 percent room tax on resort hotel rooms and a 3 percent charge on motels and commercial hotels. Plans called for an immediate bond election to fund initial construction until enough room taxes could be collected to amortize the debt and provide capital for future expansion. Following the agreement, hotelmen were delighted by the announcement that the Floral Delivery Association and American Mining Congress had already agreed to hold major conventions in the new hall.[35]

Both city newspapers helped rally community support for the project. Despite its well-deserved reputation as a newspaper given to investigative reporting and political exposés, the *Las Vegas Sun* often played the role of booster organ. Indeed, Hank Greenspun supported the convention center project, street improvements, a modern jet airport, and other public works—although somewhat less lavishly than Cahlan. To boost the project, Greenspun featured pictures of the new convention center on page 1 of a November 1956 special edition entitled "Las Vegas Unlimited." The multipage sections touted a variety of other local assets, including Lake Mead water sports, Clark County minerals, Basic Magnesium's chemical output, the Southern Nevada Industrial Foundation, plans for the new expanded McCarran Airport (complete with nearby locations for companies dependent upon air freight), plans for the new Interstate 15, the city's fabulous resort hotels and, of course, the new convention center.[36]

Still, Cahlan remained the undisputed dean of Las Vegas boosters. Since 1935, his *Review-Journal* had emphasized the importance of conventions to the city's resort economy. So, it was no surprise that Cahlan staunchly supported efforts by city and county leaders to build conference facilities in the 1950s. As a longtime town promoter, he was particularly effective in neutralizing the opposition of some businessmen and spending critics who opposed spending millions to attract convention business away from major cities. In a 1957 column, he dismissed the objections of naysayers, arguing that in the 1920s, "had the pioneers stopped to think about problems which attended plans for expansion, [Las Vegas would have remained] a sleepy little village where visitors paused only long enough to get gas and a sandwich before going on their way." According to Cahlan, the city's success had been built on a series of bold schemes: Hoover Dam, Basic Magnesium, the Air Gunnery School, and Nellis; the convention center was simply the most recent gamble.[37]

The evidence clearly supported city and county leaders. According to a 1958 report published by the Las Vegas Convention Bureau, America's "meeting industry" was booming. Thanks to increased affluence, expense allowances, and favorable tax deductions, 10 million delegates were attending 20,000 conventions in the United States annually. And the figure was growing. According to statistics, 50 percent of conventioneers' spending went to the host city's hotel-motel owners, 15 percent to restaurants, another 15 percent to retail stores, and 5 percent to taxes. All of this was welcome news to area businessmen, the majority of whom supported the room tax plan and subsequent bond issues to fund expansions. Already in 1958, even before the convention hall opened, government officials proposed a supplemental bond issue of $1 million to finance construction of an exhibit hall. As with the 1956 bond issue, the new project would cost taxpayers nothing; the debt would be paid off by room tax revenues. Originally, local officials had planned to build the exhibit hall later, but America's meeting industry was undergoing dramatic changes. Increasingly, groups were using their periodic get-togethers to showcase new products. Las Vegas convention officials had discovered already that several large groups would not consider Las Vegas until it acquired a spacious exhibit facility. As both the *Review-Journal* and *Sun* noted, voters had little choice in the matter; the town's future as a major convention site was at stake. A "no" vote was unthinkable, but an affirmative response would, in Al Cahlan's words, make Las Vegas "the new convention center of America." Voters ultimately approved the measure and in April 1959 the new convention center, with its modern domed meeting hall, opened for the World Congress of Flight.[38]

Supplementing conventions and tourism was the town's blossoming defense industry. Throughout the 1950s, Cold War defense spending energized the urban sunbelt as well as southern Nevada. As mentioned previously, the old gunnery school had been renamed Nellis Air Force Base in 1950. At first its size was modest, with a force of 1,700 men and an annual payroll of $12 million. The Korean War, however, accelerated the growth of operations. By 1953, the force grew to 5,200 and the payroll approached $50 million. In a matter of months Nellis became a major center for tactical air combat training. The impact on Las Vegas was considerable. As in the days of World War II, local rents soared as available housing constricted. These events were beneficial, however, because they encouraged developers from southern California to build more tracts in Las Vegas. To a great extent, the Korean War teamed with the Strip's development to fuel a building boom which produced 10,000 new homes in the decade following Japan's surrender. Nevertheless, the private sector could not handle the demand for dwellings, especially in the Nellis vicinity.[39]

To ease the strain, air force officials announced plans in November 1950 to build the $8 million Wherry Housing Project near the base for 400 airmen and their families. The development required Las Vegas officials to donate 1,800 acres of municipal lands for roads and utility connections. While the project was welcomed, businessmen feared that the military might damage the local economy by erecting a base city complete with a large PX. The Defense Department quelled local fears in early February when it assured local officials that the project would contain only a small retail outlet for essential items. Nearby stores would get virtually all the business from military families. Pleased by this announcement, Mayor Cragin and the commission prepared to cede the land, but new concerns were raised by City Commissioner (and local realtor) William Peccole who wanted a "reverter clause" in the contract to force the Pentagon to return the land if base operations were ever suspended. For a variety of legal reasons, Peccole succeeded in marshaling the support of fellow commissioners, but they soon deserted him after Senator McCarran told a public meeting that "the city well could lose the entire air force installation if some of the officials continued their program of harassment." The town's cooperative spirit undoubtedly encouraged the air force a month later to propose construction of the $650,000 Nellis grammar school. The facility, to be built for the Las Vegas Union School District, was a response to the projected overcrowding caused by the arrival of military dependents. These moves, along with the construction of Nellis Hospital, substantially eased the strain on municipal services.[40]

Like World War II, the Korean conflict only re-emphasized the base's importance to Pentagon officials. Southern Nevada boasted more fair weather days than Arizona, New Mexico, Texas, and even California—an indispensable asset for fighter training. By the fall of 1954, a full year after the Korean truce, Nellis's total manpower still exceeded 5,000. As the Cold War produced new crises in Suez, Hungary, and Lebanon, the air force expanded its operations at Nellis. In July 1958, the base's overall mission for testing tactics and equipment was substantially enlarged when the Tactical Air Command replaced the smaller Air Training Command at Nellis. Las Vegas, a "martial city" since 1941, has always benefited financially from each of America's last three wars. Like Vietnam and

World War II, the Korean conflict was no exception. In the 1953–54 budget year alone, the air force built a $145,000 vehicle maintenance shop, a $175,000 laundry building, a $173,000 officers' club, a $94,000 communications and electronics building, and two maintenance hangars (at $568,000) for the base's 300 aircraft. Most of this $3.4 million construction budget went to pay local contractors and suppliers of building materials.[41]

While Nellis proved to be a valuable addition to the town's defense economy, the nuclear test site was equally welcome, although its arrival was sudden and unexpected. The process which brought the facility to southern Nevada was directly related to President Truman's increasing reliance upon the nuclear deterrent. In 1950, the Atomic Energy Commission (AEC), anxious to reduce the logistical problems encountered with atomic testing in the far Pacific, chose a portion of the Nellis bombing range for America's continental test site. The zone's geological structure, Las Vegas's patriotic support of the Pentagon, the Korean War, and a variety of other factors combined to award southern Nevada this facility. Within a year, the federal government hastily constructed Camp Mercury as the primary base for operations. In the months preceding the first detonation in January 1951, over 1,500 workers handled the construction with Las Vegas again serving as the supply hub just as it had earlier with the dam, air gunnery school, and Basic Magnesium.[42]

At first, local residents were ambivalent toward these events. The obvious enthusiasm for the project's financial benefits was offset by major concerns over radiation and accidental explosions. Some even feared that the tests might discourage tourism. The AEC, however, was quick to respond. In mid-January 1951, the agency sent Dr. Alvin Graves, chief of the Los Alamos Test Division, to Las Vegas. In a series of prepared statements he reassured residents that radiation would pose no threat to safety, and that the mountains north of town would "shield" Las Vegans from any danger. Following Graves's remarks, a satisfied Mayor Ernie Cragin declared he was "100 percent behind the experiment" as was the Chamber of Commerce President Vern Willis. Supporting these views was the influential *Review-Journal*, which appealed to the patriotism of local residents, reminding them that "from the Civil War through World War II, the state of Nevada has always been in the vanguard in the support of such warfare." Discounting fears of radiation, the paper emphasized that "Nevada can contribute much to the [Korean] war effort by having the atomic project within its boundaries." With community fears largely allayed, the first bomb was detonated in January 1951.[43]

During the first year of testing, the site's payroll for construction alone exceeded $4 million. Tests themselves were labor intensive; indeed, the spring of 1952 saw over 3,000 scientists, technicians, and others prepare and conduct the "Snapper Tumbler" series. Since testing was not continuous, the labor force fluctuated from year to year, but, throughout the 1950s, the test site payroll exceeded $176 million—two-thirds of which found its way into the Las Vegas economy. In 1955, over 9,000 army, air force, and navy personnel joined with 3,500 AEC and civil defense workers to conduct the "Teapot" series. In November 1958, the AEC expanded the site's role by establishing a Nuclear Rocket Propulsion Test Center. Earlier in 1956, the AEC had inaugurated Project Rover to develop nuclear-powered rockets for space travel, and Project Pluto (ended in 1964) to create a nuclear ramjet engine for atmospheric flights. Thanks to these additional programs, the AEC was able to maintain a stable, year-round force of more than one thousand people. Most of these workers resided in Las Vegas with their families and, along with the substantial number of Nellis airmen living off base, contributed to the local economies of Las Vegas and North Las Vegas.[44]

Aside from attracting a small cluster of defense contractors to town, the air base and test site contributed to President Truman's decision in 1952 to classify the Las Vegas Valley as a "critical defense area." This designation qualified the city for more FHA mortgage loan money, federal funding for a new grammar school on West Charleston, and other benefits. In 1952, for instance, officials and regional engineers of the U.S. Home and Housing Finance Administration came to town and urged Clark County, Las Vegas, North Las Vegas, and Henderson to prepare an agenda of needed public works improvements which Washington might fund. Prospects of federal help forced each government to think seriously about how it would respond to future growth. Clark County, anxious to encourage development in its southern and eastern suburbs, drew up plans to justify a $1.6 million request for a sewer system and disposal plant for Paradise Valley and an additional network for the Boulder Highway communities of Pittman and Whitney. Las Vegas wanted $3.1 million for five miles of new 36-foot-wide streets to absorb increased traffic flow, new sewer outfalls to reduce flooding, plus a new $50,000 fire station for the growing East Charleston area, while the Water District sought $6 million to fund its pipeline connecting Las Vegas with Henderson's supply of Lake Mead water. In the end, all of these futuristic projects were built. While the Korean truce postponed some until the 1960s, all were funded at least partially by the federal government. In the long run, the valley's designation (even temporarily) as a "critical defense area" helped unify local governments behind a public works agenda of systematized improvements which only promoted more growth in the metropolis.[45]

To some extent, local politics reflected the need for more responsible city government. Despite the continued growth of the tourist and defense industries, Ernie Cragin faced an uphill fight in his bid for a third term as mayor. Along with an influx of new residents, the town's soaring debt combined with Cragin's affiliation with Fremont Street interests (Cragin & Pike insured many of the town's casinos) and Senator McCarran (which angered Hank Greenspun) to diminish his chances in 1951. Particularly damaging was the spirited campaign for city commissioner waged by perennial gadfly Charles Pipkin. Pipkin, president of the Las Vegas Taxpayers' Association, denounced the "pseudo-political organization on Fremont Street" which permitted casino interests to dominate city hall. In its place, he promised to cut municipal spending and cancel requests for "emergency loans." At the same time, Pipkin pledged to build public parks to reduce the city's alarming juvenile delinquency rate. He also spiced his campaign with a time-honored ploy, denouncing Southern Nevada Telephone Company for delays in providing new phone service and ridding the community of four-party lines. And he chastized Southern Nevada Power for charging consumers on the outskirts of town the full cost of installing poles and wires outward from the existing grid.[46]

Pipkin's invective only strengthened the candidacy of Cragin's more powerful adversary, former city surveyor, C. D. Baker. A longtime resident and prominent land investor, Baker was a responsible alternative to Cragin. Sensing defeat, the mayor struggled to recapture the support of his glory years. In a last-minute bid for voter support, Cragin emphasized the town's startling growth since he took office. In particular, he pointed to "the expansion of the downtown business district with the erection of many excellent stores and office buildings, the opening of a great number of new subdivisions with their fine homes." And he linked the promise of more development to his plans for additional police and fire stations, schools, and a vast program of street improvements, including widenings, lighting, gutters, sidewalks, and sewers—all designed to boost property values and broaden the city's tax base. But it was all to no avail. In a mild upset, voters opted for C. D. Baker (2,561 to 2,288). Incumbent Finance Commissioner Reed Whipple easily outpolled tavern owner Bob Peccole (brother of City Commissioner Bill Peccole), while Rex Jarrett, a veterans' advocate, won the other seat from Robert Moore.[47]

Two years later, voters partially cleaned house again, rejecting William

Peccole. The realtor's campaign for re-election in 1953 was dominated by charges of corruption. Acting Mayor Reed Whipple sparked the debate by chastising Peccole for using his position to approve gaming and liquor licenses for properties owned by his brother. *Las Vegas Sun* editor Hank Greenspun was harsher, denouncing the commissioner for twice voting to license the Westerner Club, whose application failed to list his brother's hidden 9 percent interest. In characteristically flamboyant style, Greenspun claimed that "we would be derelict in our duty to the people . . . if this man were permitted to escape with the loot he has amassed in his term of office." Peccole, embarrassed by the publicity and desperate to transform a budding scandal into a triumph, proposed revising the city's code of ethics. To this suggestion, Greenspun stormed back, accusing Peccole of having "the barefaced, shameless gall to jump the gun in proposing a revision of the city laws." In the end, the incumbent's critics prevailed, and architect Harrison Sharp won the seat. Peccole was subsequently indicted by the Clark County grand jury for allegedly demanding a 10 percent ownership in the Forty-Niner Club in return for his vote to license the business. After the charges were later dropped on legal grounds, Peccole then filed an unsuccessful libel suit against Greenspun.[48]

Unlike Peccole, Mayor Baker's popularity remained intact because he played no part in the alleged scandal. Instead, the mayor impressed voters with his vigorous leadership in the face of unprecedented growth. Hank Greenspun undoubtedly spoke for many when he wrote that "an extremely difficult job of administering a booming city has been admirably done under the guidance of Mayor C. D. Baker." Aside from proposing a series of paving districts for street improvements in mostly new suburban areas, Baker had actually kept a 1951 campaign promise to pave key arteries in the black Westside—a move which endeared him to the city's growing number of minority voters. Besides these accomplishments, Baker inspired the public with a bold agenda. In addition to his support of the proposed convention center, Baker also endorsed a number of progressive bond issues in the May 1955 city elections, including a $600,000 fire alarm box system, $500,000 for an underpass beneath the railroad at Owens Avenue to facilitate east-west traffic flow, and additional bonds to enlarge the city's sewage treatment plant. Baker's efforts to secure a new state office building in the City Park coupled with his determination to control the route of proposed Interstate 15 and his vigorous promotion of new commercial and residential developments won the support of many voters. It was therefore no surprise when, on May 2, 1955, Baker and the bond issues scored convincing victories.[49]

While the construction of a modern fire alarm system, street improvements, and sewer expansion all served to make Baker's second term
noteworthy, his most significant initiative was perhaps the influence he
exerted over the routing of Interstate 15. Good roads had always been
crucial to isolated Clark County. By the early 1930s, the Los Angeles
Highway (now fully paved) had become Las Vegas's economic lifeline,
providing California's burgeoning gambling market access to the town's
casinos. Within the metropolitan area, the road played a dynamic role in
the forties and fifties, decentralizing the casino core from its traditional
location on Fremont Street to the new "four-mile strip" extending from the
city limits at San Francisco Street (Sahara Avenue) southward to what is
today Tropicana. While the highway continued providing easy access to
the city in the postwar years, officials realized that the two-lane artery
could never accommodate the projected traffic coming to Las Vegas in the
seventies and eighties.[50]

An antiquated road connection with southern California eventually
would have diminished Las Vegas's business. But, once again, the federal
government came to the rescue. The Interstate Highway Act of 1956,
pushed through Congress by President Eisenhower, created a huge highway trust fund which supported 90 percent federal funding (with 10
percent state matching funds) to build Interstate 80 across northern
Nevada and Interstate 15 through the south. As early as January 1955,
debate had begun on the routing of these roads. While the bill itself did
not become law until 1956, state highway officials already knew that the
main east-west freeway would branch out of Salt Lake in three directions:
northwest toward Seattle, due west to San Francisco (through Reno), and
southwest to Los Angeles (through Las Vegas). Thanks to geographical
advantages, the railroad towns would again be favored, this time with
modern superhighways.[51]

Baker, a former city surveyor, recognized the route's political implications. As early as 1957, federal engineers predicted that the highway's
most likely location would be adjacent to Highland Avenue, although they
continued to consider two alternate routes east of Highland and a fourth
west of the railroad tracks. Of the four options, Mayor Baker preferred the
Highland option, because it disrupted the downtown business and casino
district less than the other three. Seemingly unphased by the fact that the
black Westside community would lose several hundred homes to the
Highland route, Baker focused instead on traffic flow, emphasizing how
the city could "negotiate for possible tie-ins which would provide over-
passes over the railroad tracks in the downtown area." Baker staunchly

opposed an eastern route, insisting that a freeway there would "over-load . . . residential streets," whose subsequent widening would "cost the municipality a great deal of money." He also insisted that an eastern road "would reverse the city planning and displace the present industrial and commercial area." The mayor shrewdly omitted the political fallout which would have ensued if substantial numbers of white businessmen and homeowners lost property to the freeway and street widenings. Traditionally, Las Vegas had grown eastward and later southward and northward away from the baseline of the railroad tracks. Few fashionable subdivisions had yet been built to the west. So, the city's option was clear: keep the freeway out of town but close enough to feed tourists and trucks into the downtown district conveniently. To accomplish this, part of the black Westside would have to be razed and part of the community destroyed, but in 1957 blacks were the politically weakest group in town—a plight which sealed their fate.[52]

Following the freeway decision, sewer and street expansions, and the successful completion of the convention center, Baker announced his retirement from public service. His departure left the 1959 mayoral race open to two men, veteran city commissioner Wendell Bunker and political newcomer and respected businessman, Oran Gragson. The decision was a crucial one for voters, since the 1960s promised to be a decade of unprecedented growth. Taking the offensive, the veteran lawmaker employed the familiar tactic of linking his opponent with the casino interests. Specifically, Bunker claimed that Gragson was supported by gamblers "seeking to introduce women dealers into the casinos along Fremont Street." Clearly, the charge was designed to appeal to male casino workers and conservative community groups anxious to minimize female participation in the sordid gaming world. In response, Gragson, like Cragin and Baker before him, professed a devotion to none but the public interest.[53]

Like Baker and Cragin, Gragson's Las Vegas roots ran deep. Born in Tucumcari, New Mexico in 1911, he was raised in Arkansas and Texas before coming west to work on Hoover Dam. Except for a brief return to Arkansas (1933) and Oklahoma (1937–38), he made Las Vegas his permanent home. Unlike many of his cohorts, Gragson remained in town after the dam's completion, toiling on various highway projects. An entrepreneur at heart, he eventually invested in a furniture store. Following World War II, he tried the automobile service business before returning to furniture retailing and later home appliances. His successful stores established his popularity. To a large extent, Gragson in 1959 symbolized the faith of the early pioneers in the future of Las Vegas. A relative newcomer to politics, he escaped the stigma so often attached to incumbency.[54] Promising only to maintain fiscal responsibility in all spending while promoting new commercial and residential development, Gragson appealed to the mainstream of city voters who preferred neither complacency nor radicalism. The real tribute to Gragson's centrism came in May 1959, when the Democratic *Review-Journal* endorsed the Republican for fulfilling the time-honored criteria of being a man "with proven business experience who pioneered in the progress of Las Vegas." Further support came from downtown casino interests and land developers who appreciated his pro-business, pro-growth stance. Not surprisingly, Gragson emerged victorious a few days later, defeating Bunker by a sound 6,900 to 5,100 margin.[55]

By supporting Gragson, Las Vegas voters reflected a tendency common to many postwar sunbelt cities of entrusting the reins of municipal government to prominent businessmen. In fact, editor Al Cahlan's support of Cragin, Baker, Gragson, and pro-business city commission candidates was strikingly similar to what Brad Luckingham found in his study of postwar Phoenix. Beginning in the late 1940s, Eugene Pulliam, owner of both the *Arizona Republic* and Phoenix *Gazette*, consistently endorsed the candidacies of men supporting the Charter Government Committee—the political arm of Phoenix businessmen. Gragson's victory symbolized a smaller-scale version of the Phoenix phenomenon. First elected in 1959, Gragson began a sixteen-year reign as mayor of Las Vegas during which his aggressive leadership eased Las Vegas out of the still small-town days of the 1950s into a modern era which saw the community double its population and achieve metropolitan status.[56]

Despite the aggressive leadership and public improvements of Cragin, Baker, and later Gragson, Las Vegas still lagged behind older cities in the provision of some services. In his insightful study of gambling and society in America, John Findlay has argued that Las Vegans did not build a desirable "hometown," because instead they were preoccupied with creating a city which would appeal to tourists. Indeed, he has argued that by the late 1950s,

> residents slowly began to realize that development of the city was keyed primarily to the interest of tourists and the resort industry rather than to the needs of permanent residents. Townspeople opened their eyes to see plenty of new hotel rooms and casinos but too few

houses and apartments, a sparkling new airport and well maintained highways, but inadequate surface streets and poor public transit, abundant centers for adult entertainment but unsatisfactory facilities for children's education.[57]

Findlay's statement raises an important question about the relationship between casino gambling and urbanization. Must a resort city like Las Vegas or even Miami Beach or Honolulu make trade-offs in order to please tourists? Perhaps not—at least in Las Vegas. Of course, Las Vegas's schools were overcrowded in the 1940s and into the early 1960s, but this resulted primarily from the city's spectacular growth and Nevada's anachronistic approach to school funding and organization. In general, public transit was poor because Las Vegas was fast becoming an "autopia" like the towns of southern California. According to the 1970 Census, almost 93 percent of all households in the Las Vegas SMSA (Standard Metropolitan Statistical Area) possessed a car. Even Tucson's figure was only 90 percent. In effect, Las Vegas was only 3 percent behind the southern California SMSAs which led the nation in automobility. Southern Nevada's 1960 figures were undoubtedly just as high. However, bus service was substantial in the Westside, Vegas Heights, and other low-income communities whose residents could not afford to commute by car. By contrast, service was poor in Paradise, Winchester, and other opulent suburban areas created by the burgeoning Strip resorts. The reason was simple: casino gambling generated thousands of well-paying middle- and upper-income jobs which permitted a large percentage of the town's white population to own one or more cars as well as substantial dwellings. Since Las Vegas, in both area and population, was smaller than Los Angeles or New York, there was little road congestion and therefore no real need to commute by mass transit.[58]

On another front Findlay has correctly observed that in the late 1950s Clark County social services, including welfare, aid to dependent children, and indigent health care among others, were funded at comparatively low amounts, but these findings are not unique to either a resort or casino city; indeed, they reflect western-southwestern and especially sunbelt tendencies. As Peter Lupsha and William Siembieda found in their study of public services, most sunbelt cities in the sixties and seventies funded public services at generally lower levels than their frostbelt counterparts. Yet, while Las Vegas spending for health services, welfare, and other functions was admittedly low, it compared favorably with those of other sunbelt cities. According to the 1970 census, for instance, the per capita local government expenditure for health services was $2.94, while Phoenix and Tucson both surpassed $3.00, El Paso spent only $2.62, and Albuquerque $1.70. In terms of per capita local government expenditures on welfare, Phoenix spent $.05, El Paso $.88, Tucson $.16, Albuquerque a dismal $.01, while Las Vegas topped the list with $4.18. Clearly, Las Vegas did not begin to approach the level of social spending in New York, San Francisco, and other places, but the resort city was in line with its counterparts in the southwest. Low social spending in Las Vegas was more a function of the city's southwest-sunbelt status than an outgrowth of its gambling economy.[59]

Similarly, Findlay overemphasizes the role played by the presence of casino gambling in determining the quality of the town's physical plant. Obviously, the private sector built thousands of hotel rooms along with golf courses, tennis courts, and swimming pools, but that same private sector also built acres of elegant middle- and upper-income housing for employees of the town's service-oriented economy. True, the new airport and highways were funded by the public sector, but highway funding was primarily state (and therefore gerrymandered by rural forces) and federal. And, while a modern airport was a vital priority for a resort city, the community's substantial amount of "inadequate surface streets" should not be blamed on Las Vegas's resort economy. All fast-growing cities face unavoidable lags in infrastructural development. My own past research into nineteenth-century New York found that city struggling to build enough streets, sewers, waterlines, and gas mains to service its exploding population. For five decades public schools suffered while education boards struggled to fund construction.[60] Moreover, this lag in public works and municipal services was repeated in virtually every American city. What Findlay found in the Las Vegas of the fifties and sixties was less a tradeoff for the tourists than the result of a transition period when the town's population suddenly ballooned from 40,000 to 240,000—a growth rate which would have overwhelmed the physical plant of any city. In terms of roads, utilities, and schools, had Findlay extended his study to 1980 instead of 1960, he would have seen many of the basic physical problems resolved. Thanks to strong leadership in municipal and county government, legislative reapportionment, a broader tax base, and more federal help, the Las Vegas metropolitan area would substantially improve its physical facilities and quality of life in the sixties and seventies.

Achieving
Metropolitan
Status

Following the postwar boom, Las Vegas solidified its gains in the 1960s
with additional resort construction and expanded operations at Nellis and
the test site. Continued economic expansion resulted in the creation of a
full-fledged metropolitan area. Nellis and the test site supported the
growth of North Las Vegas and Sunrise Manor, while defense production
at BMI powered Henderson, and new resorts like Caesars Palace encouraged suburban development east and west of the Strip. In the meantime,
valley residents multiplied their advantages with a new airport, more
convention facilities, and an ambitious agenda of municipal improvement
projects.

Similar to cities in California, Texas, Florida, and much of the sunbelt,
Las Vegas boomed in the 1960s. By any measure, the sixties were a
decade of extraordinary growth and development in the valley. The statistics were particularly impressive after 1965 when a combination of Lyndon Johnson's tax cut, domestic programs, and the Vietnam War drove
national spending, employment, and income levels to unprecedented
heights. In 1967, for instance, the metropolitan area gained over 1,000
new residents per month! By July 1, the population hit 269,000 with no
sign of a slowdown. Almost all business indicators were up. Airport
figures reflected the surge in tourism: 2.3 million visitors in 1966 was
easily surpassed by a 1967 figure of 2.7 million. Virtually every year
thereafter saw a new record. By any standard, Las Vegas was booming. In
1967 alone, dozens of major projects were completed, including the new
$25 million Frontier Hotel, the $5 million Foley Federal Building, and

the Sahara Hotel's $3 million "Space Center"—one of the first large convention centers within a hotel. In addition, the year saw many other significant projects begun. Leading the list was Howard Hughes's soaring $12 million Landmark Tower, the $2.5 million Flamingo expansion, the new International (today Las Vegas) Country Club and golf course, the first phase of the Southern Nevada Water Project, two badly needed municipal parking garages, and significant additions at Nellis Air Force Base and the Nevada Test Site. Impressed by the town's building fever, one observer could only conclude that "Las Vegas has parlayed America's leisure time and growing desire for fun and excitement into a multi-million-dollar tourist industry that is the state's greatest economic asset."[1]

Prior to 1950, Las Vegas had been a relatively small town which had enjoyed a slow but steady population growth. By the 1960 census, however, the valley's amazing development had qualified it as a Standard Metropolitan Statistical Area (SMSA). The 1960s, in particular, witnessed further changes in the number and composition of the valley's population. Between 1960 and 1970, the Las Vegas SMSA experienced a 115 percent increase in population from 127,016 to 273,288 and, by 1980, the figure had jumped to 461,816. The city of Las Vegas saw its figure jump by 94 percent from 64,605 in 1960 to 125,787 in 1970 and 164,674 in 1980 (only 22,000 came from annexations). The sister communities of North Las Vegas, Henderson, and Boulder City also enjoyed gains. North Las Vegas, with a 1950 population of 3,875, soared to 18,422 by 1960 and 36,216 in 1970 (42,739 by 1980), thanks especially to the development of Nellis and several large annexations. Following World War II, Henderson's population had dropped substantially to 5,419 in 1950, but rose steadily as more industry filled the Basic complex. By 1960, the Henderson area claimed 12,525 people; ten years later the number reached 16,395 and, as the town dramatically expanded with major annexations, the 1980 figure hit 24,363. With self-imposed restrictions on building, Boulder City saw its population remain low, reaching only 5,223 in the 1970 census.[2]

The major growth areas were the unincorporated townships which Clark County had managed to keep within its jurisdiction. In 1930, these lands contained only 3,367 people; the dam years doubled the number to 6,025 in 1940. Resort construction on the Strip raised the 1950 figure to 10,467 and the 1960 level to 27,405. Since that time hotel construction, Nellis expansion, tax savings, business opportunities, attractive housing developments, and a score of other factors have combined to fuel a population explosion in Paradise, Winchester, Sunrise Manor, and the other county suburbs around Las Vegas. Thanks to this growth, the 1970 population hit 89,667 and the 1980 census reported a whopping 220,450—almost half the SMSA's 461,000 people. Clearly, the decentralization of business after 1960 away from downtown Las Vegas and the availability of large land tracts for shopping centers, office parks, and sprawling residential developments accelerated the suburban trend.[3]

To some extent, the Las Vegas experience has resembled patterns in other sunbelt cities. Historian Kenneth Jackson has argued that the development of America's suburbs followed a unique national pattern. Unlike their counterparts in Europe, Asia, and the rest of the world, America's suburbs host a disproportionate share of the metropolitan area's wealthy and prestigious residents. Jackson has attributed this trend to a variety of factors, including FHA-VA subsidies, freeways, building, inexpensive land, and rising income. More recently, Carl Abbott has suggested that the trend toward low-density, high-income suburbs would be even more pronounced in newer, postwar, sunbelt cities than in their frostbelt counterparts. Las Vegas would surely fit this model, although, owing to the relatively recent development of the resort economy, the heavy deconcentration of population would date from the early 1950s rather than 1945.[4]

Similar to Los Angeles, Phoenix, Tucson, and other metropolitan areas across the sunbelt, the Las Vegas SMSA witnessed a movement outward from the city to low-density automobile suburbs scattered around the valley. Between 1960 and 1970, every census tract in the metropolis experienced a population gain and thirty-nine of the seventy tracts saw their figures doubled. The city of Las Vegas itself witnessed a 94 percent increase, while the SMSA as a whole enjoyed a 115 percent jump, reflecting the suburban tendency. Employment patterns both mirrored and reinforced the trend. A 1981 survey of major office buildings constructed in the valley since 1970 physically demonstrated the movement. Only six of fifty-two buildings were located within the city of Las Vegas—all the rest were in the unincorporated townships south of town. A similar survey of shopping centers built between 1955 and 1980 found two-thirds of these outside the city, with the process accelerating in the 1980s.[5]

Aside from these trends toward growth and suburbanization, the racial composition of the population also underwent change. In 1950, for example, whites comprised 92.4 percent of the city's 44,601 inhabitants (blacks were 6.6 percent); by 1970, the white share of the SMSA's 244,538 people had dropped to 89.5 percent—despite a massive white influx to the suburbs. Contributing to this loss was the growing Hispanic population which reached 6,000 in 1970 before doubling again in 1980. In addition to the growing nonwhite component, retirees also comprised a large segment. Many were former Nellis personnel who returned to Las Vegas after their discharge; others were frequent tourists from the midwest and east who came west to retire in their favorite town. Thousands more came from California (in 1980 it accounted for 30 percent of all Las Vegas–area newcomers) to escape the golden state's congestion, pollution, crime, and taxes. Yet, despite the substantial 30 percent increase in the age-65-and-over group in the SMSA between 1960 and 1970, Las Vegas's population remained young. In 1970, 62.5 percent of the SMSA's total inhabitants were under 35. The real key was the substantial in-migration from other states. In 1961, migration accounted for 60.3 percent of the city's increase in population (the birthrate was 39.7). By 1976 it had soared to 98.6 percent of the total increase. According to 1970 figures, 26 percent of the people in the Las Vegas SMSA had lived in a different state in 1965! Of this group, the northeast accounted for 9 percent, the midwest for 17 percent, the south 19 percent and the western states a whopping 55 percent. The Las Vegas metropolitan area therefore reflected a montage of various demographic forces, dominated by a substantial in-migration of young and old, racially diverse, relatively affluent people from every region in the country, but especially from California.[6]

Rising income and employment figures combined with a growing population to reflect the overall prosperity of the Las Vegas Valley. According to the 1970 census, Las Vegas enjoyed higher personal income per capita levels ($3,546) than El Paso ($2,359), Albuquerque ($2,872), Phoenix ($3,226), and Tucson ($2,988). In the Las Vegas area, despite the increase in Hispanic (mainly Cuban and Mexican) and nonwhite minorities, SMSA incomes at all levels rose during the 1960s. The number of families with an income range between $10,000 and $14,999 almost quadrupled (5,376 to 20,271), while the number in the $15,000 to $24,999 bracket jumped from 1,600 to 14,500. To a large extent, Las Vegas reflected the metropolitan sorting patterns found by Leo Schnore, Howard Rabinowitz, and others in other sunbelt cities. Schnore, in particular, found that in younger SMSAs like Albuquerque, Phoenix, and Tucson, the central cities were generally more affluent than their suburbs; the same was also true of Las Vegas. Between 1960 and 1970, median income rose by 55 percent (from $7,010 to $10,870) in the SMSA, and 48 percent ($7,662 to $11,344) in the city proper. Yet, just as in Phoenix and other metropolitan areas, some suburbs saw their income levels surpass the cities. This would tend to support Schnore's further contention that as these young cities mature, their upper- and middle-income elites move to the suburbs. In Las Vegas, for instance, median income levels in census tracts 17 through 27 (the "Strip suburbs" south of Las Vegas) exceeded many tracts within the city. By the 1980 census, this trend would be even more pronounced because of casino gambling's influence upon urbanization.[7] Thanks to the spectacular development of the Strip resorts in unincorporated county lands, Las Vegas—like Los Angeles—is supporting the recent view of Carl Abbott that, in general, the deconcentration of employment from city to suburb is more pronounced in sunbelt metropolitan areas than in their frostbelt rivals.[8]

Because of the Strip's rapid growth, the population in Las Vegas's southern suburbs was more affluent than the city. Even though a substantial majority of the town's old business and professional elite stubbornly clung to their residences in the city's fashionable neighborhoods, the new Strip resorts generated thousands of high-paying, casino-hotel jobs which, in turn, spawned a furious development of middle- and upper-income subdivisions. By the 1970 census, the shift of wealth to the suburbs was evident. Moreover, the rapid sorting of the metropolitan populace by socioeconomic status resulted in the general confinement of low-income workers and especially blacks to the Westside and northern suburbs of Las Vegas. The growing overall affluence of Las Vegas's suburbs resulted from the area's increased employment opportunities. In 1975, local resorts employed 43,700 workers (32 percent of the total employment figure), while a healthy construction industry counted a 6,700 median annual figure. The SMSA's large service sector economy employed 27,500 people in retail and wholesale trades and over 5,000 in finance, insurance, and real estate. In addition, the state and local governments claimed 15,200 employees in education and other services, while federal agencies counted 4,200 civilians, and over 20,000 in the military.[9]

Nevertheless, the resort industry remained the dominant force in the metropolitan economy. Employment statistics are a case in point. In 1965, the valley's service industries (dominated by the hotel, motel, and casino industry) employed 37,500 workers—over 42 percent of the county's total. Trade industries and government together accounted for 26,600 positions or 30 percent of the county's total, while construction (6.8 percent), manufacturing (4.2 percent), and finance-insurance-real estate (3.8 percent) trailed far behind. Of course, finance, education, construction, and other minor industries owed much of their vitality to business and population numbers generated by the recreation industry. While the Strip successfully challenged Fremont Street's one-time hegemony in the casino industry, Las Vegas continued to dominate in other activities. In the 1960s, as in earlier decades, Las Vegas served as the administrative center of city, state, county, and federal government as well as for the various court systems. As a result of the latter, over 95 percent of all attorneys in the valley maintained their offices within the municipality. The town also continued to maintain its role as the financial hub of the metropolitan area. As late as 1977, the main offices of all major banks (except for two savings and loans) were located downtown, as well as thirty-one other branches and eight credit union offices. [10]

Housing was another barometer of the city and county's amazing growth. Between 1960 and 1970, five of every seven dwelling units built in the state were located in the Las Vegas SMSA (as were 19 of every 26 rental units). Within the city of Las Vegas, 63 percent of all dwelling units were single-family, although the figures were much lower in the unincorporated townships (30 percent in Paradise, 19.5 percent in Winchester, 31 percent in Sunrise Manor), reflecting the suburban trend toward condominiums and higher-priced apartment developments. Between 1960 and 1970, all cities and unincorporated towns reported a drop in new single-family dwellings as a percentage of total dwelling units in the SMSA. By 1975, 63 percent of Clark County residents lived in single-family homes, 18 percent in multi-occupancy dwellings, 11 percent in mobile homes, and 6 percent in condominiums. Renters occupied 98 percent of all apartments, but owners dominated single-family dwellings (93.1 percent versus 6.9 percent), condominiums (89.2 percent versus 10.8 percent), and mobile homes (89.9 percent to 10.1 percent). [11]

Perhaps the only exception to the growth trend was housing starts. Home construction fluctuated in the Las Vegas market for one major reason. In response to housing shortages occasioned by expansion of the nuclear test site and the multiplier effect of new and expanded Strip hotels, residential building permits surpassed 10,000 units by 1962. The boom, however, quickly turned to bust in 1964 as the annual license figure fell below 3,000 units for the next six years. The drop resulted from developers overbuilding the metropolis between 1960 and 1964. Liberal

FHA mortgage insurance rates and lower interest home loans had combined with increased military spending, resort expansion, and more conventions to encourage an unrealistic estimate of population growth. The mid-sixties recession was reinforced by a spiraling inflation rate (which raised FHA and bank interest rates) resulting from President Lyndon Johnson's determination to fund both the "Great Society" and the Vietnam War. Recovery finally began in 1969 and continued thereafter into the 1970s. [12]

Throughout the housing slump, the valley's economy remained strong because of resort expansion and a defense boom. Like Houston, Albuquerque, Phoenix, and other sunbelt cities, Las Vegas received a substantial boost from the military. Thanks to Vietnam and the continuing Cold War, Nellis Air Force Base saw its payrolls swell. Of course, in the ten years immediately following the Korean War, the force dropped to nearly half the peak figure of 5,200, but the 1960s revived base operations with the introduction of such sophisticated jetfighters as the F-105. Gradually, as the training programs for modern planes and weapons systems multiplied, Nellis expanded to become the nation's main tactical weapons training center. As the jets flew faster, southern Nevada's guarantee of near perfect year-round flying weather made Nellis the logical base for the nation's swiftest aircraft. By 1969, Nellis counted over 9,000 personnel and an annual payroll of over $60 million, most of which remained in the Las Vegas economy. The cost of base operations also rose from $20 million in 1950 to $30 million in 1960 and over $90 million in 1970. These figures are important because, in addition to payroll spending, the air force purchased much of its paper, food, fuel, power, and other supplies from surrounding businesses—spending which soared to record levels after 1970. By 1985, Nellis personnel numbered 13,600, of which 11,000 were military, 1,600 civilians, and 1,000 civilian contractor employees. In that same year, the annual payroll hit $211 million, an additional $33 million went to civilian workers and a whopping $98.7 million to Nellis retirees living in the Las Vegas area. The local economy benefited further from the fact that over 80 percent of all Nellis airmen owned or rented housing off base. [13]

Following the nuclear test ban treaty of 1958–59, the test site saw its 1960 budget expanded by $50 million to fund the initial stage of development of the Kiwi nuclear rocket engine—a NASA propulsion system slated for use in the future space flights to the moon. By June 1961 it was obvious that growing operations at the test site, especially at the Nuclear

Rocket Propulsion Test Center, would require the widening of the Tono-pah Highway to four lanes between Las Vegas and Camp Mercury to handle the increased commuter and truck traffic. Congress appropriated the needed $10 million just in time. By late 1963, the test site was bustling with activity thanks to Projects Rover, Plowshare, Pluto, and a variety of other programs, including a NASA effort to develop a nuclear rocket capable of landing Apollo astronauts on the moon by 1969. As a result, Congress poured millions of dollars into test site programs. With the prospects of a sharply increased work force at Camp Mercury, the AEC considered building an "atomic city" in Nye County to eliminate the 2-hour (116-mile) round-trip between Las Vegas and Camp Mercury. Nye County Commissioners of course jumped at the prospects of acquiring an "instant city," even promising to abolish legalized prostitution.[14]

Nye County, with a sparse population but a substantial supply of artesian wells, possessed enough water to service a city. Clark County, however, proved a formidable opponent. Unwilling to lose thousands of engineers and scientists, Las Vegas-area officials prepared a compelling brief. With the construction of the Southern Nevada Water Project to Lake Mead pending, county commissioners argued that the Las Vegas Valley would soon have enough water to supply a major new community. More-over, Clark County's financial base could not be matched by its rival. This consideration was made more apparent when Las Vegas–area banks tied the promise of massive, low-interest commercial and home loans to the proviso that the "atomic city" not be located at the AEC's preferred sites near Lathrop Wells or Ash Meadows in Nye County. To this end, First Western Savings President A. G. Neumeyer offered up to $100 million for construction as long as the town was built within fifty miles of Las Vegas. The Bank of Nevada's Art Smith reinforced Neumeyer's stand, assuring AEC officials that "there isn't a lending institution in southern Nevada that isn't interested in this project." Ultimately, the rocket engine pro-gram was disbanded and Mercury itself remained a small base, but the episode clearly demonstrated the resolve of local lending institutions to promote and control development in the Las Vegas area.[15]

Despite this disappointment, Las Vegas and Clark County continued to enjoy the fruits of a substantial defense industry. Aside from their direct financial contribution to the local economy, both the test site and Nellis have also helped diversify the valley's industry by attracting a range of defense contractors to town. In 1984, for instance, EG&G Energy Mea-surements, prime handler of atomic testing instrumentation at the site, counted almost 2,400 employees in Las Vegas. Another major contractor, Reynolds Electrical and Engineering (REECo), employed a force of over 5,000 who were responsible for construction, maintenance, radiation safety, food, housing, medical care, warehousing, communications, and property management at the test site. In fact, the Department of Energy remains the largest civilian employer in the Las Vegas area with a payroll exceeding 8,000 workers.[16]

However, the impact of Nellis and the test site goes beyond payrolls. For thirty years the two have actually shaped the urban configuration of the northern edge of the Las Vegas metropolitan area. The test site extended the urbanized zone farther to the northwest. In the fifties and sixties new subdivisions and apartment housing sprang up along the Tonopah Highway (the road to Camp Mercury) and on major crossing roads like Lake Mead Boulevard, Smoke Ranch Road, and Cheyenne Avenue to serve the growing band of commuters headed northwest to the test site each morning. Nellis played a similar role, encouraging development in the northeast quadrant of the metropolitan area. Throughout the fifties and sixties new subdivisions of single-family, moderately priced dwellings and apartments appeared along branch roads feeding off Carey and Cheyenne avenues, Lake Mead Boulevard, and other main thoroughfares. Since 1950, censuses have recorded consistent growth in those tracts between East Lake Mead and Nellis Air Force Base (see Map 5, p. 240).[17]

Sections south of Las Vegas developed in response to the burgeoning resort industry. Increased tourism, powered by rising income, production, and employment levels nationwide, triggered a new round of hotel construction in the 1960s. The Aladdin Hotel, formally opened in 1966, broke an eight-year drought in new resort construction. The property's roots lay in the failed effort by New York stockbroker Edwin Lowe to build a noncasino resort for those vacationers who preferred a Scottsdale-like country club in the Nevada desert. In 1962–63, Lowe built a quaint Tudor-style inn, the Tally-ho, which catered to a stylish but small clientele. His stubborn refusal to build a casino was an expensive miscalculation, as the Tally-ho went bankrupt within two years. The property then languished for several more years until Milton Prell arrived on the scene. Prell, founder of the Sahara and Mint Hotels, had sold both properties to Del Webb in 1961 before departing town for a new life in Los Angeles. Prell's love for the casino business lured him back to Las Vegas in 1966 with plans to build a new $40 million resort across from the Sahara on the site of the old El Rancho. After Howard Hughes thwarted this dream by securing the property, Prell went up the Strip and bought the Tally-ho (between the Dunes and Tropicana) for a bargain price in January 1966. Determined to end the eight-year drought of new hotels on the Strip (since the 1958 Stardust), Prell ordered the immediate construction of a large casino, lounge, 500-seat theatre, 150-seat gourmet room, and the renovation of all existing rooms. In addition, he added an 18-hole, par-3 golf course, an Olympic-sized pool, and a massive 15-story electric sign boasting 40,000 light bulbs. Built at a cost of $750,000 by the Young Electric Sign Company, the sign resembled a large Aladdin's lamp which symbolized the resort's new name. Once re-opened, Prell's hotel was a center of activity. His Baghdad Showroom drew crowds by offering three different shows twice nightly—a daring innovation. To guide the business, he hired an experienced staff, including Carl Wilson (formerly of the Mint, Sahara Tahoe, and Riverside in Reno) as casino manager. These and a series of other reforms guaranteed the resort's success.[18]

Unfortunately, Prell's failing health soon forced him to sell to the Parvin-Dohrmann Company, owner of the Fremont and later the Stardust hotels. This firm, which soon became the Recrion Corporation, managed the Aladdin until 1971, when it sold out to a group of Detroit and St. Louis investors headed by Peter and Sorkis Webbe. The next four years saw the new owners transform the Aladdin into a major Strip resort with a $60 million expansion program, which included an expanded casino, new restaurants, a 20-story tower, and the 8,000-seat Theatre for the Performing Arts. The latter, for several years the largest indoor facility in Nevada, hosted prize fights, rock concerts, and other special events. But the Aladdin did not prosper; charges of mob infiltration and skimming eventually brought state investigations. Fear of license revocation and pressure from the Gaming Control Commission forced the owners to sell. The early 1980s saw the casino nearly close several times as Wayne Newton, Johnny Carson, and others bid for ownership. Finally in 1985, a measure of stability was achieved when the Aladdin became the first major Las Vegas resort bought by a foreign national when Japanese millionaire Ginji Yasuda purchased the property. Backed by his considerable fortune, the hotel finally seemed headed for brighter times.[19]

While it took years to make the Aladdin property a money-maker, Caesars Palace was a hit from the start. Caesars was the brainchild of Jay Sarno, who had already established an enviable reputation with his highly profitable Circus Circus Casino (a hotel building came several years later) across from the Riviera. Prior to this, Sarno had distinguished himself as the designer, builder, and operator of the award-winning Cabana Motel chain. Flushed with this success, Sarno longed to build something grand and distinctive. Funding was not a major problem. While Sarno's alleged connections with Jimmy Hoffa, Allen Dorfman, and others remain obscure, he nevertheless secured a generous loan in 1961 from the Teamsters Central States Pension Fund which financed his lease of a building site. By 1962, Sarno had obtained thirty-four acres of strategic property (located directly across from the Flamingo and Dunes) owned by millionaire Kirk Kerkorian.[20]

With Caesars's land secured, Sarno then selected Melvin Grossman as architect. Grossman enjoyed a worldwide reputation; his firm had already built a string of fine resorts, most notably the Acapulco Princess. However, despite Grossman's considerable talents, Sarno insisted on dictating the resort's design. Since western, African, Caribbean, and continental styles already graced existing Strip resorts, Sarno envisioned something new and unique—a Greco-Roman palace in the desert. Not surprisingly, the project cost millions; the final price tag of $19 million set a Strip record. To achieve a realistic look, Sarno imported tons of Italian marble and stone. Obsessed with the notion that oval design promoted relaxation, Sarno not only ordered an egg-shaped casino, but also repeated the elliptical theme throughout the resort's buildings and grounds. Equally apparent was his love of romanesque fountains and statuary which he lavished upon the resort. Even in noncasino areas, the motif was maintained. Typical was a large frieze near the Noshorium Coffee Shop which depicted the Battle of the Etruscan Hills.[21]

Caesars Palace was an immediate sensation with its crescent-shaped 14-story tower of sumptuous rooms. The 800-seat Circus Maximus Theatre (patterned after Rome's Coliseum) featured Barbra Streisand, Frank Sinatra—only the top stars of show business. The eighteen huge fountains bordering the front entrance's 135-foot driveway, the imported Italian cypresses, the Florentine statuary, the extravagantly priced dinners in the Bacchanal Room, all contributed to an absurd pretension beloved by jet-setters and social climbers alike. Of course, Caesars appealed to other customers as well. The early marketing strategy targeted conventioneers, luring them with 25,000 square feet of meeting space. From the beginning, Caesars's profits were substantial. Yet, within four years Sarno and his associates decided to sell the property. Perhaps bored by his accomplishment, the ever-restless Sarno dreamed of topping himself by building the Grandissimo, a 6,000-room spectacular (near the Hacienda) intended to be the largest hotel in the world. In 1969, needing capital to finance his new venture, the Sarno investment group sold Caesars for $60 million to Miami restaurant magnates (the Lum chain) Clifford and Stuart Perlman. As the new rulers of CaesarsWorld (the parent firm), the Perlmans immediately pumped $25 million into expansion programs. In 1969, they added the north tower (280 rooms) and ten years later the 22-story Fantasy Tower (600 rooms) plus more casino and convention space. Despite another ownership change in the 1980s, Caesars's prosperous status has remained intact.[22]

The last three major resorts to be covered—the Landmark, International (Hilton), and MGM Grand—owed their existence to the actions of two celebrated millionaires, Howard Hughes and Kirk Kerkorian. By 1968, Hughes had become the largest casino operator in the state, but this ambition had not been evident in his earlier visits to Las Vegas which dated from the 1930s. While America struggled through the last years of depression, Hughes partied in the town he loved. Actually Hughes had inherited his fortune in 1923 at the age of nineteen when he acquired control of his father's tool company. A talented engineer in his own right, Hughes moved to California in the 1920s. Hollywood proved as great a lure as aerospace, and he eventually bought RKO Studios. Though he sold the movie company a short time later, he remained in southern California for many years, managing his interests in Hughes Aviation, Trans World Airlines, and other acquisitions. Finally in the mid-1950s, tired of the California scene, he moved to Las Vegas for a time. Eventually, the restless genius left town again, spending most of the fifties and early sixties traveling, pausing for brief sojourns in the Bahamas, Canada, and Massachusetts, as well as Nevada.[23]

Despite his growing eccentricity and reclusiveness, Hughes's business mind remained as sharp as ever. Throughout the 1960s, he pyramided his fortune through a variety of corporate and casino transactions. In 1966 he sold his interests in TWA for over $500 million, thereby providing a bankroll for his subsequent casino buying spree. Hughes's sudden return to Nevada on Thanksgiving Eve 1966 was characteristically mysterious. Whisked in during the middle of the night by aides from his private railroad car to the penthouse atop his old haunt, the Desert Inn, the billionaire began a self-imposed isolation which would span four years. Negotiations for Hughes's first resort deal began only weeks after his arrival when Desert Inn management, anxious to liberate his suite for incoming high rollers, invited him to leave. Determined to remain, Hughes reluctantly offered to buy the resort. By the spring of 1967, he had acquired a deed. Once Hughes's longtime fascination with the neon world of gaming had been renewed, casino ownership became an obsession. He now coveted every Strip resort beyond his window. One by one, he got them all—the Sands, Frontier, Castaways, and Silver Slipper. At the same time, he diversified his Nevada portfolio with other acquisitions, including CBS affiliate KLAS-TV (so he could enjoy western and war movies all night), Alamo Airways, Executive Air, Hughes Air Terminal (the old McCarran facility on Highway 91), the North Las Vegas Air Terminal, and Harold's Club in Reno. Like an invincible monarch, he pursued his quest to corner the casino market and transform Las Vegas into his personal fiefdom. Caesars Palace, the Riviera, and the Dunes all became targets as did Harrah's in Reno and Lake Tahoe, but Hughes never took them over. Alarmed by his monopolistic interests, state gaming control officials allied with U.S. Attorney General Ramsey Clark and the Justice Department to block Hughes on antitrust grounds.[24]

Even Hughes's warm relationship with new Nevada Governor Paul Laxalt was not enough to break the logjam in Carson City or Washington. Frustrated and angry, Hughes would suddenly depart Las Vegas on Thanksgiving Eve 1970, never to return again. But before he left, Hughes was permitted one last purchase, the Landmark Hotel. Built in sections over a period of nearly ten years, the Landmark was the progeny of Kansas City builder Frank Carroll, a wealthy contractor, who hoped to duplicate the style of the Hollywood Landmark Hotel which he had admired during a brief stay in 1957. In 1960, Carroll obtained a $3.3 million loan from the Appliance Buyers Credit Corporation (a Whirlpool subsidiary) to build a resort east of the Strip on Paradise Road near the new convention center. Since Carroll could not raise the remaining $10 million to finance construction immediately, he instead built 120 apartments and a small shopping center on the site. Then, in August 1966, after utilizing his contacts within Las Vegas and the building trades industry, Carroll secured a $6 million loan from the Teamsters Central States Pension Fund. Yet, even this sum was not enough to finish the project. Cost overruns and especially licensing problems for key casino employees led to delays which eventually forced Carroll out of the operation.

Enter Howard Hughes. Eager to extend his growing casino empire, the eccentric billionaire bought the struggling Landmark in October 1968 for a paltry $17 million. Hughes's interest in the resort undoubtedly stemmed from a desire to match the effort of archrival Kirk Kerkorian who was preparing to open his own hotel on Paradise Road. To counter this move, Hughes scheduled the Landmark's opening for July 1969, precisely the month when Kerkorian planned to unveil his new International Hotel across the street. With this in mind, Hughes rushed to complete his building. Carroll had originally intended the Landmark to be fifteen stories—the tallest building in Nevada. But, after the Mint and Sahara erected higher towers, Carroll had been forced to revise his blueprints which, in turn, boosted his costs. Since Carroll never finished the structure, that task was left to Hughes, who added the final floors and domed nightclub on the thirty-first floor by 1969. The distinctively round Landmark tower, with its pie-shaped rooms, outwardly resembled the space-age look of the Cape Canaveral missile gantries which Hughes so admired. The Landmark remained a Hughes property for several years until it was conveyed to former actress Jean Peters as part of her divorce settlement with him. Subsequent years saw the property change hands several more times until the 1980s, when respected Las Vegas attorney and former Holiday Casino owner William Morris took control and began an expensive renovation and expansion program.[25]

If any one man rivaled Howard Hughes in Las Vegas, it was Kirk Kerkorian. Like Hughes, Kerkorian pursued an early interest in aviation, first as a crop duster in California and then as a cargo pilot during World War II. Following the war, he refurbished a twin-engine Cessna and began a lucrative business, flying gamblers from Hawthorne, California, to Las Vegas. In 1947 he formed his own airline, Los Angeles Air Service, which he later re-named Trans International Airlines. As Las Vegas grew, Kerkorian's profits mounted. In the 1960s, he added a fleet of jets before selling the airline in 1968 to the Transamerica Corporation for $104 million. Using part of these profits, he then purchased 30 percent of Western Airlines and prepared to buy MGM studios in Hollywood. Also on the drawing board was a new Las Vegas hotel, the International.[26]

The original force behind the International was actually Marvin Kratter of the Paradise Development Corporation. In the mid-1960s, Kratter, along with Irwin Molasky and others, had built the International Country Club Estates and golf course. An imaginative developer, Kratter also had envisioned erecting a 4-story, 1,500-room "Plaza Hotel" on a site 500 feet west of Maryland Parkway on Desert Inn Road and connected to the country club by a short underground railway. In the end, for a variety of business reasons, Kratter did not build the project, but instead deferred to the enterprising Kerkorian, who paid the former $5 million in 1967 for

64.5 acres—part of the huge tract originally purchased by Joe W. Brown in 1955 for the proposed convention center. Kerkorian then paid another $60 million in construction costs. Supported by this fabulous sum, the International rose quickly, opening in 1969 as the world's largest resort hotel (1,568 rooms) and casino (30,000 square feet). Kerkorian began the operation with an experienced staff that he had been training for several years at the Flamingo, which he had purchased earlier in 1967. Convinced that Las Vegas's mushrooming tourist industry (14 million visitors in 1967) could support more hotel construction, Kerkorian predicted that his International would pave the way for development of a second Strip on Paradise Road "parallel to the existing neon-jewelled showplace."[27]

Like Hughes, Kerkorian's faith in Las Vegas was unbounded. Even before the International opened, he dreamed of building another great resort. The origins of the MGM Grand Hotel lie in the failed effort of New York attorney Larry Wolf to operate a successful resort on the prosperous corner of the Strip and Flamingo Road. In 1966, the Dunes, Caesars Palace, and Flamingo already occupied three corners and Wolf was determined to build a money-maker on the fourth. Throughout 1966 and 1967 work progressed on Wolf's Bonanza Hotel, a 160-room facility furnished in turn-of-the-century decor. The Bonanza opened on July 1, 1967 with television's Lorne Greene as Wolf's main attraction. By October, however, cash-flow problems had closed the resort. Unable to finance continued operations, Wolf sold the property to Kerkorian's Tracy Investment Company in September 1968. Kerkorian now owned the land on three corners (Caesars, the Flamingo, and the Bonanza). He operated the trouble-plagued Bonanza until March 1969 before selling it to Nebraska millionaire Howard S. Levin (co-owner of Levin-Townshend Computer Corporation of New York) and casino executive Nate Jacobson. Levin soon became the sole owner before a land dispute wrecked his plans for expansion. Ernest Lied, owner of the adjacent Galaxy Hotel, had earlier leased lands upon which most of the Bonanza's rooms were built. His title claims eventually led to a court order partitioning off some guest rooms as well as eighteen feet of the Bonanza's dining room! The eventual court settlement in 1969 awarded Lied title to most of the Bonanza's 160 rooms. As a result, Levin's hotel declared bankruptcy in July 1970. Kerkorian, who had wisely escaped the litigation, now returned to lease the casino and buy more of the lands not claimed by Lied. For a while, Kerkorian operated just the casino as a training center for the staff which would someday run the dream hotel he planned to build on the site.[28]

Kerkorian moved a step closer to realizing his goal when he sold both the Flamingo and International Hotels to the Hilton chain in 1970 and 1971. Supported now with a bankroll of over $100 million, Kerkorian finalized plans for his new venture, a Hollywood-style resort modeled after the classic MGM movie, "Grand Hotel." The Hollywood theme was a natural, because Kerkorian had just purchased MGM studios, including the exclusive rights to all MGM titles, memorabilia, characters, and films. The groundbreaking ceremony on April 15, 1972 attracted world-wide notice as sex goddess Raquel Welch detonated the first explosive charge before an army of reporters and news cameramen. Subsequent months saw crews work in record time using the new "fast track" method of construction, which permitted the assembly of building materials as they arrived and the refining of blueprints as construction progressed. To be sure, the approach was wasteful. In one case, miles of electrical wires were installed which ultimately were never used. While building and fire safety standards suffered somewhat from the frantic construction pace (later a factor in the great 1980 fire), the $106 million resort nevertheless opened ahead of schedule on December 5, 1973. As the largest hotel in the free world, the MGM, with its 2,100 luxurious rooms, five restaurants, two showrooms, and jai-alai court, rivaled the glamor of Caesars Palace across the street. In just nineteen months, Kerkorian had built the largest resort hotel in the world, the largest jewel on the Las Vegas Strip.[29]

Complementing resort development was the town's surging convention industry. Several key factors enhanced Las Vegas's popularity as a meeting site in the late fifties and early sixties. Prior to 1950, most midwestern and eastern groups had convened in regional population centers like New York, Boston, and Chicago; western trips were simply impractical. However, the postwar expansion of the airline industry and especially the advent of the jet age transformed the situation. As faster planes began shrinking flight times to just a few hours, more delegates flew to Las Vegas. By 1963, half of all conventioneers came to Las Vegas by air. A substantial amount also came by car, as the new interstate highway approached completion. While affordable and convenient transportation made the once-remote desert more accessible to the nation's travelers, a rising standard of living also encouraged them to spend the hundreds of dollars necessary to travel far from home. A third factor enlarging the number of meetings was a rapid, postwar trend toward group formation. Thousands of new industry associations and specialized scientific and technological societies were created as part of the American economy's overall expansion. Demographics also played a role, as the increasing population of the United States—especially the dramatic increase in white collar, corporate, and service-sector jobs—created a large pool of conventioneers. Lastly, the liberalization of the tax code, allowing substantial deductions for business travel, played into the hands of Las Vegas and other convention cities whose promotional staffs now worked overtime to lure the big groups.[30]

When Las Vegas opened its new convention center in 1959, it immediately booked dozens of future meetings. Still, Las Vegas was hardly alone in the marketplace; almost thirty other cities provided stiff competition. While most could not accommodate the larger meetings with thousands of delegates, aggressive Las Vegas increasingly targeted this bigger market. The key was an expanded airport (the new McCarran terminal opened in 1962) and more hotel rooms. Developers proved equal to the task as the 1960s witnessed feverish construction. In 1960, the metropolitan area counted almost 12,800 rooms (approximately 5,700 motel and 7,000 hotel). Five years later the figure reached 15,000 and passed 46,000 in 1980. This enlarged capacity propelled Las Vegas into the large convention market which meant direct competition with New York, Chicago, Atlantic City, Washington, D.C., and Miami. Las Vegas met the challenge. In 1970, the desert metropolis lured 269 conventions (with 269,000 delegates) which injected an estimated $63.6 million into the local economy. Five years later, 393 meetings had raised the annual figure to $91.9 million, and by 1980, 449 groups brought 656,000 visitors and $227 million in local spending. To handle the boom, the Clark County Fair and Recreation Board (renamed in 1967 the Las Vegas Convention and Visitor's Authority) more than quadrupled its own exhibition space and the larger resort hotels (like the Hilton, Riviera, and MGM Grand) built substantial convention facilities of their own.[31]

The industry's growth forced the convention authority to keep pace with new bond issues to finance expansion. Needed construction was rarely an issue. In 1968, for instance, city newspapers endorsed the authority's request for a $22 million bond issue to expand the convention center's meeting and exhibition space. Adopting a responsible tone, the *Review-Journal* backed the construction because it was "consistent with the rate of economic growth in the area" and necessary to "remain competitive in the convention market." Noting the national trend toward larger meetings, the paper warned that failure to approve the bonds "could retard the growth of Las Vegas as a convention city."[32]

Support, however, was not automatic. Witness the 1964 effort by the

Fair and Recreation Board to obtain an $18 million bond issue to pur-
chase 411 acres of Joe W. Brown's property (today the site of the Las
Vegas Country Club) behind the convention center and partially fill it with
a concert hall, stadium, and museum. Board members reasoned that the
debt would be manageable, since the 1956 bond issue of $5.5 million
used to purchase the existing facility's site would be completely paid off in
ten years. Less agreeable was the *Review-Journal* which, in a fiery editorial, opposed "giving a group of politicians control over some of the most
valuable property in the county, opening the door for all kinds of transactions, handing them a blank check to do anything they want with it."
Moreover, the newspaper objected to board concessions designed to win
Strip hotel support for the bond issue. In a daring move, the board
promised to lease none of the land to casinos for ten years. The effort by
Strip hotels to block casino construction on nearby Paradise Road (ultimately Kerkorian built the International there) prompted the newspaper
to charge that the recreation board "has no right whatsoever to decide the
zoning of this county." Several days later, voters rejected the bond issue
by a 3 to 1 margin.[33]

Aside from the construction of convention and hotel facilities south of
town, the 1960s also witnessed the emergence of a new casino center in
North Las Vegas. In late 1964, as Dunes owner Major Riddle prepared to
open his Silver Nugget Casino on Las Vegas Boulevard North (the old Utah
Highway), he raised concerns along Fremont Street. In January 1965 several executives privately expressed fears that Riddle's "giveaway house"
would draw business away from downtown Las Vegas. At the time, these
fears were realistic because North Las Vegas was rapidly acquiring the
image of a dynamic, new city. Ultimately, Riddle's move created a small
but permanent new casino core in the Las Vegas suburb. And while the
area diverted some air force personnel and civilians away from Fremont,
most tourists and residents continued to patronize the Strip and downtown. In the intervening years, neither North Las Vegas nor Henderson
has mounted any serious threat to the lucrative trade.[34]

Nevertheless, North Las Vegas enjoyed banner growth in the fifties and
sixties. Following its incorporation as a city in 1946, the area grew
steadily, thanks to both the gaming and defense industries. The 1950s
alone saw the town's population soar from 3,875 to 18,422. City fathers
struggled to maintain urban services as the expanding test site and Nellis
Air Force Base combined with the burgeoning Strip to pour thousands of
new residents into the town. Traditionally a tax haven, North Las Vegas

saw municipal spending rise in the wake of population growth. For one thing, sanitation became a major problem as household wastes began overwhelming the town's cesspools. In response, the city council reluctantly scheduled a bond election in 1952 to fund a municipal sewer system. Lacking the tax base to finance its own sewage disposal plant as well, the city negotiated an agreement with Las Vegas to use its facility for a monthly fee. The larger city had just built a large modern treatment facility and, following Paradise Valley's decision to remain in the county, had plenty of unused capacity.[35]

The Korean War created not only a sewage problem, but a street crisis as well. The ever-multiplying subdivisions poured more traffic into the older downtown section of North Las Vegas. As a rule, developers paved their new streets, but veteran residents in the older neighborhoods were reluctant to pay the high assessments and taxes needed to widen and, in many cases, pave key arteries feeding commuters to Las Vegas or even the base. So, in an effort to improve neighborhoods and minimize local opposition, the North Las Vegas commissioner of streets announced a program in 1954 to permit those homeowners in the older residential zones (many of whom built their own houses) to curb and flag (sidewalk) their properties themselves under the supervision of the municipal street department. By eliminating the need for costly assessment districts, the commissioner estimated a cost saving of almost 30 percent. The program was reasonably successful in the short run, as dozens of property owners took advantage of the offer, but the comprehensive revitalization of the downtown area awaited the 1960s.[36]

Until then, the development of North Las Vegas was hampered by chronic political instability within the government itself. Throughout the late forties into the early fifties, voters consistently ousted incumbents. The reasons were several, although failure to undertake public improvements was often decisive. Corruption also played a role. In 1952, popular Mayor Earl Webb and city councilmen proposed building a municipal sewer system. Voters supported this bond issue at the polls, but within two years Webb and three councilmen had been indicted by the county grand jury for accepting kickbacks from the sewer contractor. The only council member not charged was Dorothy Porter, who apparently had been excluded from the scheme by the men. While many prominent citizens were undoubtedly cool to the prospect of North Las Vegas having the first woman mayor in Nevada history, they nevertheless accepted it when the incumbents, fearful of being recalled, all resigned in 1955. A return to male rule in the next election hardly cleared the air. The town's political tensions rose again to fever pitch in 1960 when embattled Mayor Earl Hartke, anxious to recall three recalcitrant city councilmen, falsely claimed support from the local Veterans of Foreign Wars chapter. Normally, VFW support in an air force bedroom community would have virtually guaranteed victory, but VFW officials angrily denied the mayor's claim and instead urged his recall.[37]

The ruckus only reinforced the suggestions by some disgruntled businessmen, anxious for a broader tax base and a measure of stability, that the time was ripe for voluntary annexation to Las Vegas. Not surprisingly, in March 1960—embarrassed by a decade of political scandal and instability—a group of businessmen led by Al Britz began a campaign to collect 2,700 signatures (representing 51 percent of North Las Vegas voters) on a petition requesting the annexation of North Las Vegas by Las Vegas. While Mayor Hartke responded to the action with an icy "no comment," Al Cahlan was somewhat less restrained. A month earlier, Cahlan had announced his support for such a move. Noting that throughout the 1950s factional "controversy has been the history of the community," the editor concluded that the citizens "deserve better government than they have been receiving." Cahlan then insisted that North Las Vegas should "never have been a separate city in the first place. It was born of the depression when land prices in Las Vegas proper were high and developers opened up the desert section to the north in order to provide building lots for those who could not afford the Las Vegas prices." In time, Vegas Verdes (later North Las Vegas) should have been annexed as a natural course and, for Cahlan, that time was long overdue.[38]

Longtime residents were undoubtedly less enthusiastic about the prospects of joining their rival and widening its tax base. Thanks to substantial opposition from residents and businessmen, the annexation movement failed. Instead, voters elected a new city council and mayor (William Taylor) who set North Las Vegas on a dramatically new course which would guarantee a prosperous future. The master stroke was the hiring of former Henderson City Manager Clay Lynch, who finally brought a strong sense of leadership to the beleaguered city. Prior to Lynch's arrival, many wondered whether North Las Vegas would ever wake up and recognize, for example, the need to enlarge its fire department of eight men, or the need to undertake an ambitious agenda of street improvements and urban renewal to attract more industry. Clearly, the city had to act. The rapid urbanization of Las Vegas had not only raised property values in that city but also had forced improvements in its "bedroom suburb" to the north. North Las Vegas had to modernize its fire department to cut local insurance rates, widen its streets to liberate them from snarled traffic, and redevelop its old rundown sections to provide for new buildings and eliminate the threats of credit blacklisting by local banks and the FHA.[39]

Under the dynamic leadership of Clay Lynch, the city embarked upon an ambitious program of public improvements. In May 1963, Lynch convinced city councilmen to endorse an $8.6 million bond issue for capital improvements in nine areas, including miles of new water mains, three new reservoirs, two artesian wells and a large-diameter sewer interceptor line on Losee Road. The latter, in particular, promoted development in the emerging Losee Industrial District, where firms that engaged in warehousing, chrome plating, steel, and prefabrication were already moving in. Eager to enhance their town's capacity to lure more business and residents, voters supported Lynch's call in 1964 for a $1.6 million bond issue to pave, curb, gutter, and light over twenty miles of dirt streets near the downtown area. Also on the drawing board was the proposed $2.8 million Nellis Industrial Park complex off Craig Road and Pecos which represented "the largest investment district in the state's history." In addition to general street improvements and industrial districts on the urban periphery which raised property values and enlarged the tax base, Lynch urged the paving and widening of a major new artery, Civic Center Drive. To the east, Lynch planned to build North Las Vegas's new civic hall to house city offices and the new public library. West of the road, he envisioned the new downtown business district, "an area which [would] tie into the commercial zone stretching west from the Salt Lake Highway (Highway 91) to Dana Street."[40]

To accomplish its goals, the city actively sought federal funds. Washington had already approved $120,000 for the new public library, which was part of the $1.5 million civic hall slated for construction in 1965. Furthermore, the federal government funded costs of land acquisition and slum clearance for the Cartier Avenue Urban Renewal Project, which promised to eliminate a "major municipal eyesore." Traditionally a community which embraced laissez-faire, North Las Vegas under Lynch readily adopted modern city planning practices. As early as 1965, officials had already master-planned five of the eleven neighborhood parks on the drawing boards. Other projects included a $65,000 fire substation at Cheyenne and McDaniel and the "most modern" sewage treatment plant in Nevada to reclaim water for parks and golf courses. Moreover, the city also planned to transform over 1,000 acres of desert north of Craig Road into a "regional recreational area" and, on a larger scale, had already begun drafting a comprehensive zoning ordinance to complement the master plan for water, streets, sanitation, and flood control. Thanks to the efforts of Lynch, North Las Vegas officials finally began to recognize how a coordinated layout could promote urban growth.[41]

By 1966, North Las Vegas was on its way to a modern appearance. In October 1965, the town began construction of the $1.8 million civic center, including city hall, municipal garage, and central library. In addition, over twenty neighborhoods, part of "special assessment districts," had received new sidewalks, curbs, gutters, and lighting. Las Vegas newspapers credited Lynch, Mayor Taylor, and the council for quickly transforming North Las Vegas from a "slum community" to Nevada's third largest city in just a few years. Slum clearance was perhaps their greatest accomplishment. Two major urban renewal projects bulldozed away the old shacks and shanties, thereby liberating the city from its longtime ghetto image. Lynch had earlier applied for federal funds through the Department of Housing and Urban Development to clear land for the Rose Garden housing project. And by June 1965, Great Society funds had also cleared 110 acres of former shacks along Cartier Avenue. Under Lynch's guidance, North Las Vegas quickly assumed the appearance of a forward-reaching suburb.[42]

Like North Las Vegas, Henderson's postwar development was slow but steady. Despite the cessation of magnesium production in 1944, the arrival of Stauffer Chemical in 1945 spurred the manufacture of a new chemical, caustic soda, and demonstrated the feasibility of using the plant to make other products after the war. Prospects of continued employment, therefore, kept many people in town. By war's end, the state of Nevada's determined effort to acquire the plant encouraged many chemical workers to remain in Clark County. As previously mentioned, extended negotiations resulted in the state's purchase of the plant and town for $24 million. The Colorado River Commission then began leasing space to WEECO, Pioche Manganese, Stauffer Chemical, and other chemical firms. By 1950, Henderson's population stood at only 5,419, but rose steadily thereafter. Responding to the overall growth of the Las Vegas area, the Federal Home Development Company in 1951 built 350 new homes on Victory and Basic roads. Terms were reasonable: $700 down and $47.91 per month. Utilities were inexpensive, and the chemical firms temporarily continued the paternalistic tradition of their predecessor, supplying fire and police protection, water, power, and gas until the early 1950s, when residents finally incorporated the town of Henderson and began self-government.[43]

In 1953 the future city of Henderson consisted only of the original Basic Townsite and Pittman. The latter, known as Midway in the 1930s, had prospered as a tent and shack town during Hoover Dam's construction and played a similar role for BMI during World War II. Following the state's purchase of the townsite in 1948, the original 1,000 demountable, prefabricated houses were sold by the state to residents and new dwellings were built. Slowly, a community took shape. As population approached 7,000, residents opted for self-government. In response, the state legislature on June 8, 1953, incorporated the City of Henderson, comprising the old Basic and Pittman townsites along with some contiguous lands. The new town was small—only 13 square miles—but through a series of aggressive annexations, it was nearly quadrupled to 49 square miles by 1969. The federal government played a major role in Henderson's growth. In 1963, for instance, Congress helped enlarge the city by Public Law 88–73 which permitted the municipality to purchase 16,000 acres of vacant land for future development. Unfortunately, state and county authorities had been less altruistic, gerrymandering the huge Basic industrial complex out of the new city. The politics behind the affair are obscure, but apparently county and company officials preferred to keep the valuable factories out of the city. The manufacturer's position was understandable. After all, the chemical plants stood to gain little from joining Henderson. They already had their own waste disposal network, water and power lines, security forces, and fire protection. Since no one lived in the factories, the companies possessed no voting blocs. On the other hand, these plants would have served as a giant revenue source for the new city to tap for the large expenditures that lay ahead. Fearing this, Basic management preferred to remain in the county. As a result, modern Henderson, while enjoying the payrolls and supply economies generated by the plants, was deprived of their lucrative property tax base.[44]

The town's substantial dependence upon the Boulder Highway (which literally bifurcated the community) was also a disadvantage. While the road provided residents with easy access to the huge job zone in the Las Vegas area, its width and lack of convenient street exits tended to pour traffic through the city and past the central business district to the west. As the city planning commission noted in a 1969 report, vacant stores and offices abounded downtown because of light traffic. In response, merchants and chain stores began a second commercial district of shopping centers along the east side of the highway in the late 1960s. While these efforts provided greater access to Henderson businesses, the town remained vulnerable to potential competition from future shopping districts in the southeast quadrant of the Las Vegas metropolitan area. Despite the increase of stores, Carson City, with half the population of Henderson in 1968, had a commercial district double the size. Tourism did not compensate for Henderson's lack of a commercial and industrial base. As late as 1970, no major hotels and only a few casinos dotted the landscape. Most did a modest business, catering to locals and motorists headed up the road to Las Vegas. The culprit was the valley's recreational economy which was highly centralized in two prime locations along the Strip and Fremont Street vicinities. While small centers flourished in North Las Vegas, Henderson, and along the Boulder Highway, they were still small-scale enterprises (with the exception of the Showboat Hotel).[45]

According to the Henderson City Planning Commission, the city's biggest problem in the 1960s remained its lackluster image as a "blue collar" or "lunch pail" town. Like North Las Vegas, Henderson's image resulted largely from its nondescript appearance. Over 50 percent of the town's housing was still low income or even substandard. As late as 1969, 843 of the city's 4,800 permanent dwellings were low-rental public housing units (operated by the Clark County Housing Authority), located mainly in the old Victory Village and Carver Park projects. For the most part, these structures were run-down and therefore added little to property tax revenues. Worse still, almost 950 of the original 1,000 demountable houses that were built during the war still existed. These temporary buildings had been slated for removal by 1946, but they remained. And, while many residents had added new rooms and landscaped the premises, these dwellings also contributed little to the tax base. Another 822 trailer units hardly improved the situation. Henderson suffered from an abnormally large public and low-income housing stock, which only reinforced the community's blue collar image. In fact, a 1968 survey revealed that not one executive from any of the major chemical companies lived in town. As the city's master plan noted, Henderson desperately needed the kind of middle- and upper-income housing which developers were constructing in Paradise, Winchester, and Las Vegas.[46]

Clearly, Henderson's traditional stigma as a low-income housing zone had led a generation of builders and home buyers alike to informally redline the city. As a result, predictions that Henderson would never change became self-fulfilling prophecies. Here was the significance of the

recreational economy and the system it spawned. The Strip hosted Caesars Palace and all the classy resorts, while the suburban communities
it created mirrored the wealth and aspirations of its upwardly mobile
employees. Developers lavished their homes, condominiums, and even
apartment complexes with large pools, saunas, tennis courts, Spanish tile
roofs, glass sliding doors, reflecting pools, and lush landscaping, while
the same builders either ignored Henderson or built their cheapest line of
housing there. Finally in the 1970s, Henderson would fight back, expanding its tax base through a series of large annexations. Paradise
Valley's southward expansion finally engulfed Henderson's low-cost housing zone, inducing substantial construction of expensive dwellings.[47]

Farther to the south, tiny Boulder City enjoyed little of the postwar
growth experienced by North Las Vegas and Henderson. As late as 1970,
the town's residents barely numbered 4,200. While the population remained low, the community nonetheless matured. Churches, social organizations, Boy Scout troops, an American Legion post, a newspaper, and
the other familiar institutions of small-town America appeared in the
thirties and forties. The city even built a high school, graduating its first
senior class in 1941. Through it all, Boulder City remained a federal
town. Residents paid no state taxes and voted in no state or county
elections. Finally, in 1958, Congress approved legislation permitting
townsmen to establish self-government under Nevada law. After much
debate, citizens voted to become an independent municipality as of
January 4, 1960. Since that time Boulder City has remained a small,
largely conservative community. Though a natural tourist stop for the
thousands annually visiting the dam, the town traditionally loses most of
the overnight business to its glittering neighbor up the road. Determined
to escape the urbanization besetting the metropolitan area in the 1970s,
Boulder City promulgated a slow-growth policy which mandated that no
developer could build more than 30 dwellings annually. The city fathers
were put to a real test in 1986 when the Del Webb Corporation pitched the
idea of building a large retirement community similar to the company's
world famous development in Sun City, Arizona. Webb wanted to build
300 homes a year for twenty years—ten times the allowable number.
Unimpressed by the prospects of a vastly expanded tax base, the city
council politely declined the offer. Boulder City has always marched to its
own drummer. Closely knit and independent-minded, it remains the only
community in Nevada where gambling is outlawed and growth discouraged.[48]

Of course, the dramatic expansion of Las Vegas and its suburbs after

1960 demanded responsible political leadership at both the city and county levels. Incoming Las Vegas Mayor Oran Gragson recognized the active role he would have to play in promoting the economic growth of not only his city but the whole valley. To accomplish this, he cooperated with county leaders to support a number of key projects. Perhaps the most important was the campaign to modernize the airport. Since 1948, commercial airlines had utilized the McCarran facility south of the Tropicana Hotel just east of the Strip. By the late 1950s, however, air traffic had begun to outgrow the terminal's capacity. In 1948 an average of 12 flights per day brought 35,000 passengers to Las Vegas. Throughout the 1950s that figure soared, reflecting the growth of the Strip. By 1959, an average of 99 daily flights carried 1 million passengers annually—more than a twenty-fold increase in just a decade.[49]

The arrival of jet aircraft, beginning in September 1960, contributed further to McCarran's obsolescence. Faster, larger, and more powerful than their propeller cousins, jets required larger taxiways and longer runways which therefore meant the purchase of more land along the field's periphery. Moreover, since jets carried one hundred more passengers (props could barely handle sixty), county airport commissioners had to expand McCarran's terminal building itself, adding larger gate and cargo facilities. As the mayor and county officials repeatedly explained, a building designed to handle only a few thousand people daily could never accommodate the three million plus airline passengers projected for Las Vegas by the mid-1960s. For this reason, Gragson and county leaders joined with the chamber of commerce and many casino executives to sponsor a $5 million bond campaign to build a modern terminal. The trend toward more air travel demanded it. Beginning in September 1960, when United Airlines introduced nonstop service to Los Angeles, Chicago, and New York, jets expanded Las Vegas's gaming hinterland, making the city accessible even to east coast residents. As the new planes shattered the travel barrier, shrinking the flight time to the vast northeast market from nine hours to four and one-half, government leaders knew they had to act.[50]

It was therefore no surprise that Gragson's administration supported the efforts of Clark County commissioners to build a new terminal not at the current site, but farther east along Paradise Road on a large tract of land capable of hosting a spacious terminal. The blueprints were ambitious, calling for the construction of two, 2-story buildings. The first would house the main terminal, including ticket counters, airline offices, and baggage space, while the second would contain a restaurant, cocktail lounge, shops, baggage space, and sixteen gates to handle even the largest jets. Plans also included a new control tower, fire station, and parking lot for 1,400 cars. To be sure, spending critics were quick to oppose the scheme as premature. Perhaps the most vocal opponent was local radio personality and county commission candidate Joe Julian, who questioned the wisdom of abandoning the current Strip location for the more distant site on Paradise Road. Planners countered this objection by proposing to extend Bond Street (later Tropicana Avenue) down to Paradise, thereby providing a convenient through route to the Strip. The campaign gained momentum throughout the winter of 1960, as Gragson and county leaders teamed with the *Review-Journal*'s Al Cahlan and the *Sun*'s Hank Greenspun in an all-out effort to sway voters. Their effort was rewarded on election day, March 8, 1960, when (with only 12 percent of eligible voters participating) the airport bonds passed by a substantial 2 to 1 margin. Construction began that fall, and was completed in 1962. Thanks to the leadership of Gragson and others, Las Vegas had equipped itself with a modern, new airport capable of servicing the town's skyrocketing air traffic. Moreover, the facility was easily expandable, making it relatively simple for county leaders to more than triple its size in the 1980s when continued growth again justified new construction.[51]

To a large extent, the airport reflected Gragson's booster approach to the mayoralty. Whether it be the airport, Interstate 15, or local street improvements, the mayor actively supported any move which would promote the city's growth. Especially significant was his $2 million improvement district plan, earlier approved by voters, which helped finance miles of street paving and widening work. Gragson and city commissioners complemented these public works programs with the city's newly enacted (1959) master plan to permit the construction of more large apartment complexes and other large commercial developments near the downtown area. To a large extent, Gragson's 1963 re-election platform was really an extension of his first-term goals. Always a forthright leader, he boldly called upon the town's cost-conscious voters to approve a citywide bond issue to fund 900,000 feet of new sewers, 1,200 new streetlights, and 24 new traffic signals. Noting that in just four years he had paved, curbed, and guttered more streets than any mayor in the previous fifty-five years, Gragson credited the $2 million improvement district with having revitalized the downtown area by widening streets and easing traffic congestion. Moreover, he correctly insisted that his improvements had encour-

aged others by inducing numerous downtown firms to expand and re-
model. And, he was quick to add, the investment had actually saved
taxpayers money because improved properties and new business had
already expanded the city's tax base. Gragson, portraying himself as a
growth-oriented mayor, also noted that, despite an 80 percent population
jump since 1959, personnel in the town's police and fire departments had
only grown by 40 percent—with no loss of efficient service.[52] Backed by
many of the city's key bankers and developers as well as many ordinary
citizens, Gragson was a popular incumbent.

Impressed by the vigor of Gragson's leadership, even the normally
Democratic *Review-Journal* endorsed his re-election. The *Las Vegas Sun*,
however, was less cooperative. Still smarting from his defeat by Gragson
(and the major casinos) in the 1962 Republican gubernatorial primary,
Sun editor Hank Greenspun attacked Gragson repeatedly during the 1963
mayoral campaign, while endorsing the mayor's chief opponent, Justice of
the Peace Myron Leavitt. Citing the latter's promise of "forceful planning"
and his "aggressive, perceptive leadership," Greenspun denounced Gragson's administration for "slavery to special interests" (the casinos and
large developers). Conceding Gragson's devotion to "the promoting of a
booming economy," Greenspun nevertheless faulted the mayor for ignor-
ing flood control as well as "the orderly development of commercial and
residential areas that result from intelligent long-range planning." In the
interest of growth, city administrators had granted developers and investors innumerable variances which partially compromised the city plan.
Greenspun undoubtedly struck a responsive chord with some long-time
residents when he asserted that "apartment buildings, commercial development and the like are necessary and desirable but so is the establishment of quiet residential areas where families may be reared in peace and
comfort."[53]

Anxious to discredit its hated rival, the *Review-Journal* countered that
Leavitt was little more than a "marryin' Sam" justice of the peace who had
enjoyed "two lucrative years in which he earned an estimated $160,000 in
marriage fees." While conceding that staff salaries were paid from the
fund, editor Bob Brown (Cahlan had left three years earlier) nevertheless
characterized Leavitt's position as "the richest political office in the
state." Leavitt tried in vain to defuse the "marryin' Sam" issue by charging
Gragson with presiding over a traffic-snarled city and incompetent municipal administration which had overestimated revenue and had failed to
stay within its $1 million budget. In response, the *Review-Journal* cred-

ited Gragson with leading the fight to equip the new freeway (Interstate 15) with exit ramps at strategic streets to relieve downtown traffic congestion. Furthermore, the paper implied that Leavitt's youth (he was only 32, as was Brown) and inexperience had led him to blame the mayor for a budget deficit which was clearly the fault of Finance Commissioner Reed Whipple. In the end, Leavitt could not overcome Gragson's popularity. While Las Vegas lacked the full-blown "business government" present in Phoenix, Dallas, and other sunbelt cities, Gragson, like C. D. Baker and Ernie Cragin before him (and their commissioners), symbolized the efficient, pro-growth, pro-business administration which voters in the urban south and southwest were increasingly supporting. Although Las Vegas's political system hardly compared in size and complexity to larger cities like Phoenix, Houston, or Atlanta, sunbelt political tendencies were evident.[54]

Las Vegas's continued commercial growth once again favored incumbents in the 1965 municipal elections. Veteran commissioner Phil Mirabelli, an insurance broker, defeated a spirited challenge by Bert Leavitt, who charged Mirabelli with conspiring to fire the police chief and city manager while, at the same time, using his influence as commissioner of parks and recreation to profit illegally from parkland acquisitions. While benefiting from the initial publicity, the inexperienced Leavitt never actually proved his charges. As a result, both city voters and the newspapers showed little inclination to reject an experienced commissioner. Moreover, Mirabelli and Gragson won another victory in 1965 when voters narrowly passed a $5 million bond issue to fund construction of a large municipal parking garage to relieve the worsening parking crisis in the congested downtown area. With city hall leading the way, the seventies and eighties would see a marked improvement, as most of the downtown hotels and office buildings erected garages of their own.[55]

Under Gragson, Las Vegas not only grew through commercial expansion and new construction, but through annexation as well. Militant opposition in North Las Vegas, Paradise, and Winchester limited Las Vegas's ability to expand its borders to zones north and west of the city. While the Gragson Administration mainly emphasized the acquisition of undeveloped lands and middle- to upper-income subdivisions, the city also took in lower-income zones with an eye toward improving them. In 1964, for instance, the town annexed Vegas Heights, a black and Latino suburb just north of the municipality. Following this move, city hall acted quickly to upgrade the 160 acres of ramshackle houses and trailers.

Rather than bulldoze the 1,800 mostly black and Latino residents out of their homes, City Planning Director Don Saylor promised instead to develop a neighborhood land-use plan. Noting the community's miles of unpaved streets, its overloaded septic tanks, and bare electrical wires, Saylor promised to form an assessment district to fund improvements while also utilizing the city's "code assistance staff" to bring local homes and businesses up to fire and building standards—a move designed to ensure community safety and improve property values.[56]

As the city's population soared past 100,000 in the early 1960s, Gragson and his commissioners could not keep pace with the need for road construction. While developers helped somewhat by building new streets within their subdivisions, the municipality assumed the costly effort of widening many of the main arteries radiating out of the downtown zone. Complicating matters was the consistent lack of state funding. Thanks to Nevada's gerrymandered state legislature, the rural counties commandeered large slices of the gaming and property tax pies for their own roads. As a result, Carson City was slow to approve many vital projects in the Reno and Las Vegas metropolitan areas. In 1963, for example, when city officials applied for funding to widen the Bonanza Underpass from two to four lanes, State Highway Department officials responded that east-west traffic flow across the railroad tracks would be improved once the downtown interchange of the new freeway was built. Las Vegas city commissioners scoffed at this assumption, charging instead that state highway revenues were being diverted to the rural counties.

While Interstate 15 eventually played a valuable role in relieving traffic congestion, its success was not automatic. Like C. D. Baker before him, Mayor Gragson spent endless hours negotiating the exact number and location of the proposed on and off ramps to minimize gridlock on the city's feeder streets. As late as 1968, the highway had yet to pass West Charleston and discussion continued over exactly how the Charles T. Parker Construction Company would build the complicated downtown interchange. Through it all, state highway officials remained optimistic that, once opened, the freeway would solve most of Las Vegas's traffic problems in and around the casino core.[57]

Gragson, like the valley's other political leaders and boosters, understood that Nevada's gerrymandered legislature was the key obstacle to adequate state funding for roads, schools, and other urban services. Fortunately, the city-building process in the Las Vegas Valley coincided with the national drive in the mid-1960s to reapportion state legislatures to give urban areas more representation. Following the *Baker v. Carr* (1962) and *Reynolds v. Sims* (1964) decisions by the United States Supreme Court, Las Vegans Clare Woodbury and school advocate Flora Dungan brought suit in federal court to force the Nevada legislature to recognize the one-man, one-vote rule, thereby giving Clark and Washoe counties their full 81 percent share of all assemblymen and senators. In response, the rural-dominated body during its regular biennial session in early 1965 evaded the issue, preferring instead to await court action. Undeterred, Woodbury and Dungan persevered, confident that the federal judiciary would rule for the cities. By June, Nevada Attorney General Harvey Dickerson was clearly concerned about the urban threat. Dickerson favored the traditional method of representation which awarded each county one senator. Dickerson, like other ruralists, feared that the "unbalanced population" of 81 percent in two areas would control the spending and policymaking for a state which contained thousands of square miles of ranching, farming, timbering, and mining interests.[58]

These arguments, echoed by rural spokesmen in dozens of other states, failed to convince the courts. Facing an almost certain constitutional order, the state legislature finally met in a special twenty-day session in November 1965. Lawmakers reluctantly agreed to give Clark County eight senators and sixteen assemblymen; Washoe and Ormsby received six and twelve respectively, while the rest of the state got six senators and twelve assemblymen. Gloom pervaded the chamber as grim-faced legislators approved their own demise. Recognizing that future census figures would only boost the cities' power, Eureka County Senator Jack Bay called it a "sad moment . . . one in which I have lost all I have fought for . . . I pleaded to protect my county, but I was put down and trampled upon." Senator Rene Lemaire (a Republican from Lander County) noted that for years the rural counties had "exemplified the general interest in the welfare of Nevada," and now he urged the cities "not [to] let the counties down," adding that "we took care of them for a long time."[59]

For their part, Las Vegas Valley city and county leaders, like their Reno counterparts, were jubilant. Finally, Nevada's urban areas would receive the funding they desperately needed to finance new public construction and services. The local press was equally pleased as well as defiant. Branding Senator Lemaire's views as "hogwash," the *Review-Journal* sarcastically noted, "we don't believe that just because a person lives in Las Vegas he is something other than a 'real Nevadan.'" And, rejecting the patronizing tone of Lemaire's remarks, the editor dismissed the notion that the "loving care of the State Senate really had much to do with the growth of Southern Nevada." Having finished with Lemaire, the paper then challenged the newly enlarged Clark and Washoe County delegations to lead Nevada to new heights. Nevertheless, despite the dramatic changing of the guard in Carson City, there was no immediate fiscal relief for Nevada's cities. Thanks to political factionalism, both Clark and Washoe counties continued to receive far less in state funding than they paid in revenues.[60]

Still, a major injustice had been overturned, and Nevada's largest metropolis could look forward to more help from the state. In 1967, voters would once again support Gragson for mayor, although the city commission would experience a dramatic change. Despite the vigorous support of the *Review-Journal*, longtime City Commissioners Ed Fountain and Reed Whipple (a twenty-year veteran) lost their seats to relative unknowns. While Fountain was defeated by Wes Howery, a respected hotel executive, few longtime residents could see any comparison between Whipple, a community pillar, and his opponent, tavern owner Jim Corey. But voters as a whole saw it differently. Clearly, the rapid urbanization of Las Vegas in the 1960s had both increased and diversified the electorate. Thousands of easterners, midwesterners, and especially Californians had filled the city. In the main, they were neither Mormons nor native Nevadans, and apparently were ill-disposed to the continued rule of the town's old guard. Both Fountain and Whipple were swept out on election day, but, despite the partial house cleaning, voters were careful to retain Gragson, whose continued strong leadership was crucial in the current period of growth and change.[61]

Perhaps a clue to the electorate's rejection of the two incumbents lies in a 1965 *Review-Journal* column by respected political reporter Jude Wanniski in which he predicted that dynamic North Las Vegas City Manager Clay Lynch would never be offered the same job in Las Vegas. According to Wanniski, even though Mayor Gragson wanted to hire Lynch as early as 1963, the city commission steadfastly refused. Why? Wanniski explained that Commissioner Ed Fountain considered himself an "expert on fire and police," while Reed Whipple felt the same about finance, and Phil Mirabelli would brook no opposition on recreation. Instead of a strong city manager, Wanniski suggested that the commissioners wanted "a docile one who will stand back quietly, do their bidding, write an occasional interdepartmental memo and generally keep his seat warm. No questions asked." Clearly, Las Vegas had suffered from a constant turnover of city managers ever since the post had been created in 1943. None had provided dynamic leadership; in fact, none had even been trained for the position. As Wanniski observed, "they have either been political appointments, promotions from departments within City Hall, or hirings of secondary-level administrators from other cities." As a result, Las Vegas had lacked the vision and know-how of a Clay Lynch. And while the city's tax base and population had grown thanks to its skyrocketing tourist business, city commissioners had not matched the North Las Vegas effort to equip itself for future growth. As late as 1965, the business commissioners who controlled the municipal government opposed any move to acquire the vigorous leadership that Clay Lynch represented.[62]

As one of the faster-growing cities in the United States, Las Vegas needed imaginative policymaking and a vision of the future, not the tight-fisted, business-as-usual approach of men who had grown comfortable in their power. A new city hall building, municipal parking garages, widened roads, downtown redevelopment, and a variety of other programs demanded municipal action if Las Vegas were to keep pace with the dramatic expansion of the county suburbs. As the 1970s beckoned, the valley's mushrooming population required leadership that could meet the challenge of explosive growth. The task would have been easier had Las Vegas enjoyed the presence of a broad-based Good Government League or comparable civic group. But the city's business voice was represented by an informal coalition of sometimes competing interests rather than a formalized and united organization. Unlike Phoenix, San Antonio, and other sunbelt cities, the shaping of public policy lay mostly in the hands of the mayor and his commissioners. A stronger city manager combined with a vigorous charter government committee, along the lines of the usually united Phoenix Committee, would have strengthened policymaking at city hall. Lacking this support and broader perspective, Gragson and his sometimes contentious commissioners ran the town as best they could.

Fragmented
Government

Politically and administratively, Las Vegas is not one city but five. In addition to special service districts for education, water, and other services, portions of the metropolitan area are controlled by Las Vegas, North Las Vegas, Henderson, Boulder City, and Clark County. This fragmentation has resulted from Las Vegas's historic inability to annex its suburbs. Casino gambling was again the culprit. Unlike their counterparts in Honolulu and Miami Beach, the great Strip resorts, with their valuable casinos, repulsed all city attempts to tax their games and annex their property.

As has been shown, shortly after World War II the El Rancho and Last Frontier blocked the municipal drive to extend the city southward—a drive which might well have encompassed all of Paradise Valley and perhaps even Henderson (before the latter's incorporation in 1953). The resorts' victory forever changed the valley's political landscape, and placed Las Vegas among a minority of cities in the sunbelt. Once stalled at Sahara Avenue, the municipality lost much of its annexation momentum. This was hardly the case in San Antonio, Houston, and other sunbelt towns. Between 1950 and 1970, thanks largely to annexation, southern cities grew by 224 percent and western ones by an impressive 68 percent! Phoenix, for instance, added over a hundred square miles to its jurisdiction, as did Albuquerque. Las Vegas, on the other hand, having failed to snare any of the emerging Strip suburbs to the south, had to content itself with minor annexations to the west and northwest.[1]

The city's relative failure to expand its borders created a political vacuum which the suburbs ultimately filled. Instead of one city government for the entire metropolitan area, four cities and one county government have administered police, fire, planning, and other government functions. This political fragmentation, in turn, has led to needless duplication of services and inefficiency. Police protection is a case in point. Prior to the dam boom of the 1930s and even before World War II, crime was not a major problem in town. While Las Vegas had its share of burglaries and bar fights, police were able to control most situations because officers personally knew many of the people in town. Then too, while some crimes were committed by permanent residents, many were not. Police therefore paid special attention to the alleys off Fremont Street, the side-street bars, the cheap roominghouses, Block 16, the railroad yards, and the Westside. As a rule, the city jail handled mostly minor offenders. To keep costs down, chronic troublemakers and transients were often hustled off on a train to Los Angeles. Two separate departments enforced the law. Within the city of Las Vegas, the police chief—appointed by the city commissioners—led a force of between five and ten men. Outside the municipality, the sheriff—elected by county voters for a four-year term—patrolled the suburbs and 8,000 square miles of rural lands with a handful of officers.[2]

Prior to Pearl Harbor, neither department had uniformed personnel. Peace officers dressed in casual western wear complete with hats, boots, and side arms. There was little official training; only a passing familiarity with the fine points of the law was required. Equipment was also rudimentary. Since squad cars lacked radios until the mid-1940s, police signalled officers in the suburbs by flashing a large red light atop the Apache Hotel on Fremont Street. Later, in 1942, county officers at the Henderson substation also used lights. Fortunately, most of the serious fracases were at night.[3]

With the onset of World War II, both departments expanded their forces to control the thousands of soldiers and defense workers pouring into town. By 1942, Sheriff Glen Jones had twenty-eight men, the largest county unit in the state. The municipal force jumped to forty-eight in that same year, as Chief Don Borax struggled with bar fights, burglaries, pickpockets, and vagrants. The latter, in particular, kept city officers busy. Throughout the war, Borax's "work or fight" edict led to occasional pillages of the "hobo jungles" along the Union Pacific tracks and mass deportations to California. Many of the homeless were no doubt mistreated, but city commissioners were determined to keep the welfare rolls thin and the streets clear for tourists. The permissive attitude toward police rousting inevitably led to abuse. Throughout the thirties and forties, city commissioners complained about officers beating suspects on the streets and even in the city jail. During this period, several chiefs were even dismissed for failure to control their officers. To be sure, beatings and pistol whippings hurt the town's reputation and discouraged tourism. Particularly embarrassing was a 1943 incident when the city's lone black officer, "Poison Smith," beat a Westside black man so badly that the victim lost his eye. Police violence, while countenanced by some as a legitimate means of keeping jail costs low, was increasingly viewed with disdain by citizens and civic leaders alike, especially after the war when Las Vegans increasingly distanced themselves from their town's frontier origins.[4]

Aside from handling ordinary crimes, city and county police were also responsible for regulating the casino industry. Both the sheriff and police chief collected gaming taxes and fees. In an effort to control crime within the casino industry, they were also charged with registering and fingerprinting all casino employees, bartenders, cabdrivers, criminals, and even entertainers. To this end, the county and city forces cooperated, establishing a joint countywide file in the mid-1940s. This function combined with regular police activities to drain the manpower of both forces. Resort expansion combined with meager taxes to create a crisis in law enforcement. During the 1950s, both departments were so understaffed that they assigned most of their own officers to the protection of businesses and homes, while commissioning hotel security guards to act in official capacities on resort properties. This dubious practice was not ended entirely until the early 1960s, when city and county leaders, increasingly wary of costly lawsuits, recognized the need for more formal police training. Prior to 1959, local police received little official training. An occasional F.B.I. class, some informal instruction from a veteran officer, and a few hours on the shooting range were the norm for officers in the county and all four city departments. Finally in 1959, the city of Las Vegas established a police academy. Cadets received 270 hours of classes, including physical fitness, self-defense, and 36 hours of practice on the shooting range. The facility quickly became an asset for all policemen in the metropolitan area, as the county and four city departments used the Las Vegas center for varying degrees of training. In another cooperative move, Las Vegas and Clark County jointly operated what later became known as the Clark County Law Enforcement Training Academy. In addition, the five departments also began using the sheriff's crime laboratory for the evaluation of evidence in major crimes.[5]

Despite these unifying programs, police protection was badly fragmented in the metropolitan area. The development of one county and four
city departments was not wasteful in the thirties, forties, and fifties when
the crime rate was relatively low and populations were small and dis-
persed. But this was not the case after 1960 when the towns increasingly
grew toward one another. Once the major road networks were built,
allowing criminals to speed across the valley in a matter of minutes, five
departments became more of a liability than an asset. Without a centralized bureaucracy, the level and quality of police services varied with
the jurisdiction. In Boulder City, for instance, the force consisted of one
chief, one lieutenant, three sergeants and five officers, which left the town
of 2,000 people guarded at night by only two men—one in the station, the
other in a car. Due to Boulder City's small tax base, the department was
necessarily understaffed, with little manpower for juvenile work or special
investigations.

Ten miles closer to Las Vegas, the industrial city of Henderson employed a force of just 30 officers. This total allowed only 5 men for each
shift; and on some nights, absenteeism cut the number to 3. In 1968, Las
Vegas had the largest department with 245 commissioned officers and 52
civilian employees. There were 129 patrol officers—about 42 for each
shift, plus traffic officers and 38 men for investigative and intelligence
work. This was a distinct improvement over the 1961 situation when the
mania for low taxes and minimal spending encouraged a training program
so rigorous that few recruits survived. As a result, the police department,
budgeted for 144 men, counted only 131, while the fire department found
itself 17 men short. Throughout the early 1960s, the chronic shortage of
police and firemen, accentuated by spiraling growth, only kept insurance
rates abnormally high throughout the city. Fortunately, the pro-growth
Gragson regime ended the crisis by allocating more money for police.[6]

Las Vegas's commitment to build a substantially larger police department was not duplicated in North Las Vegas, which maintained a force of
only 35 officers and 12 civilians. With just a single commissioned officer
for every 1,000 residents, North Las Vegas had the most understaffed
department in the valley. This was the case even though it was adjacent to
Las Vegas—a city with one of the highest crime rates in the nation. In
North Las Vegas only 5 men handled the day shift and even less at night.
By contrast, the county employed a large force. In 1968, for instance, the
sheriff had 176 commissioned officers and 67 civilians to cover the
mushrooming shopping centers and subdivisions in the unincorporated

townships abutting Las Vegas, as well as the other 8,000 square miles of roads and towns in Clark County. Major crimes and syndicate-related activities on the Strip were monitored by intelligence and investigative divisions comprised of 38 men. Aside from a downtown headquarters, substations were maintained at the airport and East Las Vegas while resident deputies patrolled the county's distant towns. [7]

Valleywide police protection was further fragmented by the maintenance of separate jails in the county and each of the four cities. Clearly, this was a waste of money. After surveying the problem, a Chicago-based consulting firm issued a report in 1968 which recommended the creation of one police department to service the entire metropolitan area. Funded by an expanded tax base, such a superdepartment, the consultants argued, would be able to provide more officers for Boulder City and Henderson while also expanding patrols in North Las Vegas which really was part of the Las Vegas-Paradise-Winchester crime zone. Despite obvious financial and service incentives for such a consolidation, North Las Vegas, Henderson, and Boulder City resisted the move as a threat to their autonomy. Long accustomed to controlling the level of police protection within their own borders, residents apparently feared that their taxes would be expropriated by more populous city and county areas to put more officers on the latter's streets. Still, there was some progress; after lengthy negotiations, Las Vegas and Clark County government leaders agreed to merge their two departments in 1973. Since that time, "Metro" has provided more efficient, cost-effective police protection, although city complaints about county favoritism in manpower allocations have persisted and continue to threaten the agency's survival. For the county as a whole though, the fragmented approach to law enforcement became increasingly archaic. [8]

The formation in 1973 of a centralized police force for the Strip suburbs and city was a crucial event, because resort cities—and especially casino cities—experience higher crime rates than most other cities of comparable size. Aside from organized-crime figures, casinos attract large numbers of transients which, in turn, lead to higher incidences of larceny, robbery, assault, and prostitution. Although the Las Vegas metropolitan statistical area annually records one of the highest overall crime rates nationally (partially because F.B.I. statistics do not factor in the temporary tourist population), the Atlantic City experience even more graphically demonstrates the phenomenon. Between 1977 (the year before casino gambling was legalized) and 1981, the number of larcenies, robberies, and assaults tripled. Even more startling was Atlantic City's crime rate compared to New Jersey's. In 1979–80, the city's rate was seven times greater than the state's.[9]

Of course, all resort cities have special crime problems. Honolulu, Miami Beach, Atlantic City, and Las Vegas always record high burglary and property crime rates. Yet, the approaches to law enforcement are different. Atlantic City and Miami Beach, for instance, prefer to use municipal police departments, while Las Vegas (with resort clusters in the city and suburbs) in 1973 adopted more of the metropolitan approach used by Hawaii. Still, the subject of crime and its prevention in resort and casino cities is a complex one. While it is true, for example, that Las Vegas has an abnormally high incidence of forcible rape, Honolulu does not. Yet, at the same time, the rate in Albuquerque and Houston far surpasses Las Vegas. The same is also true for other crimes. In short, the relationship between crime and resorts is a complicated one whose resolution goes beyond the scope of this book. Nevertheless, one can argue with some certainty that Las Vegas–area voters took a giant step toward controlling their own spiraling crime rate in 1973 when they supported creation of Metro.[10]

The same cannot be said for fire protection. Like law enforcement, fire protection was also meager in Las Vegas's early days. In general, conflagrations were met with an "all-hands" response until 1924 when fifteen men formed a volunteer hook and ladder company and began operating out of an alley behind the Apache Hotel with a 1907 pickup truck and a 1917 REO Speed Wagon. For a while, this was enough. Later, following passage of the Boulder Canyon Act, the city prepared for the inevitable population influx by purchasing a new pumper truck in 1929, and another in 1935. Lacking a modern alarm system, the town relied on the Union Pacific shop whistle, gunshots, and church bells to signal an emergency. Following the population loss which marked the dam's completion, the city continued to limp along with this primitive but inexpensive approach. After all, fires were somewhat infrequent in a town of less than 8,000 people. But World War II, with its military and defense facilities, enlarged the Las Vegas population to the point where there were too many shack, tent, and trash fires each night for workingmen to get their sleep. Clearly, the time had come for a paid force. In 1942, the volunteers petitioned city hall to create a professional department. By 1943, with Las Vegas's weekend populations often surpassing 25,000, the government had no choice. Despite an acute shortage of funds, Mayor Cragin and the commission approved the formation of a paid force. For the new crew, pay and hours reflected the lack of funds. To keep expenses down, officials divided the force into two platoons. Each crew worked a 24-hour shift on alternate days and lived in the firehouse. In effect, each man worked a 72-hour week but was paid a 48-hour week's salary—an injustice not remedied until the 1960s. In those early years, not only were working conditions poor, but training was mostly on the job because there was no fire academy until the late fifties. Alarms were usually telephoned in; Las Vegas lacked an alarm system until the mid-1950s. Fire prevention programs were also limited by budget constraints. There were few building inspections for fire code violations until the 1950s, and even then the manpower was limited.[11]

While the early city department saw a relatively small-scale operation, the county effort was virtually nonexistent. Until 1944, county commissioners relied on the municipal force to fight fires in the former's jurisdiction—a practice not ended until Mayor Cragin realized that the city's insurance policy (with Cragin & Pike Insurance) did not cover injuries or liabilities sustained in county areas. Eventually, the insurance policy was modified and the county treasury paid the additional premiums, but Cragin once again withdrew fire protection in 1951 to protest the creation of Paradise Township. To thwart a potential grass-roots annexation movement, county commissioners created the Clark County Fire Department in 1953, funded by a special fire district levy on Paradise residents. Of course, the suburban tax base was still too small to fund a decent organization, so the number of stations, trucks, and men were necessarily meager. The fiscal balancing act continued into the early 1960s, as county commissioners gradually built a department capable of protecting the growing zone of valuable homes in Paradise, Winchester, and Sunrise Manor.

Just as with the police, the political fragmentation of the valley adversely affected the quality of fire protection. Prior to 1960 the small, scattered centers of population justified separate volunteer and later small, paid fire departments. In the 1960s, however, the existence of five separate agencies resulted in uneven service, a fact not overlooked by fire insurance companies. Spiraling premiums eventually prompted the *Review-Journal* to plead for city-county cooperation in fire protection. Alarmed at rising insurance premiums for properties along the municipal boundaries, the paper in 1959 urged a policy whereby the nearest fire station would respond to a blaze. But the Las Vegas City Commission

turned down the proposal, claiming its men would not respond to conflagrations in county areas (not even 100 feet from a city firehouse),
because residents of the unincorporated townships of Winchester and
Paradise had rejected annexation. County residents would continue to pay
for their intransigence by financing their own public services.[12]

Once again, as with the police, the determination to keep local control
of municipal services created a wasteful duplication. In 1968, all four
cities and the county maintained fire departments—each a separate,
budgeted bureaucracy. Boulder City employed 6 men on 24-hour shifts to
protect the town, while Henderson, with its nearby industrial complex,
kept a force of 22. Las Vegas, a city of substantial high-density building
zones, employed 240 men, while North Las Vegas, with a substantial low-
income housing stock, needed 38. The county only provided fire service
in zones where the special fire surcharge to the regular property tax was in
effect. Still, Paradise, Winchester, East Las Vegas, Sunrise Manor, and
other areas required a scattered force of 170 men. A look at Map 2 clearly
reflects the disadvantages of fragmented fire protection. While certain
high-density areas near the Strip, the railroad-warehouse zone, and some
commercial districts enjoyed overlapping service from several fire stations, large tracts of land (often containing valuable homes and shopping
centers) were 1.5 miles or more from a firehouse. As mentioned, these
gaps resulted in some county residents and businessmen paying higher
insurance premiums than others for the same tax rate paid.[13]

In 1968 the Chicago consultants deplored this unevenness of service.
In addition, they emphasized how facilities and equipment varied within
each jurisdiction. Highly populated Las Vegas had seven stations while
North Las Vegas counted only two. The county supported eight houses
while Boulder City maintained only one with two men on duty at all times.
If the number of stations may have been adequate, locations were not. As
the map shows, certain districts within specific government entities were
favored over others. One large fire department with jurisdiction over the
entire metropolitan area could have spread stations out more strategically
and saved taxpayers money on needless administrative duplications. As
the consultants suggested, a metropolitan department could have equal-
ized the quality of fire protection and prevention in a cost-effective
manner for the whole valley. As it was, the programs varied with the
jurisdiction. By 1968, only Las Vegas had invested in a fire alarm system,
even though many neighborhoods in the unincorporated towns were just
as dense.

Map 2: Fire Coverage, 1968

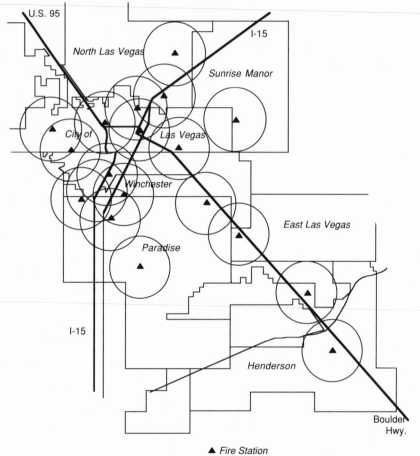

▲ *Fire Station*
Large Circles = Radius of 1-1/2 miles

The Arizona Club on North First Street, 1906.
(*Special Collections, UNLV Library*)

Fremont Street, 1908.
(*Donn Knepp*)

The Hotel Apache on Fremont Street, 1930.
(Las Vegas News Bureau)

Hoover Dam under construction, 1933.
(*Donn Knepp*)

Bungalows built for dam workers in Boulder City, 1931.
(*Nevada State Museum, Las Vegas*)

The Meadows Club on Boulder Highway, 1931.
(*Nevada State Museum, Las Vegas*)

Los Angeles City Hall superimposed on Hoover Dam to attract Southern
California tourists, ca. 1936.
(*Nevada State Museum, Las Vegas*)

Blacks in the Westside, 1942.
(*Nevada State Museum, Las Vegas*)

Flamingo entrance, 1946.
(*Las Vegas News Bureau*)

Helldorado parade on Fremont Street, 1947.
Las Vegas News Bureau)

Aerial view of the Strip, ca. 1952. Flamingo in foreground, then the Sands, Last Frontier, and Thunderbird.
(*Nevada State Museum, Las Vegas*)

Multi-story Riviera Hotel under construction, 1955. The racetrack in the background became the site for the International (Las Vegas Hilton).
(*Nevada State Museum, Las Vegas*)

Downtown during a nuclear test, 1950s.
(*Las Vegas News Bureau*)

Construction of the Las Vegas Convention Center's exhibit hall, 1958.
(*Nevada State Museum, Las Vegas*)

Dunes Tower under construction, 1964.
(*Nevada State Museum, Las Vegas*)

Caesars Palace under construction, 1965.
(*Las Vegas News Bureau*)

International Hotel under construction, 1969.
(Nevada State Museum, Las Vegas)

Aerial view of Fremont Street, 1940s.
(*Nevada State Museum, Las Vegas*)

Aerial view of Fremont Street, 1970s.
(*Nevada State Museum, Las Vegas*)

Fire prevention programs were also uneven. While the city of Las Vegas employed six men to inspect commercial buildings (including hotels and motels) for code violations annually, the county confined its inspections to the resorts; residential and even commercial buildings were only examined upon request. North Las Vegas, with its small tax base, relied on two men and occasionally an engine company to inspect a fraction of the town's many structures. Henderson and Boulder City also limped along on meager budgets. All government entities paid to use Las Vegas's fire academy. Yet, as the consultants noted, "fire training programs are conducted by every department, but they vary in scope and size." True, the four cities and county had agreed upon mutual aid pacts to assist one another in the event of large fires like the 1980 MGM conflagration, but these were no substitute for a metropolitan approach to fire protection and prevention. Nevertheless, efforts to create such a department failed as they did in Phoenix, Albuquerque, Tucson, and other fragmented towns across the west. [14]

As with police and fire protection, the political fragmentation acted for years to delay comprehensive planning for the Las Vegas Valley. Of course, there was little need for coordinated engineering and building in the early years. In fact, the first efforts to control growth were little more than neighborhood plans made by the city commissioners in the 1930s to meet the requirements of PWA, WPA, and other New Deal agencies funding sewer and street projects. Despite the expansion occasioned by dam construction, Las Vegas was still a relatively small town. But World War II transformed the situation, pouring thousands more residents into the city. Aside from military bases and BMI, each new club and resort also exerted a multiplier effect upon the town's work force and building stock. In an effort to prevent haphazard growth, city and county officials formed the Las Vegas and Clark County Planning Commission which, after conducting a preliminary survey of traffic patterns and land use, submitted a master plan to both the city and county governments in early 1944. For several reasons, however, city and county officials largely ignored the document. First, the plan was drawn up without full legal authority because the writing process itself ignored several requirements of the city and county charters; second, parts of the plan conflicted with earlier zoning laws; third, it emphasized the city and mostly ignored county lands; and finally, the plan itself was too inflexible and, if enforced, would have delayed construction of vital housing and commercial developments. As a result of these defects plus the growing mistrust between Las Vegas, North Las Vegas, and Clark County, the master plan and the so-called Regional Planning Council were largely ignored during the 1950s. All three governments acted independently of each other, although they employed the same basic policy—laissez-faire. With some exceptions, each entity promoted growth within its jurisdiction by granting variances to builders as the need arose.[15]

By 1960, as the metropolitan area's population roared past 100,000 and the town sprawled outward in a hodgepodge of developments, the need for systematic city and countywide planning became obvious. Describing the comprehensive municipal zoning ordinance of 1948 as a "Frankenstein which is nearly impossible to administer equitably," the Las Vegas Planning Commission in a 1959 report emphasized once again the weaknesses of earlier plans. To fill the gap and provide for the needs of present and future growth, Las Vegas commissioned a new city plan in 1959, designed to safeguard the casino industry location along Fremont Street, provide for hotel expansion and parking facilities on nearby streets, preserve as much of the city's retail districts as possible, allow for new residential zones, and coordinate street systems with the impending federal freeway to promote efficient traffic flow. In time, the city effort sparked a movement which spread across the metropolitan area. Boulder City drew upon its own plan in 1964. Then North Las Vegas, led by its progressive city manager, Clay Lynch, followed suit in 1965, with Henderson completing the process in 1968.[16]

The suburbs witnessed similar actions. In 1966, Clark County commissioners voted to create a comprehensive master plan for the rapidly urbanizing unincorporated townships. They commissioned Eisner-Stewart and Associates, a Pasadena, California, consulting firm, to prepare a report on existing land uses and potential zoning ordinances for the county portion of the valley. The commissioners also launched a successful effort to create a new Regional Planning Council comprised of elected officials from the county, school district, water district, and three cities to coordinate plans for valleywide road, sewer, water, and flood-control needs. To some extent, this effort succeeded in the seventies and eighties. Although the four governments continued to bypass the plan with numerous zoning variances, still the laissez-faire atmosphere which characterized urban growth in the forties and fifties diminished markedly. The Eisner-Stewart plan graphically emphasized the importance of zoning the Strip, portions of Paradise Road, and the Boulder Highway to allow room for the county's valuable resort industry to expand. Similarly, the plan demonstrated the importance of protecting the Industrial Road and Highland Avenue lands bordering the Union Pacific railroad line for warehousing and light industry. Other suggestions for the controlled development of commercial zones on major roads paralleling the Strip (e.g., Maryland Parkway, Eastern Avenue, Pecos, Decatur, Valley View, and others) also contributed to orderly growth and financial prosperity.[17] Nevertheless, the lack of comprehensive planning resulted in later problems. Take, for instance, the location of residential developments so close to the chemical plants near Henderson. In May 1988, hundreds of new homes in the area suffered structural damage when the nearby Pacific Engineering Company (PEPCON) plant was destroyed by a series of explosions.

Historically, most of the confusion surrounding governance of the metropolitan area stemmed from the fact that until the 1960s Las Vegas's city government had been the main center of political power in the valley. Not until the early 1950s did the population in the smaller cities and unincorporated areas grow to the point where the county commission played an important role in urban governance. True, the gunnery school, the BMI agreements, the new airports, and other projects were often initiated and supported by county commissioners, but prior to the mid-1950s, these men were usually residents of the city of Las Vegas. By the 1960s, however, the county board became increasingly powerful as the unincorporated suburbs comprised a city all their own.[18]

Aside from police, fire, water, planning, and other problems, there were several valleywide issues which required county attention. Flood control, in particular, became a concern as early as the mid-1950s when the city's building zone began to sprawl across natural washes, stretching eastward across the valley from Las Vegas to Lake Mead and the Colorado. Following a major flood in 1955, Nevada Senator George "Molly" Malone pushed a bill through Congress funding a preliminary flood control report for the valley by the United States Army Corps of Engineers. In October 1958, Brigadier General E. C. Itschner, Chief of the Corps, came to Las Vegas and conferred with politicians and engineers from Henderson, Las Vegas, and North Las Vegas, but no comprehensive program was adopted. Another flood in 1959 inundated homes in many new subdivisions untouched by earlier storms. This time, Democratic Senator Howard Cannon secured money for a larger engineering survey, and local politicians responded with a series of efforts, culminating in a 1961 law establishing the Clark County Flood Control District. In a related move, county commissioners also urged Nevada's congressional delegation to lobby their colleagues for more federal funds for a comprehensive survey by the Army Corps. The Nevada congressional delegation ultimately succeeded in that effort. [19]

Unfortunately, county voters rejected bond issues throughout the sixties to mitigate the flood threat. In a region where rain was infrequent and serious flooding a rare occurrence, flood control took a back seat to streets, sewers, and water projects. To complicate matters, both the county and city planners permitted developers to build new subdivisions in flood plains. This nearly criminal practice could not have continued without the approval of a generation of city and county commissioners. The result was substantial property damage and loss of life. Finally, in 1986, after a series of disastrous storms in 1984, the county commission, led by Bruce Woodbury, Manny Cortez, Thalia Dondero, and others, united with officials from the nearby cities to convince voters to raise the sales tax in Clark County to 6 percent in order to fund a multiyear, $800 million Army Corps program to reduce the flood threat in the valley. There was no choice; the urbanization of Las Vegas had forced the metropolitan building zone across all major washes, and a city of 600,000 people could no longer come to a virtual standstill every time a summer storm hit. [20]

Unlike flooding, sanitation posed a more immediate threat. Following the county's successful effort in December 1950 to block the city's annexation of Paradise Valley, commissioners began providing limited urban services for suburban residents. As already noted, county authorities levied special property taxes in Paradise to fund additional manpower for the sheriff's department and newly created county fire department. Sanitation gradually became an additional concern. For a while, cesspools and septic tanks solved the problem. However, as the resort economy blossomed and each new Strip hotel spawned additional subdivisions in Paradise Valley, commissioners reluctantly prepared to undertake the costly effort to build a sewer network, which by the 1980s would stretch as far south as Henderson. The initial step came in August 1954 when the county formed Sanitation District Number 1, which generally encompassed the zone south of Las Vegas. In less than a decade, the rapid growth of county territory east of both Las Vegas and North Las Vegas forced more action. In March 1960, faced with the problem of inadequate septic tanks and wet lots among the 800 homes and 300 trailer spaces of rapidly growing Sunrise Manor (east of Las Vegas), county commissioners created Sanitation District Number 2. Since the proposed solution to the area problem—a new 3.5-mile outflow sewer main from Cheyenne and

Nellis—would cost $8.50 per foot, commissioners also had to establish a new tax district to fund the improvement. In the meantime, the county considered banning new multi-occupancy dwellings to avoid incurring fines from the federal government for violating U.S. Public Health code standards.[21]

The county commissioners themselves did not function as the sanitation district board until the state legislature reformed the district with a series of laws in the mid-1960s. Prior to this, members of the sanitation district board ran for election. While planning and construction throughout the fifties and early sixties proceeded smoothly, the large amount of money and power centered in the board was bound to encourage abuses. Not surprisingly, the district board was often a target of critics who charged that members operated it like an empire. In a typical editorial entitled "The Sewer Boys Hire an Image Maker," the *Review-Journal* in 1964 characterized the board as "the most discredited group of public officials in the state." In the editor's view, the abuses were legion: worldwide trips at taxpayer expense to "study sewers," conflicts of interest in land transactions, construction contract awards without sealed bids, abnormally expensive consultant contracts and, worse, the hiring of an advertising agency to smooth over the board's image and discourage new candidates from running in the next district election. In raising its voice, the newspaper apparently echoed the views of others, because city and county officials successfully lobbied the next state legislature to transfer all of the district's executive power to the county commissioners.[22]

Despite this reform, the sanitation district's woes continued. For two decades the agency's major weakness was the lack of money. The relatively low value of lands along and just beyond the periphery of the county's building zone slowed construction, since many local programs were funded partially by assessments upon benefited property. Federal funding was also necessary, especially in the 1960s. As a result, the county's sewer construction schedule was often affected by national events. Moreover, a combination of explosive growth, low taxes, and diversion of tax revenues to rural areas kept Clark County chronically underfunded. Throughout the early 1960s, public works money was scarce. In 1964, for instance, county plans to widen major arteries like Desert Inn and Flamingo roads and to eliminate "dangerous dips" across flood-prone washes crossing Maryland Parkway had to be postponed because Sanitation District Number 1 lacked enough federal funds to pay its construction bills. Regardless of federal policies, however, county commissioners knew that the continued urbanization of lands surrounding Las Vegas would require a continuous effort to keep pace with building programs.[23]

If this were not enough, Clark County also had to maintain an effective facility to treat wastes before they entered Lake Mead. Throughout the 1960s, the valley's spiraling population teamed with more new hotel rooms to challenge the capacity of the county's waste-treatment plant. An immediate crisis arose in January 1969 when the Clark County Sanitation District's disposal plant malfunctioned and had to be shut down. While the Las Vegas city plant handled the county's sewage on a temporary basis, it was obvious that both governments would soon have to expand their facilities. Thanks to the valley's skyrocketing population, consulting engineers predicted that both the Las Vegas and county plants would reach capacity by 1971. Moreover, experts knew that the recently created Environmental Protection Agency would eventually enforce strict pollution standards, forcing the construction of expensive advanced wastewater treatment plants.[24]

Aside from police and fire services, regional planning, and county efforts at sanitation and flood control, the valley's political fragmentation disrupted orderly metropolitan administration in other ways as well. The existence of one county and three city governments in one valley invariably led to urban imperialism on a scale never seen before in Nevada. The famous city-county struggle over Paradise and the Strip merely served as a prelude to a series of high jinks. One of the most celebrated battles occurred in the early 1960s. On May 17, 1962, after an agonizing three-hour meeting, the North Las Vegas City Council voted to annex a twelve-square-mile area of "largely barren desert" northwest of Las Vegas—a move which overnight tripled the size of the town. Councilmen had taken roughly the same land in August 1961, but the county and Las Vegas had sued, forcing North Las Vegas to reconsider its action. Actually, the original dispute was still in court, with Las Vegas demanding one-third of the zone. At the same time, Clark County commissioners reinforced their claim by creating Thunderbird, an unincorporated township which encompassed all of the disputed land. However, North Las Vegas City Manager Clay Lynch, asserting that neither the county nor Las Vegas could take land within North Las Vegas township (the actual city of North Las Vegas occupied part of the land within the larger township), deployed his city's police along the area's roads within an hour of the vote. Not to be outflanked, both Clark County and Las Vegas rushed their police cars in too, giving the sparsely populated zone the tightest security in Nevada.

But that was not all; ensuing weeks saw apparatus from three different fire departments rush in to douse the flames of local conflagrations. While flattered by the attention, confused residents quickly saw that the disadvantages outweighed the assets. Indeed, construction in the area came to a virtual halt once developers realized they had to secure building permits from three governments to avoid costly litigation.[25]

Who was the cause of this jurisdictional circus? The *Review-Journal* blamed all three governments. According to the paper, Las Vegas for decades had been guilty of "snatching up scraps of land like a half-witted squatter." In the past, the city had been criticized for annexing neat, rectangular plots of land, because only "parts of the residents" wanted to join the city. So, to quiet spending and planning critics, the town began acquiring areas where the majority of people were favorable; as a result, "the latest annexations [were] shaped erratically." North Las Vegas pursued a different policy, taking twelve square miles of real estate "belonging to a common flood plain" but all within the broad area of North Las Vegas Township. While Clay Lynch was probably correct when he insisted that 58 percent of the residents approved the action, most of these people lived in the tiny, populated corners near the city and were not equally distributed over the area. In other words, Lynch used less than two square miles of support to grab twelve square miles of area. At the same time, North Las Vegas, which was currently claiming a water shortage, was nevertheless "attempting to add twelve vacant miles to its area and poke pipelines in another direction [toward Sunrise Manor] to service the Nellis Air Force Base area." And, the paper noted, Clark County commissioners, "worried by this ambitious burst of territorial aggrandizements," counterattacked in the name of saving "the hapless residents from the tax-hungry cities."[26]

In its appraisal of the unfolding comedy, the newspaper pointed an accusing finger at the Napoleonic county commissioners, who had, during the past five years, raised municipal fears by creating three special sewer districts which deliberately encircled Las Vegas and North Las Vegas on three sides. These districts, the paper insisted, "stand today like septic iron curtains blocking annexations in all but one direction." No wonder the two alarmed cities suddenly raced outward in panzer-like fashion to seize all available land. The county's subsequent decision to block these efforts by creating the unincorporated township of Thunderbird only reinforced the municipal paranoia. Now, the paper reported, all three governments were in court, bogged down in expensive litigation. In a plea for sanity, the *Review-Journal* urged more cooperation and "less kingdom-making among responsible officials." The editor, however, ended on a realistic note, conceding the existence of "probably greater rapport between Red China and the U.S. than . . . between the cities of Las Vegas, North Las Vegas and Clark County."[27]

Clearly, the reason for these conflicts was money. Las Vegas, in expectation of the widening of the commuter road (the Tonopah Highway) to the nuclear test site, anticipated development in the zone between Nellis Air Force Base and the Highway. As a result, the city, having already lost the Strip to Clark County, began annexing part of the Tonopah Highway before veering suddenly across the road in a quick thrust north, cutting a 6-mile swath across barren desert to Tule Springs Ranch. This aggression had alarmed the ever-vigilant Clay Lynch and sparked the crisis, which the county only reinforced. In the end, Las Vegas retained its claims to lands along the Tonopah Highway while North Las Vegas controlled parcels to the east within its township. The county also maintained a presence along the periphery of the city-held zones, although Thunderbird, which had been illegally created, was voided by the courts.[28]

Internecine warfare flared again in early 1963. This time the city of Henderson took the offensive in an effort to block efforts by the Clark County Sanitation District to lay a sewer line along Sunset Road into Henderson. In defiant fashion, Mayor Bill Byrne refused to grant an easement until the district signed an "iron-clad agreement" exempting Henderson residents from an additional $.44 levy on their sewer bills to fund construction. The city contended it already possessed sufficient sewer lines of its own and feared that the new construction was a county ploy to block Henderson's growth to the north and west. The controversy pointed up the vital role played by infrastructure in the imperialistic designs of competing urban governments. In the fragmented metropolis of the Las Vegas Valley, the county and three city governments had each financed their own water and sewer system and used it to entice adjacent new subdivisions whose additional tax base could be used, in turn, to fund still more rounds of sewer construction and annexation. These pipe networks, along with the promise of police and fire services were thus used to acquire more land along the various municipal borders. In a seemingly endless series of struggles, each government, competing for space with the others, tried to enlarge its area and tax base at the expense of its neighbors. Any county effort to build roads or extend sewer mains outward toward land near the annexable zone of the city was considered a threat to future growth. This was the case in Henderson.

Fortunately, the two entities eventually agreed to a truce on the Sunset Road sewer. The district promised not to charge Henderson residents the added sewer tax, and recognized the city's future intention of annexing a nearby country club area regardless of whether the sewer was laid. Henderson's concerns were real, because the county commissioners, recognizing that one day the vacant land between Paradise Valley and Sunset would be filled in with homes and businesses, were not anxious to see the city expand too far north and west. Having blocked Las Vegas's expansion to the south since 1950, and having slowed North Las Vegas's growth to the east and northwest by 1962, the county wanted East Las Vegas and areas east and south of the airport to remain in county hands for as long as possible. Nine-year-old Henderson, therefore, recognized a real threat to its expansion in 1962 (see Map 3).[29]

As casino gambling and defense spending fueled more urbanization, these territorial disputes continued. A dozen minor fracases punctuated the mid-1960s before a new donnybrook raised the colors once again in 1969. In the fall of that year Clay Lynch and a majority of North Las Vegas councilmen, anxious to expand the city's tax base to the east, announced their intention of annexing four areas (13 square miles) comprising Nellis Air Force Base and the growing suburban community of Sunrise Manor. The move was prompted by petitions received from two developers, the LeRoy Corporation and Park West Development, to annex one of the zones. The companies felt that only the city could provide the full range of urban services needed to enhance their property's value. While the petition pleased municipal authorities, area residents were less enthusiastic. At a public meeting on November 3, a large gathering of citizens from the affected section objected. They were joined by some North Las Vegas residents who feared the costs of extending police and fire protection along with roads, water, and sewer networks. The proposed zone was substantial, bounded by Carey Avenue on the south, Cecil on the north, Pecos on the west, and Walnut on the east. Within it were several large housing tracts, including Los Cerritos Estates, Ponderosa Manor, and Northland Gardens. Many local residents, satisfied with their limited urban services and anxious to keep their property taxes low, vowed to fight the city. Joining them were several North Las Vegas citizens who pledged their help by threatening to initiate a recall of Councilmen C. R. "Bud" Cleland, Jack Petitti, and Wendell Waite. This action, they believed, might pressure the council into ousting Clay Lynch who, in the minds of fiscal conservatives, was the real culprit. This view was perhaps best expressed by North Las Vegas's state assemblyman Dave Branch, who

Map 3: Metropolitan Political Boundaries, 1975

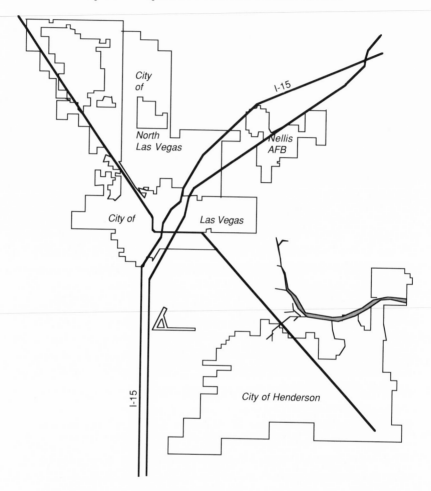

opposed the councilmen's plans because "they cannot afford it. They can't [even] afford what they have in the city limits at the present time."[30]

Of those speaking from the audience that night, only one man favored the annexation. The rest pounded away at Lynch and his allies who, in turn, countered that North Las Vegas was fiscally strong and therefore able to service its fledgling neighbors to the east. Unconvinced, Sunrise Manorites charged that North Las Vegas needed the suburbs to pay off future debts. Specifically, residents pointed to a projected $4 million bond issue and $540,000 emergency loan for the local water problem which Lynch had just proposed. "If you're so well off," one landowner challenged Lynch, then "why are you asking for the $540,000 emergency loan . . . ?" A woman then charged that "your men have been telling us our rates will go down; this is a lie." The crowd's distrust of Lynch was evident. As one man wondered, "why are you always trying to give us something? We had nothing to do with putting you in office or in compounding your problems. And we don't want to spend our money in solving your problems." The strong anti-city, anti-Lynch sentiment of county citizens was expressed best by one resident who declared, "What scares me is the way you men keep ramrodding these things through. Clay Lynch scares me. And the council sits back and lets him do anything he wants." Then came a new threat: "If we have the unfortunate luck to be annexed, I pledge all my time, money and energy in getting new councilmen at the next election." Despite the theatrics, Lynch and the councilmen remained unmoved, knowing that the audience represented only a small portion of those affected. Annexation opponents had only fifteen days to file their protests after the public hearing, and the city received none in the days immediately following the meeting.[31]

The real threat to Lynch's designs came not from the small band of protesters, but from county commissioners who wasted no time in convening a meeting to discuss the city's move. Clearly, Lynch wanted Sunrise Manor to gain an increased share of the cigarette and liquor tax revenues which were split among the county's cities on a population basis. While it was agreed that the revenue shortfall from the loss of Sunrise Manor would be offset by savings from urban services no longer provided, county leaders nevertheless saw the Lynch initiative as a dangerous precedent. In particular, they bristled at his heavy-handedness. As Commission Chairman Bill Briare noted, each of the four proposed annexation parcels encompassed portions of the others, so that if residents in one zone rejected the city's move, they would be surrounded and isolated. Conced-

ing that it was "an extremely clever design on Clay's part," Briare nevertheless lamented that even if "the people are against it, . . . they run into
blank walls opposing Clay Lynch." This view was supported by Commissioner Jim Ryan, who observed that "the protesting is done at City Hall.
Clay is the scorekeeper. If 200 people protest, he says it was 67."[32]

The county, however, awaited the outcome of a November 10 protest
meeting in which Lynch was again harangued and berated by angry
residents. Contributing to the mayhem was an announcement by Nellis
Commander Colonel Robert Anderson that the air force officially opposed
the base's annexation. Though newsworthy, the military's role in the
controversy was minimal. The Pentagon's opposition had been common
knowledge for some time but, since the base had no assessed valuation,
officers lacked a vote on annexation. In addition, since Nellis was largely
autonomous, the city had no intention of providing municipal services
anyway.

Perhaps the loudest note of the evening was sounded by County Commissioner Jim Ryan, who admonished Lynch for trying to forcibly annex
the suburb. Clearly, Ryan and his colleagues were spoiling for a fight with
Lynch and his upstart city council. Since the 1940s the county board had
fought to maintain and expand its own tax base while permitting the
limited expansion of area cities. But, following the notorious Thunderbird
incident, Clay Lynch represented the gravest threat to that policy. Lynch
had the upper hand temporarily, because Nevada law required those
owning a majority of the assessed valuation in the annexed area to protest
the city's action. Thanks to apathy and disorganization, less than a
hundred protests were received and the city annexed the zones by ordinance on December 1, 1969.[33]

As expected, Clark County commissioners, determined to thwart the
North Las Vegas initiative, acted even before the December 1 ordinance
was passed. At a November 20 meeting commissioners voted to ask the
district attorney's office to seek an injunction blocking the town's action
until after a state court ruled on the issue. The county ultimately filed suit
requesting a declaratory judgment clarifying the rights, duties, and legal
status of the county and North Las Vegas in the matter. The eleven-page
county complaint also alleged that portions of the city's annexation proceedings were illegal, and that petitions for the annexation of one zone
were used to initiate the capture of the other three. The legal battle
continued into the 1970s, with the Nevada Supreme Court eventually
voiding the city's action. Once again, suburban residents had teamed
successfully with county leaders to block municipal expansion.[34]

Aside from these occasional jurisdictional battles, the political fragmentation of the Las Vegas Valley also weakened the capacity of government to tackle valleywide problems. Dating from the aborted effort in the 1940s to form a strong Regional Planning Commission, area officials periodically agreed to confer on matters of common interest. In October 1950, for instance, Las Vegas, North Las Vegas, Henderson, and the county, put aside their disagreements over taxes and annexation to hold a conference on mutual problems. County Commission Chairman George Franklin proposed a series of agenda items, including flood control, creation of a central identification file for criminal offenders, county use of the city jail, land purchases, and revival of the Regional Planning Commission. Later years saw progress made on all these fronts. Although these ad hoc get-togethers sparked a measure of goodwill and cooperation, they were no substitute for valleywide government. Recognizing the importance of coordinated administration in the midst of explosive urbanization, County Commissioner (and later Las Vegas Mayor) Bill Briare in 1962 proposed the formation of the League of Elected City and County Officials—a permanent board designed to address major urban problems confronting the valley. Briare's effort to institutionalize some form of metropolitan government met with little enthusiasm, and in July 1964 he abandoned the scheme. In the end, the Las Vegas Valley remained saddled with a dozen governments and special service districts. And, while there were some specific boards empowered to discuss specific problems (e.g., flood control and traffic), they were, even in the eyes of partisans like Clay Lynch, "too numerous and narrow." Having won little support for his proposal, Briare changed tactics. As the county commissioner representing Las Vegas, he pushed in 1968 for the already mentioned report by the Public Administration Service of Chicago (who in 1954 had recommended limited metropolitan government for the Miami area), which surveyed the valley's urban problems and eventually recommended consolidation of services and even governments.[35]

An enthusiastic supporter of valleywide consolidation of urban services, Briare also championed a merger of the Las Vegas and Clark County governments. His position was buttressed substantially by the 1968 Chicago consultant's report, which deplored the administrative duplication of services, staffs, and budgets around the metropolis. Noting that in Las Vegas "one police, fire, street and recreation serves one side of the street, another serves the other side," the consultants characterized these "illogical service areas" as "uneconomic." Worse still, the three cities, the county, the school district, the water district, and other local governments competed with one another for property and sales tax revenues, and vied again for federal grant-in-aid programs for public housing, libraries, and urban renewal. Observing that federal agencies like HUD and HEW increasingly preferred a metropolitan approach to urban problems, the consultants argued that the fragmented and competitive approach employed by Las Vegas–area governments had already cost them a fortune in rejected grant proposals. This realization already had led town and county officials in 1966 to create the Clark County Regional Planning Council in an effort to coordinate local needs and building agendas to secure a larger share of federal programs. The financial incentive for cooperation had been lacking in the forties and fifties because property taxes were substantially less in county areas than in the cities. The growth of the Strip smashed this disparity in the 1960s, as the soaring cost of new sewers, water lines, roads, and schools forced property valuations everywhere up to the state constitutional limit of $.05 on the dollar of assessed valuation. As a result, federal funding became increasingly vital.[36]

While the consultants applauded the new, regional approach to grantsmanship, they bemoaned how the development of a politically fragmented metropolis had muddled city planning in all five communities. Although Las Vegas, Henderson, North Las Vegas, and the county had all developed master plans by the 1960s, none really considered regional factors. The consultants correctly argued that comprehensive planning for parks, open space, water, sewers, recreational facilities, flood control, traffic networks, and police and fire protection required a valleywide approach, encompassing the entire metropolitan area. Even the Eisner-Stewart County Plan of 1966 reflected this myopia. Moreover, the consultants reminded officials that all plans required constant updating and revision. While three of the governments had planning commissions, only Las Vegas had a planning department; unfortunately, most of its time and manpower was consumed investigating requests for zoning variances. In short, while the Las Vegas Valley was a clearly defined geographical area, plans only covered four distinct quadrants, zoning measures varied significantly, updating was virtually nonexistent and intergovernmental cooperation was minimal.[37]

The consultants' solution was the consolidation of North Las Vegas, Henderson, Las Vegas, and Clark County into one metropolitan government. Pointing to the recent union of Nashville with Davidson County in Tennessee, and the impending (1968) marriage between Jacksonville and Duval County in Florida, the consultants suggested the creation of one city government for the entire valley with two tax zones: an Urban Services District where residents paid the full property tax for all municipal services and a General Services District (with lower rates) along the metropolitan periphery where garbage, sewage disposal, and other functions were not essential. For his part, Bill Briare adopted a less radical stance, urging the consolidation of Las Vegas and nearby county suburbs. To some extent, Briare was resurrecting the earlier effort of Ernie Cragin to annex the Strip suburbs. It was, however, all to no avail. With the exception of the police, no significant consolidation of services or governments took place. In 1975, the year Briare succeeded Oran Gragson as mayor of Las Vegas, county voters in a referendum rejected a merger with the city.[38]

The voters were responding to powerful historical forces which had shaped the development of metropolitan Las Vegas. Despite the persuasive arguments of the consultants and other consolidation advocates, one must appreciate the factors which promoted the growth of four separate governments in the valley over time. While the fragmented-valley theme succeeds as a description of the city-building process in Las Vegas, it fails as an indictment. In terms of modern public administration and economic theory, a single, valleywide city government may forever make sense, but historically the development of five distinct urban governments was practical. The federal government itself had initiated the fragmentation when it located Boulder City and later Henderson a great distance from the Las Vegas city limits. The process was then reinforced by a variety of factors. In 1950, Las Vegas was still a small city of only 24,000 people, hardly enough to finance an expensive water and sewer network extending miles beyond the city's population core to Henderson, much less to Boulder City. Even the much-closer North Las Vegas, with its lower property values, struggled in the 1950s to fund construction of a sewer system for only 4,000 people. In those same years, while Henderson's 5,400 residents debated the need for incorporation, they never dreamed their town's water and sewer system would ever approach the Las Vegas network almost twenty miles away.

Residents of the three cities and the county began their infrastructural networks in four distinct locations and expanded them only as need arose and funding allowed. Politically and financially it made sense in the forties and fifties to develop separate police, fire, street, and parks departments. Common sense dictated that urban services and networks be kept as local as possible to guarantee the maximum service per dollar spent. The spectacular success of the valley's recreational and defense economies only seemed assured and permanent in the 1960s. In a matter of years, the boom had vaulted Las Vegas to metropolitan status. By then it was too late to unite the valley politically. Only in the sixties, as the valley's four settled areas grew toward one another along an expanding network of roads, did the existence of four large governments (and many lesser ones) become impractical. But by then, thirty years of history— thirty years of local autonomy, local pride, and mistrust of rival govern- ments' designs—had become ingrained.

Henderson residents had become conditioned to suspect the intentions of the county commissioners. And why not? County leaders had already captured the valuable Basic Plant and seemed determined to limit Hen- derson's growth westward and northward into the desert flats. Witness the county's use of the Sanitation District. Clearly, by 1970 the Las Vegas metropolitan area had grown into a sprawling organism destined to occupy the entire valley, but it lacked an efficient political and administrative nucleus to supervise the growth and services in an orderly, cost-effective manner. While earlier leaders might be faulted for lacking the vision and commitment to unify their emerging metropolis in the interest of growth, powerful economic forces acted as a constant disincentive.

There was, however, one powerful exception to the fragmentation trend—education. While schools initially reflected the parochial ap- proach common to police, fire, planning, and other municipal services, local communities eventually turned to a countywide, metropolitan re- sponse which ultimately produced the Clark County School District. Recognizing the weaknesses of a competing system of districts, civic leaders and voters in the 1950s embraced a countywide special service district capable of tapping a broad tax base to plan construction for the valley as a whole. The origins of the Las Vegas school system date from the new town's first year of existence in 1905. Even as the first buildings began rising on Fremont Street, concerned parents attended a series of public meetings in the late spring and summer to provide a school for the community's forty or more children. Eventually, citizens selected a three- member school board, which then moved quickly to secure a site (at Second and Lewis streets) and building (the four-room Salt Lake Hotel was moved to the lot for just $700). Classes began on October 2, 1905, with two teachers handling all eight grades in varying shifts throughout the day. Conditions were hectic enough, but the town's spiraling popula- tion produced an enrollment crisis. By mid-November 1905, the number of students had nearly doubled to eighty-one.[39]

Overcrowding finally forced voters in 1908 to approve a $30,000 bond issue for a larger school. This time, board officials sought a larger site capable of handling future expansion. In its typically paternalistic fashion, Senator Clark's railroad offered a two-block site (bounded by Bridger, Clark, Fourth, and Fifth streets) for a fee of $10. Following a bond issue, construction began in 1910 on a new school at South Fourth and Bridger. Blueprints called for a two-story, 14-classroom, mission-style building. In October 1911, the new Las Vegas Grammar School opened its doors to 111 elementary students and a 17-member high school class (the first high school graduation was in 1913). Senior students occupied the second floor, but, as early as 1917, grade school graduations had filled those classrooms to the point where a new high school building was needed. [40]

Residents built the new high school in 1917. Within two years, however, even more construction was necessary, as soaring enrollments forced School Superintendent A. S. Henderson to ask the board for a new branch school across the railroad tracks to service Westside students. This facility on D Street opened in 1921. Then, in 1928 as news of the impending construction of Hoover Dam drove Las Vegas's population past 5,000, residents approved bonds for a new high school to handle the prospective enrollment. With the exception of the Westside facility, all of the community's early schools were clustered in the two-block area around Fourth Street. The trend toward dispersal finally began in 1929 when the town built its new high school at Seventh and Bridger. The large, two-story structure, capable of holding 500 students, opened on September 4, 1930. Once the old high school was converted to an upper-level elementary school, officials were finally confident that Las Vegas had enough facilities to accommodate the population increase expected from the dam. The relief was only temporary. On May 14, 1934, the old high school at Fourth and Clark caught fire and many of its classrooms were destroyed. Fortunately, students had been dismissed an hour earlier and no one was hurt, but teachers were forced to conduct classes in tents for the next two years until Franklin D. Roosevelt's New Deal built a new $150,000 grammar school. The so-called Fifth Street School (today part of the Clark County Courthouse Annex), built of steel, concrete, and clay tile, was virtually indestructible and served the city for the next few decades. [41]

While the departure of dam workers in 1936 eased the enrollment crunch, the arrival of defense workers and their families during World War II created an unprecedented crisis. Throughout the 1940s, both K. O. Knudson, the town's elementary school principal (1926–59), and

School Superintendent Maude Frazier (1927–46), pleaded with board officials for more money for books, teachers, and buildings. Pressed by budget constraints and inadequate state funding, the board did its best. Although the creation of separate school districts in Boulder City, Henderson, and later Paradise Valley relieved some of the strain, Las Vegas's feverish growth during and after the war quickly offset these advantages. As school opened in September 1945, Las Vegas area residents counted eight grammar schools—six in Las Vegas, two in North Las Vegas and one still under construction in Vegas Heights (later annexed to Las Vegas). Most of the facilities housed kindergarten through eighth grade programs, although a few ended at the fourth grade. Textbooks were free except for a $2.50 deposit paid by each student.[42]

The major problem in postwar Nevada was teacher's pay; the silver state simply was not competitive with other areas. Eventually, the growing shortage of good teachers sparked an effort to raise salaries. In January 1946, the *Review-Journal* joined a chorus of voices urging pay hikes. Noting that teachers do not strike like other workers but "merely leave the field and bequeath their posts to less qualified persons," Al Cahlan, himself a former teacher, argued for more money to attract better talent to southern Nevada. With surrounding states like California, Arizona, and Utah expanding their school systems and raising salaries, the teacher drain in Nevada could have reached crisis levels. Few took solace in the report of Dr. F. W. Traner, the University of Nevada's Dean of Education, which showed that 1946 teacher salaries in the silver state were lower than in 1941. Nor was it reassuring that in 1946 instructor's pay was barely equal to the national average twenty-five years earlier when Nevada had been 34 percent above the median line. Clearly, the state, with its lack of major cities, great universities, and cultural attractions, had to pay more to lure qualified teachers. A series of increased school allocations from the legislature temporarily eased the salary problem in the late 1940s, but a new crisis arose which particularly afflicted the Las Vegas metropolitan area.[43]

As the town's postwar resort and defense industries drove the local population up to and beyond 50,000 people, lack of school space reached epidemic proportions. In April 1951, Clark County voters offered temporary help by approving bond issues to build sixty new classrooms for elementary students and a massive auditorium for Las Vegas High to house concerts, assemblies, and community events. Yet, in the face of new hotel construction on the Strip and increased defense spending at

Nellis and the test site, the new bond issue was not enough. Clark County's worsening educational crisis was reflected in the 1952 school budget, which allotted over 90 percent of all funds for salaries. As a result, additional students and teachers in 1953 only forced that budget out of balance. Even with supplementary state aid, one-fourth of Clark County's students were on half-day sessions and another quarter "were crowded into discarded army barracks and other inadequate facilities." A sympathetic Governor Charles Russell called a special session of the state legislature, which eventually allocated additional funds for the school district while also authorizing the creation of a special citizens' committee to survey the problem. However, no long-term reforms were enacted immediately.[44]

According to former Las Vegas School Superintendent R. Guild Gray, the historic origins of the crisis lay in Nevada's traditional frontier identity and the desire of wealthy Renoites to maintain the state as a tax haven. In the late 1930s voters had approved constitutional amendments prohibiting inheritance and estate taxes along with a limitation of the property tax to $.05 on the dollar of assessed valuation. The goal was to lure more wealth to the silver state. Yet, as Gray subsequently argued, while gambling and liberal divorce may have been valuable in combating the Great Depression, they were a detriment to growth in the 1950s. Nevada's famous slogan—"No inheritance, no income, no sales taxes—the tax free, one sound state"—crippled Clark County's educational system in the 1950s which, in turn, helped divert industry from the area. During the forties and early fifties, growing school expenses had been defrayed by revenues from increased gaming taxes and license fees. Casino profits could not cover the amounts needed in 1955, however, as post–Korean War inflation threatened the stability of almost every school district in the state.

No solution was popular: wealthy individuals and corporations rejected an income tax, while labor groups opposed a regressive sales tax. Worse still, Nevada's rural-based assemblymen and senators, used to viewing the world from their small-town perspective, were hardly qualified to wrestle with major urban problems. Many of the representatives came from counties with less than 5,000 people (two counties lacked 1,000 people each). As Gray noted, "some of the men who had been accustomed to dealing with an overall state population of 100,000 just couldn't project themselves into a situation where there are now as many people in one local area as there had been in the entire state." Moreover, many of the rural legislators could not believe "that every time a new hotel was constructed on the Las Vegas Strip a new school had to be constructed to take care of more new pupils than there were pupils in the entire county which they represented." While rural lawmakers marveled at the multiplier effect of hotel construction upon revenues, they bemoaned the increased road, school, and other public expenses that the resulting urbanization incurred.[45]

Progress finally came after the special legislative session in 1954 when Governor Russell's "School Study Committee" hired consultants from the respected Peabody College for Teachers to survey the state's problems and suggest reforms. Later, in a sweeping series of recommendations, the consultants urged scrapping Nevada's several hundred school districts, and replacing them with one large district in each of the state's seventeen counties. The consultants also advised overhauling the state's educational funding system. For years the Las Vegas Elementary School District was underfunded because state authorities based appropriations on average daily attendance. This practice slighted high-growth areas; indeed, during the 1953–54 school year, enrollment in the Las Vegas Union School District rose by 126 percent. This amount was not matched by average daily attendance, because the growth (in terms of daily attendance) was mostly registered late in the spring of 1954. This injustice was finally remedied in 1955 by new state legislation which basically implemented the Peabody Report's recommendations.[46]

Under the new plan, Clark County, which in 1955 hosted a confused hodgepodge of no less than fourteen school districts (Las Vegas, Paradise Valley, Henderson, Boulder City, Nelson, Searchlight, Blue Diamond, Goodsprings, and other little mining and agricultural towns had their own), was unified into a single district controlled by an elected board of trustees. In 1955, the legislature also strengthened the district's financial base by passing a 2 percent sales tax whose revenues were earmarked for educational purposes. In addition, school districts could now levy ad valorem taxes on property up to $.80 per $100 of assessed valuation, and the bonding capacity of the districts was also expanded. The latter was particularly crucial to Clark County where new construction was urgent.[47]

Already in 1953, Las Vegas voters had approved a $5.7 million school bond issue, the highest in Nevada history. Despite this action, classrooms were still overflowing with pupils. For most of the spring 1955 semester, hundreds of students attended half-day sessions until the completion of Rancho High freed up ten additional classrooms in Las Vegas High. And similar logjams afflicted grade school children as well. By 1956, continued population growth required the construction of still another high school, a junior high, and at least two more elementary schools. Yet, despite this construction, continued expansion of the city's resort economy continued to fuel population growth which, in turn, forced more school bond elections.[48]

Actually, there would have been fewer bond issues had sales tax revenues been reserved for schools in the county of origin. Instead, monies went to the state's general fund which the rural counties had the power to tap. The system effectively skewed the state's wealth from Clark and Washoe (Reno) counties where it was most needed. Eventually, this state of affairs drew the wrath of *Review-Journal* editor Al Cahlan, who blamed the local crises in water, education, and other municipal services on the lack of tax revenues for the cities. Rather than advocate higher taxes, Cahlan denounced Nevada's "cow counties" who were siphoning $9,000 per month in revenues from the new 2 percent sales tax for schools out of Clark County to fund rural facilities. Arguing that Clark and Washoe counties together generated over 80 percent of Nevada's sales tax revenues, Cahlan accused the "cows" of getting "what amounts to a free ride" in education.[49]

Rebuffed in his efforts to convince state legislators to leave sales tax revenues in the county of origin, Cahlan next suggested that the state implement the so-called Gorvine Report which had proposed dividing Nevada into five (not seventeen) counties. In his typically booster style, Cahlan insisted that "there is absolutely no valid reason why there should be seventeen separate and distinct counties in a state as sparsely settled as Nevada." For example, Nye and Esmeralda counties, with a combined population of 4,000 people, operated as two distinct governments—a wasteful practice in Cahlan's view—which was costing the taxpayers "a goodly sum each year." The same was true of Lander and Eureka counties and, "in a lesser degree, Pershing and Humboldt." Clearly, Las Vegas, with its rising population, needed a large piece of the educational revenue pie, but Cahlan's reforms were offered in vain—state legislative reapportionment was still a decade away.[50]

In its place, voters approved a series of new bond issues to keep pace with the town's growth. Even though officials built five new schools in 1962 at a cost of $7 million, they were still falling behind because ten thousand new children arrived in town that year. In a January 1963 interview with the *Review-Journal*, new School Superintendent Leland

Newcomer complained that "right now, in what we call the 'slow season' for enrollment, we wake up every Monday morning needing three complete schoolrooms and three teachers to handle the ninety youngsters coming into the system." Obviously if the trend continued, the district would need hundreds more teachers by September—a recruitment problem complicated further by Nevada's well-earned reputation for underpaying teachers. Mindful of Clark County's relatively low salaries, Newcomer noted that "we are competing with places like San Diego, Chicago, St. Louis and other big cities." Then, recognizing the long-term implications of teacher, space, and equipment shortages, he warned that, if not resolved soon, "this emergency will have a tremendous impact on the future economy and general welfare of the entire state."[51]

To meet the crisis, Newcomer urged the community to reform school financing immediately by earmarking part of a property or sales tax increase just for new school construction and teacher salaries. He reinforced this request for higher taxes with figures that graphically demonstrated the fiscal crisis. In 1962, for example, the Clark County School District paid $700,000 just to acquire sites for future schools. Of this amount, over $300,000 bought just the land for Valley High School, which the district proposed to build on Eastern Avenue. The school buildings themselves were also expensive. K. O. Knudson Junior High, for instance, cost $1,266,000, while the smaller Robert E. Lake Grammar School totaled $368,000. Such figures must have impressed voters and politicians who, in the next few years, approved more bond issues and tax increases to fund education. Clearly, Las Vegas's spectacular growth in the 1960s was not without costs. As Newcomer observed, "during the three months [summer vacation] we could build an elementary school a week—and still not meet the needs of the community."[52]

In 1965 the huge construction effort finally bore fruit. Despite a record enrollment of 54,000 youngsters, Superintendent Newcomer was pleased to announce that "for the first time in modern history we'll be on single sessions." Just three years earlier, 12,000 students had been on double sessions, but the addition of seven new grammar schools and two high schools (Clark and Valley) had cut the figure drastically. Thanks to a giant $37 million bond issue in 1964, only a few thousand students at Western High remained on double sessions. Although battles would rage in future years over the costs of new programs, additional schools, and teachers' pay hikes, county residents at least had the school space problem under control by the mid-1960s, until new rounds of population growth would force the adoption of year-round schools beginning in 1973.

Unlike the fragmentation which permeated police, fire, planning, and other municipal services, education won countywide cooperation. Crucial to this triumph was the recognition in the late forties by citizens in Las Vegas and Reno that the formation of county school districts was the only effective way to pool tax bases and abolish overlapping jurisdictions. With their children's education at stake, towns and suburbs throughout southern Nevada discarded their usual provincialism in favor of a metropolitan approach to the problem. On a much smaller scale, the same spirit of cooperation led the cities and county to form the Clark County Public Health District in the early sixties. Ruled by a board comprised of two representatives from each government, the district was charged with maintaining air and water pollution control as well as public clinics and disease prevention programs in the schools and community.[53]

Despite breakthroughs with education, and to a lesser extent police and health, metropolitan government remains weak in the Las Vegas Valley. In this respect, Las Vegas diverges somewhat from the trend in many sunbelt cities, especially places like Miami and Jacksonville where metropolitan government controls planning, building codes, parks, industrial promotion, and other functions. While Miami Beach and its hotel resorts have unsuccessfully opposed the sweeping metropolitan powers wielded by the central city of Miami and its satellite suburbs in Dade County, the Las Vegas Strip has enjoyed much greater success in fending off the central city of Las Vegas. Of course, the great hotels lining Collins Avenue have long held sway with Miami Beach politicians, but the former's overall influence has been limited by the larger metropolitan government in Dade County. On the other hand, the exotic resorts along Waikiki (within the city and county of Honolulu), have played a major role in shaping the taxation, development, and other political agendas for both the city and Oahu as a whole. Still, the county and even the state have exerted significant control over police, fire, hospital, and educational services in the Honolulu metropolitan area. In recent years communities outside of Honolulu, Miami Beach, and even Miami have increasingly enhanced their own power and influence over policymaking. The same has been true also in southern Nevada where the city of Las Vegas suffered similar power losses after 1955, as Henderson, North Las Vegas, Paradise, and Winchester increasingly thwarted Las Vegas's effort to extend regional control. In recent decades the suburbs have even hampered the city's quest for industry by developing their own building and promotion agendas. At the same time, county-based districts and authorities increasingly have controlled policy over the airport, health, flood control, schools, and even conventions. Yet, neither the city of Las Vegas nor a metropolitan government seem likely in the near future to provide the kind of comprehensive public services needed on a valleywide scale.[54]

Nevertheless, there have been joint efforts in flood control, highway planning, and other areas. While there is no doubt that the political fragmentation of the metropolis presented real problems in urban planning and service provision, the fifties and sixties nonetheless witnessed the first serious efforts by city and county authorities in southern Nevada to cooperate on issues of mutual concern. A degree of administrative maturity had been achieved, and the process of metropolitan cooperation had been set in motion.

Civil Rights
in a
Resort City

As it did in cities across the nation, racial divisions ripped Las Vegas apart in the years after 1960. From Selma to Watts, violence shattered the blue-sky, palm-tree complacency of sunbelt living. But riots and marches were especially damaging to a resort town whose glittering image was easily stained by bloodshed and violence. Yet, casino gambling only reinforced postwar segregation, because the tables and slot machines attracted thousands of southern gamblers as well as upwardly mobile eastern, midwestern, and California tourists who would have questioned the presence of black dealers, Hispanic bellmen, and Chinese bartenders. So, to preserve its hard-won image as an all-American vacation town, Las Vegas felt compelled to keep its hotels, casinos, pools, and showrooms "lily white." Racism, however, was not merely a postwar phenomenon; its roots lay deep in the city's past.

The presence of blacks and other minorities dates from the town's first years of settlement. As early as 1905, the railroad employed several black men, Chinese, and Mexicans on its local crews. By 1910, there were just under forty blacks in Las Vegas. Fearful that integrated housing might encourage more minority residence or discourage white interest in the new railroad town, Las Vegas Land & Water Company Vice President Walter Bracken tried to confine blacks to Block 17 (next to the brothels and taverns on Block 16). However, the relative lack of minority residents dampened white interest in residential segregation until the early 1940s. Nevertheless, while early Las Vegas society was relatively fluid and no formal segregationist barriers were erected, there were elements of discrimination. The town's First Methodist Church, for instance, discouraged black membership to the extent that local blacks in 1916 had to form their own Home Mission. The Methodist white minister doubled as the mission's director as well. In addition, early fraternal orders like the Elks, Masons, Eagles, and others restricted their membership to whites.[1]

Gradually, the black population inched up. By 1925, there were about fifty blacks in Las Vegas. Most men were attached to the railroad as porters or repairmen, although a few served as custodians or in other menial capacities. The working women were mostly maids and housekeepers for white families. Even into the 1930s most blacks lived downtown, clustered largely around Block 17, with the rest spread around an 8-block zone bordered by First, Fifth, Ogden, and Stewart streets. Unlike towns in Mississippi, Arizona, and even California, Las Vegas countenanced relatively little segregation except for the brothels on Block 16, the El Portal Theatre, and ultimately the Hoover Dam project. Barred by city and state laws from patronizing local brothels, blacks received their own "colored annex" on Block 16 in 1934 when the city commission granted a license to the Idle Hour Club.[2]

Gambling was a different matter. Following the legalization of the industry in 1931, clubs scrambled for business in a fiercely competitive market. Moreover, many of the casino owners had operated these clubs as taverns prior to 1931 and had regarded local blacks as regular customers. As a result, major Fremont Street establishments like the Northern Club did not begin to discriminate until the late 1930s. The only exceptions were a handful of individual clubs farther out on the Boulder Highway which catered mainly to dam workers (many of whom were southerners). In general, the relative lack of blacks in the county (fifty-eight in 1930 and under two hundred according to the 1940 census) was a major factor in allaying white fears.[3]

While blacks were few, they were not quiescent. Formation of the local chapter of the National Association for the Advancement of Colored People had already occurred in October 1918. As early as 1931, a strain of militancy began emerging after Six Companies adopted an unstated policy of excluding blacks from the Hoover Dam project. This was particularly irksome to black Las Vegans who, like their white counterparts, saw the dam as an opportunity to secure higher-paying jobs. Their frustration led to the formation of the Colored Citizens' Labor and Protective Association of Las Vegas in May 1931. The organization's main goals consisted of desegregating the dam project, while also combating the growing discrimination against black labor in all trades locally.

The dam became an immediate target because it symbolized the nascent segregationist movement in town. At the association's request, Leland Hawkins of the NAACP came to Las Vegas in November 1931 to confer with local officials. Six Companies' continued intransigence eventually prompted several visits from NAACP regional representative William Pickens in early 1932. Anxious to defuse the controversy, Mayor Cragin and other civic leaders transmitted their concerns to Senator Tasker Oddie who, along with the NAACP and the American Bar Association, pressured Interior Secretary Ray Wilbur into forcing a change in the contractor's policy. Finally, in July 1932, the first ten blacks were hired. But it was only a token response; by 1936, only forty-four individual blacks had been employed (a few several times) on the project compared with more than twenty thousand different whites.[4]

In the face of growing white hostility, blacks responded by forming a variety of organizations to knit their local community closer together. In August 1932, for instance, local veterans who were excluded from white veterans' groups formed their own Veterans of Foreign Wars post. Blacks were also active politically, creating their own "colored" Democratic and Republican party clubs. As in other western cities, blacks were barred by charter from participating in white party councils. Following the completion of Hoover Dam, however, the pressure eased, as many white workers moved on to the Pacific Northwest for the Grand Coulee project. Blacks, on the other hand, tended to remain in town, finding employment as porters, maids, and maintenance men in Las Vegas's expanding resort industry. As the city's auto courts and small hotels began to multiply, blacks were welcomed as a source of cheap custodial labor. Their job security was strengthened by the fact that other minorities did not migrate to southern Nevada in large numbers. As late as 1970, neither the Hispanic nor Asian population in Las Vegas exceeded 3,000! California, Arizona, and other western states with large agricultural economies and prosperous cities attracted most of these groups.[5]

Ironically, by the late 1930s, despite their growing importance to the community's infant resort industry, blacks faced more segregationist barriers. Although southern dam workers were gone, tourists (many of them southerners transplanted to California) increasingly expected southern Nevada to mirror the Jim Crow atmosphere of not only Dixie but the rest of the nation. In response, Fremont Street clubs increasingly barred "negroes" from the bars and gaming tables. Although the practice was not universal until World War II, it was widespread enough to prompt black leaders in 1939 to push for a race and color bill in the Nevada assembly to integrate all public accommodations. The measure died in committee after resort owners expressed fears that such a law would discourage out-of-state visitors and threaten the state's precarious economy. In the meantime, blacks now found themselves being denied service not only in hotels, but also in a growing number of restaurants and stores.[6]

As part of the evolving segregationist movement, white townsmen informally supported efforts to move blacks from Fremont Street to the old Westside section across the railroad tracks. Even before 1940, everyone knew that at least for the next two decades, most commercial and residential development would take place primarily east of the railroad lines. As a result, Westside land values had failed to keep pace with the citywide appreciation of real estate. Actually, the old McWilliams' Townsite had assumed a run-down appearance as early as 1905, when the railroad lavished its plat east of the tracks with water, electricity, paved streets, and other capital improvements. Condemned to backwater status, the Westside languished for thirty years as a "ragtown," where poor whites and a few Hispanics crowded into feeble housing often devoid of power, sewerage, and even running water. Throughout the 1930s, the Westside somehow eluded the building boom occasioned by Hoover Dam. Chronically low land values attracted only low-income or parsimonious whites.

Thus, for a town anxious to polish its image by ridding downtown of black residents, the Westside was a perfect solution to the troublesome problem. Increasingly, white Las Vegans added restrictive covenants to property deeds, limiting the sale of housing or land to "members of the Caucasian race." The black migration to the Westside began in the late 1930s and intensified during the war years. Historian Perry Kaufman has reported that Mayor Cragin's administration, in particular, promoted this informal zoning of the Westside after 1943 by refusing to renew the licenses of black-owned businesses downtown unless the proprietors relocated to the Westside. White landlords contributed further to this informal conspiracy by banning black tenants beyond the Westside.[7]

White Westsiders responded quickly to block the forced migration. In 1939, white residents petitioned city hall to limit some Westside lands to the Caucasian race only. In response, R. L. Christensen, president of the Las Vegas Colored Progressive Club, asked the city to deny the motion, which commissioners willingly did in October. Defeated in their efforts to oust the blacks, white Westsiders then demanded in vain that town authorities strictly enforce fire and building codes by prosecuting black violators. No such vigilance was forthcoming, however, because World

War II would bring an unprecedented migration of blacks to work at Basic Magnesium. As a result, white Las Vegas would need the Westside as a dumping ground until BMI built enough black housing in Henderson or until the war ended and the defense workers left town. In the meantime, there would be no effort to enforce health standards which might have forced the re-integration of the town.[8]

Confined to the Westside ghetto, blacks quickly built the foundations of a community. Physically and spiritually united by the growing tide of Jim Crow, blacks patronized their own merchants who now thrived with the trade of a captive market. Overnight, the demand for black barbers, waitresses, and salesgirls boosted the community's economy just as it had in the black, Irish, Jewish, and other ethnic enclaves throughout the country. Also contributing to this prosperity was the surge in black population. Prior to World War II, the local number of blacks was still small; only 178 lived in all of Clark County. This amount accounted for only 1 percent of the county's population. Three years later the Westside's black population exceeded 3,000, thanks to the recruitment efforts of Basic Magnesium. To handle the influx, the Defense Plant Corporation constructed additional housing for blacks near the plant.[9]

Built by the Hammes-Euclemiler Company of Los Angeles, Carver Park eased the Westside housing crunch with 64 dormitory units, 104 one-bedroom, 104 two-bedroom, and 52 three-bedroom apartments and bungalows. But it was not enough. Some workers crowded into a new black shantytown called St. Ann's off the Boulder Highway north of BMI. Most, however, preferred the friendly confines of the Westside. Unfortunately, population growth outpaced new construction, and the wartime shortage of building materials worsened an already desperate housing and sanitary crisis. Lack of dwellings forced workers and their families to live in cars, tents, shacks, and lean-tos. Yet in spite of the squalid conditions, many blacks preferred Nevada to Mississippi, where wages were low and the right to vote little more than a myth. City fathers could have taken steps to equip the 160-acre zone with more running water and toilets, but they did little, preferring instead to await the war's end—an event which they hoped would inspire a prompt black departure.[10]

In the meantime, the influx of black defense workers hardened the segregationist trend. With the exception of the Alabam Club, downtown casinos, clubs, and restaurants banned blacks in hopes of preventing violence and pleasing white customers. Fear of racial clashes was a major concern because, in addition to defense workers, World War II brought many black soldiers to town. Camp Clipper, part of the Desert Training Center south of town, contained several black regiments who frequently came north on weekend passes. Then too, Camp Sibert in Boulder City contained several all-black units charged with guarding Hoover Dam.

In an effort to avoid the racial violence erupting in Detroit and other American towns, the Las Vegas police played an active role in confining black soldiers and defense workers to the Westside and even closing clubs which catered to a "mixed trade." For their part, black leaders, with help from Catholic Charities, organized a USO near the Westside School to service the recreation needs of black troops. Yet, despite these efforts, violence flared. In August 1943, there were several injuries in clashes between black soldiers and police. A riot erupted in January 1944, after a group of black soldiers drinking in the Harlem Club moved out into the streets and eventually wrecked the nearby Brown Derby. One soldier was killed and others were injured when the police moved in. The incident resulted in an order from the West Coast Defense Command putting Las Vegas temporarily "off limits" to servicemen.[11]

Police patrols were almost the only symbols of the city's presence in the Westside. For much of the war, the town largely adopted a hands-off policy with regard to the emerging ghetto. Then, suddenly in the late summer of 1944 as Hitler's forces seemed headed for certain defeat and BMI prepared to shut down, the Cragin administration moved against Westside housing. As part of a "clean-up campaign," the municipality in September bulldozed seventy-five shacks which failed to meet building and fire codes. A few months later in 1945, the city continued its informal urban renewal program by razing another three hundred substandard structures. While the move pleased health reformers, it only promoted more overcrowding in the Westside, because black residents, banned from the Huntridge Addition and other neighborhoods, had nowhere else to live.[12]

Preferring to interpret the government's action as a benevolent effort at slum clearance and renewal and not a ruse to force blacks out of town, Reverend Henry Cooke and a group of residents in August 1945 petitioned Mayor Cragin and city commissioners to pave E Street, the community's main thoroughfare. The mayor, however, refused, claiming that the property's lack of assessed valuation would not cover the costs. Later in February 1946, Cooke again requested public improvements including the installation of fireplugs (there were only 13 for a 72-block area) and street lighting. Cragin again declined, citing low property values, but did promise a public swimming pool so that residents could refresh themselves during the hot summer months. In July 1947 a city pool opened on the Westside which, by the way, now made it possible to exclude "Negroes" from the second public pool about to open in the white section of town. [13] As the segregation and discrimination continued, it was little wonder that black business leaders in 1948 formed the Westside Chamber of Commerce in an effort to promote improvements and investment in the community.

Aside from paved streets and decent housing, the ghetto also lacked other municipal services. There was no fire station until the 1950s, and the community lacked adequate medical care. No private hospital accepted "colored" patients; and while the city facility did, wards were segregated. Moreover, Jim Crow totally dominated the town's grammar schools; black children were forced to attend grade schools in the Westside. Of all government agencies, however, the police department posed the greatest threat. As in other cities, blacks grumbled about police harassment. Incidents were myriad. In February 1945, for instance, the city's lone black officer was suspended after beating a resident unconscious. Reports of other attacks were common, as were complaints about inadequate patrols and manpower. These and other events inspired a second attempt by the Nevada NAACP to secure passage of a comprehensive state civil rights law. But, in 1949 the outcome was the same as in 1939; the bill died in an all-white committee. [14]

While the struggle for equality remained frustrated into the early 1950s, progress was made in the fight to upgrade the Westside's housing conditions. Because of the area's importance as a low-income residential zone for military and defense personnel, the Westside seemed a likely candidate for funding under the 1949 law which gave President Truman's Fair Deal limited financing to build public housing in the nation's ghettos. The Westside's chances were enhanced by a 1949 housing survey which reported that 80 percent of the community's structures were substandard. Many dwellings lacked toilets and some even the basic amenities of running water, power, and gas. In 1950, federal funding was approved, and the city announced plans to build Marble Manor, a complex of 100 rental units on a 20-acre site on the edge of the Westside. Since the land bordered a white subdivision, there was opposition. White residents of nearby Bonanza Village, fearing a loss of property values, protested the plan. After a year of negotiation, the town finally agreed to save a 100-foot-wide buffer highway (Highland Avenue) between the complex and

Bonanza Village. Only then did white opposition wane. Obviously, 100 units did little to solve the minority housing crisis. Black suggestions that officials scatter other projects around the metropolitan area to relieve pressure on West Las Vegas were greeted with the same opposition present in other American cities.[15]

In 1952 Marble Manor finally opened. In a related move, city hall further implemented its long-stated policy of reducing Westside blight when new Mayor C. D. Baker kept a campaign promise made to Westside residents and spent $10,000 to pave B, C, and E streets. The "dust bowl" was finally eliminated in 1955, when rising land values finally justified creation of a $550,000 "paving district" which eventually funded the paving, curbing, guttering, and lighting of all major Westside arteries. Then in 1956, the city planning department extended its slum clearance program by recommending that Interstate 15 be routed through part of the ghetto. By tying urban renewal to the federal freeway, Las Vegas became eligible for federal funding—a move which dampened black opposition to Baker's highway route. In 1959, the commission surveyed the Westside and began Project Madison—a program which cleared 42 acres bordered by Madison School, Van Buren Avenue, H, and J streets. Armed with $577,000 in federal funds (and $188,000 of local matching money), Las Vegas leveled dozens of run-down structures (200 families were displaced), and replaced them with 160 single-family dwellings. Of course, the black population's growth during the four years it took to plan, finance, and build the project easily offset the new housing created.[16]

While public works slowly improved the quality of life on the Westside, the drive for civil rights was less successful. In 1953, blacks, led by members of the Reno and Las Vegas branches of the NAACP, supported another state civil rights bill introduced in the assembly by Las Vegas attorney George Rudiak. The bill fared no better than its predecessors. Undaunted, Las Vegas activists then pushed for a municipal ordinance integrating all public accommodations. Their patience exhausted, black leaders increasingly took an aggressive stance to combat the growing strength of Jim Crow in the metropolitan area.

Aside from discrimination in public places, open housing was suffering new defeats, especially in North Las Vegas. Recent federal laws giving black servicemen the right to integrate off-base housing brought conflicts in air-force towns across the nation, and the Las Vegas area was no exception. On February 4, 1954, a group of North Las Vegas citizens attended a planning commission meeting to protest the integration of several apartment complexes in the Grandview and Williams Fourth additions near Nellis. Using a familiar argument, residents asserted that renting to "negroes" would lower property values. In response, North Las Vegas Planning Commission Chairman Leland McArthur suggested that residents form a "protective association" to threaten developers who rented to blacks. Speaking for the military, Colonel Gabriel Diaz, a Nellis group commander, told the protestors: "It is your problem. In the air force we have no racial segregation. We have our directives and you have your laws." In the long run, the growing federal presence in North Las Vegas eased the prejudice faced by black servicemen. And, while in the interest of maintaining friendly community relations, the military has tended to downplay its effort in this regard, more than once Nellis officials pressured North Las Vegas officials in the fifties and sixties to curb the discrimination and hostility practiced by individual store owners and landlords against black airmen and their dependents.[17]

For local black leaders, these and other events convinced them of the need for municipal ordinances mandating integration. The main effort centered in Las Vegas, where city commissioners rejected a civil rights ordinance partially on the advice of then City Attorney Howard Cannon. In an effort to reverse this stance, local blacks in January 1954 brought in San Francisco lawyer Franklin Williams, an NAACP representative, to press the argument with municipal leaders. In a packed meeting of residents and city commissioners on the Westside, Williams urged Las Vegas leaders to pass a civil rights ordinance. Requesting only the legal authority "to have a cup of coffee or throw a few nickels in the slot machines," Williams reassured uneasy commissioners that "you don't have to sleep with [me] or let me go into your home."

He then attempted to refute a December 1953 opinion by City Attorney Cannon which characterized the government's authority to pass civil rights laws as "confused." Cannon had argued that because Nevada's constitution and statutes did not specifically provide for racial integration of public places, municipal efforts to do so might be unconstitutional. Williams discounted this theory and then, in a prophetic vein, warned town leaders that "Las Vegas is a non-southern city with the pattern of the deep south. There will always be discrimination and race trouble in Las Vegas if the ordinance is not put on the books." In response, Commissioner Reed Whipple wondered loud whether such legislation might not lead to "bloodshed or other trouble"—to which Williams responded: "It's a cut and dried issue. . . . Human rights in the western states are in a vacuum." And they remained in a vacuum, at least in Las Vegas, for another six years until protests and violence brought the reforms Williams had urged. [18]

In the resort city and county, Jim Crow not only afflicted ordinary people but black stars as well. Prior to 1947, black headliners like Eartha Kitt and Lena Horne ate, slept, and gambled at the hotels where they entertained. But, as Las Vegas attracted a larger clientele from the south and east, segregationist barriers rose. Between 1947 and the mid-1950s, top black performers were forced to rent rooms on the Westside. Mrs. G. Harrison, a black landlord, ran one such operation on North F Street, although Mrs. Cartwright's rooming house was the most popular. In a later reminiscence, young Sammy Davis, Jr. (then of the Will Mastin Trio) compared the Las Vegas ghetto to Tobacco Road. Equally disturbing was the landlords' practice of charging performers of their own race exorbitant rates ($15 per night at Cartwright's while the El Rancho was asking $4 for a first-class hotel room). In spite of their disenchantment, nightclub performers like Eddie "Rochester" Anderson (Jack Benny's sidekick), Arthur Lee Simpkins, the Jubilaires, and others remained on the Westside until the mid-1950s. Conditions improved somewhat in 1955 with the opening of the Moulin Rouge, the city's first integrated resort. While black entertainers still wanted to stay on the Strip, at least they were liberated from the rooming houses. Nevertheless, top stars like Nat King Cole and Lena Horne continued to protest and finally, in 1955, the Sands became the first resort to permit black performers to stay at the resort again. [19]

Still, Las Vegas needed a place where all blacks could go. Efforts to provide black soldiers and tourists with an interracial hotel-casino date from 1942 when the Horace Heidt Corporation attempted to open the Shamrock Hotel downtown. Protests from nearby whites combined with the city's emerging Jim Crow policy to deny the hotel an operating permit. This move resulted in an organized march on city hall by several hundred blacks, but town fathers were adamant. Earlier during the war several clubs on the Westside had catered to blacks, including the Harlem Club and the Brown Derby. But the next attempt to open an interracial hotel-casino came almost a decade after V-J Day. By 1950, blacks were welcomed on a regular basis in no casino, even though they totaled over 10 percent of the city's population. To exploit the interracial gambling and entertainment market which everyone knew existed, Will Max Schwartz acquired a parcel of land on West Bonanza Road near the Westside in

1954. After adding several partners including New York restaurateur Louis Ruben and Los Angeles broker Alexander Bismo, Schwartz began building his $3.5 million hotel.[20]

When it opened in 1955, the Moulin Rouge was the only integrated casino-hotel in Las Vegas. It was also the only local resort in a predominantly residential area. In fact, when the project first was being considered by city commissioners in March 1954, Bonanza-area residents, who were mostly white, vehemently opposed its construction. Aside from the race issue, the location of the business within a neighborhood was viewed by many as a dangerous precedent. City commissioners soon discovered that, even with restrictions which forced the resort to set back almost a hundred feet from the road, homeowners were still upset. During the next few decades, city officials would be careful to restrict such places mostly to the casino district downtown.[21]

Despite the protests, Schwartz's hotel opened on May 24, 1955, catering to a mixed clientele. As noted, the integrated hotel finally liberated black stars from the ignominy of Mrs. Cartwright's rooming house. Unfortunately, the respite was only temporary: within seven months, casino losses combined with poor management to force the property into bankruptcy. Sensing a conspiracy, local blacks were quick to blame the closing on white hotel owners and bankers, and even planned a series of protest marches. But there was no conspiracy; mechanics' liens against the property testified to the fact that Schwartz had not secured enough financing originally to pay all the building contractors. Negotiations with creditors dragged on until 1957 when Leo Fry, owner of the LeRoy Corporation (a development company), bought the hotel and re-opened it. Three years later, controversy again engulfed the resort when a white patron, upon discovering that it was management policy to charge whites less for drinks than blacks, prevailed upon the local chapter of the NAACP to fight the price discrimination at city hall.[22]

The hotel which blacks had once revered now became the target of boycotts. Anxious to avoid the adverse publicity of black sit-ins, Mayor Oran Gragson and the city commission voted to revoke Fry's liquor license in 1960 and again in 1961 and 1962 (since that time, bar operations have been maintained on a leased basis). In his defense, Fry contended that he had done nothing wrong, but was rather the victim of black resentment over white ownership of the resort. His argument possessed some validity: segregation or at least racial price discrimination had been countenanced for years throughout the metropolitan area. Whatever the virtues of the case, the Moulin Rouge controversy was significant because it provided local blacks with one of their first forums for organized protests—a precedent for the larger struggles to come.[23]

The key to racial progress was power, and until the 1950s local blacks lacked the numbers and leadership needed to exert political leverage against Nevada's white power structure. Community leadership finally received a valuable boost in 1954 and again in 1956 when the town's first black physician (Dr. Charles West) and dentist (Dr. James McMillan) moved to Las Vegas. They joined with established leaders like David Hoggard, Sr., Woodrow Wilson, Lubertha Johnson, and a collection of black ministers to form a powerful core around which the local NAACP chapter would forge its successful civil rights struggle. Furthermore, thanks to the continued growth of Las Vegas's resorts and restaurants, 16,000 blacks lived in the Westside by 1955. This was significant because, for the first time in their history, Las Vegas blacks had a strong population and political base with which to fight for civil rights.

That campaign began almost immediately. Following the defeat of another civil rights bill in 1957, black leaders redoubled their efforts to strengthen their position in Carson City. Barred by charter from political intervention, the local chapter of the NAACP needed a political arm. In 1957, Drs. West, McMillan, and others formed the Nevada Voters League, an organization capable of delivering black votes to friendly candidates. Beginning in 1958, the group supplied Senate hopeful and converted civil rights advocate Howard Cannon with 1,000 crucial votes in a close election. That same year also saw the group deliver a thousand more to Democratic gubernatorial candidate Grant Sawyer.[24] However, despite these activities and the lukewarm support of some white political leaders, no significant inroads were made against the entrenched position of Jim Crow. Something dramatic had to be done to shatter white complacency.

In early 1960, following receipt of the NAACP's annual letter to local chapters urging an unrelenting effort to smash segregation, McMillan decided to challenge Las Vegas's segregation directly. Discouraged by the cautious approach of Carson City politicians, McMillan wrote a letter to Mayor Oran Gragson on March 11, 1960. In the letter, McMillan threatened massive street protests if downtown and Strip businesses did not cease discriminatory practices by March 26. With the nation already in the midst of a civil rights revolution, McMillan knew that the resort city was especially vulnerable. Threatened marches linking Las Vegas with

Montgomery and Selma would certainly have damaged the town's glittering image and cut tourism. McMillan offered Gragson the carrot and the stick. While claiming that the NAACP intended to pursue integration of public facilities "in an amicable atmosphere," McMillan refused to rule out "passive resistance" if the group's goal was thwarted. Echoing the views of many black Las Vegans, he asserted that "we want the segregation practice dropped for we feel it is the right of all people to patronize these places as long as their conduct is good." The timing of the ploy was perfect. Whatever their feelings about civil rights, hotel executives could not afford the negative publicity. While the city could not control the Strip's response, Gragson wanted to clarify the city's position regarding segregation downtown. To this end, he first called a public meeting because city officials could not legally meet officially behind closed doors. The mayor, however, abruptly canceled the meeting (scheduled for March 23) after some political and business leaders expressed fears that it could become a "fertile ground for hot-headed agitators" and possibly an excuse for violence.[25]

At this point the sequence of events becomes muddled. There are no official minutes of the behind-the-scenes negotiations which took place. Oral histories provided by major participants are contradictory and self-serving. Historian Perry Kaufman has claimed that in a 1972 interview with Dr. McMillan, the latter insisted that he attended a secret meeting with Gragson and City Commissioner Reed Whipple. According to McMillan's account, both men asked the dentist to drop his demands. In return, Whipple, a First National Bank executive, allegedly agreed to cease redlining the Westside. It was well known that the bank had granted few home loans or mortgages to the zone. So, Whipple, if he ever made such a concession, was offering a substantial economic boost. But, according to Kaufman, McMillan rejected all deals. Gragson and Whipple themselves subsequently denied that such a meeting ever took place.

Nonetheless, an agreement was reached somehow. Word came on March 26 that the city would order the integration of all public places within municipal borders and the Strip would voluntarily follow suit. At 6 p.m., McMillan's deadline, segregation barriers came down for the first time since World War II, and a major crisis was averted. McMillan then canceled the threatened sit-in march on March 26 following a meeting in the office with Mayor Gragson and Clark County Commissioners Clesse, Turner, and Olson. As an additional part of the settlement, the men agreed to form the Southern Nevada Human Relations Committee where representatives of the black community, the police, government, and business could discuss problems of mutual concern. Within days, an ebullient McMillan reported that approximately 90 percent of area hotels and casinos had already heeded the agreement and integrated—a satisfactory compliance rate at the time. Subsequent NAACP efforts would focus on securing a comprehensive state civil rights law to bring all businesses into compliance and end job and housing discrimination.[26]

First-term Governor Grant Sawyer was clearly sympathetic to the black cause, but he lacked the legislative support in 1961 to secure anything more than creation of an equal rights commission to advise the governor about civil rights problems in the state. Black hopes soon turned to scorn, though, once the commission's impotence became obvious. During a January 1962 investigation by the newly created Nevada Equal Rights Commission, hotel executives denied they had engaged in job discrimination against minority applicants. Although the hotels conceded that they employed no black dealers, waitresses, waiters, bellmen, or office personnel, and only a "scattering of Orientals," they attributed the situation to the absence of qualified non-Caucasian applicants. While the lack of black casino workers could conceivably be attributed to lack of experience, hotelmen were hard-pressed to prove that blacks were not qualified to be waiters, waitresses, and bellmen. Pressed by commission members for statistics on past hiring practices, the hotels uniformly argued that they had never kept records relating to job discrimination based on race, creed, or national origins. However, at the commission's request, executives of the Hacienda, Flamingo, and other hotels promised to collect the statistics. On the other hand, Sam Boyd of the Mint and Charles King of the Golden Nugget flatly refused. Worse still, Ed Levinson of the Fremont Hotel and officials of the Sal Sagev downtown never even accepted the commission's invitation to appear.[27]

Subsequent testimony in January 1963 revealed that most Strip hotels employed less than 20 percent non-Caucasians and they were relegated entirely to positions as maids, porters, kitchen help, and busboys; only the Riviera had two black bartenders. In response, Major Riddle of the Dunes attributed this policy to customer prejudices, observing that "four or five years ago, there would have been considerable customer opposition to negroes in [restaurant and casino] positions," but, he concluded, "things are changing." This sense of optimism was immediately challenged by NAACP activist James Anderson who demanded that Riddle and other Strip executives end the traditional "pattern of employment" in the upcoming summer hiring session.[28]

Since these and other hearings produced no reform, black frustration soon turned to anger. Tempers flared as early as January 1962 between Las Vegas black leaders and white officials in the state government friendly to the civil rights cause. On January 26, Nevada Attorney General Roger Foley denounced one "troublemaker" in the black community who had written to U.S. Attorney General Robert Kennedy making "irresponsible accusations" about Foley's supposed laxity in prosecuting civil rights violations. Las Vegas Baptist Minister Prentiss Walker allegedly wrote the letter in which he criticized both Foley and liberal Democratic Governor Grant Sawyer. Foley unofficially advised Walker and other black leaders against attacking the liberal white power structure in Carson City, and suggested instead that blacks focus their efforts on convincing the state Gaming Control Commission to consider making a casino's denial of civil rights grounds for immediate license revocation. Foley then shifted the burden to the legislative branch of government, asserting that the "only answer to the lack of civil rights in Nevada will come when the state legislature has enough guts to pass an effective law."[29]

Within a month the blacks had followed Foley's advice. In February 1962, the Reverend Donald Clark, president of the coordinating council of all Nevada NAACP chapters, provided Governor Sawyer with the wording to amend state gaming regulations to prohibit discrimination in hiring, service, or accommodations in gaming establishments. In addition, Clark sought the governor's support for a stronger state civil rights law in the next legislature. Clark, who was current president of the Las Vegas chapter of the NAACP, applied further pressure on Sawyer by threatening to sue in federal court if no positive state action was forthcoming. Referring to numerous cases of alleged hiring discrimination against black applicants for dealing and cocktail-waitress jobs, Clark insisted that "the responsibility is Governor Sawyer's. He is head of the state; I hope he will be as liberal in action as he is in conversation." Clark knew that Las Vegas and Nevada wanted no adverse national publicity, and hoped in vain that white leaders would move quickly to end job discrimination.[30]

Finally in March 1962, after a series of fruitless meetings with Sawyer to discuss the weaknesses of the state's 1961 civil rights law, Reno and Las Vegas–area blacks grew strident. In a sometimes stormy 3-hour meeting with the governor, fifteen black representatives denounced the impotence of the newly created state Equal Rights Commission, and urged Sawyer to intervene personally against racial discrimination by invoking his executive powers. Specifically, they wanted the governor to order the state Gaming Control Commission to revoke the license of any casino found guilty of discrimination. Sawyer responded that the Equal Rights Commission should be the state's main advocate of civil rights. Conceding that the commission "hasn't perhaps been as aggressive as it should have been," the governor nevertheless insisted that it was still a vigorous body—to which Las Vegas black attorney Charles Kellar angrily retorted: "It's been so vigorous that it hasn't even met. Or maybe it met once—when you greeted them." Encouraged by Attorney General Foley's view that the Gaming Control Commission could theoretically enforce casino adherence to a civil rights code, Reverend Clark again asked Sawyer to intercede. The governor instead urged the blacks themselves to approach the panel, and once again reiterated his confidence in the Equal Rights Commission's ability to combat discrimination.[31]

As Kellar and the other black attorneys knew, the Gaming Control Commission lacked the power to pressure the Control Board. For months the commission had failed to compel four Golden Gate Casino executives to testify about charges of job discrimination at their establishment. Blacks therefore ignored the commission and instead pressed for changes in gaming regulations. Sawyer was cautiously supportive, advising black leaders to seek a declaratory judgment from the courts as to whether the gaming commission had civil rights power. Foley, however, argued that the courts would only rule if the gaming commission, in a specific case, revoked a casino's license for race bias. Foley's view was vindicated a week later when the commission rejected black demands to become involved, claiming that it lacked both the power and staff to pursue racial discrimination cases. This rebuff, in turn, forced the NAACP to launch a new campaign for a comprehensive state civil rights law.[32]

Despite the integration of public places, most Las Vegas blacks in 1963 still could not live outside the ghettos, or attend grammar schools in white sections of town, or qualify for more than a menial job in most Strip and downtown resorts. As tensions mounted in the black community, Charles Kellar and other black leaders cooperated with their Reno counterparts and sympathetic whites in a determined effort to pass a new state civil rights act during the 1965 legislative session. In March 1965, with the help of freshman assemblyman Mel Close, Jr. (Democrat from Las Vegas), the campaign resulted in passage of A.B. 404, which outlawed discrimination on the basis of race, color, or creed in public accommodations and employment in places with fifteen or more workers. The bill's future was less promising in the rural-dominated senate. In an effort to pressure the body, civil rights advocates organized a massive show of support. As Bishop Robert Dwyer threw the support of the Roman Catholic diocese behind the measure, an optimistic Bill Bailey, chairman of the state Equal Rights Commission (and a Las Vegas television personality), called for mass demonstrations of support in Carson City.[33]

Anxious to demonstrate support, Protestant clergy from around the state joined with priests, nuns, and laity to organize a prayer vigil near the capitol. On March 13, Las Vegas blacks joined other Nevadans in the rally which heard both Governor Sawyer and Lieutenant Governor Paul Laxalt speak in behalf of the bill. Following this, Las Vegas–area clergymen from the Methodist, Episcopal, and Congregationalist churches (along with other denominations) wired their support of the bill to Carson City. This collective effort was rewarded finally on March 30, 1965, when the state senate approved the bill by a 12 to 4 margin, with Clark County Senator B. Mahlon Brown (the majority leader) and Lincoln County senator Floyd Lamb (later a prominent Las Vegas politician and Mormon) voting for the measure. While somewhat stronger than the federal civil rights act of 1964, the Nevada legislation still lacked an open-housing provision. Nevertheless, following passage, an exuberant Governor Sawyer told reporters that he now expected the Equal Rights Commission to provide an "active enforcement of the law and vigorous programs in defense of individual freedom."[34]

The celebrations were premature. Despite the strongly worded law, many downtown and Strip hotels continued to discriminate against blacks in employment. In April 1967, blacks staged a peaceful protest outside various resorts, but to no avail. Protest turned to militancy in early May when NAACP attorney Charles Kellar blamed the local culinary union and its secretary-treasurer, Al Bramlet, for failing to push the employment of black members. In a tersely worded statement, Kellar threatened to "cut the union down to size" by asking the National Labor Relations Board to decertify it as the hotel workers' official bargaining agent. Then, in a conciliatory move, he met with representatives of both the union and the Nevada Resort Association "to find out where the onus lies." Unwilling to compromise, Kellar demanded that more black waiters and waitresses be employed in the showrooms where tips were high, and that employees of the Desert Inn's all black-staffed Skillet Room be reassigned immediately to the hotel's other dining areas. Discussions were cordial but, from Kellar's point of view, fruitless. In the summer of 1967, Kellar appealed to the new Republican Governor Paul Laxalt for help. Laxalt was receptive and helped arrange a conference at Valley High School in early November. The day-long program of speeches and workshops featured addresses by James Farmer, the national director of Congress for Racial Equality, and several other prominent leaders, including an opening address by the governor himself.[35]

This conference had been preceded by a series of largely unproductive meetings on the Westside between concerned black and white officials. Typical was an August session at the West Owens Shopping Center attended by Henderson Mayor W. R. Hampton, North Las Vegas Police Chief Nick Janise, Las Vegas Police Lieutenant Richard Dunn, and such prominent black leaders as Dr. Charles West, Mrs. Lubertha Johnson (Director of Operation Independence, a major anti-poverty agency), and Joe Neal (an equal opportunity compliance officer for Reynolds Electric, and Nevada's first black state senator). White officials again felt the sting of black anger, as Reverend Clark and others complained loudly about white apathy toward festering Westside problems. As Clark angrily told state Equal Rights Commission Chairman William Deutsch: "You are nothing but a buffer. Why isn't the power structure here? Where is the mayor? . . . the Governor? . . . the county commissioners?" Despite the lack of progress and promises, talks continued into the fall of 1967. There was perhaps one bright spot. To its credit, the Las Vegas Police Department worked with black community leaders in placing greater emphasis upon minority group problems during police training and in developing a better community relations program on the Westside. But these reforms, while beneficial, did not remove the underlying cause of black unrest: segregated schools, housing, and employment.[36]

Continued job discrimination eventually forced the blacks to act. In November 1967, the Clark County NAACP, led by its attorney and now president Charles Kellar, filed a complaint with the National Labor Relations Board in San Francisco against the local culinary and teamsters unions as well as eighteen hotels in the Las Vegas area. As Kellar explained to reporters, "negotiations with union officials have been absolutely futile. They were so secure in their bailiwick they felt nothing could touch them. They'll soon learn otherwise." Specifically, Kellar's complaint charged the unions with "failing to place (blacks) in other but menial positions; [and] failing to upgrade them by selecting certain positions which are considered for whites only." The hotels, in turn, were charged with engaging in "unfair labor practices," discrimination in hiring, training, promotion, payment of wages (black employees were often paid less for the same work), and overtime.[37]

While the NLRB investigated Kellar's complaints, there was no immediate federal action. In the meantime, evidence mounted supporting the black position. An April 1968 report by the state League of Women Voters acknowledged that the 1965 civil rights act had opened public places to nonwhites, but criticized continued discrimination in employment and housing. As the report noted, "non-whites are beginning to be employed in stores and other consumer services, but most non-white employment remains in menial labor." The league also called for open housing and integrated schools "particularly in Las Vegas, where six Las Vegas elementary schools are wholly segregated because of housing." Again, Kellar and the local NAACP applied pressure in the form of peaceful protest marches around various hotels during the NAACP's southern California regional convention in Las Vegas. White leaders were unimpressed. In fact, both Governor Laxalt and Mayor Gragson privately urged Kellar to cancel the action, which he obdurately refused to do. Over the next few months, continued white foot dragging over discrimination against blacks only raised Westside tensions. Instances of discrimination were myriad. In November 1967, Nevada Equal Rights Commission Chairman William Laub reported the case of one black minister who had gone downtown to buy a piano for his church. He was stopped and spread-eagled against his car by Las Vegas police, called a "nigger" and warned that he was "not supposed to be on this side of town." Laub cited other examples: a black teacher who could not rent an apartment in white Las Vegas for eight months; a black college graduate offered only menial jobs—the stories abounded.[38]

Inevitably, black frustration turned to anger and then violence, as it already had in thirty-seven other American cities. The initial trouble brewed in the town's high schools all through January of 1969. Finally on January 23, a minor fracas broke out at Rancho High School, but was quickly ended by North Las Vegas police. Tipped off about potential violence, officers equipped with riot helmets, mace, and nightsticks arrived on campus an hour earlier and had no trouble quelling the disturbance. The next day, school officials joined with black and white student leaders in a series of discussions aimed at defusing the situation. Despite this effort, unrest spread to other schools. On Monday, January 27, a disturbance at Las Vegas High School began after several whites tossed a black student through a trophy case. School District officials blamed the incident partially on the presence of three news reporters and a KRAM radio announcer who were interviewing students at the scene.[39]

On the following day, in an effort to control the situation, county school chief Dr. James Mason banned the public and media from all school campuses in the metropolitan area. Two days later, violence spread to Clark High School when a three-hour "sit-in type meeting" by black students triggered a "wild melee" of "near riot proportions" involving over a thousand students. Mason closed the school temporarily and accused the newly formed Afro-American Club of fomenting the trouble. The club, a black power group comprised mostly of young blacks between the ages of 18 and 25, was led by Francis Edwards, an employee of the federally funded Equal Opportunity Board. In his assessment, Mason characterized the violence as premeditated and "part of the total racial picture that has been developing in the area high schools for more than a week." Determined to re-open the school, Mason insisted that "we will not tolerate any more of these disturbances and any students, black or white, who create trouble, will be dealt with to the fullest extent of both school rules and the law." The school chief also banned sit-ins and promised that future disturbances "would be put down by force and students would be expelled."[40]

Despite his stance, Mason was somewhat conciliatory; after a three-hour session with the dissident Afro-American Club's leaders, he agreed to grant a blanket amnesty to all youngsters involved in the Clark riot. On Monday, February 3, Las Vegas–area high schools re-opened with all but Valley High requesting large police contingents. Parents, teachers and community leaders urged a peaceful return to class. Supporting this effort was *Las Vegas Sun* editor Hank Greenspun, who, while championing the civil rights cause, urged an end to violence. In an obvious reference to Selma, Watts, and Detroit, he reminded readers that "Las Vegas is one of the few areas in the nation that accomplished integration, upgrading of jobs, and wider participation on all levels. And it has been done with few protests, minimal marches, and no violence." Insisting that "no school kid, white or black, should be terrorized or tyrannized at any time," Greenspun concluded that "just as we could not permit any extremist groups to gain a foothold, be they Minutemen, Ku Kluxers—or even John Birchers, so must we discourage black groups that advocate hatred and violence." And this view was basically echoed by the other opinion makers and community leaders.[41]

But the violence did not end. By early October 1969, trouble spread to the streets of the Westside. On October 6, gang-related assaults sent twenty-three people to the hospital, as two hundred Las Vegas police officers, supplemented by a force from the county sheriff's office, struggled to restore order. As tensions mounted, a concerned Governor Paul Laxalt reluctantly put the Nevada National Guard on alert. In the meantime, Las Vegas police took steps to quiet the situation. A 7 p.m. curfew in the ghetto at first helped preserve an uneasy peace. But the next day saw two whites assaulted by black youths at the Golden West Shopping Center at H and Owens streets. A commuter bus carrying Nevada Test Site workers was pelted with rocks as it passed nearby. Fires were set along H and J streets and rocks were thrown at responding firemen. By afternoon, Las Vegas Fire Chief Jerry Miller refused to send his crews to minor blazes and sheriff's deputies stood at Highland (today Martin Luther King Boulevard) and Washington avenues, armed with shotguns, tear gas, and pepper fog guns, awaiting city police calls for assistance. As the afternoon wore on, police sealed off the Westside and fired tear gas into groups of black teenagers in efforts to disperse them. Police sharpshooters positioned themselves atop the Golden West Shopping Center to discourage snipers.

Looting continued throughout the day at the nearby Wonder World Department Store, Western Auto, Dairy Queen, and several liquor stores. A Mexican man, an elderly test site worker, and other whites were beaten by gangs of black youths. As the violence spread southward to Bonanza Road, police ordered the closing of all Westside gas stations by 8 p.m. to discourage the making of fire bombs. Scattered disturbances continued into the night and for the next few days while police and community leaders (including the NAACP and church officials) worked feverishly to restore order. As was the case in Watts, Detroit, and elsewhere, while older blacks took little part in the violence, they played an active role in ending it.[42]

Following the unrest, black and white civic and political leaders met for days to prevent a recurrence. Yet, despite weeks of negotiations, there was no significant progress made with regard to open housing, school desegregation, job discrimination, and other festering problems. As a result, violence erupted again. A two-day "rumble" in late November 1969 at Western High ended in ten arrests, six injuries, and the school's indefinite closure. The melee involved over two hundred students and brought more than a hundred lawmen to the campus. Following the Western incident, police again were stationed at all area high schools. Their presence hardly deterred violence in the streets. Within a week, trouble gripped nearby Vegas Heights when a Las Vegas Transit bus hit a fourteen-year-old black youth. While the driver was later exonerated, passing buses were pelted with rocks, forcing the company to suspend service. This action only heightened tensions, because many black residents commuted by bus to their hotel jobs downtown and on the Strip. Nevertheless, Las Vegas Transit refused to run buses through the black and Hispanic community without a police escort. But the hard-pressed Las Vegas police demurred. As Assistant Chief John Moran explained: "we don't have the manpower to birddog buses through the neighborhood. It might have a deterrent effect if we did. Then again, they throw rocks at police cars, too." In the end, bus service resumed on a daytime basis and later, after considerable pressure from the city commission, at night.[43]

While the town was relatively quiet for the next few months, the continued lack of reform only triggered more unrest. In February 1970, violence resulting from a race-related assault following a Clark–Las Vegas High basketball game, led to a bloody melee which briefly closed Las Vegas High. Then in May 1970, nearly seventy-five students at the school, angered by the defeat of black candidates in a student election, went on a rampage. Actually, the fracas was the school's third of the year, although the others had been relatively minor. This incident, however, touched off other disturbances around town. The biggest trouble spot was again Rancho High, where over three hundred students were involved in a pipe-swinging brawl which sent nine pupils to the hospital. For the first time in Las Vegas history, police had to use mace after Rancho teachers sprayed dozens of students with fire hoses in a valiant effort to quell the violence. The Rancho riot was the worst single-day school disturbance during the entire civil rights movement in Las Vegas. It was followed the next day by another incident which saw fifty black students arrested for throwing books in the library and refusing to attend class. Beleaguered school board officials, anxious to end the cycle of violence, finally acted upon one longtime black demand, announcing plans to hire thirty more black teachers and ordering district recruiters to go as far east as Atlanta, if necessary, to get them.[44]

Following this concession, Charles Kellar and others pushed for school integration as well, but district officials neatly sidestepped this issue by singing the praises of their own "voluntary" busing plan. Actually, the struggle for school integration in Las Vegas had begun earlier in 1968 and played an undeniable role in helping to ignite black student riots. A school survey conducted in January 1968 revealed that while all junior and senior high school blacks were bused to white schools, most elementary pupils were not. The survey, required by the federal government for district funding under the Elementary and Secondary School Act of 1965, also reported a dramatic lack of minority teachers. Over 2,544 whites held teaching positions in the district, while 134 blacks, 25 Hispanics, 5 "Orientals," and 2 Native Americans accounted for the rest—this despite the fact that over 3,000 blacks alone attended local schools. Even in secretarial and custodial positions the whites dominated, claiming 1,143 of the 1,338 jobs in the district. While school authorities seemed pleased with the distribution, black Las Vegans were not. School segregation would eventually team with job discrimination and closed housing to trigger the bloody riots of 1969–70.[45]

Following a strategy session at the NAACP national convention in Boston in July 1967, Las Vegas Chapter President Charles Kellar filed suit in federal district court in May 1968 to integrate Las Vegas–area schools. Kellar's move came in response to the implacable position of Clark County School District trustees that six all-black elementary schools in the Westside were not segregated but merely "neighborhood schools," reflecting the residential segregation of Las Vegas. While Kellar recognized that school segregation resulted from the town's lack of open housing, he was not content to wait for housing reform. Citing the epic *Brown v. Board of Education of Topeka* decision of 1954 which asserted that separate education instilled feelings of inferiority in black students, Kellar insisted that, after fourteen years of foot-dragging, Clark County school officials integrate every classroom. To this end, he successfully argued before Federal District Court Judge Bruce Thompson of Reno that West Las Vegas's elementary schools were unconstitutionally segregated. In both this original decision and subsequent rulings, Thompson agreed with Kellar's view.[46]

In the spring of 1969 two local groups entered the fray, proposing their own integration plans. An antibusing organization, Parents Who Care, offered a scheme which involved some voluntary busing, but not enough to threaten the status quo. On the other hand, the Las Vegas Valley League of Women Voters suggested a more radical formula which would have ended the all-black classes in West Las Vegas. For its part, the school district pledged to obey the judge's ruling by implementing a voluntary integration plan for a trial run during the 1969–70 school year. The district offered to convert C. V. T. Gilbert Elementary School into a so-called prestige school by lowering teacher-student ratios and establishing a variety of remedial and advanced educational programs. During that year the district bused 300 white children to Gilbert, while 940 black elementary students were transported to white schools. All of the pupils who participated did so on a voluntary basis; those white grammar school students who refused to attend the integrated Gilbert School were allowed to remain in their neighborhood facility. In August 1970, Judge Thompson, though unhappy with the relatively small number of volunteers, reluctantly approved the program for a second year.[47]

Thousands of white parents, however, continued to reject the busing option. His hand now strengthened by white resistance, Kellar once again assailed the district's plan, demanding instead the complete integration of Las Vegas–area schools through busing. In December 1970 Thompson concurred, ordering the district to implement a mandatory integration plan by September 1971. The court left the exact details to school officials, but mandated that no more than 50 percent of the pupils in any class be black. While hoping that the United States Supreme Court might yet water down the Brown decision in a series of upcoming cases, the school district explored a variety of busing options. In a series of open meetings, trustees solicited suggestions from the community at large. Proposals were myriad: lotteries, the creation of seventh-grade centers, and kindergarten centers topped the list. After lengthy deliberations, trustees in April chose the so-called sixth grade centers plan, which would send all sixth grade students in the Las Vegas area to schools or centers in West Las Vegas. At the same time, every black youngster attending first through fifth grades in segregated Westside schools would be bused to white areas.[48]

Clearly, district officials embraced the plan with a marked lack of enthusiasm. Within weeks, the district's legal counsel, Robert Petroni, appeared again before Judge Thompson arguing that court-ordered integration was valid only in those school districts (mostly in the southern United States) where segregation had been mandated by law. But Thompson disagreed. White parents then tried changing the judge's mind by forming a "Bus-Out" group, and staging a one-day boycott of classes in May 1971. Despite the absence of 17,000 white students from area schools, Thompson, in a June 1971 ruling, reiterated his support for the NAACP's position that the sixth grade plan was the only effective solution to segregation. In a conciliatory move, he agreed to delay implementation until the Ninth District Court of Appeals in San Francisco had time to rule on the school district's appeal of his decision.[49]

So, the full-scale integration of Las Vegas–area schools was again delayed, but not for long. In November 1971, a three-judge panel of the Ninth Circuit Court heard Petroni's appeal but voted unanimously to uphold Judge Thompson's decision. Again, district trustees refused to give up, ordering Petroni to ask for a new hearing before all nine justices of the circuit court. In February 1972 this effort failed when every judge voted to reject the district's petition. Still, the school board clung to hope that the Nixon administration would act to weaken court-ordered busing. Their expectations rose in June 1972 when the president signed a law (endorsed by Nevada's congressional delegation) allowing school districts in the midst of appeals to delay court-ordered busing. A relieved board of trustees now planned to scuttle Thompson's program and return to the old Gilbert prestige school plan. But in August, the Las Vegas League of Women Voters petitioned Judge Thompson to hold the trustees in contempt of court and once again order the implementation of the sixth grade center plan. While not agreeing to hold the trustees in contempt, Thompson ordered immediate integration.[50]

In response, Bus-Out attorney Tad Porter appeared on September 1 before Las Vegas District Court Judge Carl Christensen, and asked for a preliminary injunction against busing. Christensen not only agreed, but delayed his ruling until September 5, the first day of school. This, in turn, forced new school superintendent Kenny Guinn to postpone all classes until the jurisdictional dispute had been resolved. In subsequent hearings both Thompson and Christensen stood their ground. As a result, the area's fifty-two elementary schools remained closed for nine days until Nevada Supreme Court Justice David Zenoff issued a stay against Christensen's injunction and set a hearing for October 9. In the interim, the state supreme court ordered the schools to open under Judge Thompson's plan.[51]

In the meantime, members of Bus-Out and Parents for Neighborhood Schools collected 30,000 signatures throughout the Las Vegas metropolitan area supporting congressional action to outlaw busing. When Las Vegas elementary schools finally opened on September 18 (the town's high schools had always been integrated and therefore had opened on September 5), absenteeism was high. While some sixth grade centers, like Kermit Booker, counted over 70 percent of their projected enrollment, others, like Jo Mackey, saw a 90 percent absentee rate. Bus-Out supporters, determined to thwart forced integration, created special Bus-Out schools for white sixth graders in secret locations around Las Vegas. Even though Bus-Out support waned by early October, school authorities nevertheless conceded that several hundred white sixth graders still were not attending regular classes.[52]

This situation finally changed in November when district officials, determined to enforce Thompson's orders (which the state supreme court ultimately upheld), warned Bus-Out parents that their covert schools were unaccredited and that no child attending such classes would be admitted to the district's seventh grade classes the following fall. This firm stand by the trustees and superintendent Kenny Guinn broke the back of the Bus-Out movement. Guinn subsequently appointed a black man, Dr. Claude Perkins, as his administrative assistant and supported the hiring of the system's first black counselors. So, after four years of litigation and grim determination, the NAACP, with help from the League of Women Voters and other concerned whites, had won the battle to integrate Las Vegas schools.[53]

Sweet as it was, this victory comprised only part of the larger battle for civil rights which raged on several fronts simultaneously. Unlike the school fight, the campaign against job discrimination in Las Vegas was more than ten years old. As noted earlier, the 1965 state civil rights law had not ended job bias against blacks on the Strip or downtown, although continuous pressure from the NAACP coupled with adverse publicity generated by the schools and Westside riots of 1969–70 had sensitized hotel executives to the need for some reform. Moreover, the hotels had to counteract charges of job bias from an increasingly vigilant state Equal Rights Commission. In January 1970, the Nevada Resort Association (a group which represented most of the town's large hotels) offered an eight-point plan to promote the hiring of blacks for nonmenial jobs in the resorts. Provisions included closer policing of personnel hiring practices, enrollment of hotel supervisors in the University of Nevada's "Minority Employment" workshops, increased funding for black trainee programs, and an outright grant of $75,000 to the local NAACP chapter for the purpose of "stimulating motivation for the training within the minority community." While the effort was a positive step, the amount of black employment in higher-paying hotel jobs continued to lag far behind black expectations.[54]

Continued intransigence by the resort industry and its unions ultimately forced the Las Vegas chapter of the NAACP to take the matter to federal court. The five-year battle to obtain a strong state civil rights law and the six-year struggle to enforce it had convinced Charlie Kellar and other black leaders of the futility of pursuing job equality through state and local channels. Throughout 1970 Kellar made it increasingly clear that he considered job bias to be a violation of the federal Civil Rights Act of 1964. At this point, the hotels and unions, anxious to avoid more adverse publicity for Las Vegas and fearful of losing in federal court, finally entered into meaningful negotiations with black leaders. On June 4, 1971, the NAACP filed its complaint with now Judge Roger Foley of the U.S. Federal District Court in Las Vegas, detailing the familiar charges of bias practiced by various unions and hotels on the Strip and downtown. On the same day, the hotels and unions signed a consent decree pledging to end all discriminatory practices.[55]

The struggle for open housing was similarly difficult and drawn out. As late as 1970, over 22,000 of the 24,760 blacks in the Las Vegas SMSA lived in the Westside, Vegas Heights, or in the other scattered enclaves within the cities of Las Vegas and North Las Vegas. The industrial city of Henderson counted 15,700 whites but only 570 blacks, while Boulder City's population of 5,195 contained only two blacks. Residential segregation was particularly blatant in the opulent suburbs surrounding Las Vegas. To the east, Sunrise Manor hosted 10,554 whites in 1970 but only 125 blacks. Worse still were the Strip suburbs of Paradise (23,887 whites and 174 blacks) and Winchester (13,755 and 46). In a resort city like Las Vegas, racial segregation not only dominated the hotels and casinos but also the suburbs spawned by the Strip economy itself. Aside from the central city ghettos, the only area in the valley where blacks were numerous was Nellis Air Force Base where 559 black airmen lived with 5,726 others.[56]

Black leaders were determined to alter the trend. Their campaign in Las Vegas began in 1965 immediately following the state legislature's deliberate omission of open housing provisions in the new civil rights act. The controversial law awarded white homeowners a "bill of rights" permitting them to sell to whomever they wished. In March 1967, Las Vegas and Reno-area NAACP leaders tried and failed to convince state legislators to pass an open housing law. A full-scale effort in 1969 was again thwarted. This time a division arose between black assemblyman Woodrow Wilson (Democrat from Las Vegas) and his female colleagues Eileen Brookman (Democrat from Las Vegas) and Mary Frazzini (Republican from Reno) who wanted to add the word "sex" to the "race, religion or national origins" section of the fair housing bill. While conceding that single women faced discrimination from landlords, banks, and mortgage companies, Wilson nevertheless opposed the change, insisting that "if we put sex in it, the bill will get shot down." Although Wilson eventually won his point, the bill was still defeated. Despite the professed support of Governor Paul Laxalt, conservative lawmakers (inspired perhaps by the high-pressured lobbying of Howard Hughes) killed the bill.[57]

Victory finally came two years later in 1971, when, under the threat of

federal court action, the Nevada legislature approved legislation effectively ending residential segregation in Las Vegas and Reno. Under a
strong open housing law, the black and Hispanic population of Las Vegas
slowly began to filter out of their traditional confines in the Westside and
Vegas Heights, but not as fast as one might expect in all areas. The
number of blacks in Henderson rose by only 10 between 1970 and 1980.
In Boulder City progress was also meager (2 to 31). The city of Las Vegas
itself witnessed a large increase (14,802 to 21,054) as did North Las
Vegas (8,785 to 16,115). Like Memphis, Houston, and other sunbelt
SMSAs, the Las Vegas metropolitan area has witnessed an outflux of
blacks to the suburbs. Paradise Township, for instance, saw its black
population jump from 174 in 1970 to 2,956 ten years later, although
Winchester's (465 to 625) increase was less spectacular. Hispanic movement to the suburbs was even more dramatic. In 1960, only 236 Spanish-
speaking residents lived in the city of Las Vegas and 578 in the SMSA.
Ten years later, thanks to Mexican immigration and Fidel Castro's closure of Havana's casinos, the figures had jumped to 3,871 and 9,937,
respectively—with most Latinos either in Las Vegas or North Las Vegas.
By 1980, however, the former's Hispanic population exceeded 12,000
with another 4,800 in North Las Vegas and over 2,100 in Henderson.
Since many were attracted to casino and hotel jobs on the Strip, the easing
of discriminatory practices spurred an outflux to Paradise (5,902) and
Winchester (1,459) where few Cubans, Mexicans, or Filipinos had lived
in 1970. The Nellis job zone also raised Sunrise Manor's Latino population from a few hundred in 1970 to 4,199 a decade later. While in some
areas, minority gains have been minimal, overall the outmigration since
1970 has been significant. Figures from the 1990 census will probably
support the recent argument of Carl Abbott, suggesting that the suburbanization of minorities since 1970 is probably more rapid in newer,
sunbelt cities than in their frostbelt counterparts. Thanks to open housing
and fair employment practices, many young Las Vegas blacks and Hispanics have moved into the elegant townhouse and condominium communities springing up in Winchester and Paradise, as well as the fashionable
single-family home developments stretching to the south and far west of
the Strip.[58]

It has been suggested by a number of observers that, prior to 1970, Las
Vegas was the "Mississippi of the West." Despite the foregoing events,
this conclusion seems a bit overdrawn. While Las Vegas was certainly no
bastion of equality, it was no worse a town for blacks than Phoenix, Salt

Lake, and most medium-sized cities in California. Indeed, segregated housing, schools, and job discrimination were common throughout the mid-twentieth-century west. So too was the rippling effect of the national civil rights movement.[59]

In Las Vegas, as elsewhere in the region, the drive for equality helped change the political climate to benefit other minorities, especially women. Unlike the Reno-Tahoe areas, Las Vegas traditionally had few women dealers. Except for the wives of a few small club owners and a brief interlude during World War II, no women dealers worked regularly on the Strip or downtown until the 1970s. True, the Santa Anita and Monte Carlo Clubs hired a few women dealers in the 1950s, but other casinos did not follow their lead. Moreover, only one dealer's school in town even allowed women to enroll.[60]

The city of Las Vegas only encouraged the trend when commissioners passed a resolution on November 5, 1958, recommending that casinos not hire women dealers. The action resulted from complaints by male dealers that some casinos were hiring women for $15 per day while the male rate was $25. The men obviously saw the trend as a potential threat to their job security. A year later, the North Las Vegas City Council went further, prohibiting the employment of female bartenders. These measures effectively limited distaff mobility, relegating all female casino employees to the so-called girl's ghetto of such lower-paying, low-prestige jobs as Keno runner, cocktail waitress, and cashier. The Civil Rights Act of 1964 laid the foundation for eventually breaking the sex barrier within casinos. In August 1970, the Silver Slipper finally broke with tradition, promoting Jean Brady, a slot machine cashier to blackjack dealer. A year later, veteran gamer Sam Boyd opened the Union Plaza Hotel (on the site of the old railroad station) and employed the first women dealers downtown. By the mid-1970s, many resorts relented under Affirmative Action pressure and in response to changing social mores. Despite the breakthrough, women, like blacks a few years earlier, continued to hold a minority of dealing jobs. As late as September 1978, women accounted for only 25 percent of the 2,616 roulette, blackjack, and baccarat dealers at the Strip's twelve major hotels. Furthermore, women held only 15 of the 410 blackjack floor supervisor jobs on the Strip. During that same month, females claimed only 2 percent of the 1,299 craps dealers jobs at Caesars Palace, the MGM Grand, and other Strip resorts. Clearly, casino gambling not only shaped the economic development of the resort city but its discrimination patterns as well. Mirroring the values of postwar America and eager to please their customers, casino executives viewed the smoky, green felt world of gambling as the preserve of white males. Black customers were banned for a generation while black labor was relegated to culinary and custodial positions. White females, while encouraged to play at the tables, had little chance of becoming dealers or supervisors. The pattern finally changed in early 1981 when nineteen Strip hotels and four unions signed an out-of-court settlement with a women's group agreeing to end all sexual discrimination in hiring, training, and promotion.[61]

The cities had acted even earlier. In June 1967, the North Las Vegas City Council, responding to the local drive for equal opportunity and the national movement for women's rights, voted to repeal its eight-year-old ban against women bartenders. Then in August 1970, prodded by the militant Committee to Abolish Discrimination Against Women Dealers and threats from the federal government's Equal Employment Opportunity Commission, the city of Las Vegas lifted its twelve-year policy against women dealers in downtown casinos.[62]

The improved climate for minorities in the 1970s also benefited Asians and Hispanics. While the latter numbered several thousand people in 1970, their population jumped by more than tenfold in the two decades thereafter. And, thanks to the black civil rights victories, both groups were able to live in integrated neighborhoods, send their children to integrated schools, and secure a large share of nonmenial jobs in the resort industry. Twenty years later problems still remain. Indeed, black leaders like Dr. James McMillan can point to many areas where racism still lingers or is even reviving. But the advances made in the 1960s changed Las Vegas forever. For all its tension and violence, the civil rights struggle made Las Vegas a more egalitarian, democratic place to live. By diversifying the resort industry racially, ethnically, and sexually, this legal revolution actually strengthened the town's resort economy by significantly enlarging the number of customers and workers for the hotels.

The Struggle
for Industry

Following passage of the Boulder Canyon Act in 1928, Las Vegans confidently expected a virtual stampede of industry into their valley. Surely, they reasoned, cheap land, water, and power would prove an irresistible lure. Yet, despite these advantages and the later success of its resort and defense industries, Las Vegas largely failed to secure a substantial manufacturing and processing base. Considering its prime location and natural advantages, the Las Vegas Valley snared little of the industry migrating westward in the decades after Hoover Dam's completion. While hundreds of companies flocked to California, Arizona, New Mexico, Texas, and other nearby states, southern Nevada was mostly bypassed. A number of factors conspired to divert many traditional industries from Las Vegas. Casino gambling was an obvious culprit, but so was the city's lack of water, power, gas, annexable suburbs, and a good university. Still, local boosters put up a brave fight and worked hard to promote their town. While many urban historians have traditionally dismissed the booster activities of local businessmen as self-serving, one must recognize that the barren desert area of Las Vegas could never have grown into a major metropolis without the determined effort of a growth-hungry business community.

As early as the 1930s, Las Vegas leaders were anxious to expand their tax base by attracting both heavy and light industry. As the dam neared completion in the mid-1930s, residents eagerly awaited the arrival of Southern Nevada Power's new transmission line. Of course, it was not until the early 1940s that federal authorities began developing the valley's manufacturing potential with Basic Magnesium. Following the state's purchase of the factory in 1948, the local campaign to find industrial tenants for Basic and other potential sites began in earnest. Spearheading the effort was longtime booster and *Review-Journal* editor Al Cahlan who, as an outspoken member of the Colorado River Commission, had helped lead the fight to buy the Basic plant and secure additional power from newly completed Davis Dam downstream. In his columns, Cahlan repeatedly exhorted Las Vegas to look beyond chemicals, defense, and gaming to diversify its portfolio with more industries. Convinced that an increasingly affluent America would eventually patronize other play spots around the country and world, Cahlan warned in 1948 that "if the day comes when the great hordes will find a new playground . . . then the more industry we have in this area and the more diversified it is, (then) we will not be too greatly affected by the fall-off in tourists."[1]

With this in mind, the local chamber of commerce undertook a determined campaign to lure manufacturers to southern Nevada. In 1948, the organization's "Industrial Committee" published an 81-page, lavishly illustrated brochure entitled *Story of Southern Nevada* to point up "the many advantages peculiar to Clark County . . . that might apply to, and be a natural for certain industrial or commercial requirements." In particular, the chamber targeted firms in the mining industry—a likely strategy in view of Nevada's mining tradition. Depicting the Las Vegas Valley as a "new industrial frontier," the brochure touted the benefits of low-cost Hoover Dam power which justified the processing of even low-grade ores. Throughout this pamphlet as well as later publications, the chamber used the Basic complex as a symbol of Clark County's industrial potential, with repeated references to the successful processing of even low-grade magnesium ore throughout the war.[2]

The Basic plant itself headed the list of potential industrial sites in the 1948 publication. Its advantages were myriad. As the pamphlet noted, a move to Henderson could eliminate "costly time consuming building programs," thereby permitting almost immediate production. Moreover, the chamber bragged that although Basic was designed for the high speed production of magnesium, there was "flexibility to allow for conversion to other processes." Already, the Western Electro Chemical Corporation was producing potash, sodium chlorate, and other compounds. Then too, the boosters were quick to note that "many raw materials are within close proximity and markets for many products are within easy reach." Clearly, the chamber expected to benefit from the western migration of population and industrial processing, both of which had been accelerated by World War II. Increasing dependence upon the midwest and east for steel, electrical equipment, chemicals, and even finished products was decreasing as California and other western states made more goods for their own growing markets.[3]

Clark County hoped to play a role in this process. Thanks to the Basic plant, the metropolitan area enjoyed immediate success in attracting some processing industries. In 1945, Stauffer Chemical came to Basic and retooled to make chlorine, caustic soda, and hydrochloric acid. Using Basic's railroad spur, Stauffer shipped the soda to Los Angeles soap makers and oil refineries. Chlorine was a raw material for many industries, while much of Stauffer's hydrochloric acid eventually went next door to Basic Titanium to help process the new wonder metal. Western Electro Chemical (WEECO) occupied part of the Basic plant even before World War II ended. By the mid-1950s WEECO had expanded its operation to manufacture a variety of chemicals, including JATO (jet assisted takeoff) fuel for the air force, manganese dioxide for heavy duty military batteries, and sodium chlorate for weed killers and paper bleaching. Titanium Metals also used a portion of the Basic complex to manufacture titanium for aircraft production. Tons were produced at Henderson, although trainloads of the materials were shipped east to Allegheny Ludlum where the metal was converted into bars, sheets, strips, and extrusions.[4]

Eventually, the U.S. Lime Corporation opened two lime quarries and two plants at Basic and Sloan, Nevada. The company soon became the largest lime processor in America, supplying various customers, including the sugar beet, glass, steel, and chemical industries. In addition, tons of mason's lime were produced for construction contractors around the west. Another firm, Manganese, Inc. (a Basic tenant and operator of the Three Kids Mine nearby), produced large amounts of manganese for steel mills around the country. While most industry was concentrated in Henderson, the Blue Diamond Corporation was a notable exception, operating a gypsum mill in the hills twenty miles southwest of Las Vegas. The plant, whose capacity was doubled in 1954, processed gypsum into ultra-modern plaster and wallboard to supply California's booming construction industry.[5]

Both Manganese, Inc. and Blue Diamond Corporation illustrated a major local advantage emphasized by the chamber. Area mines contained a wide variety of minerals used as raw materials in the manufacture of other products. Indeed, the *Story of Southern Nevada* listed over one hundred minerals mined in the county, including clay, cobalt, magnesite, marble, molybdenum, tin, zinc, and many others. Access to raw materials was only one of many Clark County assets. Cheap water, power, and land were supplemented by strategic railroad connections which awarded those sites zoned for light industry across the tracks from Fremont Street an "exceptional value" to manufacturers "shipping parts into this area for assembly into finished products and distribution to the vast, western Pacific coast or export markets to the Orient." And there were other conveniences: levelness of terrain mitigated the "expense of grading in preparation for building construction"; mild winters eliminated "the cost of snow removal and its impeding of production or transportation"; abundant year-round sunshine and lack of dense vegetation combined to keep the atmosphere "free of germ and destructive insect life for either factories or laboratories," while the arid climate in general reduced absenteeism while also holding "in check the corrosive action of rust."[6]

According to the chamber, labor and market conditions offered additional advantages. Factory construction in Clark County was relatively inexpensive because, since the days of Hoover Dam, the "unprecedented development in public works and private building" had attracted a large pool of labor "skilled in the building trades, sheet metal work, welding, heavy equipment operation, etc." Moreover, building materials would not have to be shipped in, because Las Vegas already hosted several manufacturers of cement building blocks. Lastly, while skilled labor was available, the boosters noted that since historically no one industry dominated the valley, there had been less emphasis on job specialization, so that the "average Clark County worker (was) generally equipped to perform more than one line of industrial activity." And, as the chamber proudly observed, this flexible labor force was also relatively compliant, being "notably conservative in its relation with management." While the building trades, chemical, and resort industries had been partially unionized, strikes had been few in the city's history and, more importantly, passage of Nevada's right-to-work law was only a few years away.[7]

In its typical upbeat manner, the chamber even credited the resort industry (including casino gambling) with enhancing Las Vegas's industrial potential. After observing that western population movement and vacation areas were "creating markets—ever widening in scope," the chamber's 1948 pamphlet emphasized the importance of Las Vegas's population, whose per capita income, home ownership, savings accounts, bond holdings, and insurance were at a high level. Added to this were the thousands of weekly tourists who, "by expenditures for foods, shelter, transportation and entertainment more than double[d] the (resident) population's buying power." This was an obvious pitch to food processing industries whose business the chamber craved. Every effort was made in the 1948 brochure to appeal to this group. Pictures of turkey farms and celery beds in nearby Logandale combined with tributes to the Mormons who pioneered the local soil to help buttress grand generalizations about the "eastern and midwestern food packer, processor and canner (who) has long recognized the fine quality and hardiness of Clark County seedling plants." On a broader scale, the chamber boasted that "here today, vast acreage exists; technical skills are provided; irrigation waters are at hand, and local, state and federal provisions have been set up to utilize this water on demand." Finally, the town's modern air freight facilities (at the almost-finished McCarran Airport) stood ready to deliver "the product to the grower and food processor in a matter of hours."[8]

Aside from these advantages, the chamber listed dozens more favorable factors in its ambitious postwar effort to diversify the region's economy: cheap (Hoover and Davis Dam) power, water, industrial (oil) fuel, land, and abundant raw materials combined with the city's salubrity, efficient business government, road, and rail connections, schools, churches, hospitals, and civic organizations to make a compelling argument for Las Vegas as the site for industrial development. In addition, Nevada's liberal tax structure, featuring no state income, inheritance, gift, corporation, or sales taxes, was also a powerful incentive. Beginning in the mid-1950s, the chamber of commerce published the annual *Las Vegas Report* (later the *Digest*) which provided updated statistical information concerning bank deposits, postal receipts, retail trade sales, water consumption, building permits, employment, demographics, and a dozen other economic indicators in a valiant effort to portray the valley as a dynamic new site for industry.[9]

To some extent, the campaign succeeded. By 1970, firms specializing in light industry and warehousing gradually filled many of the available parcels between the railroad tracks and Industrial Road. Not surprisingly, the Basic plant enjoyed more immediate success. As early as 1951, the advantages of cheap power, water, railroad connections, and a convenient townsite nearby had combined to fill all ten cells of the sprawling complex. Yet, in many ways Las Vegas failed to realize its industrial potential. True, major chemical firms settled at Basic, but this trend was common in other western cities, too. Invariably, the large industrial plants built during wartime by Uncle Sam and later sold off as surplus for a fraction of their value, provided a savings which many companies eagerly exploited.

Had the federal government never built Basic, one wonders whether heavy industry ever would have come to Las Vegas.

While the late forties, fifties, and sixties were a period of substantial industrial growth in the southwest, Las Vegas did not secure its fair share of the pie.[10] Despite its proximity to Hoover Dam and the large California market, the resort town lost much industry to rival cities in the southwest. According to a 1976 survey of Standard Metropolitan Statistical Areas (SMSAs), Las Vegas counted only 204 "manufacturing establishments" with a total of 4,975 employees. At the same time, Albuquerque had 492 and 14,929 respectively, El Paso 333 and 32,528, Tucson 300 and 11,629, and Phoenix a whopping 1,506 establishments employing 72,456 workers. More specifically, Las Vegas trailed its competitors in a variety of key industries. In the manufacture of electric and electronic equipment, Las Vegas employed less than 500 workers while Tucson's number was nearly double, Albuquerque's was four-fold higher and Phoenix led all with better than 18,000 on its payrolls. In other major categories like the manufacture of primary metals, fabricated metal products, nonelectrical machinery and other industries where a year-round arid climate provided an advantage, Las Vegas lagged behind its rivals in production and employment.

In textile processing, despite a substantial cotton hinterland to the west in Nye County, Las Vegas counted only 6 plants employing less than 70 workers, while Phoenix (3,754), El Paso (19,348), and even Tucson (299) were ahead. Similarly, in trucking and warehousing, Las Vegas (456) trailed El Paso (1,724), Albuquerque (about 2,000), Phoenix (4,808), and Tucson (1,024), even though Nevada was a freeport state like Arizona and New Mexico. Fortunately, Las Vegas's minority role was not total; thanks to the Basic complex, the resort town's chemical industry was second only to Phoenix in employment (648 to 1,667). Still, as late as the 1960s and even the 1970s, Las Vegas had not realized its true industrial potential.[11]

As figures indicate, Las Vegas's rivals in the southwest (and especially California) built substantial industrial bases during and after the war. Obviously, many companies intent on a southwest location bypassed Las Vegas. But why? A brief comparative look at developments in Albuquerque, Phoenix, and Tucson clearly reveals why Las Vegas lagged behind in the struggle for industry. Like Las Vegas, Albuquerque limped along for years as a railroad town until the 1930s, when it began acquiring a large share of federal regional offices as well as dozens of hospital and medical research firms clustering around the University of New Mexico's Medical School in town. Then, as in Las Vegas, World War II provided the key economic boost. In 1941, the War Department transformed the town's small municipal airport into Kirtland Air Force Base and the nearby Manzano Base. These facilities, with their large payrolls, stretched the urbanized zone to the south and east just as the aerial gunnery school stretched Las Vegas's building zone to the northeast, energizing the development of North Las Vegas. While the army air corps exerted a powerful multiplier effect, Albuquerque's economy would ultimately be transformed by events at nearby Los Alamos, where J. Robert Oppenheimer and his team of scientists were building the first atomic bomb. Already a medical, administrative, financial, and military hub, Albuquerque now became a supply center and research adjunct to the Manhattan Project. Following the war, the city's role grew to major proportions, as scientists from Los Alamos established the Sandia Laboratories on the outskirts of town. With the advent of the Cold War, Pentagon officials poured millions into nuclear research and special weapons development at the research center.[12] Blessed with these advantages, aggressive city and state leaders pursued federal research projects while also upgrading the University of New Mexico's engineering and science programs to provide the technical training for a labor pool which, in turn, would lure hundreds of high-tech firms and subcontractors to the city. Key municipal and state taxes were lowered and low-cost building sites were made available for prospective businesses. The effort paid off; by 1960, the atomic economy had transformed the city. The air base and Sandia Laboratories alone accounted for nearly 30 percent of Albuquerque's work force. By 1980, Albuquerque, like Phoenix, Tucson, Austin, and Los Angeles, had become one of the premier high-tech cities in the United States.[13]

To the west, a similar story unfolded in Phoenix, where much of the Sun City's phenomenal postwar growth was fueled by the new industry it attracted. Like Las Vegas, Albuquerque, Tucson, El Paso, and other southwestern cities, Phoenix parlayed wartime air bases and government-financed factories into a postwar bonanza. In 1941, thanks to the influence of Senator Carl Hayden, the military ringed the area with pilot-training bases, including Luke Field (today Luke Air Force Base), Thunderbird Field (near Glendale), Williams Field (near Chandler), and Falcon Field (near Mesa). Even the navy came to the Phoenix area, opening a training base at Litchfield Park. Civilian aerospace firms came as well, including the Goodyear Aircraft Company, the Garrett Corporation, and others. Like its southern Nevada rival, Phoenix also developed a chemical industry during the war. Alcoa Aluminum came to town in 1943 to operate a giant aluminum extrusion plant built by the Defense Plant Corporation, while Allison Steel, a Phoenix firm since the 1920s, won a federal contract to build portable bridges for the army. [14]

Following the war, Phoenix businessmen used their control of the city's Charter Government Committee (whose candidates were swept into office in November 1949) to promote industry. Bankers, corporate executives, and city officials helped form the Industrial Development Corporation of the chamber of commerce to promote industry. While Las Vegas struggled along with a dedicated but understaffed and undertrained industrial committee in its chamber of commerce, the city of Phoenix controlled the promotion bureaucracy. Members of the Industrial Development Corporation contacted prospective transplants, met key executives at the airport, and worked with the town's major banks to discuss specific terms of venture capital loans. Companies were not just given brochures and a pep talk; instead, major city officials, bank executives, and even developers discussed potential building sites and bank loans as part of an overall package for firms considering Phoenix. In the two decades following World War II, Phoenix attracted a veritable Who's Who of defense contractors, as Reynolds Aluminum, Motorola, General Electric, Sperry Rand, and other giants flocked to Arizona's capital. [15]

Like Phoenix and Las Vegas, Tucson benefited from federal spending during World War II. In 1941, the government began converting the municipal airport into a key military installation, Davis-Monthan Army Air Base, which became headquarters for the air corps' First Bombardment Wing. Tucson also hosted the Marana Basic Flying School, thirty-five miles north of town, and Ryan Field, sixteen miles to the west, for primary pilot training. In February 1942, as part of Washington's program to decentralize vital war industries, Consolidated-Vultee Corporation of San Diego came to Tucson and employed six thousand employees. As was the case in Phoenix, a clustering of electronics and aerospace firms occurred, with Hughes Aircraft (after earlier rejecting Las Vegas) leading a migration of defense contractors. Thus by 1970, while Las Vegas struggled along with EG&G and a few smaller firms servicing the nuclear test site, Tucson, Phoenix, Albuquerque, El Paso, and Austin all blossomed into high-tech centers. Electronics was the perfect industry for the urban southwest because it required dry weather for testing, needed little water for manufacturing, and produced high value but low-weight products which could be easily shipped over the mountains to the east, north, or west. [16] Of course, Tucson, Phoenix, and Albuquerque all enjoyed a more productive agricultural and mining hinterland than Las Vegas, which gave them a decided edge in prewar population and development. Nevertheless, these cities were clearly more successful after the war in enlarging their physical size and diversifying their economies with new industries. Historically, several key factors were crucial to their success: water, power, gas, higher education, aggressive annexations, and the lack of casino gambling.

Water was especially significant in the arid southwest. Albuquerque, Phoenix, and Las Vegas all faced water shortages in the immediate postwar years, but the former acted more quickly to solve the problem. In 1947, the same year that Nevada's legislature authorized creation of the Las Vegas Valley Water District, Albuquerque began a ten-year master plan for developing watersheds and extending its water and sewer system from downtown outward to newly annexed communities to the east and south. In 1951 voters passed a $3.5 million bond issue to fund construction. Subsequent years witnessed additional bond issues which kept the city's water supply in step with projected demand. The Phoenix effort was even more spectacular because the city's growth outpaced the dreams of its most fervent boosters. [17] Prior to the city's population explosion after World War II, the Roosevelt Dam Reservoir Project provided Phoenix with the water it needed until 1946 when the Arizona metropolis, like Las Vegas to the north and Albuquerque to the east, experienced water shortages and rationing. While Las Vegas took almost ten years to secure additional supplies from Lake Mead through a small Henderson line, Phoenix acted quickly. In the twelve years following World War II, the metropolis issued over $10 million in bonds. By 1957, Phoenix supplied water to over 70 square miles of the metropolitan region—double the city's area. Eventually, the city negotiated the purchase of water from the Salt River Valley User's Association at agricultural rates which permitted the municipality to keep prices low for home and industry. Then in May 1957, at the urging of the charter government and the Phoenix Growth Committee (a 464-member committee comprised of the town's major business leaders), voters approved a giant $70 million bond issue to purchase all remaining water companies and thoroughly modernize (by building more pumping stations and laying large-diameter mains) the city's water system on a metropolitan basis. While it took Las Vegas thirty years to go thirty miles to Lake Mead for a substantial water system to support its growth, Phoenix had largely completed its work a decade earlier.[18]

The struggle for water moved more slowly in Las Vegas than in Phoenix and elsewhere. Prior to World War II, water had been plentiful in the Las Vegas Valley. The railroad initially guaranteed the community an abundant supply when it bought the 1,800-acre Stewart Ranch together with water rights to the "Big Spring," west of the proposed townsite. Several years after the 1905 auction of lots, residents were delighted to learn that Las Vegas was actually located in an artesian basin. In fact, the Las Vegas Land & Water Company, the railroad's subsidiary, subsequently drilled what became the third largest artesian well in the world. It was little wonder then that many contemporaries shared the optimistic view of one Salt Lake reporter who in 1905 predicted that Las Vegas would "one day be the center of an agricultural region of wondrous wealth." With a more than ample supply, the town had little difficulty servicing residents and businesses even during the population surge occasioned by Hoover Dam. Throughout the 1930s, landowners or the water company itself met the increased demands by simply drilling more wells. Moreover, Boulder City and later the Basic Magnesium factory and townsite each had their own supplies, relieving the strain on Las Vegas.[19]

The first expressions of concern were voiced in the early 1940s, when weekend tourism combined with military and defense workers to boost population to unprecedented heights. As weekend populations surpassed 25,000, more hotels, motor courts, and restaurants equipped with pressurized faucets and flush toilets encouraged more total and per capita consumption. As a result, local reserves were drained; water tables fell across the valley, and the daily flow from normally dependable wells declined markedly. In an effort to determine its actual reserves, the Union Pacific in 1944 ordered a hydrological survey of the valley. For years rumors had circulated about a mysterious underground supply running from Lake Tahoe under the Great Basin to Las Vegas. The railroad's hydrologist soon dispelled this myth, warning of sink holes and dry wells if the drilling did not stop. He also cautioned Las Vegans about their continued reliance upon local aquifers, warning that "it will only be a matter of years when this artesian flow ceases altogether." Nevertheless, townsmen continued to drill; the valley's 125 wells in 1924 had grown to 450 by 1944 and threatened to surpass 500 by 1950. Experts had already calculated that the mountains ringing the city could not continue supplying Las Vegas's water needs much longer.[20]

Concerned about the worsening crisis, state authorities acted. Most of the town's business and political leaders were present at the November 1944 meeting of the chamber of commerce at the El Rancho Vegas when State Engineer Alfred Merritt Smith reported that artesian well supplies were being overdrawn. In stunned silence they heard him warn that unless plans were made soon to bring Lake Mead water to Las Vegas, he would consider restricting the drilling of more wells—a move which would have crippled Las Vegas's postwar growth. In response, the community turned its ire against Walter Bracken, the Union Pacific's special representative in Nevada and vice president of the Las Vegas Land & Water Company. The symbol of railroad intransigence regarding water, Bracken finally resigned in April 1946 under mounting public pressure. His ouster hardly altered the railroad's regressive water policies. Las Vegas was operating under an obsolete system. Long ago, the railroad had lost interest in extending its water system to develop the town. Since much of the land undergoing urbanization in the 1940s was not railroad property, the water company had little incentive to invest in new lines. [21]

Farsighted leaders recognized that Las Vegas's future hinged upon the capture of Lake Mead water. To this end, the *Review-Journal*'s Al Cahlan, an enthusiastic member of the state's Colorado River Commission, urged the formation of a "vigorous committee" in 1944 to pursue the acquisition of Basic Magnesium after the war. Indeed, he valued the factory's water line to Lake Mead as much as its production capacity. Fearful that public apathy might delay Nevada's purchase of BMI, Cahlan warned residents that prompt action was needed now, "not because of any critical shortage of water in the area at the present time, but as protection for the future of the valley." As the crisis worsened in the immediate postwar years, Al Cahlan, Ernie Cragin, car dealer Archie Grant, and other business leaders spearheaded a movement to create a special service district in the metropolitan area with bond-issuing power to finance the eventual take-over of the Las Vegas Land & Water Company. Plans also called for construction someday of a water line between Lake Mead and Las Vegas. Such a line was feasible because in 1941, Al Cahlan and Ed Clark, president of the First State Bank, had persuaded BMI's Howard Eells to increase the planned diameter of his plant's water main to forty inches to permit extra capacity should Las Vegas someday need a supply of Lake Mead water. [22]

At the urging of the Clark County delegation, state legislators in 1947 passed an act which enabled county voters to create a water district. Following the action of lawmakers in Carson City, Archie Grant presided over a mass meeting of citizens in Las Vegas on August 19, 1947, to initiate the petition drive for a ballot question to create the district.[23] A vigorous publicity effort followed, led by the *Review-Journal*. Column after column touted the benefits of a "water district." In prophetic words, Cahlan advised that "we must solve the water supply problem . . . if Las Vegas is to grow." Rejecting the suggestions of some that drilling new artesian wells was the answer, the editor insisted there was "no other way to solve the problem except by bringing water in from Lake Mead." And, he warned, "we had better do it than be out of water." Responding to those Las Vegans who wondered why they should be taxed to bring water from Henderson, Cahlan explained that full production at Basic Magnesium would benefit Las Vegas in that "the largest development, so far as housing and business is concerned, will be Las Vegas proper, because most [chemical] companies do not want to house their employees so close to the job as Henderson"—an observation which in time proved only partially correct.[24]

Thanks to the efforts of Cahlan, local service leagues and the banks (which stockpiled petitions at the tellers windows), over 1,000 signatures had been obtained by June 1948—more than twice the amount required by law. At a special election on October 19, 1948, voters approved creation of a water district by a staggering vote of 4,171 to 538. The people also chose a seven-member board of directors. Despite strong opposition in Henderson, Pittman, Whitney (East Las Vegas), and other outlying communities, an overwhelming vote in the Las Vegas area carried the day. Following the election, district board members immediately authorized engineering surveys and other studies which eventually culminated in a historic 1952 agreement with company officials at Basic Magnesium. The pact called for Basic to pump up to 13 million gallons of water per day to Las Vegas, once the district had built a connecting line and had enlarged the local distribution network. In 1953, following three years of intense negotiations, the district bought the Las Vegas Land & Water Company's equipment and system. Then in September 1953, voters approved an $8.7 million bond issue for the two-fold purpose of building the line between Henderson and Las Vegas and extending service to North Las Vegas to supply Rancho High School. Part of the money also funded a pumping station at Whitney on the Boulder Highway and a huge 30-million-gallon receiving reservoir for Las Vegas. After two years of feverish construction, Lake Mead water flowed into Las Vegas for the first time ever on September 22, 1955.[25]

Public support for these efforts swelled in response to the worsening crisis between 1948 and 1953. The water shortage posed an immediate threat to the town's economy. Referring to the construction of the Thunderbird and Desert Inn Hotels, Union Pacific Vice President Frank Strong tersely announced in 1948 that the railroad would provide no water for properties south of the city limits. His reasoning was clear: "Our facilities and the underground supply in the area from which we take our water are such that we can with reasonable safety serve the city, but we are certain that such supply is not sufficient to serve the surrounding areas." The railroad even refused to provide water lines for fire hydrants to protect the valuable Strip hotels. As a result, the hotels had to dig their own wells. The El Rancho, Last Frontier, and Flamingo were already draining the reserves under their properties when Marion Hicks and Cliff Jones ordered the drilling of wells on Thunderbird property to supply a 20,000-gallon tank. And these actions would be duplicated first by Wilbur Clark at the Desert Inn and later by all the new hotels rising on the Strip. Conservation measures were also undertaken within the city of Las Vegas. In 1950, the municipality began restricting lawn watering. During the next two years the city employed the alternate day method, allowing homeowners with lots facing north and east to water their grass on even-numbered days of the month and the rest on odd.[26]

Beginning in 1950, the crisis affected not only resorts and residents but the town's defense industry as well. In November 1950, air force officials announced their intention of drilling wells to supply the projected demand of Nellis's Wherry Housing Project slated for completion in 1951. The Pentagon, recognizing that the base's current consumption of 1 million gallons of water per day would double once the housing project opened, had hoped the newly created water district would solve the problem. But events moved too slowly. For a while, air force officials considered the expensive proposition of building a water line around Sunrise Mountain to Lake Mead, but federal surveyors discovered a new aquifer (separate from Las Vegas's) on the base with a high water table. As a result, artesian wells immediately ended the Nellis shortage. This was fortunate, since the Korean War substantially increased the base's population.

The war also promoted construction of a water main to Lake Mead for civilian use. When the Truman administration declared the Las Vegas Valley a "critical defense area" in 1952, the federal government encouraged the county and cities to draw up an agenda of needed public works projects. While roads, sewers, and schools were high priorities, Las Vegas emphasized the water line to Lake Mead. Thus, water district director Thomas Campbell joined with Mayor Baker in requesting a $6 million water main connecting the Basic plant in Henderson with Las Vegas. As Campbell advised John Lamb, regional engineer of the U.S. Home and Housing Finance Administration, if constructed, the project would become "an integral part of the ultimately envisioned direct line from Lake Mead to Las Vegas." District engineers had already warned that if growth continued for another seven years, a $13 million line would be needed by 1960. In view of this prediction, federal funding was made available, and Washington shouldered part of the cost for the 39-inch line connecting the city with BMI and, as noted, Lake Mead water finally flowed into Las Vegas by September 1955.[27]

The relief was only temporary. By 1960, the town's inadequate water supply once again threatened to short-circuit growth. Clearly, Las Vegas suffered from the delay in receiving Lake Mead water. Throughout the fifties and sixties the city was engaged in a race with time. Experts knew that the growing metropolis could no longer rely on the underground water supplied by the surrounding mountains; only water from the Rockies could support the frantic urbanization which the resort-defense economy was fueling. The magnitude of the crisis became evident in 1961 when the water district stopped construction of a major housing development on San Francisco Street between Maryland Parkway and Paradise Road because the neighborhood lacked enough water to supply the complex. The district then triggered a major controversy with Clark County's state legislative delegation when it asked for clarification of its taxing power to fund new construction. The board incensed Clark County politicians by raising the prospects of either increasing water rates by 70 percent or directly taxing valley residents. Although city and county commissioners fumed, the board was struggling with a major problem. In 1960 alone, it laid over 25,000 feet of new mains. Then, just a year later, the rapid urbanization of Las Vegas's western suburbs forced it to spend another $242,000 for pumping stations at Twin Lakes, the Strip, Charleston Heights, and the Bonanza and Hyde Park areas. As in the 1950s, the key problem was that Las Vegas's mushrooming growth far outstripped its water system. The district simply lacked the money to finance the rapid extension of the distribution network required by the city's leapfrog growth, which saw developers jumping over thousands of acres of vacant land to build subdivisions and shopping centers often a mile beyond existing mains.[28]

The worsening crisis forced citizens and leaders alike to recognize the need to end the traditional stop-gap approach to water shortages. Beginning in 1961, Governor Grant Sawyer and Nevada's congressional delegation began lobbying for federal help. The San Francisco Street incident had only strengthened their case. Clearly, with Soviet-American relations increasingly dampened by the Bay of Pigs invasion, the Cuban Missile Crisis, and the Vietnam War, the Kennedy administration would tolerate no threat to the growth potential of areas bordering Nellis and the test site. Not surprisingly, seed money for preliminary engineering surveys was contained in several Kennedy budgets. A variety of congressional delays blocked action until January 6, 1965, when Senator Alan Bible introduced legislation to fund the Southern Nevada Water Project. After a year and a half of spirited debate in Congress, it became law on July 20, 1966, when signed by President Lyndon Johnson. The first phase of the project provided for mains to carry 132,000 acre-feet of water annually to Clark County. Funded by an initial grant of $7 million, the first water line to Las Vegas was dedicated in June 1971. Ultimately, a $120 million federal loan at 3.5 percent interest combined with $460 million in state bonds to fund the entire project whose final phase was finished in April 1982. Thanks to the Southern Nevada Water Project, Nevada at last received its full legal share of Lake Mead water as provided by the Colorado Compact of 1922. After nearly two decades of struggle, Las Vegas finally had enough water to support its burgeoning economy.[29]

Lack of water was not the only handicap facing Las Vegas in its postwar struggle to attract industry. Electricity was also in short supply. This was not the case in Albuquerque, Tucson, and Phoenix. The Arizona capital, for instance, recognized early the value of cheap power and actively pursued a reliable supply. Indeed, the young town granted its first utility franchises in 1886. After 1900, as population rose, Pacific Gas boosted supplies by purchasing power from the Salt River Valley User's Association and later from the nearby Arizona Power Company. Pacific Gas later sold out to the Central Arizona Light and Power Company (CALAPCO), which in 1924 joined the American Power and Light Company, whose giant network supplied over four hundred southwestern utilities. This move enabled the former to modernize its network with much-needed capital available from a big utility with a wider income base. Even as Phoenix expanded its power capacity, Las Vegas remained isolated, content to tap a limited supply of Hoover Dam power through its small local utility. While the town had derived its early prosperity through a working relationship with a large California-based railroad, townsmen did not seek out-of-state help to boost its kilowatts. In 1955, Las Vegas finally opened its first steam-generating plant to supplement the dam; Phoenix, foreseeing the need for power to attract industry to the depression-racked state, had finished a similar facility in 1930![30]

Las Vegas's battle for electric power dates from the town's infancy. As early as 1905, some Las Vegans were troubled by the fire hazard posed by the use of gasoline lamps; two disastrous fires that year only confirmed these fears. In 1906, Charles "Pop" Squires, an enterprising business-man, promoted a scheme to utilize the spare generator in the Armour Ice Plant to transmit power around town. While residents waited in vain for a group of California investors to fulfill their pledge to provide Las Vegas with electricity, Squires and several associates secured redwood poles from a nearby lumberyard and several thousand feet of heavy copper wire. A month later, local men had already strung wire from the ice plant across Main to First Street and then north along an alley to Stewart. Within months the primitive network had been extended to most of Clark's Townsite, and Las Vegans began exchanging their gasoline lamps for 31-candlepower carbons.[31]

To meet the demand for electricity, Squires, banker John S. Park, and several other businessmen formed the Consolidated Power & Telephone Company on March 28, 1906. As early as 1907, demand had outstripped supply, and the heavy copper wire could not supply enough power to all the town's customers. Service declined steadily due to the power drain, forcing the utility to purchase "Old Betsy," a 90-horsepower, single-cylinder engine (with two flywheels over six feet in diameter) capable of generating 2,300 watts. Subsequent improvements included the replace-ment of the network's heavy copper street lines with more efficient, thinner wire. Still, service was inadequate. Electricity was only available at night for lighting and cooking; gas powered the town by day. Although capacity was nearly doubled in 1912 with the purchase of a second generator, full-time service only came in 1915, when Consolidated Power contracted to buy all of the town's electricity from the railroad's newly constructed powerhouse. This arrangement served the town's needs until the mid-1930s, when Hoover Dam took over. The only exception occurred during the national railroad strike of 1922 when the Union Pacific shut down the local powerhouse, forcing the pro-labor town into a humiliating dependency upon kerosene for light and ice for refrigeration.[32]

Consolidated Power & Telephone split into two distinct entities in 1929. Renamed Southern Nevada Power, the utility remained in the hands of Samuel J. Lawson, Cyril Wengert, Ed Clark, C. L. Ronnow, and other investors who comprised the city's old-time power structure. Service improved markedly in the 1930s. Fearful of Mayor Leonard Arnett's intention of creating a municipally owned power system, the firm aggressively built lines to Hoover Dam and extended its low-cost electricity into every neighborhood. The existing network was modernized with new transformers and other equipment to handle the Hoover Dam flow which began in 1937. However, once Arnett and the public power movement were safely defeated, the utility steered a more independent course. According to historian Perry Kaufman, President Lawson, a highly conservative businessman, disliked investing company profits for new equipment and construction. Following the completion of Basic Magnesium, for instance, he refused to extend power lines into the newly built Huntridge and Biltmore additions, because he expected that a postwar exodus of workers would empty the neighborhoods. Lines were strung only after a court order and a threatened city lawsuit. Following the war, Lawson and his comrades kept a tight grip on construction projects, installing new lines only when a substantial base of consumers filled a new zone. Despite projections of continued growth in the wake of Strip hotel construction and community efforts to attract more industry, Lawson refused to build steam-powered electric plants to supplement the town's Hoover Dam supply. As a result of these short-sighted policies, the town surpassed the dam's power capacity in early 1950. Shortly thereafter, under pressure from Wengert, Ronnow, and other business leaders, Lawson resigned.[33]

Lawson left, but not before his policies created an energy crisis which literally threatened the town's economy. As early as 1947, Las Vegas's growth had so outpaced generating capacity that the utility banned the use of electric space heaters in new commercial buildings. For the next few years the situation steadily worsened, as more hotels were built and the air base was reactivated. Then in November 1951, the utility won the state Public Service Commission's approval of a ban on space heaters in all new residential buildings. When the agency approved the motion on December 1, 1951, a storm of protest ensued. Mayor Baker and city commissioners convened a special meeting to investigate the crisis. On December 9, Lloyd Compton, the utility's assistant manager, told a packed room at city hall that the ban was necessary to conserve power. An angry Mayor Baker responded by accusing Compton's firm of failing to project future demand and plan for the future. As a stop-gap measure, Baker suggested buying additional power from the new Shasta Dam.

Compton dismissed the notion, insisting that Shasta power would cost double the price townsmen were paying for Hoover Dam electricity. Moreover, California needed all the kilowatts it could generate and had none to spare for Nevada. In the end, California Edison rejected Baker's request.[34]

Questioned closely about the crisis, Compton blamed the local energy shortage on "an unprecedented and wholly unexpected increase in the local system during the month of October [1951] which indicated that the amount of power presently available for distribution would not be sufficient to carry any additional heating." Compton's protestations aside, political and business leaders recognized the emergency's potential impact upon town efforts to attract new industries and residents. Already the Federal Housing Administration had begun rejecting mortgage insurance for new homes affected by the space heating ban. Apparently, the agency considered the power shortage an investment risk which threatened property values. Already worried about the town's water shortage, the chamber of commerce's Industrial Committee was concerned but helpless.[35]

Frustrated in their efforts to sway the seemingly intractable utility, Mayor Baker and City Attorney Howard Cannon on January 4, 1952, threatened to instigate legal proceedings against the company unless it provided more power. Revoking the firm's license, however, was not the answer; even a new utility would have required considerable lead time to bring added capacity on line. So, despite political pressure, the space heater ban continued. Fearing a threat to its own economic development, the state of Nevada also got involved. Following lengthy negotiations, Governor Charles Russell in May 1953 approved an agreement with the Arizona Power Authority to buy from 22,000 to 32,000 kilowatt hours of electricity (from the new Saguaro steam plant) during the "off-peak" months from October to March. While helpful, the action provided an unreliable source of power for industry in the winter and none in the summer when cooling systems drew the highest loads. Desperate state officials also sought federal help. In October 1952, Nevada Senator George Malone brought the Senate Public Works Committee to Henderson for hearings regarding the power shortage in southern Nevada.[36]

Undoubtedly, Malone hoped to use Korean War production as a pretext for building more electric generating capacity which Las Vegas could use for future growth. The testimony was impressive. Executives from Western Electro Chemical, the nation's chief producer of "JATO" (jet-assisted takeoff fuel), complained they were 50 to 68 million kilowatt hours short of required capacity. WEECO's complaints were echoed by Arthur Newell of Stauffer Chemical who claimed a shortage of 84 million kilowatt hours and a staggering 267 million kilowatt hours if the firm expanded to meet increased demand for chlorine (needed by California chemical plants), caustic soda (used to make aviation fuel), and muriatic acid (used to make titanium for the aerospace industry). In a similar vein, Manganese, Inc., pleaded for an additional 12 million kilowatt hours of electricity to make its valuable products. The Senate committee recognized the need for more power, an event which only reinforced the government's determination to build the Glen Canyon Dam. While the Korean truce ended the immediate crisis, more dams were built in the later 1950s to prevent future shortages from curtailing intermountain war production capacities.[37]

Still, the solution to Las Vegas's immediate problem was the ouster of utility president Samuel Lawson and the immediate construction of steam-powered generating plants to supplement Hoover Dam. Southern Nevada Power's energetic new president, Reid Gardner, immediately began a feverish construction program in 1953 to expand the firm's capacity. By February 1956, the utility's first steam-powered generating plant, Clark Station Number 1, was operational. Its 44,000 kilowatts enabled the utility to lift the ban on space heaters. At the same time, construction of the $8.4 million Clark Station Number 2 (with its 60,000-kilowatt capacity) was expected to be finished in 1957. With this in mind, local newspaper advertisements once again touted the virtues of an "all-electric home." Appliance and air conditioning sales soared and F.H.A. concerns over the valley as a mortgage risk disappeared. To keep pace with the city's growth and prevent any future crises, Gardner ordered more construction. To supply the area's 35,000 consumers (by 1959), Southern Nevada Power built Clark Station Number 3. Later, to meet the mushrooming demand for power in the neon metropolis, the company broke ground in 1963 for the massive coal-powered "Reid Gardner Electric Generating Station" in the Moapa Valley 45 miles northeast of Las Vegas. Unit 1 came on line in 1965, a second in 1968, a third in 1976, and a fourth in 1983. By the late 1970s, as the number of customers surpassed 200,000, the firm bought 14 percent of the Mojave Generating Station and 11 percent of the Navajo Station in Arizona—thereby guaranteeing enough electricity for the near future.[38]

Aside from water and power, natural gas was a third factor which awarded Las Vegas's rivals a critical advantage in the struggle for industry. Prior to 1930, Phoenix received mostly petroleum-based gas from

CALAPCO, but local industry, anxious to cut costs, wanted to tap the rich gas reserves of eastern New Mexico. Shortly after 1930, representatives of Phelps-Dodge, Calumet, and Arizona mining companies negotiated a loan from a New York finance company to build a natural gas pipeline across New Mexico to Douglas, Arizona. The depressed economy delayed the project until 1933, when the Reconstruction Finance Corporation granted additional funds to the Western Gas Company of El Paso to extend the pipelines from Douglas 230 miles west to Phoenix and Tucson. By January 1934, twenty years earlier than Las Vegas, the Phoenix and Tucson areas had secured substantial natural gas supplies which cut fuel costs for residence and industry by up to 50 percent. This awarded Phoenix, Tucson—and even earlier Albuquerque and El Paso—a critical advantage over southern Nevada in the fight to lure new industry.[39]

While efforts had been ongoing for several years to bring natural gas to southern Nevada, no formal action was taken until March 1949, when Nevada Natural Gas filed incorporation papers in Carson City, allowing it to build a 114-mile gas pipeline from Topock, Arizona, to Las Vegas. According to plans, El Paso Natural Gas Corporation would build a 433-mile line from its eastern New Mexico gas fields to Topock; Nevada Natural would then deliver it to the local utility who would distribute it through its underground pipe network. At first, progress was slow. Engineering snafus delayed the El Paso company's incorporation in Nevada until October 15, 1950, but construction proceeded at full speed thereafter and Las Vegans rejoiced at the prospects of future service. And why not? For decades townsmen had settled for a primitive gas network of pipes. Liquefied petroleum gas had been available for years, but it was expensive, inefficient, and the supply was unreliable. The town now stood on the verge of a revolution. Not only would natural gas cut commercial and residential prices, but it also raised the possibility of attracting more industry because the gas could be used to generate cheap electricity, thereby supplementing Hoover and Davis Dam supplies.[40]

This is what happened. By mid-1953 the line was completed and natural gas began cutting power costs around the valley. More importantly, it helped solve the town's power shortage as well. Southern Nevada Power had already begun construction of the first of its several steam-powered generating stations. Engineers had been reluctant to make steam by burning coal to avoid polluting the valley, which was subject to large-scale temperature inversions in fall and winter. Natural gas was the practical, low-cost alternative for making steam. As a result, Clark

Station Numbers 1 and 2, plus their successors and even the Sunrise Unit near Vegas Valley Drive (built in 1965), used gas. Coal was used only in the Reid Gardner complex, because it was located far away from the city on an Indian reservation. Natural gas, therefore, was crucial to attracting new industry while also keeping the town's air clean.[41]

Not only were Las Vegas's utilities slow in securing water, power, and gas, but the telephone company was also derelict in expanding and modernizing its operations to handle the potential needs of industry and commerce. Once again, the chief obstacle to improvement was Samuel Lawson who, as a major partner in the Southern Nevada Telephone Company, largely controlled management policy. As with the power company, Lawson opposed modernization efforts designed to put service on a par with Phoenix, Los Angeles, and other nearby cities. For example, he resisted suggestions by lesser executives to adopt the dial system, clinging instead to the archaic operator method to protect the legions of women he had hired over the years from losing their jobs. As a result, it often took several minutes to get an operator to make a local call. With the town's population mushrooming, telephone conditions became intolerable, especially for the resort hotels. In 1954, the state Public Service Commission finally pressured Lawson out by threatening to revoke the utility's license. New leadership came in 1955, and the ambitious program to modernize equipment, install the dial system, and eventually abolish four-party lines was begun.[42]

Aside from these shortcomings, Las Vegas's lack of a decent university also discouraged industry. Clearly, fine institutions of higher education were crucial to Albuquerque, Tucson, and Phoenix in their quest to attract high-tech businesses. By the mid-1950s, the University of New Mexico, Arizona, and Arizona State enjoyed substantial enrollments, large campuses, and advanced engineering programs. All three schools, while definitely not on a par with Cal Tech or M.I.T., nevertheless had programs which provided a strong base for future expansion when training and research needs became clearer. The Phoenix area led the way in this regard. By the 1960s, even the community colleges around Phoenix (Maricopa County) had developed a curriculum of basic courses in engineering and computer science to service local employers.[43]

Owing to its recent emergence in the southwest's "tournament of cities," Las Vegas lacked these advantages. Prior to 1950, it would not have been practical to establish a college campus at Las Vegas. Historically, the majority of the state's population had clustered around the old railroad-

Comstock center of Reno-Virginia City-Carson City. Even in 1950, Reno still outnumbered its upstart rival to the south in population (32,497 to 24,624). But the rapid growth of Las Vegas's resort and defense economies pressured state authorities to take action. As early as 1950, Nellis Air Force Base petitioned the Reno campus for extension courses in Clark County. Rebuffed in this effort, the military, in a surprise move, contracted with the University of Southern California for the classes. New pressure came from teachers in Clark County's rapidly expanding school districts for advanced courses to fulfill state requirements. Fears that either southern California- or Utah-based universities would eventually invade southern Nevada, prompted the board of regents to take action. In 1951, the University of Nevada went beyond the concept of extension courses and instituted a formal program in Las Vegas. James R. Dickinson, a junior member of the Reno English department, agreed to move south and teach freshman courses. He and two part-time instructors offered the first classes in the fall of 1951. About thirty students enrolled that year, attending class in space donated by the local school board. Despite low attendance, the board of regents, fearful that Brigham Young or U.S.C. might still enter Clark County and thus threaten support for the state university, voted to establish a full junior college program at Las Vegas.[44]

On October 7, 1954, at the first-ever regents' meeting held in Las Vegas, the board announced its support for a future campus in town while, at the time, warning residents that most higher education money in the upcoming budget would be channeled to the Reno campus. This announcement only strengthened the resolve of Clark County boosters to push for a school immediately. The resulting storm of protest led regents to reconsider their position, and, at its December meeting, the board voted to request a $200,000 appropriation for a building to house the Las Vegas program. In 1955, the lawmakers tied their support of the plan to a proviso that local residents demonstrate their good faith by raising over $100,000 for a campus. In response, citizens organized the Nevada Southern Campus Fund Committee to solicit donations. Chaired by Clark County School Superintendent R. Guild Gray with help from former school superintendent Maude Frazier, the group kicked off its so-called Porchlight Campaign with a one-hour telecast on May 24, 1955, featuring Strip entertainers, civic leaders, and university officials, all imploring the community to help.[45]

Ensuing weeks saw the chamber of commerce solicit funds from local businessmen, while high school and college students canvassed every home from North Las Vegas to Boulder City. The effort was a smashing success, with over $135,000 raised. A month earlier, the campaign had received a major boost when Mrs. Estelle Wilbourne, a former resident and wife of a Modesto, California, real estate dealer, promised sixty acres of land along remote Maryland Parkway "behind the Flamingo Hotel" on condition that the university purchase an additional twenty acres from her for $35,000.[46] The local fund-raising, combined with Wilbourne's offer, convinced lawmakers to appropriate the $200,000 for a Las Vegas college. Following the celebration sparked by this event, spirits were somewhat dampened by the news that Mrs. Wilbourne had actually purchased the land a few years earlier for about $100 thanks to loopholes in the state's land laws. So, what originally seemed like a reasonable deal for $440 an acre (other land in the vicinity had been appraised for up to $2,000 an acre) quickly became a local embarrassment. Nevertheless, the state proceeded with construction of the first building. In April 1956, Maude Frazier, who as an assemblyman had fought to obtain legislative support for a southern branch, turned the first blade of soil. Appropriately, when the building opened in 1957, Nevada's regents named it in her honor. A second structure, Archie Grant Hall, opened the following year, providing students and teachers of the newly named Southern Regional Division of the University of Nevada with enough classroom space for the foreseeable future.[47]

For a while it seemed that after the construction of the second building, the state's commitment would end. A year earlier, consultants had advised university President Minard Stout to emphasize the campus in Reno. Their report, however, brought a quick reaction from Las Vegans who were uncomfortable about Reno authorities determining the future of higher education in the south. In a fiery editorial in October 1956, the ever-vigilant Al Cahlan scolded the University of Nevada Survey Committee recommendation that Nevada Southern should remain a "junior or community college until 1965 at least." Conceding that in the 1940s southern Nevadans had not pushed for a Las Vegas campus "because the University of Nevada needed all the money possible for its support" from a legislature that was "extremely niggardly" in funding higher education, the editor asserted that Las Vegas's growth now justified a campus. According to Cahlan, in the last legislative session Maude Frazier had pushed through a bill establishing Nevada Southern; as a result, the northern-dominated board of regents "had little else they could do but set up the college here." He then blamed the obvious lack of enthusiasm and funding for the campus on current Nevada Governor Charles Russell. Complaining that southern Nevada was "getting a little tired of being treated like the poor relation," the editor urged Clark County citizens to register to vote in the next state election. Why? Because it was "not too early for residents . . . to start action on ganging up on the northern Nevada politicians."[48]

Local outrage combined with the region's continuing economic growth to fuel added enthusiasm for expanding the local campus. Regents acted to appease the south. In 1957, William D. Carlson, a Stout protégé and former dean of men and student affairs at Reno, was assigned to run the Las Vegas campus. Yet, despite administrative reorganization and program expansion, the school continued to be underfunded. Though surrounded by a mushrooming city, Nevada Southern limped along with a meager budget into the 1960s. In the face of modest state funding, local support was crucial to the school's future. In May 1962, Carlson helped organize a seven-member foundation to raise funds for campus expansion. But the main prerequisite was substantial state support not only for buildings and faculty but for more land itself.[49]

Despite these efforts, the school grew slowly, not graduating its first senior class (only 29 students) until 1964. While thousands of dollars were spent annually to develop the campus, many Las Vegans nonetheless accused the gerrymandered state legislature of foot dragging. Even the regents were not exempt from the wrath of the *Review-Journal*'s new editor, Bob Brown. In a 1962 column, he decried the inferior status accorded the school in the regents' proposed 1962–63 university budget. Noting that the Reno campus stood to get 90 percent of the budget (despite only a 10 percent enrollment increase) while the Las Vegas campus had enjoyed a 20 percent student jump, the editor reprimanded the regents for "rubber stamping" the pro-Reno policies of university President Charles Armstrong. Moreover, the fact that Nevada Southern (with a total proposed budget of only $448,000) had to absorb 15 percent of the budget cuts while garnering only 10 percent of spending increases, infuriated Brown. "We never said that money alone is going to build a university here," he declared. "It will [also] take an obvious need and sincere desire [for a school] by the people of southern Nevada." Obviously, a meager 10 percent allotment from the university budget indicated that the regents were "not convinced that this exists in Las Vegas."[50]

Nevertheless, progress was made. The town's growth only reinforced the importance of the fledgling university while legislative reapportionment restored some balance to funding. As enrollment grew, building projects began to multiply, especially after local bankers E. Parry Thomas and Jerry Mack helped form a foundation in 1968 to fund the acquisition of another 300 acres of land for campus expansion. As enrollment passed 5,000 students in 1969, the board of regents, in a dramatic move, forever removed the stigma of inferiority by dividing the state university into two campuses and renaming the southern program the University of Nevada, Las Vegas. The school received another boost that June when newly appointed President Roman Zorn announced regent approval of the far west's first College of Hotel Administration. The infant hotel program which had been part of the College of Business and Economics was now liberated and free to build vocational ties to the city's resort industry.[51]

Yet, in spite of these efforts, UNLV could not begin to compete with Arizona, Arizona State, and the University of New Mexico, especially in computer science and engineering. A variety of factors, including the opposition of northern Nevada legislators, delayed construction of UNLV's engineering school until 1987. Even then, many northerners still wondered aloud why millions of dollars should be spent for this when the Reno campus already had such a facility. To a large extent, it was this kind of thinking, coupled with Las Vegas's late development, which delayed construction of the kind of university that Motorola, General Electric, and other major companies wanted near their plants.[52]

Aside from utilities and schools, Las Vegas's early failure to annex more of its valley also served to fragment the promotion of industry. As early as the 1960s, Henderson and Las Vegas were direct competitors in the battle to attract firms to the valley. The county too had an interest in widening its tax base to supplement the enormous revenues provided by the Basic complex. To a large extent, this fragmentation and competition was minimal in Albuquerque, Tucson, and Phoenix. These cities had already succeeded in capturing large portions of their metropolitan areas. In Albuquerque, for instance, town fathers launched an aggressive annexation drive as early as 1940. Support from local newspapers boosted the chances for success. While the *Review-Journal* did little to promote Ernie Cragin's effort to annex the Strip, the influential *Albuquerque Journal* played an active role, arguing in 1940 that "to all intents and purposes, the entire built up community that surrounds Albuquerque IS Albuquerque." Buoyed by this support, city fathers invited homeowners to join the town. Some areas capitulated immediately; others came later after municipal leaders cut off fire and water service.[53]

To a large extent, the campaign succeeded. Albuquerque's area of 11 square miles grew to 16 by war's end, 24 by 1948, and a whopping 82.2 by 1973! While Las Vegas labored in vain to annex a couple of hotels just across San Francisco Street, Albuquerque commandeered miles of valuable tracts upon the great mesa east of the Rio Grande, while casting a proprietary glance at the undeveloped west mesa, too. Crucial to this success was the cooperative spirit of the New Mexico legislature, which, unlike Nevada's, recognized the value of allowing cities and not counties to manage events in urban areas. Recognizing that many corporations respected a municipal government that was both responsive to business and capable of controlling its metropolitan area, New Mexico legislators in 1963 passed a law prohibiting the incorporation of any community within five miles of a city. This effectively prevented Bernalillo County commissioners from blocking the growth of Albuquerque to safeguard their own power base. While eastern and midwestern cities (and Las Vegas) lost a substantial tax base to their suburbs, Albuquerque captured the wealthy Anglo neighborhoods to the north and high-tech sections to the south and east. Thus, supported by these revenues, the municipality easily expanded its street, power, and sewer systems outward, which, in turn, only attracted more firms to town.[54]

Like Albuquerque, Phoenix acted to prevent the excessive fragmentation of its metropolitan area. Boosted by the wartime development of Luke Air Force Base, Goodyear Aircraft, and other job centers, Phoenix saw its population jump from a 1940 figure of 65,000 to 106,000 ten years later. Despite this growth, Phoenix still occupied only 20 square miles. As historian Michael Konig has observed, "the city faced the possibility of geographical stagnation if outlying sections were incorporated as independent villages or towns." Already, Scottsdale, Tempe, and Glendale lurked on the urban periphery as potential predators. Phoenix officials, however, were equal to the challenge. Unlike Henderson and Las Vegas, the Arizona city snared burgeoning industrial districts with forthright moves. In 1957, the town launched a campaign to annex valuable factory and yard lands to the southwest. Like the hotels south of Las Vegas, the Reynolds Metal Company (a division of Reynolds Aluminum), Allison Steel, and the Del Webb Corporation, joined by a series of smaller firms, initially resisted the effort. But Phoenix officials persevered, offering a series of shrewd concessions which included relaxed fire and building codes, and cancellation of city sales taxes on certain business goods. Like San Antonio, Houston, Albuquerque, and other sunbelt cities, Phoenix recognized that the short-run waiver or even cancellation of certain fees and taxes would be offset in the long run by an expanded tax base. Las Vegas might have made a similar deal with the El Rancho, Flamingo, and Last Frontier, relaxing its building codes and temporarily deferring city property taxes and even table fees as a gesture of goodwill, but it did not.[55]

Thanks to an aggressive annexation policy, Phoenix expanded from 17 square miles (106,000 population) in 1950 to an impressive 180 square miles (and 400,000 people) by 1960 (in 1985 Las Vegas comprised less than 40 square miles). This substantial increase in territory and population fattened town coffers. Of course, the process was far more complicated than can be pictured here. Indeed, Tempe, Scottsdale, and other suburban cities pushed aggressive policies of their own. But in the main, the capital city's expansionist efforts were highly successful, especially in nearby residential areas. Beginning in the early 1950s, Phoenix created an annexation division headed by an annexation manager in the City Planning Department (while Las Vegas barely had a planning department at all). This division constantly monitored building activity along the urban periphery and targeted likely candidates for annexation. Then too, like Albuquerque and various Texas cities, both Phoenix and Tucson benefited from state legislative help. In 1961, the Arizona passed the so-called Anti-Incorporation Statute which banned the incorporation of any new community within six miles of an existing city or town whose population exceeded 5,000 people. As the Director of the League of Arizona Cities and Towns recently noted, "if it had not been for this law, . . . we would have had three or four times the number of incorporated places in both metropolitan areas."[56]

While New Mexico and Arizona state legislators supported existing cities, their counterparts in Nevada did not. At the local level, Las Vegas officials also bore responsibility for the city's failure to expand its borders. The lackluster pursuit of annexation can be attributed partially to the town's rapid jump to metropolitan size. In 1930, Las Vegas was a struggling town of 4,000 people; just twenty years later it was a viable candidate for SMSA status. Yet, even into the 1960s, the municipality continued to be run by the old elite—consisting mainly of longtime businessmen who, though well meaning, were novices at big-time city building. Men like John Russell, Ernie Cragin, and even C. D. Baker had lived in Las Vegas for thirty years or more, as had many of the city commissioners and chamber of commerce officials. These leaders, while eager to promote the area, nevertheless tended to view urban problems through a small-town lens. To some extent, the steady growth of Las Vegas's resort economy was enough progress for them. Anxious to maintain their control, the old guard was slow to turn on one of their own even if it were for the community's benefit. Witness the tolerance shown Samuel Lawson. While Phoenix, Albuquerque, and other cities in Texas and California sought out-of-state talent to coordinate their utilities and run their government, Las Vegas tended to promote from within. Typical was the policy toward city managers: between 1943 and the mid-1960s, candidates for this most important office were mainly recruited from within the city's own government. Proven talent from other states was not sought.[57]

Finally, Las Vegas possessed one more liability in its struggle for industry: casino gambling. While many observers today might dismiss the deterrent effect of gaming upon industry, the moral climate of the forties and fifties cannot be denied. Reservations about Las Vegas even afflicted Howard Hughes, who had embraced the town as his personal playground in the forties and fifties. Beginning in the forties, Hughes acquired over 40,000 acres of land south and west of Las Vegas. At the same time, he was negotiating with federal authorities to construct an international airport at nearby Mormon Mesa to guarantee more air space for TWA and other airlines servicing southern California. According to his plan, passengers would be transported to and from the terminals by high-speed trains running between Las Vegas and Los Angeles. On a grander scale, he intended to transform Las Vegas into an aerospace center. According to the then Clark County Commission Chairman George Franklin, by 1946 Hughes had almost convinced Boeing Aircraft to leave Seattle for southern Nevada. Apparently, Boeing was dissatisfied with the pro-union climate in postwar Seattle and wanted to escape. Hughes told Franklin that he intended to sell or lease 20,000 acres to Boeing and perhaps use the rest for Hughes Aviation. After several months of inaction, Franklin pressed Hughes for more details and was then told that the deal was off. While southern Nevada's climate and tax structure were appealing, both Hughes and Boeing apparently became concerned about the prospects of 10,000 aerospace workers cashing their paychecks in casinos. As a result, Boeing remained in Washington, and Hughes's Summa Corporation gradually subdivided much of the land, making millions in real estate.[58]

Hughes's view was shared by other industrialists. BMI's Howard Eells had voiced similar concerns earlier in 1940–41 when he tackled the question of where to house his projected work force. At a series of meetings in Washington, Eells opposed Las Vegas as a site for BMI housing. In fact, just six days after the Washington meetings, J. D. Platt, a BMI manager, wrote a memo to Eells recommending a strong stand against building employee housing in Las Vegas because of the "wide open condition of booze, gambling and brothels." Yet, despite American industry's obvious aversion to the casino city by the dam, Las Vegas undertook no effort to outlaw gambling. According to longtime newspaperman John Cahlan, even in the 1930s there was no group in town which advocated "killing the goose that laid the golden egg." While he and others conceded that wide-open gambling probably discouraged many companies "especially from the east, midwest and bible belt" from moving to Las Vegas, there seems to have been no second thoughts about the town's historic support of the resort economy.[59]

Las Vegas eventually mounted a concerted effort to capture industry. In 1956, following the closing of the bankrupt Royal Nevada and Stardust hotels, local businessmen acted. Alarmed by stories in the national media proclaiming an end to the Las Vegas boom, gas company president Harold Laub led a movement to form an organization capable of attracting industry and convincing investors that southern Nevada's economy was still healthy. In summer 1956, Laub joined with insurance broker Harley E. Harmon, Harry Manente, Julian Moore, Spencer Butterfield, Herbert Grier, Dwight Gravett, and other leading businessmen to form the Southern Nevada Industrial Foundation to develop a nonresort industrial base for the area. The nonprofit organization supported itself through donations from local businesses. Within weeks of its birth, the foundation commissioned Duff, Anderson and Clark, a respected industrial research firm from Chicago, to conduct an industrial survey of the metropolitan area. To no one's surprise, the company produced a 64-page report touting Las Vegas's industrial potential. The foundation mailed copies to dozens of firms inquiring about a potential move to southern Nevada and followed up that effort with annual publications brimming with favorable statistics concerning manufacturing output, commercial growth, and new investment opportunities. As early as the fall of 1956, the foundation had succeeded in largely reversing the city's negative economic image. Furthermore, the Duff industrial survey combined with other publicity to encourage inquiries from dozens of chemical, plastics, and electronics companies considering new locations for their assembly plants.[60]

A decade later, the organization was strengthened by a new generation of leaders, including Valley Bank's E. Parry Thomas, Southwest Gas President William Laub (Harold's son), hotelman Frank Scott, Bruce Beckley, and others. They were ably assisted by John Cahlan, brother of longtime *Review-Journal* editor Al Cahlan, who served as manager. It was Cahlan who actively participated in national organizations devoted to industrial development and, through this experience, instructed the foundation (later renamed the Nevada Development Authority) on the successful recruitment techniques being used by Phoenix, Albuquerque, and other cities. Beginning in the late sixties and early seventies, the foundation began courting high-tech, processing, and distribution firms at promotional dinners hosted by newly elected Governor Paul Laxalt. Moreover, E. Parry Thomas and other bankers were on hand to discuss potential loan terms for the purchase of industrial sites and plant construction. Of course, it did not match the size and intensity of Arizona's development programs, but Las Vegas at least had begun to promote industry with a major-league effort.[61] In the seventies and especially the eighties the movement gained momentum, as over 450 local businesses joined and contributed to the Nevada Development Authority. By 1985, the N.D.A. would lure such corporate giants as Citicorp, Levi Strauss, and Ford Aerospace to the Las Vegas Valley, helping to dispel the region's traditionally unsavory reputation in corporate circles.

Still, considering all of its natural advantages, Las Vegas lagged badly in the struggle for industry in the urban southwest. Hoover Dam and BMI had awarded the town an invaluable start. By 1942, over 13,000 workers toiled at the giant factory. But, at no time since the war has Basic employment surpassed 2,000. To some extent, Las Vegas suffered a unique disadvantage because, prior to the 1970s, its major industry did not support diversification. More than one casino executive expressed private reservations about filling the valley with capitalists to whom gambling was anathema. Up and down the Strip there were concerns that, in an effort to protect factory workers from the dangers of gambling, drinking, and absenteeism, industrial executives might eventually form a new political constituency comprised of themselves, church leaders, company wives, and thousands of pious employees to restrict or even outlaw casino gambling in Clark County. At the least, Las Vegas's recreational economy, with its aversion to air pollution, limited the potential growth of heavy industry in southern Nevada. As the writer Christopher Currin recently noted, "Bugsy Siegel, Meyer Lansky and the other hotel-casino builders upstaged Howard Eells, Major Ball and [a] host of governors and congressmen. . . . When politicians of that generation imagined the region's future, they saw something like Pittsburgh in the desert, not Baghdad on the Strip."[62]

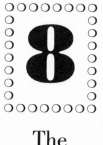

The
City-Building
Process

Like other cities, Las Vegas grew physically in response to the needs of its major industries. The location of stores, homes, and offices—even the direction of town expansion itself—was dictated initially by the railroad and later by the resort and defense industries. These economies determined where the job zones and commuter suburbs would be. Casino gambling was more than a unique form of leisure, it was a powerful force which shaped the urbanization of Las Vegas. As early as the 1950s, the great casino hotels on the Strip played a major role in determining the direction of road networks, apartment complexes, and shopping centers in the southern part of the metropolitan area. The blossoming of a resort sector along the Los Angeles (south) side of town left the Salt Lake (north) side of Las Vegas available for military operations. By the 1950s, the emerging military complex beyond Lake Mead Boulevard influenced the configuration of growth to the north. Besides the federal government, several other agents also guided the city-building process, including major developers, the water and sewer districts, key bankers, and even underworld investors.

In the early decades, when transportation was the town's major industry, Senator Clark's railroad orchestrated the physical growth of Las Vegas. Beginning in 1905, the railroad tracks acted as a baseline, encouraging development to the east and west. Like other young cities, Las Vegas grew in a helter-skelter pattern following the opening of the original Clark's Townsite in May 1905. Actually, the first townsite antedated this event. J. T. McWilliams, a surveyor and valley resident since the 1890s, began a town on the west side of the tracks in March 1905 even as two more "paper towns" were also being planned. Unfortunately for McWilliams, the railroad tracks proved to be a formidable barrier to wagon traffic. As noted earlier, once Senator Clark opened his townsite and station east of the tracks, the McWilliams community soon lost most of its inhabitants. Such was not the case with Peter Buol's subdivision east of the tracks. Buol, a former railroad chef, foresaw that if the nascent town were successful, it would grow well beyond the 1,200-acre capacity of Clark's plat. In a daring move, Buol had purchased land as close to Clark's future townsite as possible, and laid out Buck's Addition. Buol's development, stretching east from Fifth to Tenth and north from Ogden to Linden streets, also antedated the Las Vegas auction of May 15, 1905. On that day, however, his success was not yet assured. While McWilliams had stores, bars, and three newspapers serving his community, Buol counted little more than a few unseemly squatters and tent dwellers who could not afford housing near the railroad. [1]

The situation changed dramatically in a few months. By June 1905, a disgruntled McWilliams saw business and residents flock across the tracks to the new Las Vegas townsite. As Senator Clark's plat filled with tents and buildings, Buol's subdivision became an instant suburb. The next few years saw building activity ignore the west completely and spread directly east into Buol's land. Not yet discouraged, McWilliams maintained his faith in the Westside, and in June 1905 actually extended his community by platting Wilde's Addition between A and E streets from Elm to Pine—a move which ultimately failed to challenge the axis of growth down Fremont.

Buoyed by the rapid development of lots to the east, Buol quickly platted the Grandview, Fairview, and Pioneer Heights additions, all in June 1905. The Fairview tract represented a natural extension of Buck's, running north of Fremont to conform to the northeast-southwest tilt of Clark's Townsite which had been laid out at N 27 degrees, 45 minutes E of true north (see Map 4). The Grandview Addition broke the pattern. Located just above Buck's and Fairview, streets in Grandview ran almost true north and south. This was a critical move by Buol, because Grandview created a base for north-south arteries which other developers could extend. Indeed, the Stewart Addition, Fourteenth Street City Addition, and the Boulder Dam Townsite Addition of the late 1920s north of Fremont Street along with the Gibson, Jones, Sunrise, and other additions south of Fremont, adopted the north-south street precedent of Grandview—an

Map 4: Las Vegas, 1940

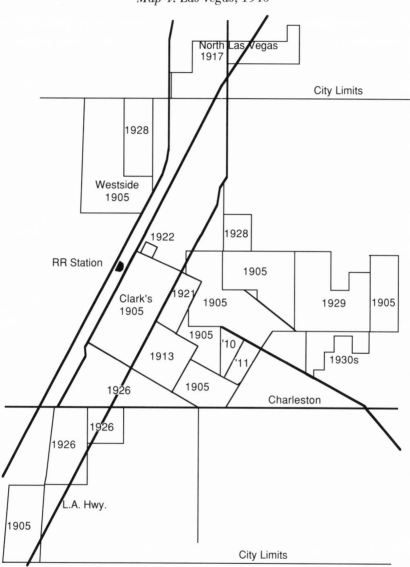

early pattern which shaped the directions of Maryland Parkway, Eastern, Pecos, and other major arteries of the later metropolis.[2]

By 1930, the Hoover Dam boom and, to a lesser extent, the legalization of gambling encouraged more development to the east and south. As tourism rose and the casino industry expanded downtown, many lots in these zones were filled in with homes. Of course, the town's early "developers" merely subdivided parcels and laid out streets; they did not erect houses for sale. It was not until the war boom of 1940–41 that Las Vegas saw its first subdivision where homes were built upon the land and sold as a package to the buyers. The Huntridge Addition, as it was called, extended from the Charleston Boulevard area south to near San Francisco Street. Previous additions southward had run along either the Los Angeles or Boulder Highways, but Huntridge boldly cut a new path south along Maryland Street (Parkway).

The development comprised only a small part of the 4,000 acres south of town controlled by speculator Leigh Hunt. He and his wife Jesse had come to Las Vegas in 1923, having already made and lost several fortunes speculating in Korean gold mines, Sudanese cotton, American newspapers, and Canadian wheat. Hunt saw in Las Vegas a potential winter haven for the wealthy, comparable to Palm Springs and Tucson. So, in the years following the disastrous railroad strike of 1922 but before the Boulder Dam announcement, he bought thousands of acres from the federal government and speculators who had given up on the town's stagnant economy. Hunt, who died in 1931, never lived to develop the resorts he planned. Unwilling to pursue their dream, his wife Jesse gradually liquidated the estate by selling off tracts to Thomas Hull and others. Today, the former Hunt lands host virtually every Strip hotel, the Convention Center, and Las Vegas Country Club, as well as Huntridge, Eastwood, Richfield Village, Crestwood, Meadows Acres, Southridge, and other major subdivisions south of Charleston into Paradise Valley. Hunt's massive holdings were surpassed only a few years later by Howard Hughes who, beginning in the 1940s, acquired over 40,000 acres from the Bureau of Land Management (often for less than $2.50 per acre)— tracts which today comprise most of Henderson west to the Spring Mountains.[3]

Despite the investments of these men, the actual city-building process in the years after 1940 was directed by a group of new developers who followed the Huntridge model, laying out subdivisions with homes and utilities to attract the throngs of discriminating homeowners drawn to Las

Vegas by the town's resort economy. Some of the new builders were
California transplants. Typical was the case of R. J. "Bob" Kaltenborn, a
San Bernardino native who came to the valley in 1932 to begin a wholesale auto parts business. Several years later, he became active in promoting the town and eventually presided over the chamber of commerce. Like
other business investors, he envisioned a prosperous postwar future for
Las Vegas and anticipated a strong residential growth pattern west of the
railroad tracks. In the 1940s, Kaltenborn and his friend Bob Griffith
"scraped up" $2,000 and began purchasing land in what is today one of
Las Vegas's most fashionable sections, Rancho Circle. Ensuing years saw
the partners, with the help of banker Nate Mack and Murray Wollman,
purchase acres of Union Pacific land in the area "awful cheap" and
develop the one- and two-acre lots which eventually hosted the elegant
mansions of the city's elite.[4]

On a larger scale, Ernest Becker, following in the footsteps of his
father, began his career in the home-building business after World War II.
During the next three decades, he built tracts in Texas, Georgia, and
southern California, as well as Las Vegas. He came to town in 1945 and,
like Kaltenborn, exploited the new growth trend to the west. Over the
course of the next thirty years, he erected eight major shopping centers
and over 2,500 homes in Charleston Heights, Stratford Estates, Mayflower Estates, and Charleston Estates. As Becker noted in a 1985
interview, "the opportunities are as great and even greater now. But it was
easier in my time because I could buy a piece of ground much cheaper. I
could buy an acre for $500. Today, if you buy 20 acres here, you can pay
$200,000 an acre." Becker built these tracts in the forties and fifties
despite the lack of a sewer and water system. Undeterred, he drilled
artesian wells and formed his own water company to service home buyers.
While Becker's homes for the most part enjoyed sewer service, others in
the western suburbs did not. Fortunately, this was not yet a major problem
to new construction, because septic tanks provided a temporary solution
until sewer mains finally crisscrossed the zone in the 1960s.[5]

By 1960, thanks to the efforts of Becker and others, building began to
spread far beyond the old downtown core, stretching south and then
eastward and westward using the Strip as a baseline. After 1940, Las
Vegas complemented the original east-west grid with a north-south street
system of blocks and lots which joined the old townsite in a contrived
form. In the forties, fifties, and sixties, developers superimposed an
automobile city over the old railroad town. As one building preservation-

ist recently noted, "within this grid of traffic arteries [was] a patchwork of residential subdivisions, shopping centers, gambling casinos, office and industrial enclaves and vacant land."[6]

The lack of planning was obvious. But city and especially county policy was designed to promote development with a minimal amount of government interference. As a result, "in-filling" was not required and zoning variances were common. Speculators sitting on vacant land were not forced to erect streetlights (even on main roads like Flamingo and Tropicana near the Strip) and no special taxes or penalties were levied for failure to improve the lot's value with a building. The policy only promoted leapfrog growth, which often forced developers to go a mile or more farther out to find available building land. This development pattern ultimately resulted in expensive extensions of gas, water, and sewer mains (blasted through incredibly hard desert clay) to service the town's new, low-density, affluent residential zones. In addition, the growth pattern south and east of Las Vegas created, in the words of consultant Charles Paige, "a checkerboard effect" dominated by "large residential subdivisions connected by commercial strips along major streets and separated by equally large squares of undeveloped land."[7]

Despite the lack of orderly physical development, Las Vegas real estate boomed. Witness the case of Maryland Parkway, today one of the valley's main commercial thoroughfares. In the late 1950s, Irwin Molasky, a Missouri transplant, teamed with Desert Inn general manager Moe Dalitz, casino executive Allard Roen, and grocer Merv Adelson to form the Paradise Development Company, a firm designed to promote commercial and residential building projects in the growing, unincorporated suburbs south of Las Vegas. The group's first major project was the construction of Sunrise Hospital in 1959 on Maryland Parkway, a formerly obscure, two-lane, direct road meandering southward from the populous Huntridge section of middle- and upper-income homes. Flushed by the success of their hospital venture, Molasky and associates began to glimpse a grand vision of what Maryland Parkway could become, if developed. Within a few years they transformed the area into a medical center by flanking the hospital with three and later four professional buildings. Also in the early 1960s, the men began acquiring large tracts on both sides of the north-south artery which, by 1962, linked Sahara Avenue with the newly completed jet runways at McCarran International. During the next fifteen years, Paradise Development built a variety of projects which transformed the road into the metropolitan area's premiere commercial strip.

Aside from Sunrise Hospital, construction included Maryland Professional Buildings I and II (largely medical offices to service Sunrise), the sprawling Las Vegas International Country Club (consisting of a championship golf course bordered by middle- and upper-income townhouses), multi-storied Regency Towers luxury condominiums bordering the golf course, the Sunrise City Shopping Center, the Commercial Center shopping complex near the Sahara city line, and in 1967 the Boulevard Mall. The latter, the town's first modern indoor mall, stretched for almost a half mile along Maryland Parkway and brought large Sears, J. C. Penney, and Woolworth stores to the suburbs for the first time. Molasky later added other shopping centers until his developments stretched for three miles between Sahara Avenue and the University of Nevada, Las Vegas campus near Flamingo. At the same time, Paradise Development also built other projects, including Valley Bank Plaza downtown, Westwood Homes, Colony Townhouses, and the Stardust (later Sahara-Nevada) Country Club, but Maryland Parkway was its greatest triumph.[8]

As late as the mid-1980s, Maryland Parkway remained the town's dominant commercial strip. The Molasky group's success lay in its ability to project and reinforce the southward march of commerce and suburbanization. As Map 5 indicates, the great casino hotels dominated the Strip, with their sprawling golf courses and parking lots reaching out to the railroad and Interstate 15 on the west and to nearby Paradise Road on the east. Industrial Road and Highland Avenue on the west naturally hosted the construction yards, small manufacturing firms, wholesalers, warehousing, and shipping firms which required a location near the train yards. Farther west of Industrial, the next major north-south artery was Valley View and then Decatur, but in the early 1960s they were beyond the town's central building zone. Moreover, neither the sanitation district nor the water district had yet extended enough large-diameter mains that far west to service a major commercial zone. East of the Strip, Paradise Road was an excellent parallel artery, but its land use was mixed—a patchwork of resort, commercial, and even residential buildings. Furthermore, by 1962, it had become the main road to the new McCarran airport terminal. Molasky and his associates therefore chose the next parallel artery to the east, Maryland Parkway.

The southward trend of building was also obvious to them. Since the 1950s, subdivisions had mostly filled in the east-west grid of lands within the city of Las Vegas. Development in North Las Vegas and to the northeast in county lands near Nellis, while substantial, consisted mostly

Map 5: Principal Streets, 1980

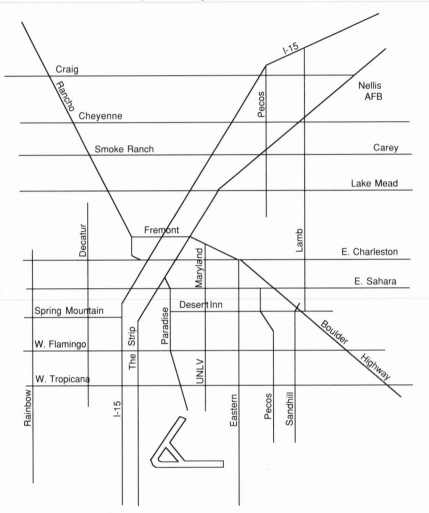

of low- and middle-income residential housing. So, in 1960, the Molasky group saw a clear trend to the south and east. In fact, Pardee, Chism, and other major developers were already building expensive new subdivisions of attractive townhouses and apartment complexes in a zone south of the Sahara city line between Paradise and the Boulder Highway as far south as Tropicana.[9]

The Molasky group surely figured that the airport's runways would pose a temporary barrier to residential growth farther south until the seventies and eighties. But east of the Strip, Paradise and Winchester were fast becoming the new residential center for Strip commuters, teachers, doctors, lawyers, professors, and businessmen. By establishing the shopping, medical, and university facilities so quickly, the Molasky group awarded Maryland Parkway an invaluable head start over parallel thoroughfares to the east. Indeed, the late sixties and seventies would see most residential developments fill in tracts behind the mall. Gradually, Eastern, Pecos-McLeod, Sandhill, Mountain Vista, and other arteries parallel but east of Maryland would attract some commercial centers; however, they would be limited primarily to intersections. Home, condominium, and apartment developments bordered by residential access roads would mostly line these streets. Later, in the early 1970s other developers would duplicate Molasky's success on Valley View Boulevard (the Meadows Mall in 1978), Decatur, West Sahara, West Charleston and, to a lesser extent, on Rainbow. But the city and county grew westward only after new streets opened access to the area.[10]

In addition to few roads, the lack of an adequate water and sewer system also limited growth to the west for many years. While some developers like Ernie Becker secured enough artesian well lands to form their own water company and directly service home buyers, most were less fortunate. As a result, subdivisions west of Valley View (especially in the county areas with limited urban services) were few and far between. A major boost to development finally came in the late 1960s when Pardee Construction Company acquired 1,160 acres of the old Stardust International Raceway west of Rainbow Boulevard to begin southern Nevada's first master-planned community, Spring Valley. A plumbing subcontractor, Bob Ruppert, recalled that in 1969 Spring Valley had no water, gas, or power. Undeterred, the resourceful Pardee brothers, J. Douglas, Hoyt, and George M., equipped their model homes with "bottled gas, and water . . . drawn from a tank set up about a quarter of a mile away. The sewer was run into a pit. At the time they [the Pardees] brought the sewer line all the way up Tropicana from the other side of the freeway." Despite these primitive conditions, the credibility of the brothers' project lay in their company's prestige and past success. Pardee, a southern California firm, first came to Las Vegas in 1953. Acquiring sites within the city's borders, Pardee built College Park Homes largely for returning veterans. The $10,500 structures were sold to them for as little as $1 down. The mid-1950s saw the firm build its "forever homes" (so-called because of their cinder block construction, steel doors, and rock roofs) in Francisco Park near Sahara and Maryland Parkway. In the later fifties and sixties Pardee followed the suburban shift to Paradise and Winchester, building larger versions of Francisco Park off Eastern Avenue and in-filling Molasky's Maryland Parkway zone with the Casa Vegas Apartments behind Sunrise Hospital. So, with its reputation firmly established, the company's ambitious development to the far west triggered a migration of developers outward toward the mountains. [11]

Of course, no discussion of the city-building process in Las Vegas should omit the heavy capital investment made by "the mob" and its reputed lieutenants. As has been shown, organized crime figures played a major role in hotel financing, tax skimming, and other illegal rackets. To be sure, they speeded up Strip development in the 1950s, especially at the Dunes, Stardust, Flamingo, Riviera, Tropicana, and Sands. The various gangland factions made and lost millions, first building and then overbuilding the Strip in the late forties and fifties. In turn, these huge capital investments invigorated the town's relatively small-scale resort industry, exerting a substantial multiplier effect upon the community's economy. Indeed, the city's payrolls, supply industries, housing market, school enrollments, local revenues, and bank deposits were fortified for thirty years by these major hotels. In fact, it has been estimated that in Las Vegas, each new hotel room added between four and five jobs to the metropolitan economy. [12]

But the contribution of reputed underworld figures goes beyond their hotel-building activities. To some extent, these men even influenced the suburban development of the metropolitan area. In December 1950, for instance, former Siegel associate Gus Greenbaum (who is generally credited with saving both the Flamingo and Riviera from bankruptcy) led the movement to create the unincorporated township of Paradise City. Elected as the chairman of the town board, Greenbaum, as "Mayor of Paradise," spearheaded a variety of local efforts for streets, sewers, schools, and other improvements to launch the new community and keep its residents independent of Las Vegas. On another front, the Dunes's Major Riddle, an alleged beneficiary of mob funding, fought a determined battle to save that resort. Part of this effort involved securing an ample water supply for the hotel's golf course. In 1961, he teamed with Moe Dalitz of the Desert Inn and J. Kell Houssels of the Tropicana to pressure Governor Grant Sawyer and the state engineer, Ed Muth, for more well water. While county commissioners argued that the supply used by the three courses could service over a thousand new apartments, Riddle, Dalitz, and other executives recognized the value of golf courses to the area's recreational economy. In a resort city, numerous golf courses adjacent to the hotels were essential to the recreational scheme. In terms of profits for the community, golf courses brought more big spenders to town than low-rent apartments. In the end, it was thanks to their vision that Las Vegas, like Miami Beach and later Honolulu, maintained a system of golf courses adjacent or close to its major resorts. [13]

Critics like Ovid Demaris have also emphasized the role played by Jimmy Hoffa in the city's development. Obviously, the Teamster chief made valuable contributions to the growth of Las Vegas. In 1959, he used his position as a trustee for the Teamsters Central States Pension Fund to approve a loan for much-needed Sunrise Hospital (today Humana Hospital Sunrise). The capital provided by Hoffa, at the urging of Desert Inn boss Moe Dalitz, not only built the medical facility, but partially helped boost the investment careers of several men who in the sixties and seventies would become major town builders: Nathan Adelson, his son Merv, and Irwin Molasky.

Even though Demaris and reporter Ed Reid in their national bestseller, *The Green Felt Jungle*, juxtaposed the names of these men with Hoffa's to insinuate an unsavory series of deals, such was not the case. Whatever the Teamster elite's motives for financing Sunrise and other projects, for the Las Vegas side of the story, Adelson and Molasky helped the community as a whole by building the needed hospital (which served as a low-cost medical center for Teamster and Culinary Union members as well as the general public). In addition, Teamster officials made other legal investments in community building projects with Molasky, Adelson, and other legitimate investment groups. While writers like Demaris and Steven Brill have rightly emphasized the overinvestment of the pension fund in real estate and the unsavory character of Hoffa, Teamster investments in Las Vegas casinos, housing developments, and other projects nonetheless injected desperately needed capital into both the resort industry and surrounding community. Molasky and other legitimate businessmen then used the profits derived from these projects to re-invest many times over in the city-building process. Over the years, Teamster money and casino profits from alleged and former mob properties have supplied Las Vegas with the capital needed to develop. Reputed mob associates boosted the economy of Las Vegas just as they did earlier in Miami Beach, Havana, New York, Chicago, and virtually every major city in the United States.[14]

Still, no matter the investment group, plans for residential, commercial, and especially resort development could not have progressed as successfully as they did in Las Vegas without the cooperation of local bankers. From the earliest days when John S. Park and his First State Bank (later First National and today First Interstate) extended loans to local clubs and merchants, banks were crucial to the growth of Las Vegas. As in the case of many small cities, Las Vegas needed the added capital of larger out-of-state banks to finance major commercial and residential development projects. But because of the city's notorious image, most American banks withheld funding for hotel construction and expansion between 1940 and 1980. This explains the town's partial reliance upon Teamster and syndicate loans.[15]

There was only one local bank whose willingness to extend credit for casino construction benefited the community as a whole. The Bank of Las Vegas (reorganized as Valley Bank in 1964) began granting casino loans shortly after its founding in 1954. Recognizing Las Vegas's need for another bank, especially one with more liberal lending policies, business leaders like Nate Mack (father of Jerry Mack), Bob Kaltenborn, Jake Von Tobel, Bruce Beckley, Herb Jones, and E. Parry Thomas, plus Salt Lake City bankers Walter Cosgriff and Ken Sullivan, joined with several local physicians to form the Bank of Las Vegas in January 1954. The bank grew quickly, with the forward-thinking Thomas as vice president of loan production. Ensuing years saw Thomas and Mack lead the bank to substantial profits, with a major portion of the bank's portfolio consisting of casino loans to struggling resorts. In some cases the bank merely administered mortgage and other financial arrangements for loans made by others. But, in either capacity, the bank's list of accomplishments on the Strip was remarkable. In 1958, for instance, Thomas handled a $4 million Teamster loan to help save the Dunes Hotel; later, other resorts benefited from direct Valley Bank loans. Over the course of the next thirty years, Thomas and Mack (Jerry replaced his father Nate), through their lending policies, were largely responsible for the success of many Las

Vegas casinos, most notably the Golden Nugget and its flamboyant proprietor, Steve Wynn.[16]

Valley Bank's portfolio also included many mortgage loans for commercial buildings, shopping centers, and residential subdivisions. Beginning in the late seventies and eighties, other banks like First Interstate cautiously entered the casino loan market both in Nevada and New Jersey. But in the earlier decades, Las Vegas had faced and survived a unique crisis when no bank would underwrite the development of its casino economy. The formation of Valley Bank demonstrated the foresight and resolve of local businessmen to funnel the deposits of local residents into a fund which could be used to promote the physical development of Las Vegas both in the casino core and in the outlying suburbs.

Aside from the developers, mob investors, and bankers, other factors influenced metropolitan development. Three elements were especially crucial to the city-building process: the federal government, the water infrastructure and casino gambling. For its part, the federal government literally created a metropolitan area, and, through its military and public works programs, actually shaped the physical configuration of the urbanized zone. First, in the 1930s Hoover Dam and Boulder City stretched the urbanized area far out to the southeast, connected with Las Vegas by the federally funded Boulder Highway. The 1940s saw this trend reinforced by construction of the Basic Magnesium plant and Henderson townsite. Also in the 1940s, the military induced metropolitan growth in the valley's northeast sector with the air gunnery school and later Nellis. Then, beginning in 1950, the Defense Department stretched the urbanized zone to the northwest quadrant with the development of the Nevada Test Site. Growth to the southwest (toward Blue Diamond) was encouraged by Oddie-Colton funding of the Los Angeles Highway and later Interstate 15, which together have catalyzed the growth of Paradise Valley and the Strip. The fifth point in the emerging star-shaped city was formed in the mid-1970s when federal land grants and highway funds opened portions of the Oran Gragson (Las Vegas) Expressway, which promoted suburban growth to the west. But, aside from shaping the points of this star, Washington also influenced growth and development within and along the edges of the star through the sale of public lands (by the Bureau of Land Management) to literally hundreds of investors from Howard Hughes and Leigh Hunt to the smallest homesteaders.[17]

Federal road-building programs were particularly crucial to the emerging resort city. Fortunately, the town's transportation arteries partially offset the lack of a strong industrial base by improving access to Las Vegas which, in turn, reinforced the mushrooming recreational economy. Even more than the railroad, highway links to southern California were vital to the city's economic and physical growth. Beginning in the 1930s and thanks to federal road funds, the Los Angeles Highway became Las Vegas's economic lifeline, providing California's burgeoning gambling market access to the town's casinos. Within the metropolitan area, the road revolutionized the town's growth patterns, decentralizing the casino core from its traditional location on Fremont Street to the new "four-mile strip" extending from the city limits at San Francisco Street southward to Tropicana. The new Los Angeles road bordered vast tracts of barren desert bypassed by the railroad. As noted earlier, unlike the lots occupied by the downtown clubs, these suburban lands were inexpensive and offered enough room for large resorts with their space-consuming pools, tennis courts, gardens, spas, bungalow units, and parking lots. The El Rancho, Hotel Last Frontier, and Flamingo had all appeared by 1947, followed by even bigger, more lavish resorts in the next decade.[18]

Despite its utility, the two-lane road would have been overwhelmed by the weekend throngs commuting to Las Vegas in the seventies and eighties. An antiquated highway connection with southern California eventually would have diminished Las Vegas's business. So, the construction of Interstate 15 was particularly crucial to the development of the resort city. Completed in the early 1970s, the latter cut the trip from Los Angeles to Las Vegas to under five hours. This smooth, wide road, with gentle banked curves and a center median for added safety, permitted drivers to travel at speeds in excess of 70 miles per hour. But Interstate 15 played another key role, encouraging the sprawl of Las Vegas westward toward the Spring Mountains. Prior to the 1960s, most of the town's main roads stretched from Fremont Street south to Tropicana and from the railroad east to Boulder Highway. Only Charleston Boulevard reached westward all the way out to the mountains. While Bonanza, Owens, and several other crosstown laterals ran a mile or so west of the railroad tracks, there were few main arteries from which developers could build branching roads to provide access to prospective subdivisions far west of the city.

Interstate 15 transformed the situation. First of all, the superhighway did not require the creation of expensive assessment districts. This was fortunate, because many of the lands west of the railroad and especially south of town had few buildings and lacked the value to support burdensome assessments. Instead, the federal government paid 90 percent of the road's cost while the state covered the rest. Second, Interstate 15, once built along a route closely paralleling the northeast-southwest axis of the railroad tracks, provided a substantial artery into which major east-west thoroughfares could feed suburban traffic.[19]

Engineers and planners reasoned that if a short freeway could be built to plug traffic from the western desert lands into Interstate 15, then the latter, which would run parallel to the Strip, could easily transport gaming and hotel employees to their jobs, provided exits were located strategically at Charleston, Sahara, Flamingo, Tropicana, and comparable places in downtown Las Vegas and North Las Vegas. In effect, the federal road would deliver not only tourists from the south but commuters from the west, opening a new real estate frontier in the process. To a large extent, this is exactly what happened. By 1978, the new east-west Oran K. Gragson (formerly the Las Vegas) Expressway combined with a growing number of major crosstown roads (which already had encouraged dozens of subdivisions east of the Strip) to connect with and leapfrog over Interstate 15 to support new road networks and housing systems to the west. As a result, the seventies and eighties saw Tropicana, Spring Mountain Road (Sands Avenue), Sahara, and eventually Flamingo-Dunes Road stretch far to the west. This movement, in turn, inspired the extension of major north-south laterals into the county. Thus, Rancho, Valley View, Decatur, Jones, and even Rainbow began to march southward from their historical confinement north of Sahara down to and in some cases beyond West Tropicana.

The urbanization of lands west of the Strip was influenced further by the expansion of the valley's water system. Crucial in determining the pace of growth were the building policies of the water district which, beginning in the late 1950s, began buying out smaller water companies, enabling the former to acquire more wells and expand (see Map 6). Slowly, as the district enlarged its tax base west of the railroad, it built up assessment districts large enough to fund the extension of large-diameter mains several miles west of the railroad line. This, in turn, permitted the construction of still more subdivisions in anticipation of the Southern Nevada Water Project coming on line. The intensification of residential and commercial construction west of the railroad also promoted the financing of sewer mains. As power, gas, water, and roads rushed westward along Tropicana, Sahara, Spring Mountain, and branched off into subdivisions, the Clark County Sanitation District and city sewer depart-

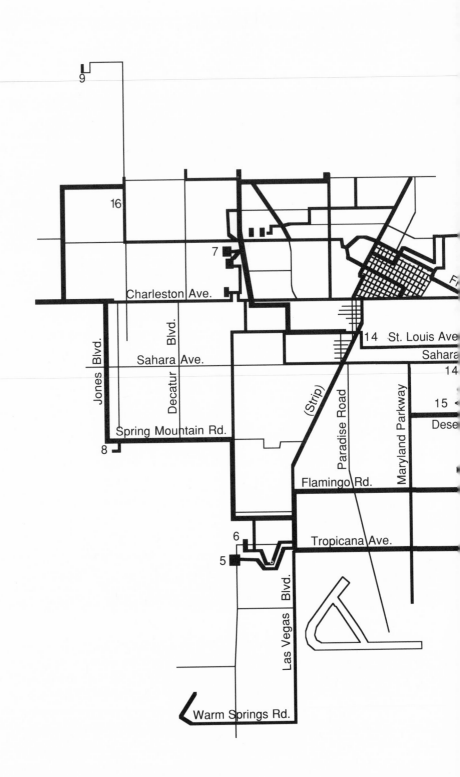

Map 6: Major Water Lines

1. Whitney Pumping Station No. 2, $495,000.
2. Flamingo Reservoir, $1,610,000.
3. Flamingo Pumping Station No. 1, $850,000.
4. Flamingo Pumping Station No. 2, $1,465,000.
5. Tropicana Reservoir, $920,000.
6. Tropicana Pumping Station, $557,000.
7. Charleston Heights Reservoir No. 2, $1,035,000.
8. Spring Mountain Pumping Station, $207,000.
9. Gowan Reservoir & Pumping Station, $345,000.
10. Flamingo Transmission Main, $455,000.
11. Sandhill-Tropicana Transmission Main, $2,493,000.
12. Sandhill-Lamb Transmission Main, $1,620,000.
13. Sandhill-Desert Inn Transmission Main, $1,862,000.
14. St. Louis-Campbell Transmission Main, $926,000.
15. Eastern & Desert Inn Feeder Mains, $187,000.
16. Jones Feeder Main, $83,000.
17. Tropicana East Transmission Main, $893,000.

Legend

Pre-1962	
1962-68	
Streets	

ment received the increased property valuations they needed to form assessment districts and plug the west end of the valley into the vast eastern network.[20]

Clearly, the extension of a utility infrastructure was as important to western growth as the building of Interstate 15. The water district, in particular, played a crucial role in this process. Beginning in the mid-1950s, one of the district's major goals was to consolidate the water systems scattered around the valley by purchasing as many private water companies as possible. Many of these private firms were the progeny of developers whose subdivisions lay beyond the district's distribution zone. Unfortunately, service was very uneven. In the summer of 1955, for instance, twenty-seven houses in the Parkridge subdivision went without water because the Pure Water Company's well was condemned by health authorities due to high concentrations of manganese and calcium sulphates. The nearest water district main was 9,000 feet away and the cost of laying a connecting pipeline was prohibitive because of the subdivision's small tax base. Ultimately, the water district bought the private firm and laid a line, but this was a typical case of the water barrier to residential, commercial, and especially industrial growth in Las Vegas.[21]

Aside from having to span great distances with a limited bonding capacity, the district often bucked the opposition of powerful water companies. In 1955, for example, the district went to court seeking permission to provide water to the area just north of Sahara in the southwest city limits. The Michelas Water Company had operated in the zone for several years under a Certificate of Public Convenience and Necessity from the Nevada Public Service Commission. Owner Theodore Michelas, like officers of other private firms, was determined to control water distribution within his service area. Anxious to maintain profitable operations, Michelas and other companies bitterly resisted the district until a series of court rulings against them eventually forced a sale.[22]

On another front, the district battled for half a decade with prominent developer Ernest Becker, owner of the Charleston Heights Water Company. Becker, who owned several wells and a substantial pipe network, augmented his supply with district water. In 1961, when Becker announced plans to develop another 480 acres in the Charleston Heights area, district officials informed him that they would not service the new subdivision without a new pumping station to enable the water to reach homes on the higher lands of the tract. Becker complained that the projected $100,000 cost of the station put an excessive burden on him.

Yet in the end, Becker, like the others, saw the futility of protracted opposition and sold his water company and equipment to the district in 1964.[23]

While developers and city officials often considered district policies to be ruthless and growth limiting, district authorities believed that they reflected sound management. In the late fifties and early sixties the district was seeking to transform the dozens of autonomous, uncoordinated water systems of the earlier town into an integrated structure for the emerging metropolis. While political opposition from municipal entities and developers temporarily slowed the process, centralization was inevitable. To a large extent, the Las Vegas of 1960 was, in the words of historian Sam Bass Warner, a "private city," where thousands of investor decisions over the years had decided the configuration of lots, buildings, streets, and utility lines. The 1960s would see the first substantial efforts by city and county planning agencies, the sanitation district, the gas and power companies, and especially the water district to bring order both to the central city and to the retreating edges of the urban periphery along Decatur, Tropicana, Smoke Ranch Road, and east of the Boulder Highway.[24]

Ironically, in the late fifties and early sixties the valley's cities often viewed the water district as a barrier to growth. Typical was the case of developer Louis Miranti of American Homes, who in 1959 complained to the Las Vegas City Planning Board about the water district's refusal to provide water for his proposed $6 million housing project adjacent to the city golf course off Decatur. The district responded that it had offered service to Miranti under the standing refund agreement which forced developers to bear the initial expense of extending mains, to be refunded later as water revenues were paid by homeowners. Miranti, however, objected to district requirements that he first build and pay for a larger main than he needed—one large enough to serve the needs of future subdivisions planned for Decatur.

Naturally, Las Vegas city commissioners, anxious to promote growth and expand the tax base within municipal limits, objected to any requirement that might discourage developers. After lengthy negotiations, the district agreed to a precedent-setting rule change, charging Miranti only the proportionate share of the cost of a main—larger than the one he would need—based upon a per acre charge for each parcel to be served. Eventually, the district bore the construction expense of as yet unused portions of the main reserved for future developments. Of course, agreements like these, especially for mains servicing the relatively unoccupied western desert lands, were not commonplace because the district's bonding capacity was still meager in the early 1960s compared to later in the decade.[25]

Aside from delays resulting from political infighting, other obstacles temporarily blocked the extension of water service outward to new subdivision systems, especially on the western edge of town. During the period of 1968–70, for instance, the time-consuming effort to create Assessment District Number 5 was slowed by the withdrawal of two key areas in the district when a majority of property owners opposed the levy. While many developers favored connecting their new projects to a centralized water system, they were often opposed by many local residents who deliberately lived on the edge of town to escape the cost of urban services. Pockets of cost-minded residents therefore could disrupt the systematic expansion of a coordinated infrastructure. Engineers were also frustrated by zones of low-income housing and vacant lots. Such was the case, for instance, with Assessment District Number 6 in 1969, when the low assessed valuation of property in the area forced the cancellation of main and pump construction.[26]

Despite these problems, the water district progressed with a bold construction program in most areas. As Map 6 indicates, residential and commercial building activity in the eastern and especially the western part of Las Vegas was reinforced by the arrival of sewer and water mains. By the mid-1960s, water line construction was either completed or progressing along Spring Mountain, Sahara, and Charleston west of Decatur toward Rainbow, permitting commercial and residential projects north and south of those arteries to plug into their water lines. Similarly, the sanitation district had largely extended its giant east-west sewer mains along Tropicana, Sahara, and Charleston west of the Strip toward Decatur. And while more construction was needed west and southwest of the Strip, most of the basic network had been installed. In just a decade or so, water and sewer district master planning brought a coordinated and orderly infrastructure to the western part of town, which promoted continued in-filling of the area (see Map 7). Water and sanitation district engineers now examined all developers' plans with an eye to the future. In those cases where the districts foresaw continued growth west of a subdivision, their boards ordered the construction of large-diameter mains, but only charged the developers for the smaller diameters required to service their abutting subdivision. Thus, reinforced by the westward extension of the water and

Map 7: Major Sewer Lines, 1971

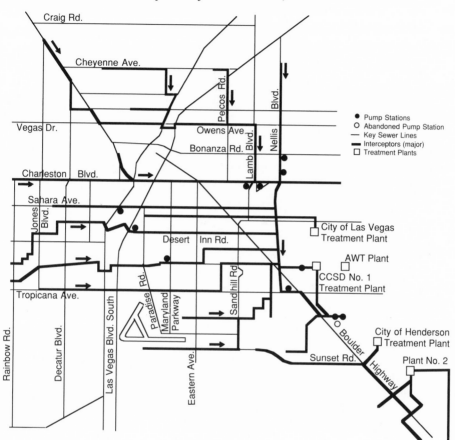

sewer system and by the freeway and other auto corridors, this section witnessed a substantial building boom in the seventies and eighties.[27]

Along with the federal government and water district, casino gambling played a major role in shaping the physical development of the resort metropolis. This process can be recognized in a number of ways. First, in Las Vegas as in other cities, land use slowly changed as the central core urbanized during the three decades following the announcement of Hoover Dam. Gradually, the railroad city gave way to its casino successor. The changing land use patterns are graphically illustrated by the fire insurance company maps drawn for Las Vegas first in 1928 and updated in 1959. In 1928 Fremont Street, the town's business hub, was lined with concrete office buildings and stores from the railroad station down toward Fifth Street. Three decades only served to reinforce the trend, although the stores, banks, and other business concerns had mostly been replaced by casinos and larger emporiums. Indeed, J. C. Penney and Sears now dominated most of the lots north of Fremont between Fourth and Sixth streets. To the north, stretching from Fremont past Ogden to Stewart and from Main to Ninth Street, small hotels and motor courts teamed with parking lots and apartments to replace the mixed neighborhood of lumber yards, building supplies, and frame houses which stood in the 1920s.[28]

Similar land-use patterns governed development along streets south of Fremont. In 1928, the lots south of Fremont between Main and Eighth down two blocks to Bridger featured a few frame dwellings and many empty lots. Thirty years later, most of the lands had been filled with frame houses, although parking lots consumed the lands behind the Golden Nugget, Pioneer, and other clubs south to Carson Street. While Fifth Street (the Los Angeles Highway) was still largely residential in 1928, thirty years later it served as the major artery connecting the Strip with Fremont. Reflecting this new-found commercial importance were solid rows of concrete stores and office buildings. In fact, thanks to the presence of the county courthouse at Carson and Third, many of the former dwellings in the court zone had been converted to offices for attorneys and bailsmen. And the arrival of the new federal building and courthouse on Carson and Fifth only reinforced this office trend in the sixties and seventies. Lands farther south of Bridger down to Clark had hosted only frame dwellings in the 1920s (many of the bungalows housed railroad employees). By 1959, however, the area contained a creamery, numerous concrete dwellings, and some cheap hotels as well as boardinghouses. As a rule, the 1960s would see the construction of still more motels, small hotels, rooming houses, and parking lots in the old downtown residential zones.[29]

As the resort economy grew, it priced surrounding residential lots out of existence, forcing homeowners to sell out and move south or east to the newly emerging suburbs on the city's periphery. As one observer has noted: "Under the pressure of rising property values and unprotective zoning, the surviving old residential neighborhoods [were] eroded by high-density apartments and commercial uses which no longer need to cluster downtown as they used to." Insurance agencies, real estate offices, low-cost motels, and dozens of small apartment complexes increasingly packed the lands south of Fremont to Charleston. North of Fremont, parking lots, cheap accommodations, and offices to service the city hall complex filled the lands up to Bonanza.

Immediately west of the railroad tracks where the Union Pacific roundhouse, repair shops, and yards stood in the 1920s, a small zone of light industry prospered. Union, Standard, and Shell oil tanks continued to border the railroad tracks, receiving daily tank car shipments from Los Angeles refineries for distribution by truck to local industries in the valley. Beyond the oil tanks along newly emerging Industrial Road, rows of warehouses, brickyards, and other light industries prospered. Farther west, frame dwellings increasingly filled all available lots on the Westside between H and F streets from Bonanza to Morgan and beyond, partly reflecting the substantial growth of Las Vegas's black population during the 1950s. As cheaper frame dwellings tended to dominate the black zone, more substantial concrete homes graced the winding, new, white subdivisions along St. Louis Avenue, Paradise Road, and other suburban arteries to the south.[30]

In terms of the physical city itself, a recreational economy combined with the area's relative lack of industry to control Las Vegas's economic geography. By 1950, the resort industry was largely centralized in two distinct zones—downtown and the Strip. Unlike the automotive, steel, or petrochemical industries, gambling supported few local supply industries which could reinforce the town's economy. Although food processing (including soda and beer bottling) plants enjoyed a substantial presence in town, there were few other factories of any size except for BMI. In addition, the town's water shortage really prohibited the clustering of additional industries near the BMI complex or even around the valley. Once the last BMI cells were occupied in 1952, there was not enough water, power, or even natural gas to support the construction of factories—not in Henderson, nor along the railroad tracks in Las Vegas, much less farther out in the vast tracts of cheap land west of town. Even the groundwater provided by the mountains which ringed the city began to diminish as over a thousand private wells and the water district's own fields dropped the valley's water table to dangerously low levels. The urbanization of Las Vegas only worsened the crisis. Lack of industry limited not only the economy, but the city-building process itself. There simply were no factories or processing centers to anchor the major roads and create economic subcenters around town. Instead, the resort economy filled the void as best it could, with most commercial and residential zones clustering south of Fremont Street and, until the late 1950s, east of the steadily growing Strip.

Although Nellis Air Force Base and the nuclear test site supported substantial building in North Las Vegas and northwest along the Tonopah Highway, the major developments in the valley after 1950 were south of Fremont Street and, especially, south of Sahara. As the Desert Inn, Dunes, Sands, Stardust, and Tropicana joined the Flamingo, Last Frontier, and El Rancho, the old Los Angeles Highway became a major job zone. With hotel construction flourishing into the sixties and seventies, the Strip became a powerful baseline for growth—a commercial axis encouraging suburban growth to the east and west. Just as the railroad had encouraged urbanization to the east and south in early Las Vegas, so too the emerging Strip steered postwar commercial and residential building south of Sahara and east of the Strip over to the Boulder Highway. By the 1960s, as the water district and road construction made the zone west of the railroad more accessible, shopping centers, apartments, condominiums, and single-family dwellings began covering the emerging checkerboard to the west. A new suburban frontier had been opened for the resort economy.[31]

While Las Vegas's casino industry played a major role in partially determining the direction of growth, the industry spawned a different building pattern from Atlantic City. New Jersey gambling operations began in 1978, and by 1985 their profits were impressive. Yet, while Atlantic City's eleven casinos drew nearly 30 million visitors (more than double the Las Vegas count), paid $750 million in wages and benefits and $63 million in property taxes, the community itself seemed strangely unaffected by the boom along the oceanfront. The stark contrast between the casino district and the rest of the city inspired one observer to describe it as "eleven Taj Mahals in the midst of a war zone." Beyond the fabulous resorts and their fleets of charter buses, lay a town continuing its three-decade plunge into decay. Abandoned stores, run-down tenements, empty lots—the perennial symbols of blight continued to litter the city-scape. Casino gambling had not transformed Atlantic City as promised, but instead promoted stagnation through the hotels' investment policies. Typical was the case of Resorts International, the largest casino in town. For over five years, Resorts plowed its profits into a massive land-buying spree. By 1985, the company owned almost half of all the developable parcels in town, including one-third of the Boardwalk area zoned for casinos. Yet, the casino giant had developed no commercial centers or low-income housing centers downtown. The other resorts also contributed to the process, tying up strategic parcels in the inner city and leaving them undeveloped. At the same time, Harrah's, Bally's, and the others, with their noisy lounges and cheap buffets, destroyed much of Atlantic City's local bar, restaurant, and entertainment industry. In short, Atlantic City resort operators, faced with a decaying, blue-collar and minority-dominated town not of their own making, have displayed a marked unwillingness to invest heavily in downtown revitalization.[32]

As in Las Vegas, casino gambling exerted pressure upon the entire urban fabric. As early as 1980, the great seaside resorts had displaced thousands of longtime Atlantic City residents. In their frenzy to attract better-paid casino workers, local landlords systematically coerced exist-ing tenants out. Between 1978 and 1981, a casino-driven gentrification movement saw hundreds of (even substandard) dwelling units renovated into condominiums. Lack of space was the key. Hemmed in by the ocean and environmentally sensitive wetlands, Atlantic City had no place to put its poor. A housing and social services crisis was thus inevitable. With resources limited, casino gambling's sudden development inspired a boomtown economy which exacted a heavy toll upon blacks, Hispanics, the elderly, and other vulnerable groups.[33] Only in the late 1980s did conditions begin to change. Casino profits are finally providing a substan-tial capital fund for inner-city improvements, and upscale neighborhoods catering to casino workers are being built on the city's periphery. It will, however, be many years before the seaside town realizes the dreams of its promoters.

Aside from Atlantic City, Las Vegas's physical development also dif-fered from other American resort cities like Honolulu and Miami Beach. The Strip was built on vast stretches of tumbleweed desert upon a broad valley floor. Environmental concerns were initially minimal because the hotels bordered no river, lake, or ocean. Such was not the case in Honolulu. Boosted by the support of industrialist Henry Kaiser and the advent of the jet plane, the city initiated a vigorous promotion campaign in the fifties and sixties to expand its tourist appeal. Lacking environmental or architectural oversight agencies, Honolulu virtually ceded its oceanfront to Hilton, Hyatt, and other hotel operators who covered Waikiki Beach with high-rise structures. The result was a city which looked more like Rio de Janeiro than San Francisco. Instead of imposing height restrictions upon buildings along the surfside and easing them as the mountains north of town were scaled, growth-hungry city officials virtually gave the resorts free rein. With environmental and planning considerations largely ignored, Honolulu became a tourist ghetto in less than twenty years. More than Las Vegas, Honolulu fit John Findlay's model of a city where leisure and tourism usurped the hometown environment for local residents. Hawaiians literally built a city for vacationers. Housing was a case in point. Like postwar Las Vegas, Honolulu built housing for tourists, not for residents. In 1970, Honolulu ranked sixth among America's largest cities in new construction, but last in new housing for families. Despite a colossal military complex at Pearl Harbor (62,000 military personnel in 1970) and a vibrant pineapple and sugarcane processing economy, Honolulu vigorously pursued the resort business, permitting hotelmen to barricade the city from its bay with a wall of hotels, stores, and golf courses.[34]

Miami Beach officials did much the same. As early as the 1920s, the city began surrendering its magnificent oceanfront to the resort makers. Dismissing concerns about the danger of hurricanes, developers filled the low-lying coastlands with a maze of hotels, auto courts, and golf courses. Not only were the beaches covered, but so were miles of inland property as well. In the scramble for space and profits, the resort industry literally pushed the city aside, forcing business and residents away from the ocean and leaving little room for other industries.

In Las Vegas, the resort sector, though powerful, exerted less of an adverse influence upon the city-building process. No scenic vistas were blocked, and no sensitive lands were immediately threatened. While the Strip encouraged residential and commercial growth south, east, and west of the city proper, there was plenty of room for low-rise, low-density building. Unlike other resort cities like Honolulu or Miami Beach, no major hills or inland waterways had to be traversed. Yet, there were similarities. All three cities were physically dominated by a tourist infrastructure of considerable proportions, with Las Vegas's spilling over into the suburbs as well. Furthermore, reliance upon a resort economy tended to discourage other industries. Even in Honolulu, where fruit processing had long been a staple of the local economy, Dole and the other fruit companies were increasingly overshadowed by resorts. To some extent, the companies themselves promoted tourism. Indeed, Dole and other Oahu landowners made millions leasing and selling lots to developers for hotel-commercial growth.

In all three cities the resort economy colored the urbanization process itself. Not only did it control the space allotted for resorts, offices, and housing, but it even affected culture. Neither Honolulu, Miami Beach, nor Las Vegas developed early the kinds of libraries, museums, or concert halls found in many commercial and industrial cities. In each of the three cities, bands of concerned citizens, eager to polish their area's cultural image, worked in the sixties and seventies to upgrade the nearby university and establish a respectable number of theatres, galleries, and other cultural venues both on campus and off.[35]

Perhaps the most troubling problem for municipal officials has been the suburbanization of these resort cities. Relatively new cities like Las Vegas and Honolulu have been especially hard-hit. After almost four decades of frantic urbanization and hotel building, both places have seen growth slow in the central city. Between 1970 and 1980, for instance, the city of Honolulu's population rose by only 12.4 percent while Oahu's as a whole surpassed 21 percent, thanks to a vigorous suburban trend. The industrial-residential Ewa Beach area near the airport and Pearl Harbor grew by over 600 percent after 1970. Other communities all over the island witnessed substantial gains, too. Like the city of Las Vegas, Honolulu proper saw its growth slowed by the rising cost of land. The urbanization of Waikiki, similar to that of Fremont Street and Collins Avenue, produced a commercialization of lots which discouraged new residential construction. Moreover, the environmentalists' success in blocking new commuter highways through scenic mountain passes cut Honolulu off from nearby bedroom communities, forcing a shift of jobs and companies to the suburbs west of Pearl Harbor, where geography made access easier. Roads played a similar role in Nevada. The construction of Interstate 15, the Las Vegas Expressway, and wider Strip feeder arteries like Flamingo, Desert Inn, and Tropicana avenues made hotel-casino and even nonresort jobs more available in the suburbs. The same was true for the military sector of the metropolitan economy. While new highways made civilian jobs at the

Pearl Harbor base more accessible, Interstate 15, Nellis Boulevard, and other thoroughfares were discouraging many air force base commuters from a Las Vegas city residence.[36]

Still, casino gambling has made the Las Vegas story somewhat unique. Even its casino rival to the north, Reno, has developed along different lines. Forced to share the smaller northern California gaming market with their nearby rival, Lake Tahoe, Renoites have diversified their economy by exploiting the state's freeport law to warehouse goods bound for California. In addition, Reno, with colder weather and a smaller market than Las Vegas, was slow to enter the resort business. While Las Vegas gambling exploded out of the central city and into the spacious suburbs by 1941, Reno's casino core hugged downtown Virginia Street until the MGM's (now Bally's) opening in 1979. The city's convention center and more hotels are planned for the suburbs, but Reno will never grow as large as her southern counterpart. Surrounded by mountains and short of water, Reno, like Atlantic City, lacks enough resources.[37]

More than anywhere else, casino gambling shaped the urbanization of Las Vegas. Unlike Reno and Atlantic City, Las Vegas grew with the infant industry. As in Phoenix, Albuquerque, San Antonio, Los Angeles, and many sunbelt (and especially southwestern) cities, Las Vegas had plenty of vacant land. It was therefore easy in the late forties and fifties for hotel owners, bankers, and developers—along with other investors—to superimpose a sprawling, low-rise city upon the old railroad town. Casino profits fueled a real estate boom which built a city of endless condominiums, elegant townhouses, and posh country clubs—a landscape of Spanish mission elegance to complement the spa-like image of the city's recreational economy. Even the cheaper apartments bordering the Strip, for low-income workers unable to afford a car, rated far above the housing for their counterparts in the garden state.

As noted earlier, the dominance of casino gambling and a resort economy, along with a sunbelt location, substantially affected the demographics of the Las Vegas area. In general, the economy attracted a relatively youthful, skilled, affluent, and upwardly mobile population. To provide for their own needs and expectations, Las Vegans built a city remarkably similar to those in Arizona and southern California—a city boasting wide roads, ubiquitous shopping centers, and above-average housing, with more than its share of swimming pools, jacuzzis, and palm-covered gardens. In little more than half a century, casino gambling helped transform a barren little whistle-stop into one of the most glittering resort cities in the world.

Epilogue:
Growth and
Diversification
Since 1970

The seventies and eighties witnessed the continued growth of Las Vegas's gambling industry along with an intensified effort to expand the area's industrial base. Despite a mild recession in gaming, the Las Vegas area continued to enjoy prosperity. Construction was a major barometer of growth. Between 1970 and 1981, developers built fifty major office buildings in the immediate Las Vegas–Paradise Valley area and almost as many shopping centers. Hotel expansion was also significant, with the construction of new towers at the Aladdin and Desert Inn. Despite a gaming recession, resort development continued unabated into the 1980s. Between 1978 and 1983, twelve major resorts either had planned or begun major construction projects (mostly new high-rise towers) including the Golden Nugget, Caesars Palace, MGM (now Bally's) Grand, both Hiltons, Circus Circus, the Holiday Inn, Union Plaza, and Landmark hotels. Moreover, in the years after 1970, new resorts were built on or near the Strip, including the Marina Hotel, the Maxim, the Imperial Palace, the Bingo Palace (now Palace Station), Vegas World, the Barbary Coast, Bourbon Street, the Gold Coast, Alexis Park, and others. At the same time, university (including a community college), hospital, city, county, and convention-center projects contributed further to the growth. On the whole, residential building permits also reflected the upward trend, climbing from 5,784 in 1970 to a valley record of 14,478 in 1978. And while the recession of the early 1980s lowered that figure by more than a third, the 1984 recovery quickly eliminated the deficit. [1]

Southern Nevada's gaming recession resulted from a variety of events, including a sluggish national economy, the MGM (1980) and Las Vegas Hilton (1981) fires, and the loss of Nevada's historic monopoly on America's casino industry. The state's dependence on gambling had long been a source of concern, but the absence of competition had always encouraged a sense of complacency. That complacency was shattered in the 1970s, when New Jersey legalized the industry and centralized it along the

Boardwalk in Atlantic City. At first, Las Vegas casino operators seemed outwardly unconcerned. But the feeling changed as more Boardwalk hotels opened and the number of eastern visitors to Las Vegas dropped. In 1983, the last nonstop airline flights between New York and Las Vegas were cancelled. Clearly, Atlantic City was the culprit. This new gaming hub, conveniently located near Philadelphia, New York, and other populated urban centers in the great northeast megalopolis, initially cost Las Vegas thousands of eastern tourists.[2]

The mid-1980s saw a return to prosperity and a revised view about the impact of Atlantic City. Today, the consensus among marketing experts is that, in the long run, Atlantic City has probably enhanced Las Vegas tourism by familiarizing thousands of novice eastern gamblers with the basic games of chance. In the 1980s, surveys have found that thousands of visitors (including many convention delegates) who normally would not have ventured west to Las Vegas, are coming and playing in the silver state with experience gained in Atlantic City. Moreover, resort executives generally agree that the recession of the early 1980s benefited southern Nevada in a number of other ways. The lean years taught them the value of slashing costs by eliminating waste. Gone are the extravagant salaries automatically paid to big-name entertainers who could not fill the showrooms, and gone too are the bloated payrolls which overstaffed the gaming tables, gourmet rooms, and upper echelons of management.

On another front, Atlantic City has succeeded in legitimizing gambling in the minds of many easterners—a feat not achieved by Las Vegas in a half century of effort. As former Nevada Gaming Control Board Chairman Jim Avance noted, Atlantic City's mere proximity to New York, Philadelphia, Boston, and other citadels of eastern banking, industry, and culture has brought a new measure of respectability to the controversial industry. Due to the publicity campaigns of Resorts International, Trump Plaza, and other gaming palaces in the garden state, thousands of easterners who formerly rejected gambling as a legitimate leisure activity at least now tolerate it. Moreover, casino executives like Robert Mullane of Ballys have argued that the spread of state lotteries in the seventies and eighties has further legitimized gambling in the minds of many Americans while also defusing campaigns to legalize casino gambling in many states. To some extent, this more liberal atmosphere has even permitted some eastern-based firms to consider a move to the silver state. Indeed, changing mores undoubtedly played a role in Citicorp's decision in 1984 to build in Las Vegas.

Citicorp provided a real impetus to the so-called Southern Nevada Industrial Revolution when it agreed to build a $40 million credit card processing plant in the Las Vegas area (employing up to 2,000 employees). In return, the Nevada legislature revised the state's banking laws to permit the New York–based giant to establish a bank of its own in the state. Since 1984, the presence of such a distinguished firm as Citicorp has brought a measure of respectability to Las Vegas which the "wide-open town" had never previously enjoyed. The Citicorp move, along with the legalization of gambling in New Jersey, has helped remove some of the tarnish from Las Vegas's traditional image. As a result, many firms, for the first time, have begun to consider a southern Nevada location.[3]

Of course, the business influx cannot compare with Phoenix and other large competitors but, with the gaming albatross increasingly less of a factor, Clark County has become more of a desirable location for business. To some extent, the improved climate has enabled the Nevada Development Authority to lure dozens of major firms to the valley and expand the number of industrial sites in the metropolitan area. Thanks largely to the efforts of Sherman Miller, board chairman of Nevada Savings and a driving force in town promotion, the N.D.A. (a privately funded agency) has seen its budget soar from $20,000 in 1977 to nearly $1 million in 1986. Among its more notable achievements, N.D.A. convinced GTE-Sylvania in 1981 to locate a plant in Henderson to manufacture lithium batteries for the Minuteman Missile System. During the productive tenure of N.D.A. president Tim Carlson, the organization enticed dozens of companies to relocate in the valley, including Ethel M (Mars) Chocolates, Tungsten Carbide, Capital, and Merillat Industries, CPI Film Processing, Morrisey Aircraft, and many smaller firms.

The N.D.A. has received valuable help from area cities and the state. Anxious to expand their tax bases, both Las Vegas and North Las Vegas have acted to provide industrial centers within their borders for out-of-state corporations. In 1985, Las Vegas city commissioners voted to establish the 400-acre Las Vegas Technology Center to encourage the location of firms engaged in the research and development of high technology activities in aerospace, energy, and defense-related systems. This effort was rewarded a few months later when Ford Aerospace, a division of the Ford Motor Company and a prime Nellis contractor for aerial combat systems, announced plans to build a 26,000-square-foot research facility employing over a hundred workers. Financed by a $1.6 million loan from

Nevada National Bank, the building was completed in 1986. North Las Vegas enjoyed a similar triumph also, luring Aerojet General, a major defense contractor based in La Jolla, California, to the new Southern Nevada Industrial Center off Losee Road. Moreover, the company will build another plant in Henderson to manufacture hardware for the Midgetman Missile System.[4]

State assistance has also been crucial. The Las Vegas metropolitan area took a major step toward securing a larger share of the electronics industry when the state legislature approved construction of the $15 million Howard R. Hughes School of Engineering and Computer Science on the University of Nevada, Las Vegas campus. Pushed by a lobbying effort spearheaded by local business leaders and university President Robert Maxson, the state legislature finally recognized the crucial role played by universities in securing this type of industry in Albuquerque, Phoenix, Tucson, and other sunbelt rivals.

Aside from state and city initiatives, the federal government also threatened to boost local revenues by locating the nation's first high-level nuclear dump at Yucca Mountain (on the test site), one hundred miles north of Las Vegas. While controversial, the $6 billion project, if built, would employ at least 6,000 workers (with a projected yearly payroll of $110 million) and would pump at least $1 billion into the local economy through the purchase of goods and services. Once completed, the facility's required maintenance would probably add at least 20,000 permanent residents to the valley.[5]

The county government has also played a major role in promoting growth through its airport and highway projects. Beginning in 1980, county commissioners started a twenty-year construction program to expand the airport for the throngs expected in the twenty-first century. Already, McCarran 2000 has produced an elegant addition to the main terminal (complete with glass elevators to a multistoried parking garage), a new wing of gates connected to the main terminal by monorail (with plans for more monorails and eventually eighty gates), another main east-west runway, and other facilities designed to enhance Las Vegas's chances of becoming a hub city for several airlines. Clearly, the Clark County commissioners are overbuilding the airport, but the strategy is plain: Las Vegas is one of the few metropolitan areas which is using its airport to promote economic growth.[6]

Like Miami and Honolulu, Las Vegas has witnessed phenomenal growth in the lands immediately surrounding its international airport—

lands not within the central city's boundaries and tax base. Clark County commissioners have reinforced airport expansion with key road projects to transform the zone south of the airport into a new-growth area. The $3.2 million widening of Sunset Road from two to six lanes between Eastern Avenue and Mountain Vista Drive—a three-mile stretch just east of Maryland Parkway—combined with other widenings east of the Boulder Highway to provide the area south of McCarran Airport with a major new east-west artery, connecting the Strip with the Boulder Highway in Henderson. This new ribbon of concrete provides commuters from the Strip with greater access to the sprawling Green Valley residential center. In addition, the road, along with the 1988 opening of the new freeway connecting the zone with the administrative, financial, and casino centers downtown, has enhanced the commercial value of lands south of the airport. In particular, expressway access will entice more developers into what has been traditionally vacant desert. Already, light industry has begun to invade. The U.S. Post Office built a massive $27 million facility in 1986 on 40 acres off Sunset east of Paradise Road. Anxious to transform Las Vegas into a major air freight hub for the southwest, federal officials explained that the postal service chose Sunset because of its "good location in a growth area and its accessibility to the airport."[7]

In a similar vein, Howard Hughes Properties selected East Sunset for its massive Hughes Airport Center because, in the words of company president John Goolsby, the site allowed "for access to the four major modes of transportation—air, rail, the postal service, and Interstate 15." By 1985, the firm had already begun to develop 110 acres of the 350-acre parcel with construction of a 50,000-square-foot building for EG&G, a test site contractor, and three general-purpose buildings totaling 150,000 square feet. The post office and Hughes developments followed the initial success of Green Valley Business Park, which opened on Sunset in 1979. Tenants in the 1,120-acre park included Ethel M (Mars) Chocolates, the Shastar Corporation and others. Developers followed this in 1980 with Green Valley Plaza, a 110,000-square-foot shopping center at Sunset and Green Valley Parkway. Then in 1983, construction began at Park 2000, a 118-acre complex with buildings totaling more than 1.5 million square feet of space. By 1985, the center already hosted Quail Park, a million feet of new office and warehouse space, several more shopping centers, and dozens of new residential subdivisions including Whitney Ranch, a 360-acre project branching north off Sunset near Stephanie Street. In short, Sunset Road has extended the metropolis several miles south of the old Hacienda line, opening up vast new tracts south of the airport for development, and this trend to the south will probably continue into the next century when the mountains are finally reached.[8]

Thanks to this growth southward and eastward beyond the old Strip suburbs of the fifties and sixties, the county-controlled suburbs below Sahara have actually reached Henderson, fifteen miles away. Part of the reason is Henderson's own growth to the west. Since the early 1970s, the Green Valley area has been a major center of residential growth between Henderson and McCarran International Airport. These once-barren flats, purchased years ago by Howard Hughes, Hank Greenspun, and other speculators for only a few dollars an acre, are worth millions today. In 1977, for instance, the Collins Brothers development firm purchased 1,000 acres near Green Valley Parkway for $40 million with an eye toward future development. By 1986, they already had an 8,000-acre master-planned community on the drawing boards. Blueprints call for several thousand homes, two 70-acre parks, a 50-acre retirement community, two shopping centers, several churches, and schools. Construction has already begun. And, as was the case in the original Green Valley, other area developers have been invited to build several subdivisions. The Collins Brothers and their associates have already sold 160 acres to Pardee-Phillips to promote construction of dwellings ranging from $100,000 and up.[9]

A second high-growth area, Summerlin (formerly Husite), is developing just west of Las Vegas on land controlled exclusively by Howard Hughes Properties—part of the lands which the billionaire intended for Boeing Aircraft in the 1940s. The area will eventually host Del Webb's massive Sun City development, which will establish the retirement industry as a major new dimension of Las Vegas's economy. In December 1986, the city of Las Vegas formally approved the annexation of over 5,600 acres of the 25,000-acre Husite lands. Howard Hughes Properties, an affiliate of the Summa Corporation, had requested the move to secure basic urban services for its development, especially sewers. The property, located about a mile west of the existing city border, was too far from the county's waste network. The city of Las Vegas, however, was a logical choice because of its substantial east-west sewer system located conveniently nearby. The annexation potentially represents a major extension of the city's tax base, since developers are planning to build almost 20,000 homes in the area along with the usual shopping centers, office parks, and light industry buildings. Ultimately, Las Vegas might get the entire

25,000-acre tract, a windfall which would more than double the city's tax base and population. Furthermore, once the municipality extends its sewer system (and adds a new wastewater treatment plant) in the northwest quadrant of the valley, this new network will serve as a powerful base for future city expansion northwesterly up the Tonopah Highway toward the test site. When one considers Henderson's recently successful move to annex Green Valley, it appears that the valley's major cities are finally beginning to outflank the county in the race to control newly developing areas.[10]

All of this success has encouraged an ambitious—perhaps overly ambitious—approach to growth. The city of Las Vegas, for instance, is supplementing its annexation efforts with downtown revitalization as part of its overall growth strategy. In 1986, the city began construction of the Downtown Transportation Center (DTC), a complex designed to accommodate the loading and unloading of city buses as well as a planned fleet of motorized trolley cars which will be looping the downtown area in the near future. By 1990, the town expects to complete its monorail system linking Fremont Street's hotels with the new Cashman Field Complex and convention center. This futuristic enterprise will feature a pair of magnetically levitated, electromagnetically propelled monorail vehicles which, according to projections, will lure more small conventions away from the Las Vegas Convention Center near the Strip to downtown hotels. If the network proves successful, planners are hopeful that county and Strip resort officials will embrace the idea and extend the monorail from the city down the Strip to the Tropicana Hotel and then southeastward to McCarran International. Las Vegas would then become the first American city providing visitors with direct rail links between the airport and their hotels.[11]

The DTC and people mover comprise only half of the city's futuristic plans. The third project involves the conversion of Fremont Street into a pedestrian mall as part of the total redevelopment of the downtown area, featuring a new 28-acre city plaza adjacent to the DTC and Church Street Station, a festival marketplace centered on North Main Street and Bonanza. The latter, a 200,000-square-foot complex of restaurants, nightclubs, and specialty shops, will be a glamorous version of the tourist-oriented shopping entrepots which first appeared along the Embarcadero in San Francisco. The last of the four projects anchoring Las Vegas's future plans involves the construction of the so-called bullet train, a German-made, magnetically levitated vehicle capable of speeds approaching 300 miles per hour. If built, such a train could transport tourists from Los Angeles to Las Vegas in an hour, thereby eliminating the tiresome, ten-hour round trip by bus. The Strip, too, will continue expanding. In 1989, Golden Nugget owner Steve Wynn will open the largest hotel in the world, the Mirage, on a site across from the Sands. In the following year, Circus Circus will unveil the Excalibur, its European castle resort near the Tropicana, while south of the Hacienda, a group of investors will be finishing Southstar, a cluster of at least ten hotels. [12]

Clearly, there will be overbuilding and other costly mistakes if the boosterish mania for growth and promotion are not balanced by careful planning in the 1990s. As early as 1988, the motorized trolley system had lost thousands of dollars and the decline of pedestrian malls in cities like Fresno was raising new questions about the Church Street Station project off North Main Street. Moreover, limitations on water supply and other environmental factors will ultimately curtail population and resort growth early in the next century. Still, all of these plans reflect the fact that residents have not been content to rest upon the achievements of earlier decades. The explosive growth of the fifties and sixties has fed an obsession to continue the boom. Although the fifty years' reliance upon casino gambling as the major industry shows no signs of ending, business leaders are more determined than ever to diversify their economy. All of these efforts reflect the vision which inspired the early pioneers to transform their railroad town into something grander—a city, a metropolis, a "diamond in the desert."

Appendix

Table 1: Resort Jobs (Hotels, Motels, Tourist Courts)

1948

	Hotel	Paid Employees (November)	Tourist Courts	Paid Employees
County	35	719	123	126
Las Vegas	26	160	No city data available	

1958

	Hotel	Paid Employees (November)	Motels and Tourist Courts	Paid Employees
County	58	6,551	171	820
Las Vegas	41	793	113	331

1967

	Hotels	Paid Employees (March)	Motels and Tourist Courts	Paid Employees
SMSA	97	18,816	187	919

Source: U.S. Department of Commerce, *Census of Business, 1948, 1958, 1967*

Table 2: Population

Las Vegas	Total	White	Black	% Black	Hispanic
1910	947				
1920	2,304				
1930	5,165		150		
1940	8,422		178		
1950	24,624	21,736	2,725	11.1	
1960	64,405	54,261	9,649	15.0	236
1970	125,787	109,923	14,082	11.2	3,871
1980	164,674	134,330	21,054	12.8	12,787

SMSA	Total	White	Black	% Black	Hispanic
1950	48,283	44,601	3,174	6.6	
1960	127,016	114,925	11,005	8.7	578
1970	273,288	244,538	24,760	9.1	9,937
1980	461,816	390,021	46,064	10.0	(approx.) 34,998

	Las Vegas	North Las Vegas	Henderson	Boulder City	Unincorporated Suburbs
1970	125,787	36,216	16,395	5,223	89,667
1980	164,674	42,739	24,363	9,590	220,450

Source: U.S. Department of Commerce, *Census of Population, 1910–1980*

Table 3: Size of Budget

	Las Vegas	Clark County
1940	$388,358	$930,719
1945	997,164	2,289,525
1950	1,936,562	5,576,683
1955	2,874,721	18,125,293
1960	4,628,385	36,107,929
1970	17,361,308	91,658,392

Source: Las Vegas and Clark County *Statistical Reports*

Notes

Prologue: Before the Dam

1. For more comprehensive coverage of early Las Vegas history, see appropriate sections of: Stanley Paher, *Las Vegas, As it began—as it grew* (Las Vegas: Nevada Publications, 1971); Elbert Edwards, *200 Years in Nevada* . . . (Salt Lake City: Publishers Press and Mountain States Bindery, 1978); Ralph Roske, *Las Vegas: A Desert Paradise* (Tulsa: Continental Heritage Press, 1986). For a capsulized version, see Frank Wright, *Clark County: The Changing Face of Southern Nevada* (Reno: Nevada Historical Society, n.d.). Also see Charles P. Squires, *Las Vegas, Nevada: Its Romance and History*, 2 vols. (Las Vegas: n.p., 1955).

2. Edwards, *200 Years*, 117–118; Paher, *As it began*, 11–18; Roske, *A Desert Paradise*, 23–26.

3. Edwards, *200 Years*, 117–121; Paher, *As it began*, 19–30; Roske, *A Desert Paradise*, 26–29. For the Mormon influence in early Las Vegas, see Ray Reeder, "The Mormon Trail: A History of the Salt Lake to Los Angeles Route to 1969" (unpublished Ph.D. dissertation: Brigham Young University, 1966); Francis Leavitt, "Influence of the Mormon People in the Settlement of Clark County" (unpublished master's thesis: University of Nevada, Reno, 1934). Also consult Glen S. Dumke, "Mission Station to Mining Town: Early Las Vegas," *Pacific Historical Review* XXII (1953): 257–270.

4. Edwards, *200 Years*, 243; Paher, *As it began*, 32–55; Roske, *A Desert Paradise*, 30–38.

5. Roske, *A Desert Paradise*, 39–46; Paher, *As it began*, 55–57.

6. Roske, *A Desert Paradise*, 52–60; Paher, *As it began*, 65–77; Wright, *The Changing Face*, 12. For an informative view of the railroad's development of the town, see *Las Vegas Review-Journal*, May 11, 1980, 8AA, 27AA. The *Las Vegas (Evening) Review-Journal* (hereafter referred to as *Review-Journal*) published morning and afternoon editions beginning in the 1950s. Unless otherwise stated, all citations are from the morning edition.

7. The original for Map 1 can be found at the Nevada Historical Society, Las Vegas; Roske, *A Desert Paradise*, 55–56, 92; Wright, *The Changing Face*, 13.

8. *Review-Journal*, January 2, 1976, 26–27—Georgia Lewis provides a good account of early Las Vegas subdivisions. See also Florence Lee Jones, "Las Vegas, Golden Anniversary Edition," *Review-Journal* special edition for February 28, 1955, "Las Vegas First Edition," 10–12; "Las Vegas Second Edition," 5–6; Roske, *A Desert Paradise*, 55–56.

9. Roske, *A Desert Paradise*, 56–57; Paher, *As it began*, 92–104.

10. Roske, *A Desert Paradise*, 59, 64, 70.

11. Florence Lee Jones and John Cahlan, *Water: A History of Las Vegas. History of the*

Las Vegas Land and Water Company, 2 vols. (Las Vegas: Las Vegas Valley Water District, 1975), I, 29; *Review-Journal,* November 12, 1978, 3J.

12. *Review-Journal,* January 2, 1976, 26; Jones and Cahlan, *Water,* I, 32.

13. Jones and Cahlan, *Water,* I, 36–37; Roske, *A Desert Paradise,* 60, 64; Wright, *The Changing Face,* 16; Paher, *As it began,* 105–110. Promoters also published several pamphlets boosting local business conditions. See, for instance, Las Vegas Chamber of Commerce, *Las Vegas and Clark County: A Brief Review of Climate, Resources and Growth Opportunities* (Las Vegas, 1917), 24 pp.; Las Vegas Promotion Society, *Nevada: Las Vegas and Vegas Valley* (Las Vegas, 1909). Also see Patricia Holland, "Las Vegas Business District, 1905–1930" (unpublished paper). Also consult Perry B. Kaufman, "The Best City of Them All: A History of Las Vegas, 1930–1960" (unpublished Ph.D. dissertation, University of California, Santa Barbara, 1974), 15–20.

14. Michael S. Green, "A Partisan Press: The Las Vegas Newspapers and the 1932 Election" (unpublished paper), 2–5.

15. Roske, *A Desert Paradise,* 69–70; Wright, *The Changing Face,* 20–21. For a typical chamber of commerce publication in the 1920s, see Las Vegas Chamber of Commerce, *Las Vegas and Clark County, Nevada* (Las Vegas, 1927).

16. Road improvements can be traced almost year by year in Jones, "Golden Anniversary Edition." For aviation, see Roske, *A Desert Paradise,* 69; Jones and Cahlan, *Water,* I, 61; *Las Vegas Age* (hereafter referred to as *Age*), March 7, 1914; Wright, *The Changing Face,* 19–20.

17. Jones, "Golden Anniversary Edition," "Construction Section," 8; Jones and Cahlan, *Water,* I, 52, 60, 61.

Chapter 1: The Federal Trigger

1. A good overview of the federal influence upon the southwest between 1920 and 1940 can be found in Bradford Luckingham, *The Urban Southwest: A Profile History of Albuquerque—El Paso—Phoenix—Tucson* (El Paso: Texas Western Press, 1982), 53–74.

2. For a brief chronology of events leading up to the decision to build the dam in Black Canyon, see *Review-Journal,* March 2, 1932 for the Bureau of Reclamation's "History of the Colorado River Conquest." See also Norris Hundley, *Water and the West: The Colorado River Compact and the Politics of Water in America* (Berkeley: University of California Press, 1975), passim. The best review of the town's preparations and Secretary Wilbur's actual visit can be found in Jones, "Golden Anniversary Edition," "Boulder Dam and Travel Section," 2. Also consult Chris Moran, "Las Vegas: 1918–1928, Years of Transition" (unpublished paper); and appropriate sections of Leon Rockwell, *Recollections of Life in Las Vegas, Nevada, 1906–1968* (University of Nevada Oral History Project, 1969).

3. Jones, "Golden Anniversary Edition," "Transportation Section," 6–8.

4. For a quick review of events, see Angela Brooker and Dennis McBride, *Boulder City: Passages in Time* (Boulder City: The Boulder City Library, 1981), appropriate sections. Another useful source is Marion Allen, *Hoover Dam & Boulder City* (Redding, CA: C.P. Printing & Publishing, 1983); Erma Godbey, *Pioneering in Boulder City* (University of Nevada Oral History Project, 1967); as well as the official government publication: U.S. Bureau of Reclamation, *The Story of Hoover Dam* (Washington, D.C.: U.S. Government Printing Office, 1966 ed.); and Paul Kleinsorge, *The Boulder Canyon Project* (Palo Alto: Stanford University Press, 1941); also consult Raymond Wilbur, "Boulder City: A Survey of Its Legal Background, Its City Plan and Its Administration" (unpublished master's thesis: Syracuse University, 1936). Also see Joseph Stevens, *Hoover Dam: An American Adventure* (Norman: University of Oklahoma Press, 1988), passim. For an excellent pictorial summary of DeBoer's plan, see "Boulder City Historic District Walking Tours," a pamphlet published by the city itself.

5. Roske, *A Desert Paradise*, 77; "Boulder City Historic District Walking Tours."

6. For early Boulder City, see Allen, *Hoover Dam*, passim; Stevens, *An American Adventure*, passim; Brooker and McBride, *Passages in Time*, passim. An especially insightful study of the Wobbly labor conflict is Guy Louis Rocha, "The I.W.W. and the Boulder Canyon Project," *Nevada Historical Society Quarterly* (1978), 3–24. For a sympathetic view of Sims Ely, see "The Nevadan," *Review-Journal*, May 15, 1988, 6.

7. *Review-Journal*, January 3, 1934, 1; Perry Kaufman, "The Best City," 41.

8. For more on the construction of the dam itself, see Imre Sutton, "Geographical Aspects of Construction: Hoover Dam Revisited," *Journal of the West* (1968), 301–344; Las Vegas Chamber of Commerce, *Las Vegas and Boulder Dam, Nevada* (Las Vegas, 1939); William Gates, *Hoover Dam* (Las Vegas: Wetzel Publishing Company, 1932). See also Richard G. Wilson, "Machine-Age Iconography in the American West: The Design of Hoover Dam," *Pacific Historical Review* (1985), 463–493.

9. See p. 11 of Florence Lee Jones's Las Vegas history in the "First Annual Report of the City Manager for 1949" contained in the *Review-Journal*, January 16, 1949.

10. Jones, "Golden Anniversary Edition," "Transportation Section," 12.

11. The development of gambling in Nevada is traced in Ralph Roske, "Nevada Gambling, First Phase, 1861–1931" (unpublished paper); as well as Russell Elliott, *History of Nevada*, 1st ed. (Lincoln: University of Nebraska Press, 1973), 248, 278–279; and James Hulse, *The Nevada Adventure*, 4th ed. (Reno: University of Nevada Press, 1978), 250–256.

12. Roske, *A Desert Paradise*, 84–86.

13. *Review-Journal*, May 1, 1931, 1, 3.

14. Jones, "Golden Anniversary Edition," "Transportation Section," 12–13.

15. Ibid., 16; *Review-Journal*, January 1, 1935, 1; Robert Friedman, "The Air-Conditioned Century," *American Heritage* (1984): 20–33. For the importance of

air conditioning in the urban southwest, see Luckingham, *The Urban Southwest*, 69–70. The Jones reminiscence can be found in *Review-Journal*, January 16, 1949, 11.

16. *Age*, April 30, 1931, 3.

17. *Review-Journal*, May 4, 1931, 8; May 2, 1931, 5.

18. Ibid., May 4, 1931, 8; *Age*, April 28, 1931, 2; *Review-Journal*, May 6, 1931, 1.

19. *Review-Journal*, January 4, 1932, 1. Early local efforts to deal with the unemployment crisis are covered in Edward Quinn, "Coping with Crisis: Las Vegas and its Indigents, 1930–1931" (unpublished paper).

20. Luckingham, *The Urban Southwest*, 63–73; *Review-Journal*, May 5, 1931, 1; February 7, 1932, 1; June 13, 1933, 1–2. For a clear view of the trend in regional government expenses and operations in the 1930s, see the *Annual Report of the Clark County Auditor, Showing Receipts and Expenditures* (1933–1938). *Review-Journal*, September 7, 1933, 1, 4. Board of Las Vegas City Commissioners, *Minutes*, III, September 8, 1933, 300. *Review-Journal*, October 18, 1933, 1. Federal expenditures in southern Nevada were substantial. For a breakdown of individual programs, consult Office of Government Reports, *Nevada: County Reports of Estimated Federal Expenditures, March 4, 1933–June 30, 1939* (Washington, D.C.: Government Printing Office, 1940).

21. For overall coverage of what public works programs Las Vegas received from the Roosevelt Administration, see Eugene P. Moehring, "Public Works and the New Deal in Las Vegas, 1933–1940," *Nevada Historical Society Quarterly* (1981): 107–129.

22. *Review-Journal*, April 2, 1934, 6; City Commission, *Minutes*, III, January 7, 1935, 358–359; January 14, 1935, 359–360; September 12, 1935, 398; *Review-Journal*, February 21, 1940, 1; City Commission, *Minutes*, IV, March 8, 1940, 236; *Review-Journal*, August 7, 1940, 6.

23. For the golf course, see City Commission, *Minutes*, III, February 21, 1935, 363; *Review-Journal*, February 9, 1936, 6; April 20, 1936, 6; October 20, 1936, 1, 6; December 10, 1937, 1. For the airport effort, consult *Age*, May 23, 1933, 2; *Review-Journal*, June 13, 1935, 6; July 22, 1935, 6; April 17, 1936, 1, 2. City Commission, *Minutes*, III, December 20, 1935, 420; *Review-Journal*, April 17, 1936, 1, 2; April 22, 1936, 6; June 8, 1936, 1; February 16, 1939, 1; September 25, 1940, 1.

24. *Review-Journal*, May 2, 1935, 1, 6.

25. For the political charges and countercharges in the 1935 mayoral election, see ibid., April 30, 1935, 6; May 2, 1935, 6.

26. Ibid., May 7, 1935, 1; City Commission, *Minutes*, III, July 11, 1935, 389; *Review-Journal*, August 31, 1935, 1; October 5, 1935, 1, 2. City Commission, *Minutes*, III, October 4, 1935, 401; *Review-Journal*, October 5, 1935, 1, 2. For Barry Dibble's report, see Barry Dibble, *Boulder Dam Power for Las Vegas, Nevada* (Las Vegas: *Las Vegas Age*, 1935).

27. City Commission, *Minutes*, III, January 20, 1937, 492–493; *Review-Journal*, February 16, 1937, 1; May 5, 1937, 1. The power bond vote was further divided into two groups, both of whom passed the issue: property owners (490 to 485), and nonproperty owners (551 to 389).

28. *Review-Journal*, November 3, 1937, 1; City Commission, *Minutes*, IV, September 5, 1940, 261; *Age*, April 8, 1938, 4; City Commission, *Minutes*, IV, May 4, 1938, 110; *Review-Journal*, May 5, 1938, 1, 2.

29. For Helldorado, see *Review-Journal*, April 27, 1935, 6; November 3, 1936, 1.

30. The significance of the Gable-Langham divorce for Las Vegas is covered in *Review-Journal*, December 28, 1986, 14CC and Kaufman, "The Best City," 109–111.

31. *Review-Journal*, May 1, 1939, 4; May 3, 1939, 8.

32. For the Russell crisis, see *Age*, January 3, 1941, 1; January 10, 1941, 6; City Commission, *Minutes*, IV, January 4, 1941, 295–297; *Age*, January 10, 1941, 1; January 17, 1941, 6; City Commission, *Minutes*, IV, January 16, 1941, 298–299; *Age*, January 31, 1941, 1, 6; February 7, 1941, 1; February 14, 1941, 6; March 31, 1941, 1; May 9, 1941, 1, 3; May 16, 1941, 4; May 30, 1941, 1; *Review-Journal*, May 3, 1939, 8; City Commission, *Minutes*, IV, May 12, 1941, 331–332.

33. See Gerald Nash, *The American West Transformed: The Impact of the Second World War* (Bloomington: Indiana University Press, 1985). Jones, "Report of the City Manager," *Review-Journal*, 11.

34. *Review-Journal*, June 26, 1940, 1; July 24, 1940, 1; December 14, 1940, 1; *Age*, March 14, 1941, 1; City Commission, *Minutes*, V, September 4, 1942, 11; June 7, 1944, 162.

35. *Review-Journal*, October 10, 1941, 6.

36. Ibid., December 23, 1940, 1; November 10, 1941, 3; Roske, *A Desert Paradise*, 89.

37. Luckingham, *The Urban Southwest*, 75–83. An especially useful source tracing the origins of Basic Magnesium is Christopher Currin's article on BMI in the *Review-Journal*, May 1, 1983, 6L–7L. See also Maryellen Sadovich, "Basic Magnesium, Incorporated and the Industrialization of Southern Nevada during World War II" (unpublished master's thesis: University of Nevada, Las Vegas, 1971).

38. *Review-Journal*, May 1, 1983, 6L–7L.

39. Ibid. Sadovich, "Basic Magnesium," passim.

40. *Review-Journal*, May 1, 1983, 6L.

41. Ibid., December 8, 1941, 1.

42. Ibid., May 1, 1983, 6L–7L. See also appropriate sections of Sadovich, "Basic Magnesium," and William Dobbs, "Working for BMI: Reflections on Life and Labor at America's Largest World War II Magnesium Plant" (unpublished paper).

43. Dobbs, "Working for BMI," 6–7.

44. Roske, *A Desert Paradise*, 91.

45. *Review-Journal*, September 4, 1942, 2; May 4, 1944, 18.

46. Jones and Cahlan, *Water*, I, 99; *Review-Journal*, April 5, 1943, 12.

47. *Review-Journal*, October 15, 1942, 2; February 6, 1943, 5.

48. Kaufman, "The Best City," pp. 80–84; Roske, *A Desert Paradise*, 92–94.

49. Kaufman, "The Best City," 80–84.

50. Jones and Cahlan, *Water*, I, 114–116 covers the water crisis in the Biltmore and Huntridge additions.

51. For a brief survey of the scrap drives, casino curfews, meat rationing, and the overall reaction of the community to the war, see Eugene P. Moehring, "Las Vegas and the Second World War," *Nevada Historical Society Quarterly* (1986): 1–30.

Chapter 2: A City Takes Shape

1. *Review-Journal*, January 3, 1942, 5; Jones and Cahlan, *Water*, I, 117; Kaufman, "The Best City," 421–426.

2. Kaufman, "The Best City," 168–170; Roske, *A Desert Paradise*, 87–88.

3. *Review-Journal*, April 4, 1941, 8; Kaufman, "The Best City," 170–172. In 1979, George Stamos wrote an informative series of articles on the major hotels for the *Las Vegas Sun Magazine*—for the El Rancho, see *Las Vegas Sun Magazine*, April 1, 1979, 6–10; Roske, *A Desert Paradise*, 8, 94, 95, 106, 107; Ovid Demaris, *The Last Mafioso* (New York: Bantam Books, 1981), 60–61, 230.

4. *Sun Magazine*, April 1, 1979, 8–10.

5. Ibid.

6. Kaufman, "The Best City," 172–174; *Review-Journal*, October 29, 1942, 11; *Sun Magazine*, April 8, 1979, 6–11; Roske, *A Desert Paradise*, 88, 98, 105, 106, 112, 113; Demaris, *Last Mafioso*, 189, 246, 389. See William J. Moore, *Papers*, for the blueprints.

7. *Sun Magazine*, April 8, 1979, 6–11.

8. Ibid.

9. Ed Reid and Ovid Demaris, *The Green Felt Jungle* (New York: Pocket Books, 1964), 20–22, 27–28, 30–38; *Sun Magazine*, April 22, 1979, 6–11; Kaufman, "The Best City," 176–185; Roske, *A Desert Paradise*, 98, 105, 106, 113; Demaris, *Last Mafioso*, 51–54, 57, 58, 104–105, 247.

10. Reid and Demaris, *The Green Felt Jungle*, 30–38; *Sun Magazine*, April 22, 1979, 9–11.

11. John Findlay, *People of Chance: Gambling in American Society from Jamestown to Las Vegas* (New York: Oxford University Press, 1986), 134.

12. Reid and Demaris, *The Green Felt Jungle*, 2, 26, 128; *Sun Magazine*, May 6, 1979, 6–10; Kaufman, "The Best City," 188–189; Roske, *A Desert Paradise*, 106–109; Demaris, *Last Mafioso*, 129.

13. For more on McAfee's accomplishments, see his obituary in the *Review-Journal*, February 21, 1960, 1 and Kaufman, "The Best City," 168–170, 185.

14. *Review-Journal*, March 12, 1979, 1B; March 3, 1986, 13B; *Las Vegas Sun*, "Backstage," March 16–22, 1979, 14–15.

15. Kaufman, "The Best City," 190–192. See also Lester "Benny" Binion, *Some Recollections of a Texas and Las Vegas Gaming Operator* (University of Nevada Oral History Project, 1973).

16. Russell Elliott, *History of Nevada*, 1st ed. (Lincoln: University of Nebraska Press, 1973), 281–282, 313–318.

17. Reid and Demaris, *The Green Felt Jungle*, 14–29; Demaris, *Last Mafioso*, 82–84. The literature on organized crime in the forties and fifties is vast. Some helpful works are: Carey McWilliams, "Legalized Gambling Doesn't Pay," *Nation*, 171 (November 25, 1950), 482–483; Hank Messick, *The Silent Syndicate* (New York: MacMillan, 1967); David Hanna, *Bugsy Siegel: The Man Who Invented Murder, Inc.* (New York: Belmont Tower Books, 1974).

18. Kaufman, "The Best City," 244–246; Demaris, *Last Mafioso*, 50–57, 82–83. For newspaper reaction to the mob takeover, see *Review-Journal*, November 1, 1948, 1; and the editorial on November 2, 1948, 16.

19. Kaufman, "The Best City," 246; *Review-Journal*, December 1, 1947, 4; April 15, 1948, 1.

20. Kaufman, "The Best City," 246; Elliott, *History of Nevada*, 281–282; 316–317; *Review-Journal*, December 30, 1948, 1; December 9, 1952, 1.

21. Kaufman, "The Best City," 272–277; Elliott, *History of Nevada*, 328–337; Mary Ellen Glass, *Nevada's Turbulent '50s: Decade of Political and Economic Change* (Reno: University of Nevada Press, 1981), 25–38. For the struggle to regulate gaming, see appropriate sections of John Cahlan, *Reminiscences of a Reno and Las Vegas, Nevada Newspaperman, University Regent, and Public-Spirited Citizen* (University of Nevada Oral History Project, 1970); Oscar Lewis, *Sagebrush Casinos: The Story of Legal Gambling in Nevada* (New York: Doubleday, 1953); Frank H. Johnson, *Legalized Gambling in Nevada* (Carson City, 1970); Jerome Skolnick, *House of Cards: Legalization and Control of Casino Gambling* (Boston: Little, Brown, 1978); Paul Ralli, *Nevada Lawyer: A Story of Life and Love in Las Vegas* (Dallas: Mathis, Van Nort & Co., 1946).

22. Findlay, *People of Chance*, 155. Nevada's taxation of casino gambling is ably summarized in Ward H. Gubler, "Las Vegas: An International Recreation Center" (unpublished master's thesis: University of Utah, 1967), 73–80; Glass, *Nevada's Turbulent '50s*, 25–27. Carl Abbott, *The New Urban America: Growth and Politics in Sunbelt Cities* (Chapel Hill: University of North Carolina Press, 1981), 249.

23. *Review-Journal*, January 6, 1953, 1; April 19, 1957, 4; Gubler, *Recreation Center*, 82.

24. *Review-Journal*, May 1, 1943, 9; May 3, 1943, 1; May 5, 1943, 1–2.

25. Ibid., January 16, 1949—see "Report of the City Manager," *Review-Journal*; also May 3, 1943, 1, 13; May 5, 1943, 1.
26. *Review-Journal*, September 12, 1945, 1; September 13, 1945, 20.
27. Ibid., May 9, 1945, 1; May 5, 1947, 1; May 6, 1947, 1.
28. Ibid., May 7, 1947, 1. See also Cragin's advertisements in Ibid., April 21, 1947, 6.
29. Ibid., September 5, 1945, 14.
30. Ibid., July 2, 1948, 18; Kaufman, "The Best City," 450–451.
31. "Report of the City Manager," *Review-Journal*, 18, 4.
32. *Review-Journal*, January 5, 1946, 1.
33. Ibid. For newspaper reaction, see ibid., January 7, 1946, 16.
34. Ibid., January 13, 1947, 1; April 29, 1954, 1; Reid and Demaris, *The Green Felt Jungle*, 99–110; *Review-Journal*, April 29, 1954, 1; *Sun*, January 7, 1955, 1.
35. Roske, *A Desert Paradise*, 100; *Review-Journal*, September 10, 1945, 1; September 25, 1945, 1; November 1, 1946, 1.
36. For the initial reaction, see Clark County Board of Commissioners, *Minutes*, November 7, 1946. For later events, consult the *Review-Journal*, January 14, 1947, 16.
37. *Review-Journal*, April 22, 1947, 1; April 23, 1947, 1; April 28, 1947, 18. For the election, see May 2, 1947, 1.
38. Ibid., February 27, 1948, 20; Kaufman, "The Best City," 67–71; Roske, *A Desert Paradise*, 102.
39. "Report of the City Manager," 11; *Review-Journal*, February 20, 1948, 20; Roske, *A Desert Paradise*, 102–103; Kaufman, "The Best City," 72–74; *Review-Journal*, May 1, 1986, 6L–7L.
40. *Review-Journal*, January 23, 1946, 1, 8.
41. *Age*, May 2, 1941, 6; *Review-Journal*, November 13, 1945, 1.
42. *Review-Journal*, January 10, 1947, 1.
43. *Age*, October 1, 1944, 6; Roske, *A Desert Paradise*, 98–100; Kaufman, "The Best City," 118–131; *Review-Journal*, September 22, 1945, 12; January 18, 1948, 12B.
44. Roske, *A Desert Paradise*, 99–100.
45. Ibid., January 11, 1947, 2. For more on Las Vegas promotion and postwar tourism, see Perry Kaufman, "Public Relations Men, Images and the Growth of Las Vegas" (unpublished paper), later refined into "City Boosters, Las Vegas Style," *Journal of the West* (1974), 46–60; Jonreed Lauritzen, *Las Vegas, Nevada for Fun and Sun* (Las Vegas: n.p., 1947); Wesley Stout, "Nevada's New Reno," *Saturday Evening Post*, 215 (October 31, 1942), 12–13, 68–71. Earl Pomeroy develops some helpful themes in his book, *In Search of the Golden West: The Tourist in Western America* (New York: Knopf, 1957).
46. "Report of the City Manager," 4, 11.
47. *Review-Journal*, April 27, 1949, 13; April 29, 1949, 9.

48. Kaufman, "The Best City," 463–472.
49. *Review-Journal*, April 6, 1946, 1. For the actual debate, consult City Commission, *Minutes*, V, April 6, 1946, 409–410 and especially May 8, 1946, 418–421.
50. *Review-Journal*, May 9, 1946, 1, 2.
51. Ibid., May 22, 1949, 1; November 15, 1950, 4; Clark County Board of Commissioners, *Minutes*, December 8, 1950.
52. *Review-Journal*, April 28, 1949, 17; April 29, 1949, 7. In particular, William Peccole's realty company was an opponent of postwar rent control and public housing; company advertisements characterized them as "socialism"; see *Review-Journal*, May 2, 1949, 2.
53. Ibid., May 1, 1949, 10, 12B; May 4, 1949, 1; Abbott, *New Urban America*, 63.

Chapter 3: "Boomtown in the Desert"

1. The chapter title derives partially from Gladwin Hill's "Atomic Boomtown in the Desert," *New York Times Magazine* (February 11, 1951), 14. For Las Vegas and American cultural trends, see John Findlay's three chapters on the Nevada city in *People of Chance*. The popular literature regarding the postwar popularity of Las Vegas is vast. Without doubt, John Findlay's endnotes and bibliography provide the most comprehensive listing. In particular, see Julian Halevy, "Disneyland and Las Vegas," *Nation* (June 7, 1958), 510–513; "Las Vegas: It Just Couldn't Happen," *Time*, LXII (November 23, 1953), 30–34; Ed Reid, *Las Vegas: City Without Clocks* (Englewood Cliffs: Prentice Hall, 1961); Mary K. Hammond, "Legalized Gambling in Nevada," *Current History*, XXI (1951), 177–179; Gladwin Hill, "Klondike in the Desert," *New York Times Magazine* (June 7, 1953), 14–15, 65, 67; Gladwin Hill, "Las Vegas is More Than the 'Strip,'" *New York Times Magazine* (March 16, 1958), 19, 31–32; Lucius Beebe, "Las Vegas," *Holiday*, XII (December 1952), 106–108, 132–137; Katharine Best and Katharine Hillyer, *Las Vegas: Playtown U.S.A.* (New York: D. McKay Co., 1955); William F. French, "Don't Say Las Vegas is Short of Suckers," *Saturday Evening Post*, 228 (November 5, 1955), 12; "Gambling Town Pushes Its Luck," *Life*, XXXVIII (June 20, 1955), 20–27; "Gambling: Wilbur's Dream Joint," *Time*, LV (May 8, 1950), 16–17; Paul Ralli, *Viva Vegas* (Hollywood: House-Warven, 1953); Jack Murray, *Las Vegas: Zoomtown U.S.A.* (Phoenix: Lebeau Printing, 1962).
2. *Sun Magazine*, May 20, 1979, 5–11; Kaufman, "The Best City," 189–190; Michael Drosnin, *Citizen Hughes* (New York: Holt, Rinehart & Winston, 1985), 55–56, 77–78, 128, 496, 498; Roske, *A Desert Paradise*, pp. 106, 113, 120, 121, 123; Demaris, *Last Mafioso*, 58–59, 131, 228–229. Las Vegas held a particular fascination for wealthy men like Howard Hughes and Kirk Kerkorian along with thousands of ordinary people. The relationship of gambling to society

has been ably examined by Findlay, passim, but also see Charles W. Fisher and Raymond J. Wells, *Living in Las Vegas: Some Characteristics, Behavior Patterns and Values of Local Residents* (Las Vegas: n.p., 1967?); William T. White, Bernard Malamud and John E. Nixon, *Socioeconomic Characteristics of Las Vegas, Nevada* (Las Vegas: UNLV Center for Business and Economic Research, 1975); Don R. Murphy, "The Role of Changing External Relations in the Growth of Las Vegas, Nevada" (unpublished doctoral dissertation: University of Nebraska, 1969); William R. Eadington, ed., *Gambling and Society: Interdisciplinary Studies on the Subject of Gambling* (Springfield, IL: Thomas, 1976); Henry Sciullo, "Las Vegas: A Study of Short and Long-term Economic Effects on a Community of Legalized Gambling" (unpublished paper); Philip Richardson, "Effects of Legalized Gambling on Community Stability in the Las Vegas Area" (unpublished paper: sponsored by Twentieth Century Fund, 1974).

3. *Review-Journal*, April 24, 1950, 1, 2; *Sun*, May 20, 1979, 7–11.

4. *Sun*, December 1, 1952, 2; *Sun Magazine*, June 3, 1979, 6–11; Kaufman, "The Best City," 196; Roske, *A Desert Paradise*, 94, 106, 108, 118, 119.

5. *Sun*, December 2, 1952, 1; Kaufman, "The Best City," 196–198; Reid and Demaris, *The Green Felt Jungle*, 76–79; *Review-Journal*, December 15, 1952, 1; *Sun*, December 15, 1952, 1; Roske, *A Desert Paradise*, 113, 121, 122; Demaris, *Last Mafioso*, 83, 129, 228, 246–247.

6. *Sun Magazine*, September 2, 1979, 6–11; Kaufman, "The Best City," 198–199. For the zoning changes regarding the Showboat, see City Commission, *Minutes*, IX, January 5, 1955, 371, 372.

7. *Review-Journal*, April 25, 1955—see the 16-page special section; Reid and Demaris, *The Green Felt Jungle*, 34, 40–46, 51; Susan Berman, *Easy Street* (New York: The Dial Press, 1981); Kaufman, "The Best City," 200–201, 203; Roske, *A Desert Paradise*, 109, 113, 121; Demaris, *Last Mafioso*, 129, 132, 322; Steven Brill, *The Teamsters* (New York: Simon & Schuster, 1978), 219.

8. *Review-Journal*, May 23, 1955, 17–25; *Sun Magazine*, July 15, 1979, 6–11; Reid and Demaris, *The Green Felt Jungle*, 2, 19, 36, 89–90; Kaufman, "The Best City," 201–202; Roske, *A Desert Paradise*, 109, 113, 118, 119; Demaris, *Last Mafioso*, 132, 228, 310, 526; Brill, *The Teamsters*, 145, 213, 241, 251.

9. *Sun Magazine*, July 15, 1979, 7–8.

10. Ibid., 10–11; *Review-Journal*, April 22, 1988, 1.

11. *Sun Magazine*, August 12, 1979, 6–11; Kaufman, "The Best City," 208; Roske, *A Desert Paradise*, 121; Demaris, *Last Mafioso*, 132, 239, 252, 320, 436.

12. See Robbins Cahill, *Recollections of Work in State Politics, Government, Taxation, Gaming Control, Clark County Administration and the Nevada Resort Association* (University of Nevada Oral History Project, 1973), see passim for his various comments on gaming control and resort development in Clark County.

13. *Sun Magazine*, August 12, 1979, 9–11.

14. *Review-Journal*, May 17, 1956, 32; May 18, 1956, 1; *Sun Magazine*, July 29,

1979, 6–11; Kaufman, "The Best City," 207–208; Demaris, *Last Mafioso*, 228, 319, 436, 444, 525; Brill, *The Teamsters*, 213, 237, 241–242, 246.

15. *Review-Journal*, July 1, 1958, 17–27; *Sun Magazine*, September 9, 1979, 6–11; Reid and Demaris, *The Green Felt Jungle*, 50, 53, 58, 61–62, 64–69; Kaufman, "The Best City," 210–211; *Review-Journal*—see Sam Boyd's section March 13, 1981, 9D; March 12, 1979, 1B; Roske, *A Desert Paradise*, 118, 119, 121; Demaris, *Last Mafioso*, 178, 246–248, 435–436, 444; Brill, *The Teamsters*, 213, 237, 241–242.

16. *Sun Magazine*, September 9, 1979, 7–11.

17. *Review-Journal*, April 4, 1957, 13–22; *Sun Magazine*, August 26, 1979, 6–11; Reid and Demaris, *The Green Felt Jungle*, 2, 73, 74; Kaufman, "The Best City," 208–209; Roske, *A Desert Paradise*, 113; Demaris, *Last Mafioso*, 130, 132, 444, 502–503. The economic slowdown in Las Vegas in the mid-1950s is covered in a variety of sources, including: "Las Vegas Hedges its Bets," *Business Week* (August 11, 1956), 157–158.

18. *Sun Magazine*, August 26, 1979, 8–11.

19. Ibid.

20. *Review-Journal*, October 28, 1952, 15; June 16, 1959, 1; November 6, 1964, 1. The open shop law was passed by voter initiative.

21. Clark County Commissioners, *Minutes*, December 8, 1950. For more on the reasons why the Strip resisted annexation, see *Review-Journal*, April 4, 1957, 1, 3.

22. Abbott, *New Urban America*, 249.

23. *Sun*, December 19, 1950, 1, 2.

24. *Review-Journal*, March 23, 1951, 1.

25. Ibid., January 6, 1953, 1; April 19, 1957, 4.

26. For coverage of the Kefauver hearings in Las Vegas, see ibid., October 12, 1950, 1; for Keating's bill, consult *Review-Journal*, January 10, 1955, 1.

27. Senator McCarran's influence crested in the early 1950s when he allied with Senator Joseph McCarthy. Indeed, no less an authority than the *Washington Post* characterized McCarran in 1952 as "the most important member" of Congress—*Washington Post*, July 10, 1952 as cited in Jerome Edwards, *Pat McCarran: Political Boss of Nevada* (Reno: University of Nevada Press, 1981), 142. Kaufman, "The Best City," 488–489. See also appropriate sections of Michael S. Green, "Where They Sat, Where They Stood: The Las Vegas Newspaper War of the 1950s" (unpublished paper). Tom Mechling, "I Battled McCarran's Machine," *Reporter* (June 9, 1953), 21–25; Edwards, *Pat McCarran*, 155–172.

28. Kaufman, "The Best City," 495–502, 503–508; Green, "Newspaper War," 10–23; *Sun*, October 25, 1952, 1, 2; December 4, 1953, 1, 8; December 9, 1953, 1, 2; January 12, 1954, 1, 2; June 11, 1954, 1, 2; July 12, 1954, 1, 8.

29. The *Sun*'s sting effort was in response to a libel suit filed by the sheriff against the newspaper. Reid and Demaris, *The Green Felt Jungle*, 92–124; *Sun*, April 27,

1951, 1, 4; May 1, 1951, 1, 2; July 31, 1952, 3; April 12, 1954, 1, 13; April 30, 1954, 1; January 28, 1955, 1, 2. For the Thunderbird hearing, see January 22, 1955, 1. Also see appropriate sections of Hank Greenspun and Alex Pelle, *Where I Stand* (New York: D. McKay Co., 1966). For Cliff Jones's version, see *Review-Journal*, "The Nevadan," October 4, 1987, 3–5, 11.

30. *San Francisco Chronicle*, November 5, 1950, editorial page; November 9, 1950, 1; see November 8, 1950, 6, for state and countywide totals on the gambling referendum.

31. *Review-Journal*, September 1, 1950, 8; September 3, 1953, 1; September 8, 1953, 1; September 15, 1953, 1.

32. Ibid., January 11, 1955, 1–2.

33. Ibid., January 18, 1955, 1. For Las Vegas's support of state legislation authorizing a convention board, see City Commission, *Minutes*, March 2, 1955, 437.

34. *Review-Journal*, January 10, 1957, 1; City Commission, *Minutes*, X, March 14, 1957, 445. For the bond authorization, see Clark County Board of Commissioners, *Minutes*, February 7, 1956—Ordinance No. 67.

35. *Review-Journal*, January 16, 1957, 1, 3.

36. *Sun*, November 19, 1956, "Las Vegas Unlimited"—special edition.

37. *Review-Journal*, November 26, 1950, 1 contains early comments on industry. January 18, 1957, 4; October 31, 1958, 4.

38. Ibid., October 28, 1958, 2; October 31, 1958, 4; May 31, 1959, 4 and see the *Sun*'s special section: "Las Vegas, Nevada Now the World's Most Exciting Convention City," May 31, 1959.

39. Roske, *A Desert Paradise*, 102–105.

40. *Review-Journal*, November 13, 1950, 1; January 4, 1951, 1; October 15, 1952, 1.

41. Ibid., October 31, 1954, 20; Kaufman, "The Best City," 76–80.

42. *Review-Journal*, June 4, 1986, 9C, 12C (contains an informative interview with Harold Cunningham, President of Reynolds Electric, who first came to the test site in 1952). Kaufman, "The Best City," 84–100; Roske, *A Desert Paradise*, 103, 104, 105, 110.

43. *Review-Journal*, January 12, 1951, 1; January 16, 1951, 10. See also U.S. Atomic Energy Commission, *The Story of the Nevada Test Site* (Washington, D.C.); Gladwin Hill, "Desert Capital of the A-Bomb," *New York Times Magazine* (February 13, 1955), 22, 38, 40; Edgerton, Germeshansen & Grier, Inc., *The Nevada Test Site and Southern Nevada* (Las Vegas, 1961). A. Costandina Titus, *Bombs in the Backyard: Atomic Testing and American Politics* (Reno: University of Nevada Press, 1986).

44. *Review-Journal*, February 25, 1985, 11D reviews the test site's early years.

45. Ibid., January 5, 1952, 1.

46. Ibid., May 8, 1951, 2; Edwards, 157.

47. *Review-Journal*, April 27, 1951, 8; May 9, 1951, 1.

48. Ibid., May 4, 1953, 2; May 6, 1953, 1; *Sun*, May 2, 1953, 1; January 18, 1957, 1.

49. *Review-Journal*, January 4, 1954, 3; January 13, 1955, 1; *Sun*, May 2, 1955, 14.

50. *Review-Journal*, January 9, 1955, 1. The best recent work covering federal road building policies is Mark Rose, *Interstate: Express Highway Politics, 1941–1956* (Lawrence: The Regents University Press, 1979). For Oddie-Colton and the Federal Aid Road Act in Nevada, see Elliott, *History of Nevada*, 275, 300.

51. *Review-Journal*, April 17, 1957, 1.

52. Ibid., January 4, 1957, 1; April 15, 1957, 4; April 25, 1957, 4.

53. Ibid., June 1, 1959, 1.

54. Roske, *A Desert Paradise*, 128; *Review-Journal*, May 26, 1959, 11; June 3, 1959, 1.

55. *Review-Journal*, June 1, 1959, 1.

56. Bradford Luckingham, "Phoenix: The Desert Metropolis," in Richard Bernard and Bradley Rice, eds., *Sunbelt Cities: Politics and Growth Since World War II* (Austin: University of Texas Press, 1983), 318–319.

57. Findlay, *People of Chance*, 177.

58. Ben-Chieh Liu, *Quality of Life Indicators in U.S. Metropolitan Areas: A Statistical Analysis* (New York: Praeger, 1976), 232, 246–247.

59. Peter Lupsha and William Siembieda, "The Poverty of Public Services in the Land of Plenty: An Analysis and Interpretation," in David C. Perry and Alfred J. Watkins, *The Rise of the Sunbelt Cities* (Beverly Hills: Sage Publications, Inc., 1977), 169–190; Liu, *Quality of Life*, 235, 239, 248–249, 252–253.

60. For the infrastructural lag in New York, see the appropriate sections of Eugene P. Moehring, *Public Works and the Patterns of Urban Real Estate Growth in Manhattan, 1835–1894* (New York: Arno Press, 1981).

Chapter 4: Achieving Metropolitan Status

1. *Review-Journal*, January 1, 1968, 3 reviews 1967 growth.

2. Las Vegas Planning Department, *Population Profiles: Population, Income, Housing, Occupation, Education, Analysis of the 1970 Census, Las Vegas SMSA.* (n.d.), 3; Gubler, "Recreation Center," 133.

3. Gubler, "Recreation Center," 133; *Population Profiles*, 3.

4. Carl Abbott, "The Suburban Sunbelt," *Journal of Urban History* (1987), 276–281 discusses Ken Jackson's thesis.

5. *Population Profiles*, 3; Nevada Development Authority, First Interstate Bank and *Las Vegas Review-Journal*, *Las Vegas Perspective*, 47.

6. *Population Profiles*, 1; *Las Vegas Perspective*, 16, 19.

7. Liu, *Quality of Life*, 232, 246; see Howard Rabinowitz, "Albuquerque: City at a Crossroads," in *Sunbelt Cities*, 255–267; *Las Vegas Perspective*, 12–15; *Popula-*

tion Profiles, 4, 23. Leo Schnore, "The Socioeconomic Status of Cities and Suburbs," *American Sociological Review* (1963), 76–85; Philip Hauser and Leo Schnore, *The Study of Urbanization* (New York: John Wiley, 1965), passim; Abbott, "Suburban Sunbelt," 283–284.

8. Abbott, "Suburban Sunbelt," 285.

9. *Las Vegas Perspective*, 12–16, 34–41.

10. Betty Yantis, *Fact Book for Las Vegas and Clark County* (Las Vegas: UNLV Center for Business and Economic Research, 1977), 8–1 to 10–1. A revealing study of the impact of casino gambling upon the economy is Robert E. Willard, "The Quantitative Significance of the Gaming Industry in the Greater Las Vegas Area" (unpublished doctoral dissertation: University of Arizona, 1968).

11. *Population Profiles*, 5, 39–40; *Las Vegas Perspective*, 28–33; Yantis, *Fact Book*, 9–1.

12. Gubler, "Recreation Center," 113–151.

13. *Review-Journal*, January 1, 1970, 4; see February 25, 1985, 3DD for a review of Nellis's historical contribution to Las Vegas. Kaufman, "The Best City," 76–80.

14. *Review-Journal*, March 8, 1960, 7; June 7, 1961, 1.

15. Ibid., January 1, 1963, 1.

16. Ibid., June 4, 1986, 9C, 12C (reviews EG&G and REECo operations).

17. Gubler, "Recreation Center," 143–148.

18. *Sun Magazine*, September 23, 1979, 6–11; Demaris, *Last Mafioso*, 310, 319, 444, 526–527.

19. *Sun Magazine*, September 23, 1978, 8–11.

20. *Review-Journal*, August 5, 1966, 25–30; Roske, *A Desert Paradise*, 114, 119, 123, 137; Demaris, *Last Mafioso*, 377, 382, 432, 443–444, 475; Brill, *The Teamsters*, 211, 213, 240. For more on the connection between Jay Sarno and the Teamsters, see ibid., 215, 221. For some interesting observations about Strip architecture, see John Pastier, "The Architecture of Escapism: Disney World and Las Vegas," *American Institute of Architects Journal*, 67 (December 1978): 26–37. Robert Venturi, *Learning from Las Vegas: The Forgotten Symbolism of Architectural Form* (Cambridge, MA: MIT Press, 1977 ed.).

21. *Sun Magazine*, October 14, 1979, 6–9.

22. Ibid., 10–11.

23. Hughes's Landmark Hotel opened at 9 p.m. on July 1 and Kerkorian's International opened the next morning at 10 a.m. For the Landmark's opening, see *Review-Journal*, July 1, 1969, 10, 14; and *Sun*, July 1, 1969, 7, 26; July 3, 1969, 1–2.

24. Michael Drosnin, *Citizen Hughes*, 332–333, 523; Demaris, *Last Mafioso*, 223–228, 246; Brill, *The Teamsters*, 213, 360.

25. *Sun Magazine*, December 9, 1979, 6–11. Drosnin, *Citizen Hughes*, 332–358. For another view of Howard Hughes, see Ron Layton, *Up Against Howard Hughes* (New York: Quadrangle Books, 1972).

26. *Review-Journal*, January 1, 1968, 3; April 24, 1986, 1D–2D.

27. *Sun*, July 1, 1969, 6, 26; July 2, 1969, 18; *Sun Magazine*, November 18, 1979, 6–11; *Review-Journal*, January 1, 1968, 3; November 1, 1968, 1.

28. *Sun Magazine*, December 23, 1979, 5–11; *Review-Journal*, November 1, 1968, 1; April 24, 1986, 1D–2D.

29. *Review-Journal*, December 5, 1973, 28; *Sun*, December 6, 1973, 11.

30. Gubler, "Recreation Center," 107–108; *Review-Journal*, June 1, 1967, 1.

31. *Las Vegas Perspective*, 52–53.

32. *Review-Journal*, November 4, 1968, 38.

33. Ibid., January 5, 1964, 42.

34. Ibid., January 6, 1965, 21.

35. Gubler, "Recreation Center," 133; *Review-Journal*, December 4, 1951, 2.

36. *Review-Journal*, October 26, 1954, 1.

37. Ibid., December 4, 1951, 1. The idea of building a sewer system for North Las Vegas was originally proposed by former Mayor Ken Reynolds in 1951. Ibid., January 1, 1954, 1. See also February 22, 1955, 1; February 23, 1960, 1–3.

38. Ibid., February 24, 1960, 6; March 28, 1960, 3.

39. Ibid., May 2, 1957, 1.

40. A review of North Las Vegas's public works projects after 1962 can be found in ibid., January 3, 1965, 13; January 2, 1966, 10. See also North Las Vegas City Manager, *Annual Report for 1963–64* (1964); North Las Vegas City Council, *Community Renewal Plan*, Vol. 1 (1972).

41. *Review-Journal*, January 2, 1966, 10.

42. Ibid.

43. Roske, *A Desert Paradise*, 102, 103, 109, 121, 125, 126–128. Also see Henderson City Planning Commission, *General Master Plan of the City of Henderson, Nevada* (1969), 4–5. For some early background material, consult Sadovich, "Basic Magnesium," passim and "Henderson—From Desolate Desert to a City of Destiny," *Nevada Highways and Parks*, XI (1951), 1–15; as well as the appropriate sections of Henderson City Council, *Minutes* (1954–). As early as 1954, Basic Management had become less cooperative about helping the newly incorporated city with fire, water, and waste removal services, see *Minutes*, January 20, 1954.

44. *Henderson Master Plan*, 4–5, 6–7, 12.

45. Ibid., 12–14.

46. Ibid., 15–16.

47. Ibid.

48. *Las Vegas Perspective*, 5; *Review-Journal*, December 16, 1986, 8B. For Boulder City's problems in the late 1940s, see Harry Reining, *Boulder City, Nevada: A Federal Municipality, a Report of a Survey Made under the Direction of the Bureau of Reclamation of Problems Affecting Boulder City* (Washington, D.C.: Government Printing Office, 1950).

49. *Review-Journal*, March 3, 1960, 3; March 17, 1960, 2.

50. Efforts to improve the airport in the mid-1950s resulted in two bond issues. See Clark County Commission, *Minutes*, July 1, 1955 and April 20, 1956. *Review-Journal*, February 25, 1960, 5, 6; August 25, 1960, 30; *Sun*, March 5, 1960, 6. In order to boost support for the bond election for the new McCarran terminal, county leaders were careful to obtain an exciting and futuristic building design. For a key meeting with the architects, see Clark County Commission, *Minutes*, March 6, 1959.

51. *Review-Journal*, March 3, 1960, 3.

52. Ibid., June 2, 1963, 2.

53. Ibid., June 2, 1963, 1; *Sun*, November 6, 1962, 1; June 3, 1963, 1.

54. *Review-Journal*, May 27, 1963, 12; June 2, 1963, 2; June 3, 1963, 1. For Phoenix, see Michael Konig, "Toward Metropolitan Status: Charter Government and the Rise of Phoenix, Arizona" (unpublished doctoral dissertation: Arizona State University, 1983), 52–76.

55. *Review-Journal*, June 6, 1965, 1.

56. Ibid., June 15, 1964, 3.

57. Ibid., January 1, 1963, 1; January 4, 1968, 14.

58. Ibid., June 4, 1965, 1.

59. Ibid., November 15, 1965, 1; For reapportionment, see Gilman Ostrander, *Nevada: The Great Rotten Borough* (New York: Knopf, 1966), passim. Eleanor Bushnell, *Sagebrush & Neon: Studies in Nevada Politics* (Reno: Bureau of Governmental Research, 1973), 93–116.

60. *Review-Journal*, January 15, 1965, 1; June 16, 1965, 16.

61. Ibid., June 4, 1967, 1; June 7, 1967, 1.

62. Ibid., January 7, 1965, 4.

Chapter 5: Fragmented Government

1. See, for instance, Richard Bernard, "Cities, Suburbs and Sunbelts: The Politics of Metropolitan Growth," *Journal of Urban History* (1983), 85–92; Howard Rabinowitz, "Growth Trends in the Albuquerque SMSA, 1940–1978," *Journal of the West* (1979), 65–66; Michael Konig, "Phoenix, Arizona, 1920–1940" (doctoral dissertation: Arizona State University, 1983), 109–114.

2. Kaufman, "The Best City," 426–428. The concept of urban fragmentation has been discussed in various works. For a good bibliography and a picture of southern California's problems, see Robert Fogelson, *The Fragmented Metropolis: Los Angeles, 1850–1930* (Boston: Harvard University Press, 1967) and Jon Teaford, *City and Suburb, The Political Fragmentation of Metropolitan America, 1850–1970* (Baltimore: The Johns Hopkins University Press, 1979) for excellent background coverage.

3. Kaufman, "The Best City," 427–428.

4. Ibid., 428–430.

5. Ibid., 436–440. Public Administration Service, *Local Government in Clark County, Nevada* (Chicago, 1968), 95–96.

6. *Local Government*, 89–95; *Review-Journal*, January 10, 1962, 1.

7. *Local Government*, 89–95.

8. Ibid., 105.

9. George Sternlieb and James W. Hughes, *The Atlantic City Gamble* (Cambridge, MA: Harvard University Press, 1983), 134–136.

10. See the various crime rates per 100,000 people in Uniform Crime Reporting Section, Federal Bureau of Investigation, U.S. Department of Justice, *Crime in the United States* (Washington, D.C., July 1, 1986), 335–363 for a recent study of crime trends.

11. For the early history of the fire department, consult Jones, "Report of the City Manager," *Review-Journal*, 7; Kaufman, "The Best City," 447–449. A site for a fire station for the populous Huntridge area southeast of downtown was not even selected until 1958; see City Commission, *Minutes*, XI, July 2, 1958, 166.

12. *Review-Journal*, May 5, 1959, 4; May 6, 1959, 1; *Local Government*, 105–106.

13. *Local Government*, 107. For Map 2, see the map between pp. 109 and 110.

14. Ibid., 109–112; Kaufman, "The Best City," 449–450.

15. Kaufman, "The Best City," 421–426.

16. Ibid., 425–426; *Local Government*, 83–85. Eisner-Stewart and Associates, *Proposed General Plan: Las Vegas Valley* (1966); Ibid., *Land Use Inventory and Analysis* (1966). See also Henderson City Planning Commission, *Henderson Master Plan*; Las Vegas Planning Commission, *Capital Improvement Program, 1969–1974*; Las Vegas Planning Commission, *Las Vegas Plans its Future, Master Plan* (1959); Clark County Planning Commission, *Comprehensive Plan, Clark County, Nevada*, 6 vols. (1981) is an updated and expanded version of the earlier plan. For the water district, consult Las Vegas Valley Water District, *Master Water Plan, Las Vegas Valley* (Las Vegas: Boyle Engineering, 1970).

17. Eisner-Stewart, *Proposed General Plan*, passim. As early as 1951, Las Vegans agreed to share funding for the new Regional Planning Commission with North Las Vegas, see City Commission, *Minutes*, VII, October 17, 1951, 456.

18. Gubler, "Recreation Center," 133; *Local Government*, passim.

19. *Review-Journal*, October 17, 1958, 4; October 24, 1958, 1; March 18, 1960, 2. See also Clark County Board of Commissioners, *Clark County Road and Flood Control Needs Assessment* (April 1981). Also see City Commission, *Minutes*, XI, August 5, 1959, 507 and September 16, 1959, 531.

20. *Review-Journal*, September 3, 1986, 1.

21. Ibid., March 3, 1960, 1–2.

22. Ibid., July 21, 1964, 26.

23. Ibid., January 5, 1964, 1.

24. Ibid., January 4, 1969, 13.

25. As early as 1956, Las Vegas was opposing county efforts to create an unincorporated township to the east; see City Commission, *Minutes*, X, December 5, 1956, 376. *Review-Journal*, May 17, 1962, 1–2; May 18, 1962, 5.

26. *Review-Journal*, May 16, 1962, 20; May 17, 1962, 1–2.

27. Ibid., May 16, 1962, 20.

28. Ibid., May 22, 1962, 10. For a modern look at municipal borders, see *Front Boy's 1983 Greater Las Vegas Street Directory*, XVI edition.

29. *Review-Journal*, January 4, 1963, 1; January 5, 1963, 1–2. For Map 3, see Metcalf & Eddy Engineers-Montgomery Engineers, *Facility Plan Las Vegas Valley Regional Secondary Treatment Facilities: Clark County, Nevada* (1976).

30. *North Las Vegas Valley Times*, October 30, 1969, 1; November 3, 1969, 1, 8; November 6, 1969, 1, 10; November 10, 1969, 1, 8; November 13, 1969, 1, 12; November 17, 1969, 1.

31. *Sun*, November 4, 1969, 11.

32. Ibid., November 7, 1969, 6.

33. Ibid., November 11, 1969, 1.

34. Ibid., November 21, 1969, 1; Clark County Board of Commissioners, *Minutes*, November 20, 1969.

35. *Review-Journal*, October 24, 1950, 1–2. See July 19, 1964, 4; January 1, 1971 for Bill Briare's efforts to annex Paradise and Winchester as a means of expanding Las Vegas's tax base and consolidating government functions. Raymond Mohl, "Miami's Metropolitan Government: Retrospect and Prospect," *Florida Historical Quarterly* (1984), 30–31.

36. *Local Government*, 59.

37. Ibid., 73–74, 85. The Clark County Regional Planning Council was finally created in April 1966 to help satisfy federal grant requirements. For Henderson's discussion and approval, see Henderson City Council, *Minutes*, August 8, 1966; For Las Vegas, consult *Review-Journal*, August 4, 1966, 2.

38. *Local Government*, 63–79. A useful study of the need for government consolidation in the Las Vegas Valley in the mid-1970s is: Local Government Study Committee, *The Report on Local Governments in Clark County* (1973). Also see Andrew Grose, "Las Vegas—Clark County Consolidation: A Unique Event in Search of a Theory," *Nevada Public Affairs*, vol. 14 no. 14 (1976); Franklin J. Bills and Associates, *Local Government Services Crisis, Clark County, Nevada: Feasibility Report—Alternative Courses of Action* (Las Vegas, 1968); Clark County Board of Commissioners, *A Workable Blueprint for Local Government in Clark County, Nevada* (March 1969).

39. *Review-Journal*, December 4, 1951, 2. For a brief but informative survey of early Las Vegas schools, see ibid., November 12, 1978, 3J–5J as well as Mary B. Kieser, "A History of Las Vegas Schools, 1905 to 1956" (unpublished professional paper: University of Nevada, Las Vegas, 1977) and Susan Kendall, "Education in Las Vegas, 1905–1934" (unpublished paper).

40. *Review-Journal*, November 12, 1978, 3J–4J.

41. For the new grammar school, see Moehring, "Public Works and the New Deal in Las Vegas," *Nevada Historical Society Quarterly* (1981), 117–118.

42. *Review-Journal*, August 31, 1945, 4.

43. Ibid., January 16, 1946, 18. A number of sources provide useful discussions of the postwar education crisis, especially Kieser; Elbert Edwards, *Memoirs of a Southern Nevada Educator*, 2 vols. (University of Nevada Oral History Project, 1968); R. Guild Gray, "The Organization of a County School District: A Case Study of . . . District Consolidation and Administrative Reorganization" (unpublished doctoral dissertation: Stanford University, 1958).

44. *Review-Journal*, April 25, 1951, 1; Glass, *Nevada's Turbulent '50s*, 49–60.

45. Gray, 32–34. See also Peabody College for Teachers, *Public Education in Nevada, Digest of the Survey Report* (Nashville, 1954), 4–5.

46. Gray, "County School District," 170–171.

47. For the reform legislation, see *Statutes of Nevada* (1955), chapter 402, section 44; for the funding formula, see ibid., chapter 443, section 6.

48. *Review-Journal*, January 12, 1955, 1; Gray, "County School District," 176.

49. *Review-Journal*, January 1, 1956, 4.

50. Ibid.

51. Ibid., January 1, 1963, 1–2; January 1, 1965, 1–2.

52. Ibid., January 1, 1963, 1–2.

53. *Local Government*, 168–171.

54. For Dade County, see Raymond Mohl, "Miami's Metropolitan Government," 28–33 and Edward Sofen, *Miami's Metropolitan Experiment* (New York: Doubleday, 1966), passim. William Graves, *Hawaii* (Washington, D.C.: National Geographical Society, 1970), passim. Thanks to its growing resort economy, Atlantic City is currently locked in a bitter struggle with Atlantic County over control of the municipal airport. With millions of dollars in expansion funds at stake, the county wants to form a regional airport authority; see *Review-Journal*, October 11, 1987, 5C.

Chapter 6: Civil Rights in a Resort City

1. U.S. Department of Commerce, Bureau of the Census, *Nevada, 1910*, 53–62. Kaufman, "The Best City," 326; Roosevelt Fitzgerald, "Black Entertainers in Las Vegas, 1940–1960" (unpublished paper), 4. For general background, see Rita O'Brien, ed., "West Las Vegas at the Crossroads: A Forum" (1977)— transcript of a discussion; Elizabeth Nelson Patrick, ed., "The Black Experience in Southern Nevada," *Nevada Historical Society Quarterly* (1979), 128–140, 209–220; ibid., "The Black Experience in Southern Nevada" (UNLV oral history transcripts, 1978).

2. Kaufman, "The Best City," 326, 333.

3. Roosevelt Fitzgerald, "Black Entertainers in Las Vegas, 1940–1960" (unpublished paper), 7, 32.

4. Kaufman, "The Best City," 328; *Age*, November 18, 1931, 1; January 20, 1932, 2; June 18, 1932, 4. See also Roosevelt Fitzgerald, "The Impact of the Hoover Dam Project on Race Relations in Southern Nevada" (unpublished paper), passim.

5. *Age*, August 18, 1932, n.p.; *Review-Journal*, March 31, 1934, 1.

6. *Review-Journal*, February 15, 1939, 1; Fitzgerald, "Black Entertainers," 7–11. For more on southern dam workers, see Fitzgerald, "The Evolution of a Black Community in Las Vegas, 1905–1940" (unpublished paper), 16; Kaufman, "The Best City," 331.

7. Kaufman, "The Best City," 355. In October 1943, over two hundred blacks walked off the job at BMI to protest the company's discriminatory policies. See *Review-Journal*, October 20, 1943, 1.

8. Ibid., October 17, 1939, 2; Kaufman, "The Best City," 338–339.

9. Fitzgerald, "Black Entertainers," 11–13.

10. For Carver Park, see ibid., 340–345 and Dobbs, "Working for BMI," 10, 17–20 for treatment of black workers at BMI.

11. Fitzgerald, "Black Entertainers," 5; *Review-Journal*, July 1, 1943, 1. For the riot, see August 1, 1943, 1 and August 2, 1943, 1; City Commission, *Minutes*, V, December 22, 1942, 47; February 4, 1943, 62; March 4, 1943, 67; February 10, 1944, 440; *Review-Journal*, November 1, 1944, 2. Al Cahlan defended the city's action in the black riot, see ibid., January 13, 1944, 6.

12. *Review-Journal*, September 22, 1944, 2; April 10, 1945, 7; Kaufman, "The Best City," 354.

13. *Review-Journal*, August 8, 1945, 4; February 6, 1946, 6; July 3, 1947, 3. See also C. B. McClelland Co., *Report of Las Vegas, Nevada, Housing Survey, December 1947* (Riverside, CA: 1948).

14. *Review-Journal*, February 1, 1945, 1; Kaufman, "The Best City," 356.

15. Kaufman, "The Best City," 360; *Sun*, August 2, 1950, 1–2; April 24, 1951, 1; *Review-Journal*, October 21, 1957, 1–2; see also Las Vegas Housing Authority, *Housing Survey of Selected Areas, Las Vegas, Nevada* (1950).

16. Kaufman, "The Best City," 376–378; *Sun*, May 24, 1956, 20; *Review-Journal*, October 16, 1959. For some of the Westside's street improvements in 1955–56, consult City Commission, *Minutes*, X, February 1, 1956, 173–174; February 20, 1957, 412; May 7, 1958, 129. For "Project Madison," see ibid., XI, October 15, 1958, 225; February 4, 1959, 295; October 15, 1959, 55.

17. Ibid., February 25, 1953, 3; Kaufman, "The Best City," 363–365; *Review-Journal*, February 5, 1954, 3.

18. Ibid., January 8, 1954, 1.

19. Fitzgerald, "Black Entertainers," 37; Kaufman, "The Best City," 367.

20. Gary Elliott, "The Moulin Rouge Hotel: A Critical Appraisal of a Las Vegas Legend" (unpublished paper), 5.

21. *Review-Journal*, March 4, 1954, 1. Foxy's was the only Strip restaurant which regularly served blacks in the 1950s—Kaufman, "The Best City," 368, 374.

22. Elliott, "The Moulin Rouge," 6–10; *Review-Journal*, May 18, 1961, 1–2. For more on the city zoning needed to accommodate the hotel's construction, see City Commission, *Minutes*, IX, March 29, 1954, 36.

23. Elliott, "The Moulin Rouge," 6–10; *Review-Journal*, May 19, 1961, 20.

24. Kaufman, "The Best City," 379–382; *Review-Journal*, February 14, 1957, 1.

25. *Review-Journal*, March 17, 1960, 1; March 25, 1960, 1.

26. Kaufman, "The Best City," 391–394. *Review-Journal*, March 27, 1960, 2.

27. *Review-Journal*, January 5, 1962, 1–2.

28. Ibid., January 6, 1963, 4.

29. Ibid., January 27, 1962, 6. A number of oral histories provide good coverage of various local civil rights activities in the late 1950s and 1960s. See, for instance, Elizabeth Nelson Patrick, ed., *Oral Interview of Cora Williams* (UNLV oral history interview, 1978); *Oral Interview of Reverend Prentiss Walker* (UNLV oral history interview, 1978); *Oral Interview of Lubertha Johnson* (UNLV oral history interview, 1978).

30. *Sun*, February 24, 1962, 1.

31. *Review-Journal*, March 9, 1962, 2.

32. Ibid., March 21, 1962, 1; *Sun*, March 15, 1962, 14.

33. *Review-Journal*, March 19, 1955, 6.

34. Ibid., March 20, 1965, 11; July 1, 1965, 13.

35. Ibid., April 21, 1967, 11; May 5, 1967, 13; May 17, 1967, 1; November 2, 1967, 29.

36. Ibid., August 1, 1967, 1; October 25, 1967, 1; November 23, 1967, 33.

37. Ibid., November 22, 1967, 2. Named in the complaint were the Fremont, Mint, Horseshoe Club, El Cortez, Sahara, Thunderbird, Riviera, Stardust, Frontier, Sands, Flamingo, Caesars Palace, Dunes, Bonanza, Aladdin, Hacienda, Las Vegas, and California clubs.

38. Ibid., November 23, 1967, 33.

39. *Sun*, January 28, 1969, 1.

40. Ibid., February 1, 1969, 1.

41. Ibid., February 5, 1969, 1–2.

42. Ibid., October 7, 1969, 1, 4.

43. Ibid., November 26, 1969, 1; December 4, 1969, 9; December 9, 1969, 1.

44. *Review-Journal*, February 17, 1970, 1; February 18, 1970, 1; May 19, 1970, 1; May 21, 1970, 1.

45. *Sun*, January 29, 1968, 3.

46. *Review-Journal*, July 13, 1967, 21; *Sun*, October 17, 1968, 1–4. For a description of the school district's plan, see Clark County School District, *An Action Plan for Integration of Six Westside Elementary Schools . . . prepared by Superintendent James I. Mason* (Las Vegas, 1969).

47. *Sun*, January 22, 1969, 2; June 1, 1969, 3.

48. *Review-Journal*, May 12, 1972, 8; the entire story from 1968–1972 is reviewed in ibid., September 17, 1972, 5.

49. Ibid., September 17, 1972, 5.

50. Ibid., May 17, 1972, 1; August 25, 1972, 2.

51. Ibid., September 6, 1972, 1.

52. Ibid., October 17, 1972, 11.

53. Ibid., September 17, 1972, 5; September 23, 1972, 2. The *North Las Vegas Valley Times* praised the sixth-grade plan also, see February 23, 1973, 17.

54. Ibid., January 22, 1970, 1.

55. Consult the federal complaint filed by the U.S. Justice Department in behalf of civil rights groups on June 4, 1971. The U.S. District Court, District of Nevada, "Civil LV No. 1645, Complaint." Then see "Civil Action LV No. 1645 Consent Decree." Copies of both documents are available from the court clerk's office at the Foley Federal Building in Las Vegas.

56. *Population Profiles*, 11; Joseph Crowley, "Role and Residence: The Politics of Open Housing in Nevada," in Bushnell, *Sagebrush & Neon*, 55–73.

57. *Review-Journal*, March 7, 1967, 2; *Sun*, March 13, 1969, 1; April 17, 1969, 11. Michael Drosnin has asserted that Howard Hughes played a backstage role in blocking the 1969 fair housing bill: Drosnin, *Citizen Hughes*, 188–189.

58. Crowley, "Role and Residence," 70–73. Compare *Population Profiles*, 11 with 1980 figures in *Comprehensive Plan, Clark County, Nevada*, I 128. Abbott, *New Urban America*, 281–283.

59. Local NAACP members referred to Nevada and even Las Vegas as the "Mississippi of the West" as has Perry Kaufman: see *Review-Journal*, April 14, 1954, 1. The notion that other southwestern cities were also hostile to minorities is briefly covered in Konig, "Toward Metropolitan Status," 187–188; Robert T. Wood, "The Transformation of Albuquerque, 1945–1972" (unpublished doctoral dissertation: University of New Mexico, 1980), 335–336. Also consult *Review-Journal*, June 6, 1967, 1; November 1, 1970, 2.

60. For the debate surrounding Las Vegas's decision to ban women dealers, see City Commission, *Minutes*, XI, November 5, 1958, 233–235; Roske, *A Desert Paradise*, 122; *Review-Journal*, March 19, 1981, 17D. The complaint was filed on January 13, 1981 and is entitled "U.S. Equal Employment Opportunity Commission v. Nevada Resort Association et al.—Case No. CV-LV-81-12 RDF." The consent decree was filed on January 26, 1981. It was in effect until August 13, 1986, when it was rescinded after both parties agreed that the resorts and unions had reformed their hiring, promotion, and pay practices to the point where complaints were no longer valid.

Chapter 7: The Struggle for Industry

1. *Review-Journal*, September 23, 1948, 24.

2. Industrial Committee of the Las Vegas Chamber of Commerce, *Story of Southern Nevada* (Las Vegas, 1948), 10–11.

3. Ibid., 11–12. See also Charles N. Stabler, "Fades and Factories: Las Vegas and Reno Want More Industry to Back Dice Tables," *Wall Street Journal* 56 (January 22, 1957), 1, 12; Los Angeles Bureau of Municipal Research, *Economic Base Study—Las Vegas, Nevada* (Los Angeles, 1958).

4. Las Vegas Research and Statistical Bureau, *Las Vegas Report, 1957*, 12.

5. Ibid., 13.

6. *Story of Southern Nevada*, 13, 15, 43.

7. Ibid., 8, 9.

8. Ibid., 10, 27.

9. Ibid., 57–63.

10. See also the "industrial sections" for *Las Vegas Report*, later called *Las Vegas Digest*, for 1961, 1963, and 1964.

11. U.S. Department of Commerce, Bureau of the Census, *County Business Patterns: Standard Metropolitan Statistical Areas, 1976* (Washington, D.C., 1976), 6–7, 67–68, 119–120, 171–172, 227–228.

12. Luckingham, *The Urban Southwest*, 76–77; Rabinowitz, "Growth Trends," 62.

13. Rabinowitz, "Growth Trends," 62–63; Luckingham, *The Urban Southwest*, 76–77.

14. Luckingham, *The Urban Southwest*, 80–84; Konig, "Toward Metropolitan Status," 198–213.

15. Konig, "Toward Metropolitan Status," 212–216.

16. Luckingham, *The Urban Southwest*, 77–78, 105–106. For coverage of Phoenix's efforts up to 1980 to lure industry, see *Review-Journal*, February 19, 1985, 1A and 4A, which examines the "Sun City's" success. For Tucson's promotion efforts, see Tucson City Council, *The Comprehensive Plan for the City of Tucson, Pima County* (1975), chapter 6: "Economy," 6, 12–13.

17. Wood, "Albuquerque, 1945–1972," 132–134; Michael Kotlanger, "Phoenix, Arizona: 1920–1940" (unpublished doctoral dissertation: Arizona State University, 1983), 490–492.

18. Konig, "Toward Metropolitan Status," 286–291.

19. *Review-Journal*, January 15, 1961, 1; *First Annual Report of the City Manager*, Jones, "Report of the City Manager," 11.

20. Jones and Cahlan, *Water*, I, 127–129.

21. Ibid., II, 4–5.

22. *Review-Journal*, November 4, 1944, 18; Roske, *A Desert Paradise*, 109; Jones and Cahlan, *Water*, II, 4–5. See also George Maxey, *Well Data in Las Vegas* (1946); ibid., *Geology and Water Resources of Las Vegas* (1948).

23. Jones and Cahlan, *Water*, II, 4–9.

24. *Review-Journal*, October 3, 1948, 1; Jones and Cahlan, *Water*, I, 142.

25. *Review-Journal*, October 20, 1948, 1; Jones and Cahlan, *Water*, I, 14.

26. *Review-Journal*, January 15, 1961, 1–2 reviews the water crisis from the 1940s into the 1950s. For the city's sense of helplessness regarding the water shortage, see City Commission, *Minutes*, VII, August 15, 1951, 408.

27. *Review-Journal*, November 6, 1950, 1; January 5, 1952, 1.

28. Ibid., January 16, 1961, 1, 4; January 17, 1961, 1–2; Jones and Cahlan, *Water*, II, 91–92.

29. Jones and Cahlan, *Water*, II, 167–174; Roske, *A Desert Paradise*, 126.

30. Kotlanger, "Phoenix, 1920–1940," 500–505.

31. *Review-Journal*, November 14, 1982, 6L–7L.

32. Ibid.; Kaufman, "The Best City," 460–463; see also Charles Squires, "The Glory of Light: A Half Century of Service" (Las Vegas: n.p. 1955), and Jones, "Golden Anniversary Edition," "Las Vegas—1st Edition," 13; "General Section," 16.

33. Moehring, "Public Works in Las Vegas," 123–128; Kaufman, "The Best City," 460–461.

34. *Review-Journal*, December 9, 1951, 5; December 25, 1951, 1; January 2, 1952, 2.

35. Ibid., December 9, 1951, 1.

36. Ibid., January 4, 1952, 1; May 4, 1953, 1.

37. Ibid., October 13, 1952, 3.

38. Ibid., October 13, 1952, 3; January 4, 1956, 1; January 13, 1956, 3. November 14, 1982, 6L–7L reviews the utility's construction projects from 1953–1965.

39. Kotlanger, "Phoenix, 1920–1940," 504–506.

40. *Review-Journal*, March 11, 1949, 1; October 21, 1952, 1; October 22, 1952, 1.

41. Conversation with Sid Burns of Nevada Power Company, October 17, 1986.

42. Kaufman, "The Best City," 461–463. For city efforts to monitor the progress of telephone installations in new neighborhoods, see City Commission, *Minutes*, X, January 18, 1956, 161 and February 1, 1956, 165.

43. *Review-Journal*, February 19, 1985, 1A and 4A reviews the role of higher education in Phoenix's development efforts.

44. James Hulse, *The University of Nevada: A Centennial History* (Reno: University of Nevada Press, 1974), 62–63.

45. *Review-Journal*, May 24, 1955, 3.

46. *Review-Journal*, April 29, 1955, 2.

47. Hulse, *University*, 64–65; see also the section on UNLV's development in *Review-Journal*, April 17, 1982, 2C–7C.

48. *Review-Journal*, October 30, 1956, 4.

49. Hulse, *University*, 62–66; *Review-Journal*, March 9, 1960, 4; May 20, 1962, 38.

50. *Review-Journal*, January 9, 1962, 14; January 3, 1965, 13.

51. Ibid., January 2, 1968, 11; January 1, 1970, 4; see May 20, 1962, 38 for creation of Nevada Southern University's foundation.

52. Ibid., February 18, 1985, 1A, 4A. UNLV's engineering program itself began in 1984.

53. Rabinowitz, "Growth Trends," 64. Also see the *Albuquerque Journal*, January 30, 1940, 6; January 23, 1940, 6 suggests easing Albuquerque's strict building code to slow construction in the county. The newspaper pushed city interests on

other fronts as well. In early 1940 see, for example, January 17, 1940, 6, which boosts construction of the new post office in order to promote employment. Also see January 21, 1940, 8, which urges recruitment of more air carriers to service Albuquerque's airport.

54. Rabinowitz, "Growth Trends," 65–66.

55. For San Antonio, Texas see Arnold Fleischman, "Sunbelt Boosterism: The Politics of Postwar Growth in San Antonio," in *Sunbelt Cities*, 151–161.

56. Konig, "Toward Metropolitan Status," 109–114. John D. Wenum, *Annexation as a Technique for Metropolitan Growth: The Case of Phoenix, Arizona* (Tempe: Institute of Public Administration, Arizona State University, 1970), 66–70; Luckingham, "Phoenix," in *Sunbelt Cities*, 317–319. A.R.S. 9–101.01 enacted in 1961 and partially amended in 1968. The director's quotation can be found in a letter from Jack DeBolske to Eugene Moehring, dated January 13, 1987.

57. *Review-Journal*, January 7, 1965, 4; see John Cahlan's memo dated March 25, 1971, 4 in *Cahlan MSS.* at the Nevada Historical Society in Las Vegas. Given the old elite's control of the local government, Las Vegas does not fully fit the "professional government" models of sunbelt cities fashioned by historians and political scientists. A good review of the literature can be found in Abbott, *New Urban America*, 140, and other sections.

58. *Review-Journal*, December 1, 1951, 1; for a reminiscence, see George Franklin's column, ibid., December 30, 1986, 5B.

59. See memorandum of J. D. Platt, assistant to Howard Eells, dated July 21, 1941 as well as other memos from 1941 dated July 15, July 22–24, and December 12, all in the Howard Eells *Papers* at Special Collections, James Dickinson Library, University of Nevada, Las Vegas.

60. Duff, Anderson and Clark, Industrial Investment and Financial Analysts, *Las Vegas and Clark County, Nevada: An Economic and Industrial Analysis* (Chicago, 1956). Also see Arthur Little, Inc., *Business Opportunities in Southern Nevada* (San Francisco: n.p., 1970). Las Vegas Chamber of Commerce, *Where is Las Vegas Going? Get the Full Facts on the Present and Future Economy of Las Vegas* (Las Vegas: 1974); Larry Smith & Co., *Clark County Economic Analysis prepared for the Southern Nevada Industrial Foundation* (Seattle: 1960); Robert E. Willard, "Significance of Gaming," passim; Las Vegas Chamber of Commerce Research and Statistical Bureau, *A Compendium of Statistics and Social Facts of Las Vegas* (1952–1975). See also Albin Dahl, *Nevada's Southern Economy* (Carson City: University of Nevada Bureau of Business and Economic Research, Report No. 8, 1969), passim. For city efforts to provide office space for the Southern Nevada Industrial Foundation, see Board of City Commissioners, *Minutes*, X, January 20, 1957, 412 and March 27, 1957, 446. John Cahlan comments on the relative lack of enthusiasm of certain northern Nevada politicians for the Southern Nevada Industrial Foundation, see *Cahlan MSS.*, letter dated March 25, 1971, 4.

61. For a brief summary of the Nevada Development Authority's highlights, see *Review-Journal*, February 17, 1985, 15A; August 4, 1986, 5B.
62. Ibid., May 1, 1983, 7L.

Chapter 8: The City-Building Process

1. See Georgia Lewis's informative article in *Review-Journal*, January 2, 1977, "The Nevadan," 26–27. A devastating fire also depopulated the McWilliams' Townsite in 1905.
2. Ibid., 27. Map 4 is from C. D. Baker's *Map of Las Vegas, October 1, 1940*.
3. *Review-Journal*, September 11, 1977, 3J–5J; December 30, 1986, 5B. For more on Howard Hughes, see Omar Garrison, *Howard Hughes in Las Vegas* (New York: Dell Publishing Company, 1971).
4. *Review-Journal*, January 22, 1978, 1K–2K.
5. Ibid., August 11, 1985, "Homes," 1–2.
6. Charles Paige & Associates, Inc., *Historic Preservation Inventory & Planning Guidelines: City of Las Vegas* (San Francisco, 1978), 15; see also Findlay, *People of Chance*, 185. As Findlay notes, Las Vegas bore a striking resemblance to Los Angeles. Some of the physical and cultural similarities are obvious from reading Christopher Rand, *Los Angeles: The Ultimate City* (New York: Oxford University Press, 1967), passim.
7. Paige & Associates, *Inventory & Planning Guidelines*, 15–16.
8. *Review-Journal*, April 24, 1983, 1J–2J. The source for Map 5 is *Front Boy's 1983 Greater Las Vegas Street Directory*.
9. See, for instance, the "Homes" section of the *Review-Journal*, March 1, 1976.
10. See *Las Vegas Perspective*, 57–59, for the patterns of commercial growth. Earlier patterns can be derived by comparing city directories published at various times in the forties and fifties. Map 5 courtesy of Monique E. Kimball.
11. For the rezoning of San Francisco Street parcels to accommodate Pardee's early subdivisions, see Board of City Commissioners, *Minutes*, IX, January 5, 1955, 372. *Review-Journal*, July 21, 1985, "Homes," 1–2.
12. Reid and Demaris, *The Green Felt Jungle*, 34–38.
13. Jones and Cahlan, *Water*, II, 91–92.
14. Reid and Demaris, *The Green Felt Jungle*, 85–88, 90, 82–91; Brill, *The Teamsters*, 213–219. Hoffa and Joseph Dorfman provided casinos with low-interest pension fund loans in return for "skimming" privileges and/or kickbacks.
15. For Las Vegas's shortage of bank loans, see Vern Willis's column in *Review-Journal*, February 20, 1983, 3J.
16. Reid and Demaris, *The Green Felt Jungle*, 85–88; Peter Wiley and Robert Gottlieb, *Empires in the Sun: The Rise of the New American West* (New York: G. P. Putnam's & Sons, 1982), 198–208; *Review-Journal*, February 20, 1983, 3J.

17. For the urbanization of the northeast and northwest sectors of Greater Las Vegas, see Gubler, "Recreation Center," 143–149; consult, for example, the real estate map in *Review-Journal*, August 29, 1976, 8A.

18. Paige & Associates, *Inventory & Planning Guidelines*, 18–21.

19. Eugene P. Moehring, "Eagle over Main Street: The Federal Presence in the Las Vegas Metropolitan Area" (unpublished paper).

20. For Map 6, see Las Vegas Valley Water District, *Proposed Major Construction Program* (Las Vegas: Montgomery Consulting Engineers, 1964).

21. Jones and Cahlan, *Water*, II, 41, 57. For a typical complaint about water service, see Board of City Commissioners, *Minutes*, IX, June 16, 1954, 202.

22. Jones and Cahlan, *Water*, II, 41, 59, 60.

23. Ibid., 63, 85.

24. Sam Bass Warner, *Streetcar Suburbs: The Process of Growth in Boston, 1870–1900* (Boston: Harvard University Press, 1962), 153–165.

25. Jones and Cahlan, *Water*, II, 53, 60, 62, 115. For city cooperation with the water district, consult Board of City Commissioners, *Minutes*, X, March 27, 1957, 445; for complaints, see ibid., XI, August 27, 1958, 201 and September 3, 1958, 205.

26. Board of City Commissioners, *Minutes*, XI, 141.

27. Las Vegas Valley Water District, *Master Plan*. Also consult R. W. Beck and Associates, *System Study of the Clark County Sanitation District No. 1 of Clark County, Nevada* (Seattle: 1972) for Map 7.

28. *Insurance Maps of Las Vegas, Clark County, Nevada* (Sanborn Map Company, 1928, 1961 updated), 4–5, 6–7, 8–9, 12–13. For locational trends in the 1940s, see Las Vegas Chamber of Commerce, *Directory of Las Vegas and Vicinity, 1943–1944* (1944); many business directories are available for later decades.

29. *Insurance Maps*, 1–3, 11–13, 20–21.

30. Paige & Associates, *Inventory & Planning Guidelines*, 21.

31. See the general land use map in Eisner-Stewart, *Proposed General Plan*.

32. See Scott Kraft's column on Atlantic City in *Review-Journal*, September 10, 1984, 1E, 3E; March 2, 1986, 1A, 14A.

33. Sternlieb and Hughes, *The Atlantic City Gamble*, 111–117. See also Francisco Troncaso, *Report of the Impact of Casino Gambling on the Welfare of the Poor, the Minorities and the Elderly in the Inlet Section of Atlantic City* (Philadelphia: Temple University, May 23, 1977), 1–11; Marea Teski et al., *A City Revitalized: The Elderly Lose at Monopoly* (Lanham, MD: University Press of America, 1983), passim; and Michael Hawkins, *The Atlantic City Experience: Casino Gambling as an Economic Recovery Program* (Reno: University of Nevada Bureau of Business and Economic Research, 1981), passim.

34. William Graves, *Hawaii* (Washington, D.C.: National Geographic Society, 1970), 55–58.

35. Ibid. In fact, Miami Beach was engaged in a continuing controversy with Miami

and Dade County's metropolitan government over administrative functions and taxation: Mohl, "Miami's Government," 33.

36. University of Hawaii, Department of Geography, *Atlas of Hawaii*, 2d ed. (Honolulu: University of Hawaii Press, 1983), 126–127. See also State of Hawaii, Department of Planning and Economic Development, *The Population of Hawaii*, Report No. 113 (April 21, 1976). See also Bryan Farrell, *Hawaii: The Legend That Sells* (Honolulu: University of Hawaii Press, 1982), passim.

37. See, for instance, William Rowley, *Reno: Hub of the Washoe Country, An Illustrated History* (Windsor Hills, CA: Windsor Publications, 1984), 58, 71, 78, 81, and appropriate sections of the text.

Epilogue: Growth and Diversification Since 1970

1. Nevada Development Authority, First Interstate Bank, *Las Vegas Review-Journal*, *Las Vegas Perspective* (1981), 30, 42–43, 46–47, 58–59. For a complete list of new hotel projects, see *Review-Journal*, January 17, 1988, 1AA.

2. *Review-Journal*, September 10, 1984, 1E; March 2, 1986, 1A, 14A. Atlantic City, once the playground of wealthy Philadelphians, had suffered a decline in the 1960s thanks to low jet fares to Florida resorts. *Review-Journal*, July 13, 1987, 1A.

3. See ibid., September 10, 1984, 1E for an informative survey of the views of Jim Avance and other Nevada gaming observers who see Atlantic City exerting a beneficial influence upon Las Vegas. For Robert Mullane's comments, see ibid., January 3, 1988, 1AA.

4. Ibid., August 4, 1986, 4B.

5. Ibid.

6. For an insightful assessment of Las Vegas's future, see Harley Akers, "Las Vegas, 2001," *Las Vegas City Magazine* (November 1986), 20–25.

7. *Atlas of Hawaii*, 126–127; *Review-Journal*, November 14, 1985, 2D.

8. *Review-Journal*, November 14, 1985, 2D.

9. Ibid., March 16, 1986, 1D.

10. Ibid., December 2, 1986, 1B, 6B.

11. Ibid., November 26, 1986, 6D. Also see Burrell Cohen, *An Action Plan for Downtown Las Vegas* (1975).

12. *Review-Journal*, November 26, 1986, 6D.

Selected Bibliography

Books

Abbott, Carl. *The New Urban America: Growth and Politics in Sunbelt Cities.* Chapel Hill: University of North Carolina Press, 1981.

Allen, Marion. *Hoover Dam and Boulder City.* Redding, CA: C.P. Printing and Publishing, 1983.

Berman, Susan. *Easy Street.* New York: The Dial Press, 1981.

Bernard, Richard and Bradley Rice, eds. *Sunbelt Cities: Politics and Growth Since World War II.* Austin: University of Texas Press, 1983.

Best, Katharine and Katharine Hillyer. *Las Vegas, Playtown U.S.A.* New York: D. McKay Co., 1955.

Brill, Steven. *The Teamsters.* New York: Simon & Schuster, 1978.

Brooker, Angela and Dennis McBride. *Boulder City: Passages in Time.* Boulder City: The Boulder City Library, 1981.

Bushnell, Eleanor. *Sagebrush & Neon: Studies in Nevada Politics.* Reno: Bureau of Governmental Research, 1973.

Dahl, Albion. *Nevada's Southern Economy.* Carson City: University of Nevada Bureau of Business and Economic Research, 1969.

Demaris, Ovid. *The Last Mafioso.* New York: Bantam, 1981.

Drosnin, Michael. *Citizen Hughes.* New York: Holt, Rinehart & Winston, 1985.

Eadington, William R., ed. *Gambling and Society: Interdisciplinary Studies on the Subject of Gambling.* Springfield, IL: Thomas, 1976.

———. *The Economic Effects of Nevada's Gambling Industry.* Reno: University of Nevada Bureau of Business and Economic Research, 1974.

Edwards, Elbert. *200 Years in Nevada. . . .* Salt Lake City: Publishers Press and Mountain States Bindery, 1978.

Edwards, Jerome. *Pat McCarran: Political Boss of Nevada.* Reno: University of Nevada Press, 1982.

Elliott, Russell. *History of Nevada.* 1st edition. Lincoln: University of Nebraska Press, 1973.

Farrell, Bryan. *Hawaii: The Legend that Sells.* Honolulu: University of Hawaii Press, 1982.

Findlay, John. *People of Chance: Gambling in American Society from Jamestown to Las Vegas.* New York: Oxford University Press, 1986.

Fisher, Charles W. and Raymond J. Wells, *Living in Las Vegas: Some Social Characteristics, Behavior Patterns and Values of Local Residents.* Las Vegas: n.p., 1967.

Fogelson, Robert. *The Fragmented Metropolis: Los Angeles, 1850–1930.* Boston: Harvard University Press, 1967.

Garrison, Omar. *Howard Hughes in Las Vegas*. New York: Dell Publishing Co., 1971.

Gates, William. *Hoover Dam*. Las Vegas: Wetzel Publishing Company, 1932.

Glass, Mary Ellen. *Nevada's Turbulent '50s: Decade of Political and Economic Change*. Reno: University of Nevada Press, 1981.

Graves, William. *Hawaii*. Washington, D.C.: National Geographic Society, 1970.

Greenspun, Hank with Alex Pelle. *Where I Stand*. New York: D. McKay Co., 1966.

Hanna, David. *Bugsy Siegel: The Man Who Invented Murder, Inc.* New York: Belmont Tower Books, 1974.

Hauser, Philip and Leo Schnore. *The Study of Urbanization*. New York: John Wiley, 1965.

Hawkins, Michael. *The Atlantic City Experience: Casino Gambling as an Economic Recovery Program*. Reno: University of Nevada Bureau of Business and Economic Research, 1981.

Hinds, James. *Epitome of the History of Nellis Air Force Base*. Las Vegas: Nellis Air Force Base, 1977.

Hulse, James. *The Nevada Adventure: A History*. 4th edition. Reno: University of Nevada Press, 1978.

———. *The University of Nevada: A Centennial History*. Reno: University of Nevada Press, 1974.

Hundley, Norris. *Water and the West: The Colorado River Compact and the Politics of Water in the American West*. Berkeley: University of California Press, 1975.

Jackson, Kenneth. *Crabgrass Frontier: The Suburbanization of the United States*. New York: Oxford University Press, 1985.

Johnson, Frank. *Legalized Gambling in Nevada*. Carson City, n.p., 1970.

Jones, Florence Lee and John Cahlan. *Water: A History of Las Vegas. History of the Las Vegas Land and Water Company*. 2 vols. Las Vegas: Las Vegas Valley Water District, 1975.

Lauritzen, Jonreed. *Las Vegas, Nevada for Fun and Sun*. Las Vegas, n.p., 1947.

Layton, Ron. *Up Against Howard Hughes*. New York: Quadrangle Books, 1972.

Lewis, Oscar. *Sagebrush Casinos: The Story of Legal Gambling in Nevada*. Garden City: Doubleday, 1953.

Little, Arthur. *Business Opportunities in Southern Nevada*. San Francisco: n.p., 1970.

Liu, Ben-Chieh. *Quality of Life Indicators in U.S. Metropolitan Areas: A Statistical Analysis*. New York: Praeger, 1976.

Luckingham, Bradford. *The Urban Southwest: A Profile History of Albuquerque—El Paso—Phoenix—Tucson*. El Paso: Texas Western Press, 1982.

Maggio, Frank. *Las Vegas Calling*. Las Vegas: TAD Publishing Company, 1972.

Maxey, George. *Geology and Water Sources of Las Vegas*. Carson City: n.p., 1948.

———. *Well Data in Las Vegas*. Carson City: Water Resources Bulletin No. 4, 1946.

Messick, Hank. *The Beauties and the Beasts: The Mob in Show Business.* New York: McKay, 1973.

————. *The Silent Syndicate.* New York: Macmillan, 1967.

Meyers, Sid. *The Great Las Vegas Fraud.* Chicago: Mayflower Press, 1958.

Moehring, Eugene. *Public Works and the Patterns of Urban Real Estate Growth in Manhattan, 1835–1894.* New York: Arno Press, 1981.

Murray, Jack. *Las Vegas: Zoomtown U.S.A.* Phoenix: Lebeau Printing, 1962.

Nash, Gerald. *The American West Transformed: The Impact of the Second World War.* Bloomington: Indiana University Press, 1985.

Ostrander, Gilman. *Nevada: The Great Rotten Borough.* New York: Knopf, 1966.

Paher, Stanley. *Las Vegas, As it began—as it grew.* Las Vegas: Nevada Publications, 1971.

Perry, David C. and Alfred J. Watkins. *The Rise of the Sunbelt Cities.* Beverly Hills: Sage Publications, Inc., 1977.

Pomeroy, Earl. *In Search of the Golden West: The Tourist in Western America.* New York: Knopf, 1957.

Ralli, Paul. *Nevada Lawyer: A Story of Life and Love in Las Vegas.* Dallas: Mathis, Van Nort & Co., 1946.

————. *Viva Vegas.* Hollywood: House-Wharven, 1953.

Rand, Christopher. *Los Angeles: The Ultimate City.* New York: Oxford University Press, 1967.

Reid, Ed. *Las Vegas: City Without Clocks.* Englewood Cliffs: Prentice Hall, 1961.

————. *The Mistress and the Mafia: The Virginia Hill Story.* New York: Bantam Books, 1972.

———— and Ovid Demaris. *The Green Felt Jungle.* New York: Pocket Books, 1964.

Reisner, Marc. *Cadillac Desert: The American West and Its Disappearing Water.* New York: Viking, 1986.

Rose, Mark. *Interstate: Express Highway Politics, 1941–1956.* Lawrence: The Regents University Press, 1979.

Roske, Ralph. *Las Vegas: A Desert Paradise.* Tulsa: Continental Heritage Press, 1986.

Rowley, William. *Reno: Hub of the Washoe Country, An Illustrated History.* Windsor Hills, CA: Windsor Publications, 1984.

Shalett, Sidney, ed. *Crime in America, by Estes Kefauver.* Garden City: Doubleday, 1951.

Skolnick, Jerome. *House of Cards: Legalization and Control of Casino Gambling.* Boston: Little, Brown, 1978.

Sofen, Edward. *Miami's Metropolitan Experiment.* New York: Doubleday, 1966.

Squires, Charles P. *The Glory of Light: A Half Century of Service.* Las Vegas: n.p., 1955.

————. *Las Vegas, Nevada: Its Romance and History.* 2 vols. Las Vegas: n.p., 1955.

Sternlieb, George and James W. Hughes. *The Atlantic City Gamble*. Cambridge, MA: Harvard University Press, 1983.

Stevens, Joseph. *Hoover Dam: An American Adventure*. Norman: University of Oklahoma Press, 1988.

Teaford, Jon. *City and Suburb, The Political Fragmentation of Metropolitan America, 1850–1970*. Baltimore: The Johns Hopkins University Press, 1979.

Teski, Marea et al., *A City Revitalized: The Elderly Lose at Monopoly*. Lanham, MD: University Press of America, 1983.

Titus, A. Costandina. *Bombs in the Backyard: Atomic Testing and American Politics*. Reno: University of Nevada Press, 1986.

Venturi, Robert. *Learning from Las Vegas: The Forgotten Symbolism of Architectural Form*. Cambridge, MA: M.I.T. Press, 1977.

Warner, Sam Bass. *Streetcar Suburbs: The Process of Growth in Boston, 1870–1900*. Boston: Harvard University Press, 1962.

Wenum, John. *Annexation as a Technique for Metropolitan Growth: The Case of Phoenix, Arizona*. Tempe: Institute of Public Administration, Arizona State University, 1970.

White, William T., Bernard Malamud and John E. Nixon. *Socioeconomic Characteristics of Las Vegas, Nevada*. Las Vegas: UNLV Center for Business and Economic Research, 1975.

Wiley, Peter and Robert Gottlieb. *Empires in the Sun: The Rise of the New American West*. New York: G.P. Putnam's & Sons, 1982.

Wolfe, Tom. *The kandy-kolored tangerine-flake streamline baby*. New York: Farrar, Straus & Giroux, 1965.

Wright, Frank. *Clark County: The Changing Face of Southern Nevada*. Reno: Nevada Historical Society, n.d.

Yantis, Betty. *Fact Book for Las Vegas and Clark County*. Las Vegas: UNLV Center for Business and Economic Research, 1977.

Articles

Abbott, Carl. "The Suburban Sunbelt." *Journal of Urban History* (1987): 275–301.

Adams, Charles L. "Las Vegas as Border Town: An Interpretive Essay." *Nevada Historical Society Quarterly* (1978): 51–55.

Akers, Harley. "Las Vegas, 2001." *Las Vegas City Magazine* (November 1986): 20–25.

Beebe, Lucius. "Las Vegas." *Holiday*, XII (December 1952): 106–108, 132–137.

Bernard, Richard. "Cities, Suburbs and Sunbelts: The Politics of Metropolitan Growth." *Journal of Urban History* (1983): 85–92.

Dumke, Glen S. "Mission Station to Mining Town; Early Las Vegas." *Pacific Historical Review*, XXII (1953): 257–270.

French, William. "Don't Say Las Vegas is Short of Suckers." *Saturday Evening Post*, 228 (November 5, 1955): 12.

Friedman, Robert. "The Air-Conditioned Century." *American Heritage* (1984): 20–33.

"Gambler's Gala." *Life* (February 16, 1953): 105–107.

"Gambling: Wilbur's Dream Joint." *Time*, LV (May 8, 1950): 16–17.

"Gambling Town Pushes its Luck." *Life*, XXXVIII (June 20, 1955): 20–27.

Grose, Andrew. "Las Vegas—Clark County Consolidation: A Unique Event in Search of a Theory." *Nevada Public Affairs*, vol. 14, no. 14 (1976).

Halevy, Julian. "Disneyland and Las Vegas." *Nation* (June 7, 1958): 510–513.

Hammond, Mary. "Legalized Gambling in Nevada." *Current History*, XXI (1951): 177–179.

"Henderson—From Desolate Desert to a City of Destiny." *Nevada Highways and Parks*, XI (January–April 1951): 1–15, 30.

Hill, Gladwin. "Atomic Boomtown in the Desert." *New York Times Magazine* (February 11, 1951): 14.

———. "Desert Capital of the A-Bomb." *New York Times Magazine* (February 13, 1955): 22, 38, 40.

———. "Klondike in the Desert." *New York Times Magazine* (June 7, 1953): 14–15, 65, 67.

———. "Las Vegas is More Than the 'Strip.'" *New York Times Magazine* (March 16, 1958): 19, 31–32.

Jones, Florence Lee. "Las Vegas, Golden Anniversary Edition," a collection of articles in a special edition of the *Las Vegas Review-Journal* (February 28, 1955).

Kaufman, Perry. "City Boosters, Las Vegas Style." *Journal of the West* (1974): 46–60.

"Las Vegas Hedges its Bets." *Business Week* (August 11, 1956): 157–158.

"Las Vegas: 'It Just Couldn't Happen.'" *Time* (November 23, 1953): 30–34.

McWilliams, Carey. "Legalized Gambling Doesn't Pay." *Nation* (November 25, 1950): 482–483.

Mechling, Tom. "I Battled McCarran's Machine." *Reporter* (June 9, 1953): 21–25.

Millstein, Gilbert. "Cloud on Las Vegas' Silver Lining." *New York Times Magazine* (March 18, 1956): 17, 63–65.

Moehring, Eugene. "Public Works and the New Deal in Las Vegas, 1933–1940." *Nevada Historical Society Quarterly* (1981): 107–129.

———. "Las Vegas and the Second World War." *Nevada Historical Society Quarterly* (1986): 1–30.

Mohl, Raymond. "Miami's Metropolitan Government: Retrospect and Prospect." *Florida Historical Quarterly* (1984): 24–50.

Pastier, John. "The Architecture of Escapism: Disney World and Las Vegas." *American Institute of Architects Journal*, 67 (December 1978): 26–37.

Patrick, Elizabeth Nelson. "The Black Experience in Southern Nevada." *Nevada Historical Society Quarterly* (1979): 128–140, 209–220.

Rabinowitz, Howard. "Growth Trends in the Albuquerque SMSA, 1940–1978." *Journal of the West* (1979): 62–74.

Rocha, Guy Louis. "The I.W.W. and the Boulder Canyon Project." *Nevada Historical Society Quarterly* (1978): 3–24.

Schnore, Leo. "The Socioeconomic Status of Cities and Suburbs." *American Sociological Review* (1963): 76–85.

Stabler, Charles. "Fades and Factories: Las Vegas and Reno Want More Industry to Back Dice Tables." *Wall Street Journal* (January 22, 1957): 1, 12.

Stout, Wesley. "Nevada's New Reno." *Saturday Evening Post*, 215 (October 31, 1942): 2–13, 68–71.

Sutton, Imre. "Geographical Aspects of Construction: Hoover Dam Revisited." *Journal of the West* (1968): 301–344.

Wild, Roland. "Las Vegas." *New Yorker* (April 1953): 39–44.

Wilson, Richard G. "Machine-Age Iconography in the American West: The Design of Hoover Dam." *Pacific Historical Review* (1985): 463–493.

Newspapers

Albuquerque Journal

Las Vegas Age

Las Vegas (Evening) Review-Journal

Las Vegas Sun

North Las Vegas Valley Times

San Francisco Chronicle

Government Documents and Reports

Beck, R. W. and Associates. *System Study of the Clark County Sanitation District No. 1 of Clark County, Nevada.* Seattle, 1972.

Bills, Franklin J. and Associates. *Local Government Services Crisis, Clark County, Nevada: Feasibility Report—Alternative Courses of Action.* Las Vegas, 1968.

C. B. McClelland Co. *Report of Las Vegas, Nevada, Housing Survey, December, 1947.* Riverside, CA: 1948.

Clark County Auditor. *Annual Report of the Clark County Auditor, Showing Receipts and Expenditures.* 1933–1938.

Clark County Board of Commissioners. *A Workable Blueprint for Local Government in Clark County, Nevada.* March 1969.

———. *Clark County Road and Flood Control Needs Assessment.* April 1981.

———. *Minutes.* 1909–1960.

Clark County Planning Commission. *Comprehensive Plan, Clark County, Nevada.* 6 vols. Las Vegas, 1981.

———. *Statistical Reports.* 1958–

Clark County School District. *An Action Plan for Integration of Six Westside Elementary Schools . . . prepared by Superintendent James I. Mason.* Las Vegas, 1969.

Cohen, Burrell. *An Action Plan for Downtown Las Vegas.* 1975.

Dibble, Barry. *Boulder Dam Power for Las Vegas, Nevada*. Las Vegas: *Las Vegas Age*, 1935.

Duff, Anderson and Clark. *Las Vegas and Clark County, Nevada: An Economic and Industrial Analysis*. Chicago, 1956.

Edgerton, Germeshansen & Grier, Inc. *The Nevada Test Site and Southern Nevada*. Las Vegas, 1961.

Eisner-Stewart and Associates. *Land Use Inventory and Analysis*. South Pasadena, 1966.

———. *Proposed General Plan: Las Vegas Valley*. South Pasadena, 1966.

Hawaii. Department of Planning and Economic Development. *The Population of Hawaii*. Report No. 113, April 21, 1976.

Henderson City Council. *Minutes*. 1954–present.

Henderson City Planning Commission. *General Master Plan of the City of Henderson, Nevada*. 1969.

Las Vegas, Board of City Commissioners. *Minutes*. 1911–1959.

Las Vegas Chamber of Commerce. *Las Vegas and Boulder Dam, Nevada*. 1939.

———. *Las Vegas and Clark County, Nevada*. Las Vegas, 1939.

———. *Las Vegas and Clark County: A Brief Review of Climate, Resources and Growth Opportunities*. 1917.

———. *Where is Las Vegas Going? Get the Full Facts on the Present and Future Economy of Las Vegas*. 1974.

Las Vegas Chamber of Commerce Industrial Committee. *Story of Southern Nevada*. Las Vegas, 1948.

Las Vegas Chamber of Commerce Research and Statistical Bureau. *A Compendium of Statistics and Social Facts of Las Vegas*. 1952–1975.

———. *Las Vegas Report (Digest)*. 1956–1964.

Las Vegas City Manager. *Annual Reports*. 1949–1970.

Las Vegas Housing Authority. *Housing Survey of Selected Areas, Las Vegas, Nevada*. 1950.

Las Vegas Planning Commission. *Capital Improvement Program, 1969–1974*. 1969.

———. *Las Vegas Plans its Future, Master Plan, 1959*. 1959.

Las Vegas Planning Department. *General Plan of Parks and Recreation*. 1969.

———. *Population Profiles: Population, Income, Housing, Occupation, Education, Analysis of the 1970 Census, Las Vegas SMSA*. n.d.

Las Vegas Promotion Society. *Nevada: Las Vegas and Vegas Valley*. 1909.

Las Vegas Valley Water District. *Master Water Plan, Las Vegas Valley*. Las Vegas: Boyle Engineering. 1970.

Local Government Study Committee. *The Report on Local Governments in Clark County*. 1973.

Los Angeles Bureau of Municipal Research. *Economic Base Study—Las Vegas, Nevada*. Los Angeles, 1958.

Metcalf & Eddy Engineers-Montgomery Engineers. *Facility Plan Las Vegas Valley Regional Secondary Treatment Facilities: Clark County, Nevada.* 1976.

Nevada Development Authority, First Interstate Bank. *Las Vegas Review-Journal, Las Vegas Perspective.* 1981 edition.

Nevada. *Statutes of Nevada.* Chaps. 402, 403 (1955).

North Las Vegas City Council. *City of North Las Vegas: Community Renewal Plan.* Vol. 1. 1972.

North Las Vegas City Manager. *Annual Report for 1963–1964.* 1964.

Paige, Charles & Associates, Inc. *Historic Preservation Inventory & Planning Guidelines: City of Las Vegas.* San Francisco, 1978.

Peabody College for Teachers. *Public Education in Nevada, Digest of the Survey Report.* Nashville, 1954.

Public Administration Service. *Local Government in Clark County, Nevada.* Chicago, 1968.

Reining, Henry. *Boulder City, Nevada: A Federal Municipality . . . A Report for a Survey Made under the Direction of the Bureau of Reclamation of Problems Affecting Boulder City.* Washington, D.C.: U.S. Government Printing Office, 1950.

Sanborn Map Company. *Insurance Maps of Las Vegas, Nevada.* 1928, 1961.

Smith, Larry & Co. *Clark County Economic Analysis prepared for the Southern Nevada Industrial Foundation.* Seattle: 1960.

Troncaso, Francisco. *Report of the Impact of Casino Gambling on the Welfare of the Poor, the Minorities and the Elderly in the Inlet Section of Atlantic City.* Philadelphia: Temple University, May 23, 1977.

Tucson City Council. *The Comprehensive Plan for the City of Tucson, Pima County.* Tucson, 1975.

Uniform Crime Reporting Section, Federal Bureau of Investigation, U.S. Department of Justice. *Crime in the United States.* Washington, D.C., July 1, 1986.

U.S. Atomic Energy Commission. *The Story of the Nevada Test Site.* Washington, D.C., 1963.

U.S. Commission on the Review of the National Policy Toward Casino Gambling. *Gambling in America.* Washington, D.C., 1976.

U.S. Department of Commerce, Bureau of the Census. *County Business Patterns: Standard Metropolitan Statistical Areas, 1976.* Washington, D.C., 1976.

University of Hawaii, Department of Geography. *Atlas of Hawaii.* 2d edition. Honolulu: University of Hawaii Press, 1983.

Manuscript Collections

Aplin, Charles. *Papers, 1907–1960.*

Baker, Charles Duncan. *Papers, 1926–1972.*

Cahlan, Albert E. *Papers, 1930–1968.*

Cahlan, John. *Papers.*
Cashman, James. *Family Papers, 1901–1961.*
Economic Opportunity Board of Clark County. *Archives, 1963–1970.*
Eells, Howard. *Construction Progress: Photographs and Papers.*
Franklin, George E. *Manuscripts.*
Grant, Archie. *Family Papers, 1918–1973.*
Hicks, Marion. *Papers.*
McWilliams, J. T. *Family Papers, 1905–1960.*
Moore, William J. *Papers.*
Park, Dr. William S. *Papers, 1923–1939.*
Rockwell, R. Earl. *Papers, 1911–1979.*
Squires, Charles Pemberton. *Papers, 1893–1958.*

Unpublished Materials

Decker, Robert L. "The Economics of Legalized Gambling in Nevada." Doctoral dissertation: University of Colorado, 1961.

Dobbs, William. "Working for BMI: Reflections on Life and Labor at America's Largest World War II Magnesium Plant." Paper.

Elliott, Gary. "The Moulin Rouge Hotel: A Critical Appraisal of a Las Vegas Legend." Paper.

Fitzgerald, Roosevelt. "Black Entertainers in Las Vegas, 1940–1960." Paper.

———. "The Evolution of a Black Community in Las Vegas, 1905–1940." Paper.

———. "The Impact of the Hoover Dam Project on Race Relations in Southern Nevada." Paper.

Gray, Raymond Guild. "The Organization of a County School District: A Case Study of District Consolidation and Administrative Reorganization." Doctoral dissertation: Stanford University, 1958.

Green, Michael S. "A Partisan Press: The Las Vegas Newspapers and the 1932 Election." Paper.

———. "Where They Sat, Where They Stood: The Las Vegas Newspaper War of the 1950s." Paper.

Gubler, Ward H. "Las Vegas: An International Recreation Center." Master's thesis: University of Utah, 1967.

Holland, Patricia. "Las Vegas Business District, 1905–1930." Paper.

Kaufman, Perry. "The Best City of Them All: A History of Las Vegas, 1930–1960." Doctoral dissertation: University of California, Santa Barbara, 1974.

Kieser, Mary. "A History of Las Vegas Schools, 1905–1956." Professional paper: University of Nevada, Las Vegas, 1977.

Konig, Michael. "Toward Metropolitan Status: Charter Government and the Rise of Phoenix, Arizona." Doctoral dissertation: Arizona State University, 1983.

Kotlanger, Michael. "Phoenix, Arizona, 1920–1940." Doctoral dissertation: Arizona State University, 1983.

Leavitt, Francis. "Influence of the Mormon People in the Settlement of Clark County." Master's thesis: University of Nevada, Reno, 1934.

Moehring, Eugene. "Eagle over Main Street: The Federal Presence in the Las Vegas Metropolitan Area." Paper.

Moran, Chris. "Las Vegas: 1928–1931, Years of Transition." Paper.

Murphy, Don. "The Role of Changing External Relations in the Growth of Las Vegas." Doctoral dissertation: University of Nebraska, 1969.

Quinn, Edward. "Coping with Crisis: Las Vegas and Its Indigents, 1930–1931." Paper.

Reeder, Ray. "The Mormon Trail: A History of the Salt Lake to Los Angeles Route to 1969." Doctoral dissertation: Brigham Young University, 1966.

Richardson, Philip. "Effects of Legalized Gambling on Community Stability in the Las Vegas Area." Paper prepared for the Task Force on Legalized Gambling sponsored by the Twentieth Century Fund, 1974.

Roske, Ralph. "Nevada Gambling, First Phase, 1861–1931." Paper.

Sadovich, Maryellen. "Basic Magnesium, Incorporated and the Industrialization of Southern Nevada." Master's thesis: University of Nevada, Las Vegas, 1971.

Sciullo, Henry. "Las Vegas: A Study of Short and Long Term Effects on a Community of Legalized Gambling." Paper.

Squires, Charles. "The Glory of Light: Half a Century of Service." Las Vegas, 1955.

Wilbur, Ray. "Boulder City: A Survey of its Legal Background, its City Plan and its Administration." Master's thesis: Syracuse University, 1936.

Willard, Robert E. "The Quantitative Significance of the Gaming Industry in the Greater Las Vegas Area." Doctoral dissertation: University of Arizona, 1968.

Wood, Robert T. "The Transformation of Albuquerque, 1945–1972." Doctoral dissertation: University of New Mexico, 1980.

Oral History

Aplin, Charles W. *An Oldtimer in Las Vegas.* University of Nevada Oral History Project, 1969.

Binion, Lester Ben. *Some Recollections of a Texas and Las Vegas Gaming Operator.* University of Nevada Oral History Project, 1973.

Boyer, Florence. *Las Vegas, Nevada: My Home for Sixty Years.* University of Nevada Oral History Project, 1967.

Cahill, Robbins. *Recollections of Work in State Politics, Government, Taxation, Gaming Control, Clark County Administration and the Nevada Resort Association.* University of Nevada Oral History Project, 1973.

Cahlan, John. *Reminiscences of a Reno and Las Vegas, Nevada, Newspaperman, University Regent, and Public-Spirited Citizen.* University of Nevada Oral History Project, 1970.

Edwards, Elbert. *Memoirs of a Southern Nevada Educator.* University of Nevada Oral History Project, 1968.

Godbey, Erma. *Pioneering in Boulder City.* University of Nevada Oral History Project, 1967.

O'Brien, Rita. *West Las Vegas at the Crossroads: A Forum.* Las Vegas, 1977.

Patrick, Elizabeth Nelson. *Oral Interview of Coral Williams.* Las Vegas, 1978.

———. *Oral Interview of Lubertha Johnson.* Las Vegas, 1978.

———. *Oral Interview of Reverend Prentiss Walker.* Las Vegas, 1978.

——— and Rita O'Brien, eds. *The Black Experience in Southern Nevada.* Las Vegas, 1978.

Rockwell, Leon. *Recollections of Las Vegas, Nevada, 1906–1968.* University of Nevada Oral History Project, 1969.

Legal Cases

Baker v. Carr

Brown v. Board of Education, Topeka, Kansas

Dungan v. Sawyer

Reynolds v. Sims

U.S. District Court. *Civil LV No. 1645-Complaint and Consent Decree* (1970).

———. *Equal Employment Opportunity Commission v. Nevada Resort Association et al. Case No. CV-LV-81-12RDF* (1981).

Index